A Handful of Honey

Annie Hawes, originally from Shepherd's Bush, divides her time between Liguria in Italy, the west coast of Ireland and Whitechapel in London. Her first book, *Extra Virgin*, was a worldwide bestseller and she has written two further books, *Ripe for the Picking* and *Journey to the South*.

Annie Hawes

A handful of honey

Away to the Palm Groves of Morocco and Algeria

PAN BOOKS

First published 2008 by Pan Books
an imprint of Pan Macmillan Ltd
Pan Macmillan, 20 New Wharf Road, London N1 9RR
Basingstoke and Oxford
Associated companies throughout the world
www.panmacmillan.com

ISBN 978-0-330-45722-4

Typeset by Intype Libra Ltd
Printed and bound in Great Britain by
Mackays of Chatham plc, Chatham, Kent

Visit www.panmacmillan.com to read more about all our books
and to buy them. You will also find features, author interviews and
news of any author events, and you can sign up for e-newsletters
so that you're always first to hear about our new releases.

A Handful of Honey

Prologue

I awoke at first light, as usual, to the clang and crash of heavy metal doors, the clatter of key-chains on the guards' belts, their shouts echoing down the long tiled corridor as they headed this way on the breakfast round. *Toc'acordar! Toc'acordar!* Wake up, wake up!

The spyhole in my cell door clicked open, snapped shut: I scrambled off the narrow bed and onto the steel-tube chair a couple of feet away. The bed, in a direct line with the doorway, was not a good place to be when the day's bread ration arrived.

Here they came. With a rattle and a crash the door flew open: another, close-up roar of *Toc'acordar!* and the solid kilo loaf came hurtling through the doorway. Seriously wholemeal, hefty as a rock, it landed with a thud on the mattress, dead centre. The door slammed shut again, keys jangled, lock clunked home.

Alone again, and unscathed for the second day running. I was getting the hang of this place at last. Of the details, at least. The bigger picture still eluded me: I'd been here almost a week, and still nobody had told me what I'd been arrested for – or even, come to that, whether I was technically under arrest at all.

I waited now, poised to deploy my tin mug – the only movable item in the cell apart from the sheet – as soon as I heard the next guard, the one with the bucket of sweet black coffee, begin rattling her way down the hall. No knives or forks in here, of course. You just tore bits off your loaf, dipped them into the coffee. No toilet paper, either, though I couldn't imagine what harm you could do with that. At first I thought they'd forgotten it: banged on the cell door for half an hour. Surely loo roll was a basic human right? Wrong. There was

1

a bidet for that, they said, next to the toilet. Which had no door on it, and was also in line with the spyhole.

Early sunlight was already streaming through the window high up in the yard-thick wall. That unreachable square of luminous blue, the odd passing cloud, were all that was left of the Portugal I'd known for the last four months: a friendly village just south of Lisbon, a tiny sun-filled house daubed with generations of whitewash, leafy grapevines outside the door. Beyond the house, a field of sweetcorn and a luscious green ramble down to the sea, or up the lane to the shops and pavement bars at Sesimbra. My slightly derelict home, a spare farm building, was the den and headquarters of Octavio and his friends, the bunch of young locals my own age who had befriended me. Octavio's mother was letting me stay in the upstairs rooms, in exchange for a bit of cleaning and painting, while I looked for a proper job.

I'd found one, too, starting next month. Pointless, as it happened, because by midday today, although I had no way of knowing this, I would not only be out of this jail, but out of the country too. So far, though, there was no hint of a change. Here came the coffee. Make sure the sheet's straight, grab the tin mug. If you weren't standing by the door in full view, bed tidied, mug in hand, when the guard looked through the spyhole, she'd snap it shut again and move on to the next cell, leaving you coffee-less. And that bread was seriously hard work with no coffee to wash it down.

Strange fact: I'd never come across any kind of brown bread at all in this country until I found myself behind bars. Although the prison-ration loaf was surprisingly reminiscent of my mother's good solid home-made stone-ground, here in Portugal it was seen, apparently, as a form of punishment. Must tell the mother that. If I ever saw her again, that is. It was starting to seem horribly possible that I might never get out of this place. Who even knew I was in here, after all?

The only people to witness my departure in the unmarked car, supposedly to answer a few questions about my lost passport, were Octavio and his mother, Eugenia. Not that any of us really believed it was about my passport. These weren't the normal police from the station down the road, where I'd reported the thing lost, but the plainclothes PIDE – pronounced 'peed' – the Policia Internacional e Defesa do Estado, the grandly named International Police and Defence of the State. The dictator Salazar, though on his last legs, was still in power in Portugal at the time of these events, the early 1970s, and the PIDE was his much-feared political police force, keeping everyone in the country in a state of looking-over-their-shoulder anxiety. The PIDE's reputation was certainly not built on a tender concern for innocent visitors' lost passports.

They had come for me just before dawn, as is the habit of such organizations, battering at Eugenia's front door, across the cobbled courtyard from mine. She had startled me awake in the half-light, flanked by two strangers in dark suits, who stuck their heads round the door, peremptorily demanded my name and withdrew to stand guard while I dressed. Once Eugenia had fully grasped that the PIDE were here for me alone and not for her beloved son, praise the Lord, her main concern was – oddly enough – my outfit. No, no, not those jeans! A skirt! she hissed, snatching them from me. Jeans on a female had subversive connotations: the PIDE-men would take it as deliberate provocation. Realizing that I owned no such thing, she dashed off to return with one of her own, a navy-blue item unpleasantly reminiscent of the school uniform I had only recently escaped. She looked so panic-stricken that I didn't even argue – though, truth to tell, a few weeks off my seventeenth birthday and deeply ignorant of the ways of dictatorships, I was a lot more troubled by the embarrassing outfit than by the prospect of being taken for a spin by the secret police.

Now, naked legs exposed to the view of all and sundry – as befits a decent woman – I was driven to the harbour at Setubal, marched onto a ferry boat, handcuffed to one of the PIDE-men in case I made a dive for it: then off into another car, up a long dusty road, through a deep gateway in thick stone walls, to be deposited at last in a small khaki office deep in the bowels of this fortress.

*

I retrieved my loaf from the bed, tore off a bit of crust, dipped and started to chew, as slowly as possible. If you paced yourself right, you could make breakfast last right up to the next event in the day: the arrival of the lunch-bucket. In a mere five hours I would get to moisten the second third of my daily bread in watery soup, a dish whose principal ingredient was the huge, spiky bones of some monstrous and apparently virtually fleshless fish, bulked out with the occasional chunk of mushy potato. Nothing else whatsoever would happen till lunchtime: because nothing was allowed to happen. They did the rounds every hour or so, checked through the spyhole, and if you'd found anything remotely entertaining to do, they stopped you. On the second day, unaware of this rule, I'd decided to ward off the fear and the boredom – worst possible combination of emotions – with a bit of singing. I would work my way through my Highland granny's old Scots songs, fine wailing tunes with good fierce stories to them, mostly concerning the terrible fates that befall women who stray from the paths of righteousness. Very suitable to a prison cell, you'd say, and not too offensive to the ears of a nation brought up on the soulful wailings of the *fado*, either. I sang my way happily through the tale of the lustful Lady Margaret's liaison with Sweet William, but hardly had I left her lying in her cold, cold coffin, face turned to the wall, and begun on the story of the young mother enticed away by her demon lover – 'and a grimly guest / I'm sure was he' – when two hatchet-faced guards appeared at my door. *Não cantar*, they said sternly. And mimed zipping their mouths shut, in case my Portuguese wasn't up to it.

So I sat quietly and twiddled my thumbs until lunch: when, inspired by the vast number of giant fishbones left in my mug, I hung on to one of the long straight ones and, making judicious use of my eye-teeth, bored a hole in its broader end. Now to pull a strand of cotton from the hem of the repellent skirt and thread up my fishbone needle with it. Proudly, self-sufficiently, I set about repairing the unravelling armpit of my T-shirt. Brilliant entertainment. Compared to staring at a wall, that is, or watching the occasional cloud pass across a patch of blue sky.

The punishment for this, once spotted, was terrible. My fishbone was confiscated on the spot. (I was appalled to find tears starting from my eyes. Surely I couldn't be crying over a fishbone?) Half an hour later – worse still – I was brought some proper sewing cotton and a real needle and made to finish the job at top speed, entirely surrounded by guards. They stood silent, critically watching my every stitch, till I was done.

I gave up after that: just sat still and tried not to speculate. Would Octavio and Eugenia have guessed where I was? I didn't even know myself. Still, what could they do about it, anyway? Nothing. As far as I could tell, the entire Portuguese nation was either terrified of the PIDE or employed by them. Sometimes both. I'd soon discovered, out and about with my Portuguese friends, that I could hardly talk about anything at all without being hissed at to lower my voice, just in case it was taken the wrong way by some eavesdropper.

Weren't there an amazing number of people around here with terrible cross-eyes? I might say, for example, while sitting at a pavement café watching the world go by. And odd wonky teeth, too. Why was that? Was it a local genetic defect?

Ssssh! Of course not! It was just that they were poor, they couldn't afford doctors and dentists.

Afford doctors and dentists? A child of the Nanny State, I'd always taken free healthcare as part of the bedrock of life: like, say, tap-water. Or toilet paper. No, more like the weather: you got it anyway, like it or not.

Too poor to see a doctor? But that's outrageous, I might continue, after a rapid re-evaluation of the unsolicited doctoring and dentistry I'd been subjected to in my childhood. So what happens when a poor person gets sick? Is that why that man with no legs goes bumping up and down the Chiado on his bottom, holding a block of wood in each hand to raise him off the cobbles? Not because he's a touch eccentric, as I've assumed till now, but because he can't afford a wheelchair?

Ssssh, would come the reply. Wait till we get home . . . !

In the early days I would press on regardless, imagining that I was giving my Portuguese friends a much-needed lesson in the proud British tradition of free speech. How could they all be such cowards? Surely they couldn't think the whole lot of us were about to be arrested just for talking? Anyway, it was me that was talking, not them!

But that, I eventually grasped, wasn't the point. The PIDE didn't need to arrest people. The merest hint of disloyalty to the Salazar regime was enough – such as hanging around with a loudmouth like me. Your father might inexplicably lose his job; he might never get another. Bad things could happen to your whole family: homes lost, futures wrecked, nobody ever openly accused of anything – or given a chance to prove their innocence.

So nobody was likely to be mounting a campaign to get me out of here, were they? I hadn't seen anybody but prison guards since the day I got here, when I was escorted to that gloomy khaki office to have my photograph taken, clutching a card with a number under my chin. Next, into another identical office, where a genial man at a huge desk addressed me in French, for lack of any other common language, as he tipped out the contents of my bag and combed through them in slow motion. Ridiculous palaver, I thought, expecting in my ignorance to be back home in Sesimbra in an hour or two. What did he expect to find in there? Wasn't he going to ask me some proper questions? The PIDE-man ploughed on through hair grips, shop receipts, half-eaten packs of chewing gum, tangles of earrings, while I sat trying not to yawn and doing my best to avert my eyes from the awesomely luminous flesh beneath the horrendous skirt.

Until, that is, he picked up one last bit of paper, an old crumpled sheet that must have been lying at the bottom of the bag for weeks, and began smoothing it out with the side of his hand. Suddenly I was wide awake; my stomach gave a nasty lurch. The map. Did I not throw away the map?

Just as I'd feared. The scribbled zig-zags of the hill-path leading through the scrubland and across the border were plain to see: with the road and the position of the sentry post marked out. My job had been to walk up on foot, playing the flirtatious hitch-hiker, and keep the soldiers occupied while the two boys nipped up the slope behind them, over the ridge, and into Spain and safety. The ruse had worked brilliantly, though the job wasn't as easy as I'd imagined. It is surprisingly difficult to talk nonsense to four heavily armed men when all your attention is focused on the hillside above them – never letting your eyes stray upwards, even for a second, to check on the progress of the fugitives behind their backs. Harder still when it suddenly dawns on you that the hefty automatic weapons slung from their shoulders are intended for use in just these circumstances.

This people-smuggling outing was exactly what I had feared I was being picked up for. And now I'd put the evidence right into their hands.

Here in Portugal, as soon as a boy hit seventeen, he was drafted into three years of military service, no choice about it – unless he wanted to spend six years in prison and be branded a traitor, while the rest of his family suffered all the petty torments the PIDE could unleash upon them. Our friends Olavo and João didn't want to kill any Africans, they said: nor be killed by them, either. Two of their schoolmates had already died in Angola, and one in Mozambique. Why shouldn't Africans have their countries back if they wanted them, anyway? If the boys could just get out of Portugal and across a couple of hundred miles of hostile Spanish territory – General Franco was still in power in Spain and had no sympathy for Portuguese draft-evaders – they would be at the French border, where they would automatically get political asylum. There was a whole community of Portuguese dissidents living in France. And, as they pointed out, I was the ideal person to help. I had no family here to be persecuted if things went wrong . . .

My map, strangely enough, seemed to mean nothing to Mr Genial. Unless this was some kind of Macchiavellian double bluff?

He narrowed his eyes and stared at it for what seemed an eternity, looked up at me and paused – causing all the blood to drain from my head – and then, unbelievably, turned the paper casually over to look at the writing on the other side. Thank God. A harmless list of things I was thinking of putting in a letter to my mother. A fantasy letter, that is, because I suspected she would chuck any real letter of mine straight in the bin. I'd been nothing but trouble for years, and had trumped the lot by running off across the Channel at sixteen, the minute I'd finished my exams. Still, at least there was nothing incriminating on that side of the paper.

Think again. The list, alas, contained the two words 'No' and 'Salazar'. They were separated by a good dozen other words: but structure and syntax meant nothing to my interrogator. 'No . . . Salazar!' he announced triumphantly. *Vous n'aimez pas Salazar?*

Hard to know how to answer this. Was there any point, anyhow, in answering a man who made up my opinions for me out of random words on a scrap of paper?

Being a normal English teenager who had hitherto taken very little interest in foreign affairs, I had arrived here with no opinions whatsoever about Salazar. I didn't recall ever having heard the man's name and was surprised to discover, as I went about the country, that Portugal considered Britain to be its closest friend and ally – and had done ever since 1373, when our two countries signed their first treaty: the world's longest-running alliance. Britain, though apparently happy to keep the treaty running, was a lot less keen to publicize its connection with Salazar. It had not taken me long to gather that inside Portugal, too, most people had little esteem or affection for their Great Leader – although, with the constant fear of eavesdropping informers, only the seriously inebriated ever mentioned this openly. And I was with them all the way, drunk or sober. Salazar and his PIDE seemed positively to enjoy tormenting their people, and over the pettiest details. Trousers, for example. Pointless tyranny.

It did not seem wise to bring this up just at the moment, though.

I tried explaining, instead, that my list didn't actually say, 'No Salazar'. It was just some thoughts for a letter to my mother.

Aha! said he. My mother was a political activist, then?

What? My mother? This was getting seriously weird. Certainly not, I said.

Who, then, my interrogator asked after a long pause, were my friends in Portugal?

Well, I answered, almost entirely truthfully, I only knew people's Christian names. Portuguese surnames were beyond me.

But no, said he, smiling the genial smile. He did not mean individuals, necessarily: we could talk about that later, perhaps. He did not think it had been my own idea to come to Portugal. Was he right? I was very young: how had I come to have such extreme opinions at my age? Perhaps I had political friends back in England? Portuguese émigrés, maybe? Communist friends? Socialist friends? African friends, even, hmmm? Clearly someone had been leading me astray . . . Who had suggested I come and sow discontent in the Sesimbra countryside? Who had I given my passport to? Or sold it to, perhaps?

Extreme opinions? Africans? Communists? Politics? The man certainly was mad. I had arrived in Portugal by chance, wandering the highways of Europe, imagining myself to be some kind of a cross between Bob Dylan and Jack Kerouac – or was it Laurie Lee? – and hitching lifts from long-distance lorry-drivers.

Sowing discontent in the Sesimbra countryside, though . . . I had certainly tried my hand at that. But not at anyone else's instigation. I had done my best to make kind, patient Carmen, the human washing machine, angry with her lot. Carmen came round twice a week to do Eugenia's laundry – by hand, with a scrubbing brush, in a concrete vat in the yard – while I practised my beginner's Portuguese on her: slowly and painfully extracting the story of her life with the help of a dictionary. Painfully, because she couldn't help at all with the spelling of words I needed to look up – she'd never been to school, ever, and she still couldn't read or write at thirty-five. She'd started washing clothes for a living at nine years old. Nine years old? What was the matter with this country? Wasn't there a law against that? Eugenia told me to calm down: it was perfectly normal. Lots of simple country folk actually didn't want to go to school. What good would reading and writing do them? They would rather get on and earn some money . . .

And Carmen just tutted disbelievingly when I spoke of the free schooling and doctoring, and the prevalence of washing machines, where I came from. I'd never get away with that sort of thing here, she told me. Not in Portugal! And anyway, she needed the work.

I must have been more successful at sowing discontent than I imagined, though. Carmen had obviously bothered to pass these conversations on to someone, hadn't she? Or the PIDE would never have got to hear of them. Unless, of course, she just passed them on to the PIDE directly?

No, that way madness lies . . .

I was relieved to find, at the end of our interview, that my interrogator hadn't accused me of anything at all, far less of smuggling draft-evaders out of the country. Imagine my surprise when I was now led off, not homewards, but to be shoved into a cell and locked up. At dawn the next morning the door swung open at last – to allow some roaring madwoman to hurl a two-pound loaf at my solar plexus. I nabbed the next caller, a woman with a zinc bucket of an unappetizing brown liquid, but she had no idea why I was in here, or how long for. She was just doing her job. Did I want coffee or not?

Six days on, I had made no headway. Was I being held here under suspicion of helping Olavo and João? Of having African friends? Of selling my passport? I was never to find out. Suddenly, well before lunch-bucket time, two jailers appeared at my cell door, and the pace of life shifted from snail to overdrive. Within the hour, I would be out of here: and moreover, by the time night fell, I would – by a strange coincidence – even have some African friends. Several of them. A connection that would one day lead to my spending several months on that continent. Prescient interrogator.

I was marched away at the double now, back down to the khaki office, where a middle-aged man and a young woman sat waiting outside the door. Inside, next to the interrogator with the smile, stood a grey beanpole of a man clutching a swatch of papers, who stepped forward, reached out a hand to shake mine and addressed me in my own language. He was from the British Embassy. The Portuguese authorities had declared me *persona non grata*. I must be got out of here as quickly as possible. He had brought all the necessary documentation with him. Here, he said, detaching a thick envelope from the pile, is your train ticket to London, the price of which you will have to repay before you are issued another passport. And a temporary travel document to take its place. He was sorry that, since speed was of the essence, he had used the photo provided by the prison authorities. And he was authorized to advance me a small sum of money for the journey – perhaps twenty pounds would do? Because you'll be back in Britain within forty-eight hours, of course, he added, comfortingly.

I didn't find it any sort of comfort at all. Britain? What was I going to do in Britain? I didn't even have a town there that I would call home: our family had never stayed anywhere for more than a few years. In fact, they were in the middle of moving from Edinburgh to the Welsh borders as I left.

But this is my home, here, in Portugal, I said. I don't want to go to Britain. I want to go back to my friends, to Sesimbra. I'm supposed to be starting work next week! What are they saying I've done? They haven't accused me of anything!

Her Majesty's representative looked pityingly at me. They hadn't informed him of the details, but they didn't need to, he said. They were deporting me as an Undesirable Alien, with immediate effect. The two people on the bench outside the door were PIDE agents: they were waiting to escort me out of the country. Now.

Now? What, without my going home at all? But what about my

stuff? I asked, clutching at straws. My clothes and everything? Can't I go back to Sesimbra to get them? And say goodbye, at least?

Out of the question, alas. The PIDE had already seen to that: my bag was waiting upstairs.

Now, to make matters worse, the Embassy man wanted to get in touch with my parents. It was an official requirement, I was legally a minor. If I would just give him their name and address . . . ? I certainly would not. Yet another disgrace: deported penniless from Portugal, to throw myself on their mercy? I don't think so. I'd rather stay in here and rot, I said.

Highly exasperated, he asked whether I realized, young lady, that this place, Caxias, was one of the most notorious political prisons in the country? And that he was doing his best to get me out of it?

I didn't, as it happened. As far as I knew, political prisons were something that went on behind the Iron Curtain, in films, certainly not in countries that were close allies of my own. And I was in one? I stood and thought some uncomfortable thoughts about this. Stuck in that cell, I'd several times heard screaming and wailing from down below and congratulated myself on being made of sterner stuff than my fellow inmates. I might be young, but I could certainly handle a bit of solitary confinement without going to pieces like these emotional Latins . . .

I saw now that I was a stupid, smug idiot.

Still, this seemed a pretty conclusive reason why the Embassy man was going to have to get me out, parents' address or no. I sat on in mulish silence. It worked. All most irregular, complained my saviour, but, oh, very well . . .

And so, within the hour, I was sitting shell-shocked on a Spain-bound train, with my own personal PIDE escort. Two whole secret police agents to make sure I left their country: that's how dangerous I was. I pulled out my envelope, read the details on the ticket. Change at Ciudad Real for Paris. At Paris for Calais. Then the cold grey Channel, the ferry, and one last train to cold grey London. I had no friends or family there, nowhere to stay, and twenty pounds to last till I found some way of earning more. And a gigantic debt to pay back for this ticket I didn't want, before I could get a proper passport again. There was nothing but a yawning black hole where once my future had been. Even being locked in that cell was better than this horrible travesty of freedom.

We racketed on along the tracks, blur of green countryside, glimpses of whitewashed farmhouses, windows outlined in lapis lazuli blue – just like my own home back in Sesimbra. No. Not my home any more. Don't think about that. Some of the more tumbledown houses had blue-paint handprints round the windows and doors too, a ring of blue hands right round every opening. Not kids messing about with dad's bucket of blue wash, as I'd assumed when I first met them, but the Muslim Hand of Fatima, protecting the house from evil. Octavio told me that. Memories of Islam, he said, lingering on in countryside superstition, centuries after the religion had vanished from his land. I was missing him badly, I wanted my friends and my life back. Please let me wake up and find this was all a bad dream. For a happy moment, I imagined turning around as soon as my escort left me at the Spanish border and sneaking back into Portugal. Luckily, I'd had a bit of practice at that. But no, stupid idea. I'd never be able to leave the house, would I? I'd have to stay indoors, in hiding, for the rest of my life. Nothing for it but to ride out this miserable journey into the unknown.

I unfolded the travel document with the black-and-white convict photo, tired eyes staring bleakly out over my stencilled prison number. The PIDE-man, spotting this last vestige of control over my own destiny, stood up and took envelope, ticket and passport from my hands. The woman – girl, really, she couldn't be more than a few years older than me – sat at my side. She could speak French, while her fish-eyed colleague couldn't, and, bizarrely, she seemed to be trying to make friends with me. She was Maria do Céu, she told me – Mary of Heaven, or maybe it should translate Mary of the Sky – but I must call her Céu for short. Lovely name. Still I resolved not to call her anything at all. Why on earth would I want to make friends with a PIDE-person? How long will it be, I asked her coldly, till I'm allowed back into the country?

A minimum of three years, she said. Then you could maybe ask for permission to return.

Three years! An eternity. I would be old by then. Nearly twenty.

Still, why don't we keep in touch? said my new friend Céu brightly. If I let her know when I was thinking of coming back, she might be able to help. She hoped I realized that she didn't actually want to do this job. But there were so few openings here for graduates . . .

I was saved from answering by a portly ticket collector who now stumped into our compartment and checked our tickets, frowning. Which two passengers were getting out at the border? This was a through train, an express, he said: anyone not crossing the Spanish border had to pay a supplement.

Fish-eye slipped his hand into his breast pocket and flashed his official ID card in proper scary-PIDE style, gesturing to Mary of the Sky to do the same, evidently expecting that to be the end of the matter. The ticket collector, with much thoughtful nodding and lip-pursing, inspected the documents, compared the photos carefully with the originals seated before him, and eventually handed the cards back, apparently satisfied as to the identities of my escort. Yes indeed, he said. PIDE. Makes no difference, though, he added comfortably. You'll have to pay up, just like everybody else. More than my job's worth to allow people to travel on this train without paying the supplement. Rules and regulations: you'll know all about that, in your line of business. That'll be thirty escudos, thank you.

Delicious moment. The discomfited PIDE-man had no choice but sheepishly to pull out his wallet and pay. Just like everybody else. The ticket man gave me a sly glance and a hint of a wink as he exited in triumph. Stunning. This was the first time I'd ever seen anyone act as if it were remotely possible to stand up to the PIDE. I was nearly as shocked as my escort.

I had witnessed an early tremor in the earthquake soon to come. It would not be long till half the Portuguese nation would take to the streets in anger: and the Salazar regime would collapse under its own weight at last, along with its secret police and its bloody colonial wars.

On a deserted Spanish platform in a silent dusty station somewhere south of Madrid I waited, small and lonely, for the Paris train. The duffel bag containing all my worldly goods lay at my feet. So low was my morale that, in spite of the two-hour wait, I hadn't even opened it to dig out a less offensive garment than the vile skirt. Why bother? The skirt was just part and parcel of the general vileness that was life.

When at last, with a long squeal of brakes, the trans-Europe train drew up alongside my platform, it did not suit my mood at all. It was horribly loud and lively, bursting at the seams, every compartment packed with repellently cheerful-looking travellers. It must have begun its journey somewhere down near the Straits of Gibraltar, I deduced from the exotic outfits all around me: a distinctly African train, full of migrant workers from the ex-French colonies returning to their Paris jobs after the summer break – Tunisians, Algerians, Moroccans, Senegalese. I shoved my way gloomily along the crowded corridor, looking for a seat. Eventually, five or six carriages on, I elbowed my way into a compartment that looked marginally less overcrowded than the rest. Its occupants, five boys not much older than me, courteously shifted their lunch, their bedding and quantities of luggage to disinter a vacant corner seat, into which I collapsed, a walking casualty.

My hosts, after checking me out for a moment, leapt straight into rescue mode. Give her more space, Rashid! Karim, roll up that blanket . . . make her a cushion! Does she speak French? Is she hungry? Get the olives back out! The bread, too . . .

No, no thank you, I said, I'm not hungry, I'm fine . . .

But they were right, I realized as soon as the food was set out in front of me. I was not fine – and I was starving hungry. Soon I was wolfing down the last of my fellow passengers' olives, fragrant with garlic and coriander: paradise after all those days on bread and water. Water-with-a-hint-of-fishbone, that is. Now I followed up with several particularly tasty chick-pea-and-onion patties made for the journey by the boys' Aunt Rashida back home in Algeria – the best cook in the family. Soon I was checking out Aunt Rashida's toothsome chilli-braised chicken too, and her voluptuous soft spicy pitta-bread, and washing it all down with swigs of Hassan's mother's cold sweet lemon-mint tea from a recycled mineral-water bottle. Dessert next: a pile of tiny crunchy doughnut-things filled with dates and covered in sesame seeds. Delicious. Made by Cousin Aisha, apparently. Hard to keep up the gloom when your fellow travellers are so high-spirited, and your belly is full of tasty titbits, with plenty more waiting on your lap.

The boys were riding high: a new life awaiting them in France, and well into their second day of train travel. They were cousins and brothers, they had crossed the Mediterranean this morning from their North African home, this was their first ever trip abroad. Yesterday they'd seen the city of Algiers for the first time, their own capital city. Grandiose! And tomorrow, Paris! The Eiffel Tower! The river Seine! The Champs-Elysées! They had jobs waiting for them there, too, grown men's work starting next week, wages beyond the wildest dreams of their home town, all sorted by their kindly Uncle Kebir, who was a brilliant mason. And a place to stay as well. Mohammed, the youngest, was going to be a mason just like his uncle: it would be a great opportunity for him. The rest of them were just going to do some labouring for the year, save up to get themselves started back home.

I was envious. Why didn't I have a kindly uncle waiting in London to save me? The boys were appalled to hear that I was heading for a notional home town where I knew nobody at all. No family? No friends? Nowhere to stay? Nothing? Why didn't I just stay in Paris with them, then? Uncle Kebir, who could do anything, would surely find me a job; they would be happy to share him with me. They would simply adopt me as a sister, *et voilà*! Sorted!

I wished I could, I said. But I had no choice in the matter.

My new-found brothers shook their heads over my miserable one-week travel document. But why on earth did it have that convict photo on it?

They enjoyed the story of my imprisonment a lot. Of course the PIDE knew all about my draft-evaders, they told me. It was a classic technique, not telling prisoners what they've been arrested for. Designed to disorientate you, so you'll end up volunteering to confess to anything, just to get the uncertainty over. They should know: all five of them had grown up listening to such tales, in the bad old days of their country's eight-year-long war to get rid of the French. But now look, said my benefactors, how well Africa had repaid my good deed! I had got myself a bargain, as Europeans so often did where their continent was concerned. For two colonial soldiers fewer, I had five ministering North African angels, come to my aid with food and blankets.

The boys were pleasantly surprised to hear that France, these days, had become a safe haven for young Portuguese who didn't want to fight in colonial wars. Very good news, said Hassan. The French must truly have had a change of heart, then.

Had they? I'd never even heard of this Algerian war. But then, I didn't seem to have heard of anything much. I wasn't even sure where Algeria was.

Had I never noticed the stretch of Mediterranean coastline between Morocco and Tunisia? Well, that was Algeria, said Sayid, and it was huge, the tenth-largest country in the whole world – it stretched all the way down across the Sahara to Black Africa, to border with Mali. And the French had clung on to it like grim death for years, long after they'd given up Morocco and Tunisia: they'd even tried, for almost a century, to claim that it was part of France.

They didn't want to lose the oilfields, said Karim.

Or the cornfields, said Mohammed. And the vineyards.

So they tested a couple of atom bombs down in our desert, in revenge, said Hassan. But they still lost.

Now, as we rattled on through the midday heat in the desert-dry centre of Spain, I was treated to an intensive course in colonialism in general and the Algerians' war to get out from under the thumb of the French in particular, and had many scenes from the Battle of Algiers acted out for me, the weaponry represented by two Evian water bottles, half a baguette and a rolled-up train brochure: while in place of French Secret Service torture equipment we had the brass-and-cord luggage rack, from which Mohammed suspended himself in various impossibly painful-looking postures.

So thoroughly was my mood lifted by the eventual victory of the Algerians in the teeth of what seemed almost impossible odds – Algerians were free at last to build themselves a country of equals, a socialist Islamic republic where exploitation and oppression would have no place; and women had played a central role in the struggle, so they would be fine too – that I was able to open my duffel bag at last and seek out my beloved jeans. I was myself again. I would eliminate the evil skirt from my life for good.

Or would I? I opened the bag only to find, neatly folded right at the top, another identically horrible skirt in a gloomy dark brown: Eugenia, of course, still fearing for my freedom if I didn't learn to keep my legs respectably nude. I dissolved into sniffles.

Time, Rashid decided, for a short lesson in North African dance styles. Dancing would cheer anybody up. He performed the slinky Tunisian, then the hip-twitching Egyptian, while his brothers clapped out the rhythm. And now, see how much more beautiful is the Berber dancing of our own town, Timimoun! Round of applause . . . As night fell we were chugging on through a dark invisible France, wrapped up snug in a nest of bright North African blankets, looking at photos of Aunt Rashida and Cousin Aisha and everyone else they were going to miss from back home – and some they weren't . . .

Timimoun, they told me, lay far away on the edges of the Sahara: a small friendly town of ancient stone aqueducts and sculpted red-mud-brick arches, of hot, dusty camel-trains and cool, shady palm groves, of bright, bustling markets, where the wares of the Black south meet those of the Arab north. It was a last green outpost before the liveable land gives out and the endless sand takes over. Ancient trails led out from it, still used by the Tuareg nomads, who can live for weeks on dates and camel-milk alone, the Blue Men of the desert, their faces tinted indigo from the *chèche* that veils all but their eyes against sun and sand. Oil- and gas-juggernauts follow the same routes nowadays, twenty wheels on them at least, each one as big as your house – no, bigger, interrupted Mohammed – bringing prosperity to their country at last. Soon there will be education for all, jobs for all, said Sayid, the serious one. People won't need to leave Algeria any more to find work: there will be plenty for everyone! Mohammed and Karim gave him an ironic cheer. But it's true, said Sayid. Twelve years isn't long to build a country from war-torn ruins. Of course, it hasn't happened yet . . .

By the time we got to Paris, some twenty intense hours later, bonding was complete, and the brothers were certainly not leaving me alone in the Gare du Nord to wait all night for the Calais train. There was a whole week to go before my forced repatriation. I must come and rest at Uncle Kebir's. Get my strength up before I left to face London and the Unknown.

Do not fear, said Mohammed. You will be welcome. He has plenty of beds, beds for twelve, he said so!

Twelve bedrooms? In Paris? Was their uncle a millionaire?

Sayid dug out the precious scrap of paper, crumpled and dog-eared, with Kebir's address on it, spelt out in wobbly capitals by a hand unused to our spiky European alphabet. We showed it around, asking directions, and got plenty of black looks. *Dégueulasse!* Disgusting! A white woman with a bunch of Arabs! A confused hour later, we found ourselves in darkness at an empty echoing end-of-the-line Metro station. Now we were directed on, amid more raised eyebrows and pursed lips, to the bitter end of a dying bus route. Black drizzle here, one o'clock in the morning on an empty road: no houses now, but concrete warehouses half-derelict on rubbish-strewn land. We tramped on in silence, jackets sodden, bags weighing heavy. So much for the Champs-Elysées: no Elysian Fields here. This was not the Paris of my brothers' dreams.

At long last a pale glow through the cold mist resolved itself into tall searchlights above twenty-foot wire fencing. We rattled tentatively at looming steel gates, blinded by the glare. Beyond the wire mesh, a sea of mud, a flotilla of Portakabins. Could this be it?

Welcoming voices called out, some in French, some in Arabic. Kebir's nephews? At last! *Bienvenus! As-salamu aleikum!* The gates squealed open to admit us. Kebir! Come out! Quick! Here they are at last!

But then they saw me and stopped in their tracks. A woman! No! A woman on site is a sacking offence!

Uncle Kebir, quick thinker, whisked me in through the door of the nearest cabin: a shed filled with shovels and pneumatic drills. *Attends ici!* Wait here!

A minute later he was back with an impenetrable disguise: a neighbour's long jellaba of fine pale wool, a pair of big muddy boots – and, mysteriously, a large emerald green bath-towel. Where did that go?

Wind it round your head, of course! Your *chèche*! Perfect! *Voilà!* You'd hardly notice her at all!

And so, invisible in my huge green turban and steel toecaps, I squelched my way behind the Uncle through the floodlit quagmire to Portakabin Number Seven. Mire without, maybe: but inside our cabin was another world. Behind the anonymous grey door, warm light reflected from the dozen steel bunks: the red glow of a round clay brazier, a terracotta bowl of charcoal embers, burning bright on its low pedestal in the centre of the room, soft kelims spread all around it, gold, pink and green. And my five new-found brothers already sitting snug around its warmth, cross-legged among the firelit shadows. I joined them, while Uncle Kebir brought out our dinner, couscous to be eaten from the communal bowl at our knees. Make your own personal hollow in the fragrant pile before you, and the uncle will fill it with rich, finger-licking mutton and vegetables, steaming hot, spiced with plenty of garlic, coriander, chilli . . . yes, yes, use your hand, no cutlery required. The boys ate elegantly with their fingertips: how on earth did they do that? The couscous granules trickled warm between my fingers; the sauce dribbled luxuriously up my wrist. A thousand miles from my last cutlery-free experience, in every sense.

Soulful music serenaded us from the cassette player in the corner, Uncle Kebir's pride and joy. As we ate, he nursed a long-handled copper pan to the simmer on the charcoal brazier, and soon we were sipping tiny glasses of hot, sweet tea. Aaaaah. Who needed Paris, anyhow? This was fine by me: a home safe and sound, with five kind brothers and a generous uncle to look out for me. I could stay here for ever. Or for five days, at any rate.

In the mornings, Uncle Kebir cooks us a Proper Breakfast of eggs scrambled with plenty of crushed broad beans, tomato, onion, olive oil, served with good hot flat-bread toasted over the charcoal brazier – none of that namby-pamby French coffee-and-croissant nonsense, not here in Timimoun. Within the house the copper pot always gleams on the brazier for tea; and the teapot sits on the embers beside it, because, explains Kebir, if you have one glass, you must always have three. Don't add more tea when you refill the pot, though – just more mint and sugar. I learn many other useful things. The tea must be poured from elbow-height, yes, like that, says Cousin Hassan, who is starting university next year. It needs the oxygen or it won't taste right. How do you calm a camel that's angry from overwork, asks Rashid, who is going to buy a massive flock of sheep, the biggest Timimoun has ever seen, with his Parisian earnings, and maybe a few goats too, and, of course, a thoroughbred camel to ride while he herds them all. Simple! he says. As soon as the camel starts to make those threatening gurgling sounds in its throat, you pull off your jellaba, the sweatier the better, and cast it at the animal's feet. It will happily vent its spleen on that and not spit its bolus of fierce, burning stomach acids at you. Awesome. By night Karim fights with Mohammed over the cassette player. Will we listen to Mohammed's non-stop tapes of *Rai* music, complete with trumpets and saxophones, for my education? Or to the endless pulsating chants of the lovely Oum Kalthoum, brightest star in the traditional Arabic musical firmament? Still, the brothers are not Arabs, they tell me, not at all, whatever the French public may think. They are Berbers and proud of it: their people have dwelt in North Africa, on the southern shores of the Mediterranean, since long before the Arabs even heard of the place: since many centuries before Islam, even. You call this coastal strip, stretching from Morocco through Algeria to Tunisia, the Maghreb, which means, in Arabic, the Far West: the land of the setting sun.

So, aided and abetted by my new-found family I retreat into darkness and warmth and Timimoun, where I stay to the last possible moment of my last day of freedom.

An objective observer might see nothing but an acre of building-site-cum-concentration camp with a bare searchlight poised high at each corner: the only hint of Africa the occasional burnous-clad figure trudging from hut to hut through the grey drizzle, carrying his cross of shadows. (Could the figure be me, invisible in my green towel turban and boots, squelching my way to the bathroom block?) But look again and you may spot, in the cool whitewashed courtyard beyond our home, Aunt Rashida and the rest of the women working under the lemon tree, grinding the corn, handful by handful, between the two round flat stones, or deftly rolling the moistened flour against the reed mat on their laps, the fresh-made couscous granules trickling from their fingertips into the shallow baskets at their sides. The older women still cover their heads when they go out, says Hassan, but Rashida and the young ones have given that up, spurred on by the air of freedom in their new country. Two of his sisters were even training to be teachers. On my last night, Mohammed and Uncle Kebir sing a beautiful plaintive song, all in close harmony: the special Timimoun song for the palm groves in spring, when the whole town is busy working high in the date-palms, pollinating the long strings of date-flowers so that they will bear fruit. Nature would do the job for you herself, of course, says Rashid the farmer, but you'd have to plant a lot more trees, a male for every five females. And Timimoun doesn't have the water to waste on trees that carry no fruit, not with the encroaching desert all around. So human hands must take over her work, with the song to lighten the load.

Despite the desert, though, there is life in the burning sands beyond the high red earth walls of the precious date-palm groves. In the outlying hamlets, says Sayid, you'll still find the wise bearded *marabouts* who, if you treat them right, will take you down into their cool subterranean homes, seat you cross-legged on their floors of fresh sand, and make you up a gri-gri amulet to beat any and every ill . . .

Except, maybe, a travel document that's about to run out.

I finally left Timimoun-on-Seine a mere five hours before the thing expired. Mohammed, Rashid and Karim came to the Gare du Nord, braving more volleys of hissing and tutting, to see me off. I would be back as soon as I'd paid off my debt and got my passport back, I promised, as I hugged them goodbye on the platform and clambered up the three high steps onto the wheezing Calais train. Failing that, if it took too long, I would come and find them in the real Timimoun.

And so it came about that I found myself wandering alone, late that night, through the cold wet streets of London, asking my way to Trafalgar Square, the only name that came to mind in this unknown city, there to be swallowed up into the street life of the down-and-outs of Piccadilly. Portugal was soon forgotten in the struggle to survive; so were the brothers of Timimoun. Twenty years would pass before I would finally make it all the way to North Africa: to the fringes of the Sahara and the old home town I had never known.

1

The coincidence that would lead me at last to the far side of the Mediterranean and the shores of Africa took place – as luck would have it – just a couple of miles from the northern shores of that very sea. A couple of miles as the crow flies, at any rate, because the winding road to my present home here more than doubles the distance, climbing steeply uphill through drystone walls, vegetable patches and terraced olive groves. It occurred, in fact, under a grapevine on the sunny patio of a small stone-built shack in the Ligurian hills of Italy, where I had been living now, off and on, for almost a decade.

I never did manage to settle down full-time in London and, almost by chance, I'd ended up here in Liguria, where you could buy a home for a song – especially if you didn't mind setting up in an isolated, hillside cottage with no running water, standing in a decrepit run-down olive grove well over a mile from the nearest village. No sane local would dream of taking this place on – it was only a couple of decades since Ligurian villagers had given up the simple peasant-farming life and made their escape to a world of electricity, water closets and indoor taps; and they counted it a lucky one. That, of course, was why my house was so cheap. But surely, I'd said to myself, I could learn to make some sort of a living from the olives? Plant a vegetable garden down by the well? Keep a chicken or two, maybe? Of course I could – people round here had been doing it for centuries: just add a nice new pump to the well, a solar panel to the roof, and I'd be set up for life.

So it was here in Italy, among the steep silver-green terraces of an olive grove slowly responding to my loving kindness, that Gérard – an old friend now domiciled in the south of France – came calling. It was easily done: my place is a mere hour's drive from Nice, along the coast road or the Autoroute du Soleil. Gérard had brought a friend with him: another Frenchman, a bit shy, nice flash of a smile, large horn-rimmed specs, dark curly hair, name of Guy. A name which, in French, is pronounced 'ghee', like the clarified butter of Indian cuisine.

The guests settled down under the grapevine at my lovely new garden table – a beautiful oblong of veined white marble I'd just found in the local junkyard down in the river valley – and got on with uncorking the wine. I went in and got the pasta on. They had a surprise for me – some amazing news, said Gérard, brandishing a folded Michelin map as he brought me in a glass. And a proposition to make. No, not now! It would wait till the dinner was ready!

As soon as I'd set our three plates down among the wine-bottles, out came the surprise.

Here, said Gérard, doing his best to open the map out with a flourish, while the evening breeze from the coast did its best to sabotage him. Eventually, Gérard won: the thing was tamed, spread out, and weighted down with wine-bottles. I could read the legend.

The Michelin map, it said, of North and West Africa.

Africa? I said.

Africa, yes! said Gérard happily. He and Guy were in full mid-life crisis: they were about to leave this continent and travel from Morocco to the Ivory Coast. From the Mediterranean in the north to the Gulf of Guinea in the south, right across the Sahara. Not on some organized tour, though, nor insulated from the experience by any luxurious four-wheel-drive. Their plan was to sleep where locals slept, eat what locals ate, and travel by public transport – or whatever means local people used. They would scarcely need any money at all.

Which was lucky, said the quiet Guy, because, as it happened, they scarcely had any money at all.

Gérard had thrown in his job, he said. He would be leaving at the end of the month.

Was he serious?

He certainly was. He and Guy had already been to get their African inoculations.

I could hardly believe it. Gérard's was a fabulous job, at a French radio station. All he had to do was stay up and read the news reports as they came in through the night – an activity that made him one of the most well-informed people I knew – and choose the ones that might be of interest to the French commuting public the next morning. These would go into a small tidy pile in the News Team's in-tray: while everything else – which was, admittedly, most of the news from most of the world – he simply crumpled up and hurled into a waist-high bin in the corner of his office. Friends, me included, could pop in for a nocturnal can of beer with him whenever they liked, since the place was otherwise deserted. But Gérard had lost interest in a career in news-gathering, he said. The in-tray was tiny, the bin was always overflowing. He had a powerful urge to go off and experience, at first hand, some of the sources of all this irrelevant rubbish. And Africa was so close: just across the Mediterranean. So he had decided to start there.

So, was I coming too, then? asked Gérard, picking up the wine-bottle and emptying it into my glass. Why not?

What, come to Africa? Now? Me? It certainly wasn't the right moment to go haring off across an unknown continent, I said. I couldn't even make up my mind whether I was staying here in Italy permanently, throwing in my lot with this small, scruffy olive-farming village, carrying on trying to turn the olive grove into a going concern – a job I could make a decent livelihood from. Or should I be giving that up as a mad pipe-dream and heading back to England to put plan A into action: get a sensible home and a sensible career? Whatever the answer might be, trips to Africa did not come into the equation.

But look at the map, said Gérard in his most persuasive voice.

There was the Mediterranean, right at the bottom of this hill. Just a few miles across the water to Africa. It was nearer to us, here in Italy, than London was. Why was it an unknown continent? That was the question! It was ridiculous not to have been there already. And we had the ideal travelling partner for this trip, too. Guy had Africa in his blood. Four generations of his family had been born there. Guy himself had been conceived there, even – though he'd never actually set foot in the place. What could be more perfect?

Guy laughed. He was a positive mine of information, he said – of nostalgic hearsay, from his parents and grandparents, about a French-run North Africa of the past, a Maghreb paradise of cocktails and *cafés dansants*, of horseback promenades in the hills and picnic-baskets on Mediterranean beaches. A paradise that had been created, as far as Guy could tell, by making the place a hell on earth for its original inhabitants. He certainly wanted to see Algeria for himself at last – if only to exorcize a few ghosts.

While Gérard and Guy busied themselves with the next bottle, I looked at their map as I was bid. Gérard was right. There at the very top of the sheet were the southernmost tips of Italy and Spain: Sicily and Palermo, Malaga and Gibraltar, so close to Morocco that they were almost touching. And on the map, in the abstract, the African south coast of the Mediterranean, the Maghreb – from Tangier through Algiers to Tunis – looked reassuringly similar to the northern, European side: the same green background of arable land, the ranges of low hills, the meandering highways crossing it, marked out in red or yellow.

All well and good. But then, just look a few inches further down the sheet, below the fertile Maghreb! No green any more, just the harsh pale beige and white of endless wilderness. Nothing but emptiness: the roads all gone, replaced with the spidery black lines of tarmac-free trails. In place of the big black dots of towns, light blue dots marked the places where you might find water – and at what depth below ground. The Sahara desert. Look at the size of it. It was enormous – it took up a whole two-thirds of the map! Hardly a sign of habitation there, either, just a few microscopic green patches of oasis. How were Gérard and Guy ever going to get across that on local transport? Was there any transport? Were there any people there, even?

It was then that I saw it, slap in the middle of their pencilled-in route: the town of Timimoun. There certainly were people there. More than that, I knew some of them already. I had made a promise to go and visit them, too – even though it was rather a long time ago. When would I ever get another opportunity like this?

OK, I said. Why not? I'm coming too.

It was not that I'd had no desire to get back to Paris – or to Timimoun or Sesimbra, indeed. But it had taken a lot of concentration to dig myself out of that unpromising start in London. I had, though, watched with delight – from the safety of London – the collapse of the Salazar regime, and been filled with joy on the day the Portuguese army turned on its masters and, gun-muzzles loaded with pink and red carnations, marched arm in arm with the massed protesters calling for liberty and democracy. Two years later, every political prisoner in the country was set free. Rejoicing crowds partied in the streets, there were bonfires and mass celebrations, and I even received an official invitation to join in the fun. Anyone whose name was on the PIDE's files was welcome to come and dig out the information held on them in the secret police offices, now thoroughly vandalized by a grateful population. You could pull out your file, rip it to shreds, throw it on the celebratory bonfires, and sing and dance while the evidence burnt.

I missed all that, though. Money was still tight at the time, and the PIDE's effect on my own life was still ongoing – I would get no passport until my debt to Her Majesty was paid off.

As for Timimoun, it was beyond my wildest dreams. And from what little news you got about Algeria here, I'd gathered that things weren't going as well as the brothers – or Sayid the optimist, at any rate – had hoped. The price of oil had collapsed by two-thirds in the

1980s, and all the country's plans had gone awry. With better health-care the population was growing apace, but there was little sign of the extra housing and work all these new people needed. The new, dynamic country that Algerians had dreamed of had not materialized – nor the democratic government, either. The leaders of the heroic army that had won the war against the French were still in charge – in various semi-elected guises – of a state that was growing less and less heroic as it grew in corruption. The mass exodus of young men towards France – or anywhere else there was work to be found – continued.

Eventually, I had the price of that unwanted trip from Portugal paid. Early one spring morning the postman handed me the sturdy brown envelope I'd been waiting for. At last I was free to leave the country once more. I flicked through the passport's pristine pages, lingering over the best bit – where Her Britannic Majesty, in a beautiful copperplate hand, Requested and Required everyone, wherever I might go, to Allow me to Pass Freely Without Let or Hindrance and to Afford me such Assistance and Protection as might be Necessary. Lovely stuff. One Requests first, politely: and moves swiftly on to Requiring, with its ring of gunboats at dawn. None of the above, of course, corresponded too closely to my earlier travel experiences. But I was not put off. Nothing for it but to make my second foray from the shores of Britain.

A year later, when I returned to London, penniless again but at least not indebted, I still hadn't quite made it either to Portugal or to North Africa. I'd got stuck neatly between the two, in the south of Spain: in Andalusia, where I'd been seduced by the Moorish charms of the city of Granada. This feeble effort would scarcely be worth mentioning if it wasn't for the strange fact that, thanks to my landlord, Pedro, I had quite possibly learned as much about the Maghreb here – and about the place of distant Timimoun in its world – as I would have done if I'd actually made it across the Mediterranean.

At this time, Spain, like Portugal before it, was joyously recovering from a long and repressive dictatorship: in this case, the rule of the Generalíssimo Franco. Pedro, boldly sporting a bright red tie one morning, told me that he had never taken this piece of neckwear out of its drawer in the whole forty years of Franco's reign. Why? Because a red tie would get you a savage beating from the police, the Guardia Civil, that's why, if not a spell in the cells!

Spain's multicultural heritage, along with her citizens' red neckties, had been very much downplayed over the forty years of Franco's reign. The jewel of Islamic architecture at Granada's heart, the fabulous Alhambra palace, had for all this time been no more than a tourist attraction as far as the locals were concerned, a bizarre anomaly in a Spanish Catholic town, and certainly of no interest or significance to a good devout Franco-supporting Christian. The memory of a glorious 700-year-long Moorish culture would, of course, be as repellent to a right-wing Christian dictator as the sight of an avowed socialist. General Franco had even adopted, as his insignia, the yoke-and-fasces symbol of King Ferdinand and Queen Isabella, the fifteenth-century monarchs who had overseen the ethnic cleansing of Spain: the deportation or forced conversion of all Muslims and Jews on Spanish territory.

Now, though, hand in hand with its political recovery from the long silence of the Franco regime, Andalusia was slowly beginning to take pride in its Islamic heritage. At long last, the people of Granada could sport any colour of necktie they fancied, learn to take an interest in their city's Moorish past and – in Pedro's case – point it out to you at every opportunity. A Moorish culture of which my landlord in the red tie was extremely proud, one in which, at its height, Muslims, Christians and Jews, the three Peoples of the Book, bound by the common roots of their three religions, had lived not merely in mutual tolerance, but in active cooperation. Something that we in the modern world, as Pedro will tell you, have still not managed to achieve, in spite of all our airs and graces.

Till now, apart from those few hints in Portugal, I'd had only the vaguest notion of the Iberian peninsula's Islamic past. Here in Granada, within days I soon got a very practical introduction to this ongoing heritage. My new neighbourhood was the Albaycín, a friendly warren of narrow cobbled streets and whitewashed houses that straggled uphill towards the Gipsy quarter of the Sacromonte. It was the oldest part of town, built some five or six centuries earlier by the Moors themselves, a people born here on the Iberian peninsula from the mingling of the local inhabitants with the new Muslim settlers. And very hardy folk those Moors must have been, too. The winters here in Granada were horribly cold, and there was not so much as a fireplace in this draughty, centuries-old stone house. So I had – against the aged Pedro's express instructions – snuck an electric blower-heater into the house. Within minutes it had blown the fuses to the whole place.

Pedro came round to sort me out, bringing some fuse wire – and a bag of charcoal.

What was I supposed to do with that, I asked, when there was no fireplace?

Fireplace? Pedro tutted at me. And from the back of a kitchen cupboard he dug out a red clay brazier, identical to the one I'd met all those years ago in Paris. Uncle Kebir's couscous-cooker. Charcoal braziers might no longer be essential for cooking purposes in Granada – luckily we had gas bottles for that these days, though Pedro himself, he said, would not eat a sardine unless it was brazier-grilled – but they were still, five centuries on, essential for winter survival in the Albaycín: the only form of indoor heating in everyday use round here.

Pedro showed me how to light the thing – outside, so you didn't get smoked to death – and then slot it into the circular iron brazier-holder built in under the kitchen table: an item that I had taken for a strangely deformed foot-rest. Now then, just spread that big woollen blanket over the table – of course it's a tablecloth! What did you think it was? – and hey presto! The rest of your home may be cold as ice, but as long as you stay at that toast-warm table, with the blanket-cloth nicely tucked in around your waist, you will probably survive the short but freezing Granada winter.

Granada, my landlord soon revealed, had been the very last Muslim-run stronghold in Spain, holding out till 1492, the year Columbus set sail for America. Muslim settlers had crossed the Mediterranean during the long twilight of isolation left once the Roman Empire had crumbled away, bringing with them, incidentally, the knowledge of astronomy that would one day make Columbus' trip possible. Soon the whole of Iberia was under their control, from Portugal to Cataluña. They met with hardly any resistance until Poitiers, half way up France. The poor peasant farmers of Europe were completely bedazzled, it seems, by the sight of those stylishly caparisoned horsemen, determined bearers of North African civilization and Islamic purpose.

Soon, though, humbler settlers followed that military vanguard across the waters – Muslim and Jewish, Arab and Berber – among them the Berber farmers who, Pedro tells me, contributed to their new homeland of el-Andalus many boons and blessings, such as the mighty olive tree, the almond and the orange. It was their skilled horticulturalists, he says, who first established the pomegranate here – the heraldic symbol of Granada to this day.

Handily for the future of the decaying West, Eastern civilization was still going strong – and took a great interest in Europe's own lost classics of Greek and Roman thought, along with its scientific and technological advances. These were all a vibrantly going concern in the Islamic world, though being slowly forgotten here – irrelevant to the backward conditions of modern life in Europe, where the once proudly paved roads of Rome were slowly turning back into muddy pathways along which a wheeled vehicle could no longer pass. But once the newcomers had established themselves here, Pedro says, a sophisticated civilization soon grew. Pedro himself has seen the remains of the impressive series of high-tech water-mills built by the skilled engineers of el-Andalus, all along the river Guadalquivir, to produce the good, reliable supplies of bread flour, of olive oil, and even of henna, required by a new, city-dwelling populace. Moreover, says Pedro, the name *Guadalquivir* is nothing but a corruption of *Wadi el-Kebir*, which means, in Arabic, 'the Great River'. (Strange. Does this signify that Uncle Kebir's name is actually Uncle Great? Very apt, if so.)

Over the next few centuries, as the culture of the Moors reached its high point, the Muslims, Jews and Christians of el-Andalus formed the westward heart of an intellectual ferment that reached from the Spanish university cities of Cordoba and Seville, through those of Fez and Bejaia across the Mediterranean, all the way to the universities of Cairo, Damascus and Baghdad. Eventually, all the accumulated knowledge of the East, lost classical texts and new scientific discoveries, would seep back into European culture thanks to the multilingual Moors and the collaboration of the Peoples of the Book, to feed Europe's rebirth – its Renaissance, the first beginnings of the world as we know it today.

And how did little Timimoun come into all this? Not only important highways of knowledge, but also major routes of trade connected Islamic Spain eastwards and southwards: across the Maghreb and through the Sahara to the kingdoms of the Sudan – source of the gold that oiled the wheels of the thriving economy that funded the universities and their scholars. The jewel in the crown of this trans-Saharan trade was the great oasis city of Sijilmassa, standing in what is now south-east Morocco, on the present-day border with Algeria, and allied with the Spanish Caliphate of Cordoba. Into this city's bullish markets the gold and spices, oils and perfumes, ebony and ivory, slaves and parchments poured, to meet the merchants who would send them onwards to the great cities of the North African heartlands, or to the ports of the Mediterranean – Sicily, southern Italy, and el-Andalus.

Somewhat more obscure in this glorious tale, but a mere day or two's northward travel for those dusty camel-trains with their precious cargoes arriving from across the Sahara, was a place closer to my heart. The caravans' final watering stop, before making that last push across sun-baked dunes and stony desert to Sijilmassa, was at the green and bountiful oases of the Gourara; chief among which was a certain small fortified city of deep-red earth named: Timimoun! Not at all the secret oasis refuge, the quiet desert backwater I had imagined, nor the self-sufficient little community of date-palm farmers and goat-herds, but a sophisticated centre of far-flung connections, on the main artery of a buzzing international trade route.

Once the Inquisition had moved here to Granada, 700 years after the arrival of Islam in et-Andalus, Pedro tells me, not just the Muslim and Jewish faiths, but the entire lifestyle of the town came under attack. Cordoba had long since fallen to the Christians, as the culture of tolerance began to break down. First the Jews and then the Muslims of Spain had been given the choice of converting to Christianity or fleeing to seek asylum in foreign lands. Now the *hammams*, or Turkish baths, were banned, as was the use of henna for bodily adornment, and even the dancing of the *zambra* – though they got nowhere with that one, Pedro says gleefully: it is still danced in Granada to this very day! Moreover, he points out, although the Christian Church ruthlessly rooted out converts suspected of ongoing Jewish or Muslim connections, without the collaboration of all three Peoples of the Book, Columbus would never have made it to America. While Islamic science had provided the navigational technology, it was, as it happens, two ex-Jewish *conversos* who bankrolled Ferdinand and Isabella's Christian expedition, providing the ships and stores.

At the other end of the social scale, according to my ebullient landlord, just a very few among the ordinary Muslims of old Granada were actually asked to stay on: small peasant farmers in the villages of the Alpujarra hills, rapidly emptying now with the persecution. The Spanish Crown now requested – or do I mean required? – two Muslim families per village to remain. Their skills were urgently needed: the new Christian farmers being brought in from more back-ward parts of Spain to take their place must be taught how to use and maintain the sophisticated Moorish irrigation system. Without it, the rich crops of the south would be lost to the newly pure Christian nation.

That system is still in use to this day. Let Pedro take you for a walk in those Alpujarra hills above his town (Alpujarra is really *al-bajara*, 'the highlands' in Arabic) and ask a local to point you to the nearest irrigation channels. You will soon find yourself wandering along many miles of sturdy stone pathways, built right into the narrow rushing watercourses that cling to the steep sides of hill and valley, engineered all those centuries ago to bring security of life and harvest to the farmlands of the interior. The Alpujarra local will very likely tell you – these being post-Franco days when people can speak their minds freely – that the Moors did more for Andalusia, nowadays an isolated and poverty-stricken region, than self-centred Madrid has done in the five centuries since they left.

And as for me, settled here in Italy, several hundred miles further along the Mediterranean coast, many's the time I've stood, at the end of a hot, dry summer, gazing hopelessly into my dried-up well and watching my vegetable patch curl up and die for lack of water, heartily wishing that the Moors had concentrated a bit harder on their northern conquests. They came to the south of Italy, all right, and held parts of Calabria – where I have seen with my own envious eyes villages set in that desiccated countryside which nevertheless own a merrily gushing public fountain on every street corner – and of course the kingdom of Sicily. But the best they could do for us up here in the Diano valley was a feeble attempt at coming in by sea from el-Andalus, in the year 739. For a century, it seems, they held La Garde-Freinet, nowadays well known to me as a train-station somewhere before Nice, where the train waits an inexplicably long time – perhaps in mourning? – before departing again for Monte Carlo, the Italian border, and home. And that was that.

All we in Liguria have to show in the way of a Moorish presence are a few evocative ruined towers along the coastline, known locally as 'Moorish towers', a name that had me fooled for some time. But no: these were in truth anti-Moorish towers, watchtowers from which to keep the North Africans at bay, once Barbarossa and the corsairs had begun launching punishing raids, from their bases around Algiers, on Genoa's coastal possessions, including, in 1508, our own Diano Marina.

Here, in Liguria, we were left, by default, to the Christian monasteries, which did, three or four centuries after the Muslim arrival in Spain, introduce the olive tree to our region, for which they are heartily to be thanked. But Christian technical expertise at the time was certainly nowhere near that of Islam, and did not extend to brilliantly executed irrigation systems. If only those Moors had spent a century or two here, now, my tomato crop might get to ripen however dry the weather, and there would be no more of this sad shrivelling on the vine.

2

No sooner had I committed myself to heading off with Gérard and Guy than every friend I had, Italian or English – everyone who'd actually heard of the Maghreb – went into panic stations. Was I mad? Wasn't there serious trouble there? Riots, strikes, Islamic fundamentalists, violence in the streets?

Was there? I had no idea. I'd been too deeply sunk in what I believe someone called the Idiocy of Rural Life. The only North African news I'd heard for months had been from the plant expert down at the Farmers' Co-operative in San Pietro, when I'd taken him a few samples of miserable twisted leaves from my sickly *quattro-stagioni* lemon tree. Alas, he had said, examining my exhibits with his magnifying glass, he could not help. The definitive cure for this disease was still to be determined, though they were working hard on it at the University of Genoa. It was a new form of blight, unknown here in Italy until a couple of years previously. It had probably come over from North Africa, where it was already doing a lot of damage, in a cargo of imported lemons.

Imported lemons! From North Africa! It is hard adequately to convey the full horror of the tone an Italian horticulturalist will employ when using these phrases. Suffice it to say that riots, strikes and street violence would be infinitely preferable. Possibly Islam too.

A fearful phone call to Gérard established that among the news he had recently weighed and found wanting there had indeed been reports aplenty of riots and strikes. Not in Morocco; but Algeria, he said, had recently fallen into the clutches of the IMF and the World Bank. It was in the process of being forcibly globalized, and its people were not taking too kindly to the chill winds of the World Market, far less to the joyous commitment of their present government, known for its corruption and nepotism, to this novel form of Freedom. Thousands were jobless; people could no longer afford the basic necessities of life. Last month the Front for Islamic Salvation had won a whole quarter of the votes cast in the national elections. That might not seem a lot, but the government itself had only got twelve per cent. It had simply suspended operations, fearful of an Islamist victory, then declared a state of emergency and resigned, leaving the army in charge of finding a substitute.

And now, of course, the whole country was in uproar – not just the Islamists, but anybody who believed in democracy. Including, at a guess, the sixty-three per cent who had withheld their votes from both parties. So altogether, said Gérard, this should be a very interesting time to visit!

Should it? I didn't think it sounded too restful, myself.

Fortunately for my nerves, I now discovered that I actually had an Algerian acquaintance here in Italy: a very calming influence. I'd always assumed that Samir was Moroccan, thanks to the local habit of calling all North Africans *Il Marocchino*. But no. It now turned out that Samir, who often lent a hand at busy times in my friend Ciccio's restaurant up in the hills, was from the city of Oran, in Algeria.

Would you be afraid, asked the sensible Samir, to holiday in Ireland, because of the troubles?

Well, no, I said. Of course I wouldn't. I'd often been to Ireland.

Exactly! said Samir. Every year many people go there to relax and rest! Maybe if they would go into the ghettos of Belfast, or some such place, they could get caught up in the problems, but why would a visitor go to such a place? The argument is only between Algerians – and then, only between a few extremists on either side.

Comforting. And far from warning me off the trip, Samir and his Dutch wife, Mireille, were delighted to hear of it. I was going to love it. They now insisted on writing me out a great long list of places we mustn't miss en route, of foodstuffs we must be sure to try, and of relations we absolutely must drop in on. They had been going back home to Algeria every autumn for ten years, said Mireille. She and Sammy always spent the whole month of October there. It was the perfect place to recover from the stress and strain of the full-on summer months, spent catering for demanding Italian diners on the Riviera dei Fiori.

Much better. Never mind religion and politics. This is what you really need when you set off travelling to an unknown land. A list of attractions, relations, and tasty snacks, scribbled on the back of a restaurant napkin.

We have arrived here in Morocco on a warm, bright spring morning. It is still only March, but bright fingers of early-morning sunlight are streaming in through the curlicued grilles at the window of this tiny backstreet bar, picking out the basket of fresh croissants on the worn zinc counter and pixillating the brightly tiled walls behind it. Occasionally, as the proprietor prepares our three *cafés-crème*, a stray beam catches his grizzled stubble and turns it to gold. But there's to be no luxuriating outside in the sunshine for us three yet: not if we want our breakfasts. The inviting little tables in the street are, we have just learned, not to be used until after dark.

We have headed for the town of Tetuan straight from the Spanish ferry, to be dropped off in the main square that divides the city's ancient walled heart, the warren of narrow streets inside the medina, from the newer, colonial-built part of town. Somewhere not too far from here, the buses leave for the Rif, the rugged mountain range running right along the coast, parallel to the Mediterranean – the length of which we must travel to reach Morocco's eastern border and Algeria. A fifteen-hour ride, if we did it all in one go. But we have no plans to do any such thing. We will be taking it slow and leisurely. We've found ourselves a lift for the first leg of the journey, anyway – in the car of a certain Tobias, whom we met on the boat. He had a few errands to do here in Tetuan, he said, but he would be back to collect us in no time. We could get a coffee in the square while we waited.

As Tobias had predicted, there were several large, commodious-looking cafés around the square. But alas, not one of them was open. Were we too early? You wouldn't have thought so: there was a hum and buzz of activity around the picturesque keyhole arch that led into the medina, and it looked as if a market was well under way within the walls.

Then we spotted this little bar, on a side-alley, the shutters half-open at its doors. Above the doorway, a Hand of Fatima palm-print, keeping the Evil Eye at bay. Not in the cobalt-blue I used to see in Portugal, though, but in a kind of rust-brown. Still, it seemed to be bringing us luck. Peering inside, detecting signs of life, we took our seats at one of the three little tables in the alley, stretching and yawning in the early rays while we waited for the place to finish opening. Gérard pulled out his travel guide and set to studying the entry for Tetuan. Guy glowered and sighed loudly. The book, a French guide called *Le Petit futé* – *The Little Cunning One*, or maybe it should it translate as *The Small Wily One*, since its cover is decorated with a smug-looking fox – was already a bone of contention. Guy had announced firmly, when Gérard first produced it, that he did not wish his travels to be guided by a book: he wanted his experience first-hand, not filtered through someone else's eyes. Gérard, on the other hand, maintains that you see better when you have some idea of what you're looking at.

Leaving them to this philosophical debate, I set to checking out the scenery. A particularly rowdy scene from the Bible; that is the first thing that springs to mind when you arrive in North Africa. A thousand and one stereotypes lurch into life at your first sight of Moroccans going about their daily business. You can't help yourself. Wizards and sorcerers, Jesus and his Disciples, Barbary pirates and desert sheikhs, Ali Baba and Aladdin, the Blessed Virgin and Mary Magdalene, medieval monks and Chaucerian nuns . . . all the way on through *The Lord of the Rings* to Obi wan Kenobi. How many childhood hours can I have spent, swathing myself in tablecloths, towels and dishcloths, my head filled with a jumble of romance, mystery, and wild adventure, trying to achieve just the effects that these passers-by carried off so casually?

Across the square, two youths in cleverly twisted-and-knotted head-cloths were loading barrows stacked high with crates of bottles; closer by, a bunch of older men with dark five o'clock shadows and crocheted skullcaps clambered – in ankle-length jellabas, no problem – onto a lorry laden with chickens in twiggy wooden coops, and began unloading. A middle-aged woman in bright draperies, several layers of knotted scarf and shawl, walked elegantly through the middle of this scene, balancing upon one shoulder a massive sacking bundle of some feathery-leafed vegetable: carrots, maybe, or fennel? She turned in through the arch, showing tough bare heels decorated with henna, and crossing the path of two dignified bearded men, each wrapped in a good half-dozen toga-like yards of fine cream cloth. One of them had draped the last few feet of this garment casually across his head, and looked like nothing so much as the classic image of God himself, from some Renaissance chapel ceiling in Italy. Now came a man leading a donkey half-swamped by an eccentrically ancient-and-modern load: on one of its flanks a bundle of home-made besoms, simple brooms made of tied twigs; on the other a great tangle of multicoloured plastic sieves and colanders. Its master was a tall, cadaverous-looking man in an ankle-length burnous of rough-spun wool, his face half-hidden in the sinister shadow of its deep, pointed hood.

No, no, not sinister, of course; get a grip! Romance, mystery and wild adventure were not about to break out, in spite of the wondrous array of clothing and headgear. This was perfectly ordinary outer-wear here: the local equivalent of overalls and boiler-suits. The white toga, Guy says, is the business suit of the prosperous in these parts, made of the finest of wools. His family had one in their chest of souvenirs from their old life in Algeria: it was always protected by vast quantities of mothballs and was the only item so precious that he was never allowed to use it for his dressing-up.

A whole chest of North African souvenirs? Really? Some people have all the luck. I had only the contents of my mother's airing cupboard.

Two of the skullcap men were carrying the chicken-coops up into the market now, while another casually tossed the cargo down, crate by crate, the merchandise fluttering and squawking, red-wattled beaks stabbing through the bars. One of the wheelbarrow boys passed close enough for us to see the labels on his bottles: sinuous Arabic script, brilliant white against scarlet red. Something strangely familiar about the format, though. Of course: Arabic Coca-Cola. The next woman to pass us, with an assorted basket of aubergines, bunches of spinach, and loose eggs, wore an extra scarf veiling the lower part of her face. And on her head (could it be?) a genuine, no-doubt-about-it cotton dishcloth. The classic white glass-cloth with a red border, such as we use every day in the heartlands of Europe. The cloth was just sitting there, plain and unselfconscious, casually – no, stylishly – draped over the top of her various other layers of head-scarf. Guy and I caught one another's eye, but the mutual giggle was stifled before it was born. Something about this woman's bearing made her dishcloth, unlike our own childish dishcloths of the past – or, indeed, our green bath-towels – look utterly, proudly, authentic.

Beyond her, a pair of mules entered the arch, heavily laden with rolls of cloth. The donkeys and mules were essential here. Just like the streets of Granada's Albaycín, where you still meet beasts of burden aplenty, no lorry could possibly fit down the narrow streets of the medina. It was built in the days when donkeys and mules were the only form of transport. They would never be out of a job as long as this place survived.

Which would be for a very long time, contributed Gérard all of a sudden, taking his nose out of his book. Because UNESCO has declared the medina of Tetuan a World Heritage Site, he added, waving the publication at us triumphantly.

There! said Guy. That was a classic example of exactly the sort of pointless information a guidebook gave you! Why did we need to know that?

I for one was rather happy to hear that UNESCO had assured a future for those lovely, gentle beasts of burden. Though it didn't seem politic to mention this just at the moment.

All right, then! said Gérard, on his mettle now. Did Guy know that the medina had been built – or rather, rebuilt from the ruins of an earlier city – in the sixteenth century, by Muslims and Jews who'd been driven out of Spain by the Inquisition? And that was why the medina looked so Spanish?

Guy looked at Gérard. Then he looked pointedly at the distinctly Islamic-looking keyhole archway in the twenty-foot-high wall of the medina.

Are you mad? he said. What on earth looks Spanish about that? Bin the book!

Spanish Islamic, I contributed knowledgeably. Moorish.

I was with Gérard, I decided, on the topic of the guidebook. And as soon as I'd got some breakfast inside me, I was going to take a quick look at the works of my old friends from el-Andalus before we left town, Tobias or no Tobias.

With perfect timing, a portly gentleman now emerged from the café, ducking under the blind. But, rather than take our breakfast order as we were expecting, he gazed mournfully at us for a long moment, lowered himself into an empty chair, and finally announced that perhaps we might prefer to sit indoors.

Well, no, we said. We were enjoying it out here in the fresh morning air. We'd just like a coffee and some small breakfast snack.

It might perhaps be better if we came inside, still, said our host, inscrutably.

Why? asked Gérard. Was he expecting rain?

No, no, said our host, smiling at last. *Inshallah!* How welcome a drop of rain would be! Spring had been so dry this year . . . But the thing was, he added after another lengthy pause, with a gesture

43

towards the square, that there were many hungry, thirsty people about, who might take it amiss . . .

I took another look over the road, perplexed. It's not that I imagined Morocco was a rich country, of course, but surely people weren't actually starving in the streets here? Wouldn't we have heard? In fact, not a few of the market shoppers passing by looked somewhat on the stout side.

The proprietor quickly identified the problem. We had just arrived from Europe now, this very morning, *évidemment*?

Yes, we certainly had.

Of course! Then he must explain to us that today was the last day of the month of Ramadan – during which the faithful of Islam must fast during the hours of daylight. No food, not even a glass of water, nothing at all would pass their lips until the sun had set: in memory of the Prophet Mohammed, and in solidarity with the poor of the world. That is why his shutters were kept half-closed at the moment. Not everyone is religious, of course, and since there were plenty of Unbelievers like us about the town wanting refreshment, he was only too happy to oblige. But all those people hard at work in the market would not be eating or drinking for many hours yet. It was better to show some respect, not to flaunt our breakfasting – our breaking of the fast – before their eyes. Did we not agree?

What idiots we were. We knew perfectly well that it was Ramadan. We'd even made sure to time our arrival today for the end of the fast, in case it made travelling more complicated. We'd done our research, too. We could tell you reams of stuff about Ramadan. If you break the fast, you must pay penance by feeding a poor person; if you have marital intercourse, which is also forbidden by daylight, you have to feed fifty poor people. (How embarrassing would that be? Think of the smirk-worthiness of your situation as you went about rounding up your fifty poor people, all only too aware of exactly why you were so keen to feed them.) We knew that the fast commemorated the period when God was busy revealing His Word, the Koran, to Mohammed, and that the duty to observe it was the Fourth of the

Five Pillars of Islam. We could even, on a good day, list off all Five Pillars. But it hadn't occurred to any of us, having no actual experience of a fasting city, what that would mean in practice. Obvious: a lot of hungry, thirsty people everywhere. Rude and inconsiderate to eat and drink in front of them.

Light having now dawned, we rose with alacrity and followed our host in under the blind.

Safe indoors, he relaxed visibly. Poor man. Was he fearing that we were about to make a stand, some kind of up-yours-Islam gesture to the local populace? Maybe so. There is a lot of mindless anti-Muslim feeling in the Western world these days, after all.

He must introduce himself, he said. He was Moustafa, *propriétaire*. And he shook each of our hands ceremoniously, placing his right hand over his heart each time in what seemed an oddly melodramatic manner – though we would soon discover that this was just the normal way to greet a new acquaintance here in Morocco.

This was a much better idea, was it not? Moustafa said. All the more so since the month was nearly over, and after weeks of discomfort, people's tempers often got somewhat short!

Ah. Of course. There would no doubt be plenty of mindless anti-Western feeling in the Muslim world too.

And what, asked Moustafa, getting down to business, did we desire?

Now at last, sitting at our tiny table by the even tinier window, we were reaping our just reward: three large bowls of deliciously aromatic coffee, accompanied by a basket of those fragrant golden croissants. My travelling companions, uttering muted cries of joy, fell upon their national breakfast like starving men, sugaring and stirring the *café-crème*, tearing frenziedly into the croissants and dipping the buttery fragments into the heavenly beverage . . .

Gérard finally came up for air again two croissants later. Perfect! he exclaimed. Just like home!

Better than home, said Guy, taking another slurp. When did you last get your breakfast coffee served in a good old-fashioned bowl? Not since your mother made it! *Merveilleux!*

I sat observing this scene with some misgiving. What an advantage it is, when travelling abroad, not to have much of a national cuisine to miss. I was certainly used to Italians carrying on like this: I'd often found myself accompanying Italian friends, holidaying in Britain, on desperate – and usually hopeless – missions to hunt down the Proper Espresso without which their day could not begin. But I had thought the French were made of sterner stuff. Evidently not. After a mere two days of foreign breakfasts – Spanish breakfasts at that, nothing too exotic – they were already pining for their home comforts. And we three still had well over a thousand North African miles to travel together before the parting of our ways. Still, Gérard and Guy might be in luck. Tetuan was in the ex-Spanish zone of Morocco, and they'd done all right here. Much of the rest of the Maghreb had been run by the French themselves for well over a century. There was certainly a good chance that the rich vein of ex-colonial croissants-and-*café-crème*-served-in-a-bowl we'd struck here would extend right the way down to the Sahara . . .

Moustafa having returned to stand over us, beaming benevolently, I took the opportunity to ask him about his Hand of Fatima. Oh, that was nothing – his mother put it there, he said, looking slightly shame-faced. As well he might. I had gathered from our recent Islamic investigations that the purists of the religion, the ones who seem to be gaining the upper hand these days, frown upon all superstition of the Hand-of-Fatima type. They sound depressingly similar to the puritans of Christianity, all plain God-alone worship, no decorations, no frills: going around condemning anything at all entertaining or attractive as sinful, pagan or idolatrous. It was this kind of stuff, in its doom-laden Highland Scots version, which led to the last three generations of my family abandoning organized religion entirely, in favour of the principle of do-as-you-would-be-done-by. A fine principle, too. Entirely adequate to purpose, couldn't possibly offend a

God if there turned out to be one – and allows you to enjoy the pleasant things of life to the full.

Moustafa had never heard of a blue Hand of Fatima, he said. His was done with henna. That was how the old people always did it round here. Henna attracts the good spirits, they say, the kindly djinns, and repels the bad ones that might harm you.

These old people, as it happens, are not wrong. Back in Granada, intrigued by the Spanish Inquisition's attempts to ban the use of henna, I investigated the matter, to find that not only had henna been used since biblical times – even appearing in the love poetry of the Song of Solomon, with deeply romantic and sensuous connotations – but it was also a powerful antibacterial agent. If we are to count the bugs Candida, Staphylococcus and E. Coli as bad spirits – a good enough description to be going along with – then Moustafa's mamma was entirely right about the properties of henna. Though not, perhaps, about applying it to doorposts. Still, I hate to imagine the effect on the health of the Spanish nation when both henna and the *hammam* were banished from the scene. I imagine an Inquisition epidemiologist, had such a personage existed, would have gathered some pretty horrifying statistics.

Moustafa was now telling me that he thought we might find such a thing as a blue Hand of Fatima in Chefchaouen, a town in the foothills of the Rif that was famed for painting everything blue, even its pathways . . . Were we heading that way?

We certainly were: it was the first town we would pass on our way through the Rif, heading along the coast towards Algiers. And I was pleased to hear its mystifying-looking name pronounced aloud: Shef-show-en.

Algeria? Moustafa was not impressed. I should send the Frenchmen off alone to that godless place, he said, and stay here in Morocco. Being English, I would naturally feel more at home in a country with respect for its traditions – and for its Royal Family.

Why had I ever started this conversation? Not only did I suffer from a deep lack of interest in royalty in general, but the Moroccan king in particular did not sound like my cup of tea. His hand-picked interior minister, in charge of the Moroccan equivalent of the PIDE, was nicknamed The Butcher. Several thousand Moroccans had inexplicably gone missing over the last two decades. Need I say more? Also, I badly wanted to get at my breakfast – but how was I supposed to sit stuffing my face in front of a starving man? Not that it seemed to be bothering Gérard and Guy. The croissant-basket was nearly empty already, which made my own situation all the more desperate.

Light-headed with hunger and guilt, I must have burbled something about fasting and Ramadan, because Moustafa was now telling me that it wasn't so bad when Ramadan fell at this time of the year. The worst was when it came in high summer. Double the heat; double the thirst; and double the hours of daylight to keep to the fast in. People started keeling over in the streets, or fainting at their work.

In high summer? I knew Ramadan moved about, but had imagined it stayed within certain fixed bounds, like, say, Easter. But no. Over thirty-odd years, Moustafa explained, you will have experienced it in every possible season. The lunar months used in the Islamic calendar give a lot less than three hundred and sixty-five days to a year, and don't correspond to the seasons of the year at all. Ramadan falls roughly ten days earlier each year.

And does everyone really not touch so much as a drop of water, even in such heat? Are people allowed to slip up occasionally?

Only sick people, or women with child, or travellers on the road, answered Moustafa. Or children, of course, who don't begin joining the fast till puberty. Otherwise, nothing must pass your lips: not while your eye can distinguish a black thread from a white thread in the palm of your hand. That is the word of the Koran.

Really? I was fascinated. Did people actually go around with a pair of threads, checking, then?

Of course! Look around you later tonight, said Moustafa. Once it begins to get dark, you will see everyone out in the streets, palms outstretched, eyes fixed on those two little cotton threads; just waiting for the moment to come when they can rush indoors and throw themselves on their dinners!

But this, it turned out, was only Moustafa's little joke. You visitors love *le folklore* so much, he said. Often it is hard to resist making a little humour! But of course not! In these modern times, it is all done scientifically. Look over the road there, up on the roof: see that siren? That is how we know when the fast is over!

Moustafa went off, guffawing, back to his bar. And I grabbed a croissant.

3

My fellow travellers being men of their word – men who, when they say they will be travelling overland on local transport, really mean it – we had caught the train down to Andalusia, and the ferry from Algeciras at dawn this morning. The boat trip was a most educational experience. The ferry passenger soon discovers that the dark mysteries of distant Africa lie a mere three-quarters of an hour from the familiar Brit-packed beaches of southern Spain. Only nine miles of sea separate the two continents. The last time my world-view took such a battering was when the Berlin Wall came down, the Iron Curtain floated wide, and the fearful Communist bloc turned out to be a place you could, if you lived in Italy, just get into your car and drive to.

Still, though the distance may be short, these are some of the most dangerous and unpredictable seas in the world. The sun-warmed waters of the land-locked Mediterranean stream out here through the narrow Straits of Gibraltar, while the cold might of the massive Atlantic fights its way in: an encounter that unleashes unimaginable powers of wind and current. Turbulent seas, and a turbulent history, too. By the time we had docked on African soil and got through Moroccan passport control, it had become clear to us that the troubled past of this area had segued seamlessly into a troubled present.

Gérard takes a seat in the stern of the ship, pulls out the *The Little Cunning One* and sets to checking his coordinates. Guy and I get on with checking out the rest of the vessel, making our way through stinging sea spray up to the bows, where the rugged brown cliffs of Morocco are blurring slowly into focus. Here, in a powerful head-wind, we make our first African acquaintances of the trip.

Tobias is leaning right out over the handrail, shading his eyes against sun, wind and spray, straining into the distance. He is hoping to catch sight of his home town, Melilla, he shouts: another 140 kilo-metres eastwards along the Moroccan coastline. Sometimes you can see its headland from the boat. But it is too misty, too early in the day. No sign at all. Just his luck.

Next to Tobias, also gazing out to sea, but in an altogether less fevered manner, is a man with a gentle smile under a bushy mous-tache, a good twenty years older than him, who introduces himself as Yazid. Yazid, short, dark and a little on the plump side, certainly fits my notion of a Moroccan. But Tobias, with golden brown eyes and a great bush of auburn hair, is a most unlikely-looking North African.

Yazid, he tells us as we withdraw to a slightly less windswept corner, is from Berkane, a short way past Melilla. And although they have only just met, Tobias has kindly offered to save Yazid the tedious bus trip and give him a lift most of the way, getting him home several hours earlier. Yazid seems in a positive fever to see his wife again. He left Holland yesterday, he tells us, and since then he has rung her three times: from Antwerp, from Marseilles, and just now from Spain. Each phone call is making him more homesick! Tobias is a good man to be so neighbourly, in spite of the troubles that are afflicting him.

No serious afflictions, says Tobias, joining us in the shelter of the cabin wall. A few problems in his love life, that's all. A bracing sea crossing, some good home cooking at his mamma's, and he will soon rise above his broken heart. All the more reason, anyway, to help out another lonely man who's missing his woman.

Tobias does not only look distinctly un-Moroccan, but sounds it, too. I am beginning to suspect from his accent that his mother tongue is not Arabic at all, but Spanish.

Of course! Tobias says. That is because he is, in fact, Spanish. Melilla is a Spanish town, a Spanish enclave on Moroccan shores. The port of Ceuta where we will soon be landing is also a Spanish possession. Both towns have been Spanish since the fifteenth century – officially parts of Spain, and now outposts of the European Union on African shores.

I am startled. How come I've never ever heard tell of this African corner of Europe? Or do I mean European corner of Africa? You'd imagine, wouldn't you, that the supporters of a British Gibraltar, whenever Spain brought up the question of sovereignty over the Rock, would be emphatically pointing the finger at Ceuta and Melilla – at not one, but two Spanish cities still held on Moroccan soil – and making loud remarks about sauce for the goose and sauce for the gander?

No, on second thoughts, that might just make both parties look bad. Still, it's surprising that the Moroccans themselves don't try to claim their territory back, the way Spain sporadically does over Gibraltar, isn't it?

According to our new acquaintances, though, there is nothing at all surprising about this. His own king's government, Yazid says, wouldn't dream of offending Morocco's main trading partners – not with the Moroccan economy in such dodgy shape. And nobody, anywhere, ever, says Tobias dramatically, knows of African Spain: neither Ceuta nor Melilla. Except the mainland Spanish, that is, and in their case, Tobias would rather they didn't. Once upon a time you could be proud to be a Melillan. But not any longer. His city's main claim to fame was always its great patriotism. It was the base from which General Franco invaded his own country, accompanied by a thousand loyal Moroccan troops, saving Spain from the perils of modern democracy for the next forty years. And, let us not forget, having a seriously negative effect on the Spanish red-tie market.

In his parents' day, Tobias says, the city's loyalty to Franco was something to be proud of, but now that the Generalíssimo is dead and his name is mud, Melilla's association with his exploits does little for its image. A life-size statue still stands down on Melilla's port, he says, commemorating Franco's triumph. Nobody takes care of it any more. It is cracked and dirty, lichen-covered, surrounded by weeds, and ignored by the local populace. But still, according to Tobias, other young Spaniards assume that all Melillenses must be some kind of Fascist-supporting reactionaries. He goes over to Andalusia a lot; he has to, he says, to earn a living. He is a builder, a shuttering carpenter. He's just finished the concrete on one of the myriad British-inspired building sites of Almería – and he'll be forced to go back there soon. There's no work of that ilk to be had in his home town. And he can tell us that you get treated like a dog over there if you're from African Spain. Like a dog!

Yazid, with a wheezing chuckle, tells us that we should take Tobias' laments with a large pinch of salt. There are plenty of building jobs much closer to home than Spain. Yazid himself is building a house, he says, in Berkane, with four flats in it, one for each of his children. He is on his way home from his job on the Dutch railways: he has taken his month's holiday now, bringing his year's savings with him, especially to get work started on the second floor. He would be happy, he says, clapping Tobias enthusiastically on the back, to offer him a job in Berkane, starting immediately – just a short drive from his home – if he wants one. What about it?

Both men find this suggestion utterly hilarious. Tobias joins his putative employer in hearty laughter.

Work-shy, you see, these Spaniards! says Yazid, once they have got over the private joke, and collapses again into breathless laughter.

Perplexed, we await enlightenment.

No Spaniard, Yazid explains between chuckles, would ever dream of working on a Moroccan building site. And no Moroccan would consider employing a Spaniard – not even an African Spaniard. Their towns may be only a few miles apart, but wages in Berkane are less than a third of European ones. Tobias, born with the right to work in Europe, would be mad to take a Moroccan job. Why do we think Yazid leaves his wife and family to go all the way to Holland? Far from employing rich Spaniards, he says, he will be taking on fellow Moroccans from down in the poverty-stricken south, where people are glad to get any sort of a job. They are hard workers too, he says, not like our lazy Spanish friend; and Yazid needs to get a move on – his oldest son will be getting married next year, and the ground floor, where Yazid's own wife and the younger children are living, still isn't properly finished. Though at least he has, at long last, managed to get that telephone put in.

Yazid, we gather, is almost as keen to see his new phone as he is to see his wife. He can't wait, he says. A real telephone, all his, sitting there in his own home. The first house phone his family has ever had, and already it has improved his life beyond all measure! He will be ringing his wife again as soon as we dock in Ceuta!

Yazid has been working abroad, he tells us, since the year he got married, twenty-five years ago. And he reckons that, over all that time, he has spent less than three years altogether in his family's company. Still, looking on the bright side, he says, they certainly haven't got bored with one another! It was hard enough to keep in touch at all. When he first left Morocco there were hardly any phones in the country, and no postal service worth mentioning, either. Migrants like him would pay professional runners from their home towns to carry letters for them – and then, of course, the wife had to pay someone to read them out to her, and to write down her answer. No chance of mentioning anything private or intimate. The first phones were a lot better, but still, there Yazid would be, queueing with his workmates at some phone box – in Germany first, then in Holland – hoping against hope to get through to another in Morocco, where his wife would be waiting. Nine times out of ten something would go wrong. And then when it didn't, it cost a fortune! For a while, when audio cassettes first came out, Yazid and Naima used those instead of the phones. You could chat, relaxed, for a whole hour, for the price of the cassette and the postage stamp. And say openly what you meant. Even whisper sweet nothings, if you wanted to! But this wonderful system was soon spoilt – by jealousy and greed.

We make noises of polite enquiry. Jealousy and greed?

Yes. It's a terrible thing, says Yazid, how his own countrymen, the ones who were lucky enough to get a good start in life, to be able to stay at home in their own town – people with school qualifications and a decent career in the Post Office, for example – can be full of hatred and envy for migrants like himself. They're disgusted that a man like him, an unskilled ignoramus, can earn good European wages, afford to build a nice new home for himself and his family, a place to retire to and live happily ever after, snug among his grandchildren. They sit in their nice, clean offices, he says, muttering to one another about ignorant country bumpkins getting above themselves. The Post Office officials started demanding bribes when migrants' wives came to collect their letters or packages. Nothing too obvious; they would insist on selling them lottery tickets, stuff like that, to cover the bare-faced blackmail. If the woman didn't buy one, she would be told she had no mail that day, and go home empty-handed.

But look – all that is behind him! He has his own wonderful telephone in the house! He's had a lock put on it, of course, so his wife and children can't bankrupt him while he's away, and now he will always have peace of mind: no more anxieties about staying in touch. Best of all, he confides, is the way he can ring his wife randomly, at any time of the day or night. That way, he doesn't have to worry, the way he used to, about what she, or his daughter, might be getting lured into with no man in the house to watch over them . . .

Poor wife! She can't even use the phone herself, then. I wonder how glad she is to have it in the house?

Gérard and his guidebook now arrive at our side, Gérard having absorbed enough information from it, he tells Guy with a wicked look, to make sense of what he's looking at. While Gérard gets on, at last, with admiring the misty-morning view of the shores of Africa, where the vague outline of a small white coastal town set against lush green vegetation is starting to be visible, I check out the book to discover that there is much more to Melilla's bad name on the Spanish mainland than Tobias has let on. The only industry in Tobias' city these days, I read, apart from a small fishing fleet, is smuggling. Melilla is Mediterranean Morocco's main depot for contraband. Hashish goes north to Europe, along with would-be asylum-seekers or migrant workers, while electrical goods, avoiding heavy Moroccan taxes, come south.

Tobias is horrified to hear that all this is written down in black and white. He snatches the book from me, only to be defeated by the complexities of written French. But would the same stuff be written in an English version?

I imagine so, I say.

So the whole world can read that stuff, he says. The whole world! Why? I ask. Is it not true?

But that is not the problem. Tobias fears, he explains, that the ill fame of his town may have spread as far as the United States of America. Tobias, unlike the contented Yazid, seems a very angry man. He is only on this boat, he says, and obliged to go home to Melilla, because he has just been jilted by his fiancée – an American, from Texas. Tobias, who has now realized that I am English, appears to feel that, since I share not only a sex but also a language with this girl, I should be ready to take my share of responsibility for her actions. He was supposed to join her in the States next month, he tells me accusingly. Her parents had even stood guarantor for his visa, though they'd never met him. Tobias spent almost a whole month's wages on the ticket, and pulled out of the next job he had lined up, too. But last week, all of a sudden, Marla rang him from the States, a different person, cold as ice, to say that it had all been a mistake: now she was back home, she'd realized theirs had been nothing but a holiday romance. The wedding was off, the visa guarantee withdrawn, and his bright future on the gold-paved streets of America snatched away, leaving him adrift on the Mediterranean, minus last month's money, and on his way home to Mamma. He was just a human tourist attraction, he says bitterly, a handy Latin lover with a set of free Spanish lessons thrown in. Though now he has begun to wonder whether maybe her parents got to her – could they be racists who, once they'd worked out where Melilla was, thought he was actually an African African? But then – if everyone in the whole world can read this insulting description of his home town, maybe that was what did for him?

What else does it say? he asks anxiously, handing it back to me. I flick on through it. Nothing, I tell him reassuringly, that would put off a good American parent. All just ancient history. It says that the Spanish have, as Tobias told us, held Melilla since 1497. (A mere five years after the fall of Granada, I note: not content with exiling their Jews and Muslims, Ferdinand and Isabella, by the looks of things, couldn't resist chasing hotfoot after the other two Peoples of the Book, still living in relative harmony.) Then that Spain used the town as a penal colony for a time, as a sort of Spanish Botany Bay. A perfect place to hold your least desirable prisoners, it says: a fortress city with an unpredictable sea on three sides of it, and to landward, the Berber clans, keen to get their property back, roaming bands of ferocious armed men, just waiting for the chance to cut a few Spanish throats . . .

Yazid laughs heartily at this. It's the other way round, these days, he says. The ferocious armed men are the Spanish inside the walls of Melilla, not the Berbers beyond. Far from stopping desperate Spaniards getting out, the city spends all its time stopping desperate Africans moving in. Because, once inside, they are into the European Union. And a hard fight Melilla is having of it, too. They've put up a ten-foot barrier, right the way round Melillan territory – between his own town and Tobias' – and have brought in the Spanish army to patrol it day and night. Same goes for Ceuta – we'll see as we come in to land. Controlling the sea is harder, though. People-smugglers take big money from would-be immigrants to Europe, telling them they'll be landed on Spanish shores. Then they drop them in the water off Ceuta or Melilla, to swim for it . . .

Europe is putting up the money now to raise the fences to twice the height, Tobias tells us. Word's already out in the building trade: it could be the first decent job there's been on this side of the water for years. Obviously they can't be planning to employ cheap Moroccan labour to build a fence against – well, against themselves! Two solid barriers, five yards apart: surveillance cameras, motion sensors, floodlights. Razor wire on the top for good measure. With a sentry post every half kilometre. Because someone who's walked right across the Sahara, like a lot of those boys have, isn't going to balk at a bit of plain barbed wire for long, is he?

Still, who knows, says Tobias, if he will even get a job on the project? He would much rather be in America with his Marla. Do I think he should write her a letter? Should he keep ringing, or will silence make her heart grow fonder? Should he try to get a tourist visa and go over, even if she says she doesn't want to see him?

I do my best to rise to my new role as expert on feminine psychology, Anglo-Saxon style, but I find it hard to concentrate on Tobias' love-life. I am too distracted by the thought of that barrier. Good job Salazar didn't get round to building such a thing between Portugal and Spain! Still, imagine having made it halfway across Africa, hundreds of miles from your home, so close to your goal: only to find that last fence defeating you. A family back home waiting hopefully for news of your success. How could you not try to get over it? Of course you would. You wouldn't care if you got cut about by razor wire, would you? You'd go in the hours of darkness, try laying your clothes over it to protect yourself, maybe, jump down on the other side, bloody but certain you were in with a chance – only to find yourself trapped and floodlit, stuck in that narrow alley, and the tramp of soldiers' boots heading your way. It doesn't bear thinking about.

Tobias isn't bothered, he says. He wants the work. That's how life is. He isn't allowed into the USA. Other people aren't allowed into Europe. What do you expect?

I don't know what I expect, but surely we humans can come up with something better than an earth criss-crossed by impassable barriers separating the haves from the have-nots? From a distance, in the abstract, it may be easy to believe in their necessity. But from close up? I, for one, certainly couldn't look another human being in the eye and give him any good reason why he should have less right than me to travel the world and try his fortune.

Now that the warm morning sun is clearing away the sea mist, the Rock of Gibraltar, rearing high, is just visible again, receding into the deep blue distance. The northern Pillar of Hercules, last outpost of our own continent . . . Or maybe not, these days, when we can just shift bits of one continent to another as the fancy takes us. Which of the high African hills ahead, now looming ever closer, is the Pillar's southern twin? Does anyone know?

No. Nobody does. It's been a thousand years and more since anybody knew the answer to that question, says Tobias. Some say it is Jebel Musa, over to the west there, on Moroccan soil. But most people prefer Monte Hacho for the role, that hill straight ahead, above Ceuta – the one with the Byzantine fortress sitting on it.

I suppose it makes sense, in the tangled history of this part of the world, that the southern Pillar should have a Spanish name, and the northern Pillar an Arabic one. Just for balance. Because Yazid tells us that the real name of Gibraltar is *Jebel Tariq* – Tariq's hill. Our word is just a corruption of the original Arabic.

More intriguing than the etymology, though, was the back story. Who was Tariq? What was he up to on this hill? Why did the place get named after him? Simple. The year was 710 AD, and Tariq, a Berber leader recently converted to Islam, was assembling his forces there. He was about to launch that Islamic invasion of Iberia: the one that stopped half way up France and never did make it to my tomato patch. Strange that Franco the Spaniard should launch his invasion from the Maghreb, while Tariq the Maghrebi launches his from Spain. Does this reflect the level of welcome they were expecting to meet? As invasions of Spain go, General Franco's bitterly fought one, bringing about the deaths of millions of his fellow Spaniards, followed by a stultifying regime no longer than his own life span, was certainly a terrible failure compared to Tariq's. Franco's statue is, it seems, already rotting in Melilla a mere sixty years on, and in Spain itself there is hardly a memorial to him left standing. But the words *Jebel Tariq* will have been perfectly comprehensible to the local Spanish populace for the next seven hundred years, and Tariq's name is still going strong well over a millennium later – even if, admittedly, somewhat garbled up by us infidels.

Fettah, short for Abdelfettah, we come across – fall over, rather – when we go indoors out of the wind. He is perched on top of a colossal zip-up bag – those rectangular white-plastic plaid ones you find in street markets all over the world – and we have to clamber over three equally enormous bags, all full to bursting, to take a seat with Guy, to whom he is chatting animatedly inside this luggage barricade.

Guy introduces us. Abdelfettah, who looks about eighteen and has the most amazingly thick, curly eyelashes, is on his way home to Morocco, to Tetuan. He has been working in the greenhouses – or the plastic tunnels, rather – of the Spanish agro-industry. The Maghrebi contribution to Spain's horticulture still continues, it seems, albeit in modern guise. And this stuff in the bags is all the shopping he is taking home to the family.

Much shopping! says Abdelfettah, patting it happily.

It certainly is much shopping. And, Guy tells us, he has to get it all through customs by himself, no trolleys, no help, nothing!

But why? How on earth can he carry all that by himself?

It is necessary, says Fettah. All must go on my back! Guy passes on the explanation. The residents of Tetuan have a special dispensation on visits to the next-door Spanish territory – they pay no Moroccan import tax on any goods they can manage to carry, without help, on their backs (or any other part of their body, come to that) from the Spanish side of the border. The idea being that criminal gangs will have no incentive to go in for large-scale organized smuggling if local Moroccans can just nip over to Ceuta – to Europe, as it were – and bring back their own cheaper shopping. No scope for profiteering. Sounds a good plan, although, by the look of things, also likely to lead, in the longer term, to plenty of bad Tetuan back problems.

We could just carry one each for him, couldn't we, says Gérard, evidently thinking along the same lines as me. We've got hardly any luggage ourselves.

But no, we couldn't, because we're not residents of Tetuan, are we? If we got stopped we'd be made to pay the tax on it all! It won't be too hard, though, Abdelfettah tells us. There is always a big crowd of willing would-be porters waiting just beyond the Ceuta border. There is no work in his town, and no end of big, strong men keen to earn themselves a few dirhams by taking over a traveller's burden.

Tobias now offers us, too, a lift for the first leg of our journey. There's still plenty of room in the back seat. And he'd be glad of some more help with the petrol. He could drop us off at Tetuan – or a couple of hours further on, if we like, in Chefchaouen. Unless we'd like to come and visit Melilla, maybe? No, of course not . . .

He has a few bits of business to see to on the way, he says, but it will still save us three or four hours of bus – and a change at Tetuan. We'll get to see a few places off the beaten track, too.

What does he mean, bits of business? asks Gérard as soon as Tobias is out of earshot. Doesn't he seem a rather fishy character altogether? And much too friendly?

He certainly does if, like Gérard, you've had your nose stuck in *The Little Cunning One* for half the boat trip. Gérard shows us the 'dangers' box on the next page of the Melilla entry, with a map of the town standing right at the head of the poverty-stricken and isolated hills of the Rif. The traveller should trust nobody here: carry nothing for anyone, and accept no lifts. This is the country's main cannabis-growing area. That's what it says. And Gérard is now certain that Tobias must have some ulterior motive for wanting us along. Luckily for our chances of a lift, though, he can't quite think what this motive could be.

Surely, says Guy, even if Tobias did import hashish into Spain, as well as working on building sites – a combination that doesn't strike Guy as too likely – Gérard can't seriously imagine that he would be bringing it the wrong way across the Mediterranean, back into Morocco? Or that he would be so hard up he needed to ask for a share of the petrol?

Gérard, somewhat shamefacedly, agrees to give his fears – and his book – a rest.

We've almost arrived now, and Ceuta looks beautiful from a mile out, sitting on its ancient fortified walls, the steep hills above it crowned with their ruined fortress and dappled with the fresh green of spring, a tiny jewel of a Mediterranean town set at the blue sea's edge. The flyer we were given with our ticket tells us that this is a harbour so safe and so well placed that it has been fought over since the dawn of seafaring history. It lists the one-time masters of the town: Phoenicians and Romans, Arabs and Visigoths, Portuguese and Spanish – everybody who was anybody has had a finger in this pie. A Hollywood extravaganza with a cast of thousands – millennial battling over these narrow straits: Roman legions and Visigoth raiders, Moorish armies and crusading Normans, Barbary pirates and traders of the Levant, Elizabethan privateers and Spanish galleons, and then, all the fleets of the colonial powers, competing for the spoils of Empire . . . Finally, behind the warfarers and the moneybags, come the unsung ordinary inhabitants of both sides of the water, following the tides of history, scraping a living for themselves and their families as best they can, shifting back and forth from one continent to the other – these days, likely as not, as human contraband in flimsy fishing boats and tiny inflatables.

Once we've pulled into shore amid the clang and crash of landing gear, Tobias drives us out of the dark bowels of the ship and into the blinding sunshine of a new and indeterminate land. The continent: Africa. The country: Spain. There are signs everywhere for *churros* and *café con leche*, for *hamburguesas* and *bocadillos*. Another mile or so of

Spanish territory, and we meet Ceuta's ten-foot anti-African barriers, as advertised: a few yards further on are the somewhat lower wire fences of Morocco. Assembled on the tarmac between the two, a large crowd of people – Tetuan residents, presumably, though we can't see Abdelfettah here yet – are passing massive quantities of bags and boxes over to waiting helpers. Our queue inches forward towards passport control, and here comes Abdelfettah at last, a bag hanging from either elbow, a third clutched to his belly, and the last perched precariously on one shoulder. There are so many other heavily laden people around him that he hardly stands out from the crowd at all. We wave to him, but he doesn't see us. Not that he's in any position to wave back if he did. And he is soon thoroughly upstaged by a family who, bizarrely, are contriving to lift a full-size fridge right over the fence.

Sitting comfortably in Tobias' big, white, squashy saloon with its Spanish number plates, we roll on to join the passport queue. Our side of the border is moving pretty quick. There are only a few cars in front of us. But look at the size of the queue on foot, coming the other way! Several hundred not-very-hopefuls are being held back behind barbed-wire barriers bristling with armed men. The no-man's-land this side of the border is thronged with people standing and sitting about, not a few of them sub-Saharan Africans as predicted by Tobias, waiting in patient – or do I mean tragic? – poses that suggest they've been here for hours, if not days. None of them looks remotely prosperous. Not a few of them look positively ragged.

The four of us drive on, straight up to the sentry-post where a banner proclaims PASAPORTE EUROPA. I am suddenly seized by a powerful feeling that, in solidarity with the other Undesirable Aliens of this world, I should refuse to cross this border. Turn back and just go home.

Silly idea. What good would that do anyone?

Tobias hands our documents through the car window to the men in uniforms. A quick glance, and we're waved on out of Spain and into Morocco. Easy as pie.

4

In Tetuan, Tobias points us towards the medina. There are plenty of cafés in the square up there, he says. He'll be back by the time we've finished breakfast. Yazid, of course, is staying in the car: he urgently needs to find a phone booth.

An hour later, we're still in Moustafa's bar, and there's still no sign of either of them.

You see! says Gérard, whose worst fears are now confirmed. Of course Tobias was up to something! He was just using us as cover while he got whatever-it-was through customs! Come to think of it, maybe he and Yazid were in it together? We've only got their word for it that they didn't know one another already, after all . . .

Guy rolls his eyes meaningfully. I can see he's about to make some cutting remark about guidebook-induced paranoia.

Well, I say soothingly, it's no skin off our nose, is it? The Rif buses leave from here – we had to come to Tetuan anyway.

The boys decide to have one more coffee, just in case this is the last outpost of civilization we meet for some months. If Tobias hasn't turned up by then, we'll go and find the bus station. While they go to the bar, I nip back out under the shutter and into the street. The sunlight is blinding now, and it's starting to get ridiculously hot. I can't waste the chance to get a glimpse of a proper old-style Moorish town for the first time since Granada. Or as proper as it gets on the last day of Ramadan, anyway, if Moustafa is to be believed: with all the local inhabitants either in a temper or fainting away.

I cross the square, squeeze through the archway, now crowded with shoppers – plenty of them dressed European-style, too: the market traders must be a more traditionally minded bunch – and push my way along the alley. A few yards up, the lady with the hennaed heels has spread her wares on the cloth of her bundle and is sitting cross-legged beside it, along with several dozen other purveyors of vegetables, narrowing the already-narrow street even more. My first impression is of total chaos. So many people, so much hubbub, so much stuff, none of it ordered in any way I recognize. From all sides, a cacophony of Arabic music from tinny radios; somebody banging on a tambourine as he calls out his wares; the chat of busy shoppers; the braying of an invisible donkey. Where people have stopped to examine the goods, or to barter loudly over their price, the flow of bodies is dammed up completely: we shove past in single file. I'm caught up in the crowd now, no choice but to move at their speed, which gives me plenty of time, alas, to examine a busy butchers' street full of skinned sheeps' heads and dangling offal. Can the medina always be this frantic? Maybe it's worse during Ramadan: if you can't eat, you can at least shop? The winding alleys really do look just like the Albaycín. Whitewashed buildings, terracotta-tiled roofs, curving wrought-iron grilles protecting the windows. The rule here seems to be just one trade per street. I pass through an alley of spice-sellers now, warm perfumes strong in the air: baskets of nutmegs and of cinnamon sticks, whole sacks of cumin and of coriander, yellow turmeric and red chilli powder, a little wooden shovel in each for measuring out . . . now on to dried fruits and nuts, dates beautifully stacked and gleaming, figs strung on loops of palm-frond, a display that must take hours to do each morning; off the main drag is a tiny piazza with a bunch of old men sitting on worn stone steps, chanting what must be verses of the Koran. I try not to stare at two women covered from head to toe in *haiks*, only their eyes showing; now a gaggle of teenagers, chatting animatedly in Arabic, bursts out of a side opening: all in blue jeans, the girls with slinky jersey tops and lashings of make-up. Only one of them has her hair modestly covered up in the *khimar* scarf; the others have it blonde-streaked, curled and primped. Two worlds crushed up together in a three-foot alley.

I'll only go up as far as the mosque I keep glimpsing between the houses. Can't be too long getting back: it takes for ever to move just a few yards in this crush. I'm among olives now, buckets and bowls of them, from palest green through red-purple to black – more varieties than I've ever seen in Italy; then a whole alley of nothing but shoes, shaded by woven reed mats. A street of fabric-sellers now, packed, this one. The rolls stacked within their alcoves are jewel-bright, but every last woman fingering the cloth is wearing a plain pastel jellaba, all-enveloping, and a tightly tied headscarf. Who knows what goes on beneath the modesty? If the wares in here are anything to go by, away from the public gaze the women of Tetuan must be a positive riot of colour. Into a street of mattress-stuffers now – workshops these, deeper but still tiny, figures working away at piles of wool and bundles of straw. Another alley is all jellaba-makers at their sewing machines, then handbag- and slipper-makers. Trade once used to be arranged like this in Europe, too, I know, but I've never understood the principle. A great advantage to the buyer, being able to compare all the prices on offer so easily, all in one place, but what do the craftsmen or merchants get out of it? Clearly I am not cut out for commerce.

The streets are getting less packed. I must be nearly at the mosque, now, surely? Or am I just lost? As I hesitate, wondering whether to turn back, a woman with two children clinging to the skirts of her jellaba holds a house-door open to wait for a lagging third child. I glance past her to find that, through the dark tunnel of the entrance, I'm looking into bright sunlight beyond: a gleam of checkered floor-tiles, glimpse of greenery and trailing plants, intricate arches set on elegant pillars.

The last child is out, now, the mother looking at me askance. I suppose I would be a little surprised, too, if some Moroccan woman came and stood staring through my front door.

Sorry, I say in French, forgetting that here people are more likely to speak Spanish. It's just that your house is so lovely . . .

She answers me in Spanish anyway. Lovely, yes, she says, but *muy viejo* – very old! Too much cleaning, she adds, miming a scrubbing brush. *Limpiar, siempre a limpiar!* Always cleaning! Do you want a proper look? she asks, holding the door invitingly ajar. Go on! Don't be timid!

So I stick my head in through the doorway and look a bit longer. A central courtyard open to the sky and flooded with sun, galleried upper floors resting on the slim pillars, traceries of wrought-iron balconies sun-dappled, wound with leafy tendrils of climbers. And some kind of stone well or water fountain in the centre, a little garden of potted plants around it . . . a tiny paradise.

Le gusta? she asks. Do you like it?

I certainly do, I say, stepping back out. I would never have guessed in a million years what lay behind that door. So much space, air and light within, but outside in the street, no hint of it at all. Just this cramped setting of narrow streets and tall, almost windowless façades.

She pulls the door shut and sets off up the road, driving the infants before her, turns and waves goodbye with a hygienically hennaed palm. I stand and look up and down the street. Are all these houses like that on the inside, then? I suppose they must be. That's what a Muslim home is meant to be: the architectural equivalent of the all-concealing jellaba. Enclosed space at its heart, sheltered from sun and wind, plain on the outside, all ostentation frowned upon, the beauty of its decoration hidden within, never to impress, but for private appreciation only. It's a technically brilliant design, too: the central column of air keeps a current flowing all through the building, a natural eco-friendly air-conditioning system. They certainly do a convincing job on the plain-outside part of the equation, though, here in Tetuan. And the secret heart of the house is a lot grander than anything I ever saw in the Albaycín. Maybe I never got to know the right people?

That mosque seems to have vanished off the face of the earth. I'll just head straight back downhill, I decide. Rounding the first corner, I almost fall into a tiny shop. More of a long, deep alcove, really, than a shop. But what kind of shop is it? Indecipherable. In its narrow window – and on the tightly packed shelves within – are displayed an extraordinary array of multicoloured powders, granules, oils, liquids, piles of petals and of seeds, something that looks like slivers of translucent amber, another something that looks like pieces of twisted black twig. These unknown substances are held in every possible type of receptacle: from tiny vials to great glass demijohns, from baskets and glass bowls to tall earthenware jars. I stare on, clueless; no idea what any of it is, or why I should want it. This must be the first time in my adult life that I have been faced with a whole range of completely unidentifiable commodities: nameless Stuff whose use is entirely unknown to me. Feeling strangely disorientated and vulnerable, I peer into the similar establishment next door. It too is packed with shelf upon shelf of mystery merchandise. There is just enough room for a couple of customers to squeeze between the shelves – no more. At the very back a man in an embroidered velvet skullcap sits behind a tiny counter, pestles, mortars, and a set of small brass scales before him. He stands up and beckons me in. I dither at the door. He has already left his counter now, swishes through his shop to my side, leans forward confidentially, taking my arm.

What, Madame, is my favourite perfume? Do I like Dior? Givenchy? Gucci? Something more floral? More sharp? More sweet? More musky? Because whatever my desire may be, he will make me one up just like it – only his will be better, longer-lasting and half the price. Come on in! *Entrez, entrez!*

Declining as politely as possible, I disentangle myself and scuttle off back towards Moustafa's café. I've been away far too long as it is. Luckily, I don't want any perfume just at the moment: it's hardly high on anyone's list of travelling accoutrements, is it? I wouldn't dare try buying anything in a souk yet, anyway. There is a whole page devoted to the topic in Gérard's book: which starts by suggesting you should offer the merchant only half the price he first names. Half! It seems insulting. Like calling the seller a liar. I haven't finished the rest of the section. Obviously I am badly in need of training. I shall make sure to study it in depth, so as to be ready to bargain when I return this way. I'd love a bottle of long-lasting half-price Amerige to take home to Italy . . .

I'm hardly back out through the arch when Moustafa rushes out and nabs me. Why didn't I tell him I was going to visit the medina? See all those young men sitting on the steps over there? They are guides, waiting for nothing better than to show the likes of me around the city's secrets! Moustafa has already beckoned one of them over. This is Abdelkrim, he says. Abdelkrim knows everything, all the history of the medina. He will show you the mosques, the rich merchants' homes, the old mellah, the Jewish quarter – and the tanneries, which foreigners always find so spectacular, away on the far side. Abdelkrim is a professional *faux guide* – a False Guide.

I am too distracted by this extraordinary job title to go on listening to Moustafa's list of the sights I've just missed. What does he mean, a False Guide? Why on earth is he called that? It's hardly a very confidence-inspiring name. Does it mean he just makes it all up as he goes along?

Moustafa, horrified at the suggestion, leaps to the defence of False Guides. Abdelkrim, he says, is as knowledgeable as anyone else – as anyone possibly could be! – about the history of his town. But the local tourist authorities refuse to accredit more than a certain number of Official Guides. So everyone else is, by definition, a False Guide. And what else are these good young men to do with all their education, then, asks Moustafa rhetorically, putting an arm around his protégé's shoulder. Abdelkrim gives Moustafa's hand a soothing pat.

Of course he will take us for a tour, he says, if we have an hour or two, but it looks as if we're about to leave.

Yes. There is Tobias' car, I see now, and Tobias himself, shifting things about in the boot. Gérard and Guy have come out to pay. And the majestic personage beside Tobias, an impressive figure in a flowing white jellaba and snow-white *chèche* is, amazingly, Yazid. Not just a phone: he has found himself a genie with a lamp. The classic migrant worker in the slightly ill-fitting Western clothes has been magically transformed into a proud prince from the court of the Sultan.

We pile back into the car, complimenting Yazid on his startling makeover.

But of course, he says, he couldn't present himself in his home town in that foolish Western outfit. And then, after all these months without him, he wants his wife to be struck by his good looks! To Moroccan eyes, he explains, you look childish and infantile in Western clothes – not like a proper, manly man. Meaning, he adds hastily, no disrespect to the European company!

I sneak a look at Guy, the fashion victim among us. A certain pensive look in his eye tells me that this last remark has got to him. I must remember to place a bet with Gérard, next time we're alone, on how many miles through North Africa we'll get before Guy too is dressed as a proper, manly man.

And did Yazid find a phone? Gérard asks. How was his wife?

Yazid replies, in a strangely frosty manner, that he did find a phone, yes.

And the wife?

Silence falls.

Here in Morocco a man must never ask another how his wife is. It is tantamount to claiming some sort of dubious intimacy with her. An insult, explains Tobias. You have to ask how his home is, instead – and then he will tell you about the wife if he wants to.

Yazid decides not to be annoyed. Gérard didn't do it on purpose. Probably.

Tobias congratulates me on evading the *faux guides*. I'm not so pleased, though, to have missed out on being shown all the secrets of the medina.

Bah! You'll see plenty more medinas, says Tobias, shoving the car into gear. Every town in the Muslim world has one. Those guide boys know their way around town, all right, but once you're in their clutches there's no escape from being dragged into some carpet shop and given the hand of eternal friendship, the mint tea, and the heavy sales pitch. Come here in the summer, and they pester the lives out of people. Long may Melilla stay Spanish!

And so saying, Tobias shoots off at speed out of the square. I sneak a look at Yazid, but he seems a lot less bothered by Tobias' determination to hang on to part of his country than he was by Gérard's interest in his wife.

Yazid agrees with Tobias, life certainly is hell here in summertime. Nowadays he works all through August, the official holiday month, and comes home in spring instead. In August, he says, it can take the whole day to get through the Ceuta frontier. It is always jam-packed with the second-hand Mercedes that every last young migrant has to bring over the water to impress his stay-at-home neighbours. Yazid wouldn't dream of wasting his hard-earned cash on such nonsense. Then, once you're home, you never get a wink of sleep. Families find brides for their migrant sons, he says, while they're away working, and as soon as they get home for the holiday, everything kicks off: the streets are jammed with hooting, shouting wedding cortèges – of Mercedes, naturally – and all night long there are squealing electronic bands and endless firework displays. They spend a fortune on those weddings, he adds. And the worst of it is, they're impressing nobody. They just look like jumped-up yokels with more money than sense. Genuine, old-school-rich Moroccans don't carry on like that, and their sons don't need to emigrate to find work, either. They get set up in some cosy family business as soon as they leave school, and laugh up their sleeves at the peasants who have to leave the country to earn a living, all trying to impress one another with their tasteless displays of migrant money. Yazid doesn't know what he's going to do about his son's wedding. Look like an idiot, or look like a miser?

So what is life like up there in Holland? I ask – once I've thoroughly checked the question for potential veiled insults and concluded that it is safe. But according to Yazid, life in Holland is not like anything at all. He eats, he sleeps, he works. He doesn't socialize with the Dutch from work. Much better not. You could easily say or do something that would get you the sack. And maybe you'd never get another visa. He used to spend some time with his fellow Muslims, go to the mosque every now and then – but not any more. The new, young ones are troublemakers. They wanted him to sign a petition for a prayer-room at work! Yazid told them he wasn't in Holland to pray, he was there to earn. Full stop. They think growing beards and praying five times a day makes them morally superior to the Dutch. And maybe it does, but if they think the Dutch will notice it, they're fools.

What he does love in Holland, though, are the patisseries. Dutch cakes are good, but that's not the main attraction. Firstly, alcohol is not sold in patisseries – there is nothing worse than finding yourself in a room full of drunken Dutchmen – and secondly, the customers are mostly women. On the weekends, when the patisseries are full up, some of them are bound to sit at his table. And the Dutch women are not like the men. They like to talk; they ask him about his life back home, about Islam, about his wife and children. They tell him about their own lives. He feels good, then. The tea may be weak and horrible, but with a big fat slice of Black Forest gateau before you, and some pleasant conversation, you can manage to overlook that.

Out of town, the ground soon starts to rise, while the view from the back seat, or as much as I can see of it past Yazid's *chèche*, continues the biblical theme: acre upon acre of olive groves, plenty of fig trees, small flocks of sheep or goats herded by jellaba'd men with long staffs, often with a small child in mini-jellaba taking up the rear. These country jellabas are nothing like Yazid's smooth snow-white linen job, though: I get plenty of time to examine them as we crawl along, waiting for a chance to squeeze past the livestock. They are farmers' all-weather get-ups, home-made looking, with great long, pointy hoods that spread wide and collar-like across the shoulders, made of coarse sheep's-wool the colours of their own flocks. Wool that has been carefully separated out into its natural sheep-colours of beige, brown and cream by some tender-hearted and skilful female relative, at a guess, before being home-spun and hand-woven into narrow vertical stripes.

The dry, desert-like olive groves here are nothing like the steep and leafy terraces of olive trees I'm used to back home in Diano, with green grass and dappled sunlight beneath them. On these arid, open Maghreb slopes there is a hundred feet or more of pale, sun-baked dry earth between each tree. What a horrible, hot job it must be to look after them, come summer, out in the baking African sun. In fact, you'd hardly call them groves at all; they are wide hillsides, their rounded slopes broad and gentle, the trees planted in regimented straight lines, so that in the distance the landscape looks like some piece of French-knot embroidery, or maybe a pile of patchwork quilts, perspective cutting the parallel lines of the trees at each overlapping curve. A thoroughly Andalusian view. Were these olive plantations established by the Spanish colonists of the early twentieth century? Or four centuries earlier, by the Moorish refugees of the sixteenth? Were they already here before the arrival of Islam, perhaps, when this land belonged to the Berbers alone? No idea. Any way round, they would look the same.

To make up for my missed tour of Tetuan, Guy decides to give me a medina low-down as we drive, culled from his family's chest of memories. The mosque always has pride of place, he says, right in the centre of town, and the holier, or the cleaner, a trade is, the closer it will be to the mosque. First comes luxury stuff like candle-sellers and incense and spices, books and bookbinding, confectionery and sweets for offerings: then embroidery, clothing and fabrics, carpets and fine leather goods; then – slowly getting messier – weaving and carpentry, general hardware and ironmongers, and last of all fresh food – meat and suchlike – until you get to the really smelly and noxious things, blacksmiths' forges and butchers' abattoirs and tanneries for hides, which will be on the edges, or right outside the walls.

Yazid is nodding away approvingly as Guy speaks. But how come Guy knows all this, he asks, when he's never been to North Africa before? Guy seems as reluctant to answer this as Yazid was to share information about his wife.

Tobias is surprised to hear that there's any sort of plan to a medina at all. It always seems like plain anarchy to him. He'll remember that next time he's lost in the labyrinthine medina of Fez – follow the dirt and you might find your way out.

The principle of keeping the dirt outside the walls, it now occurs to me, may explain a mystery I encountered in the sketchy and (I admit) rather erratic reading I did to prepare for this journey. Guy lent me a family heirloom – a memoir called *Tangiers to Tunis – Adventures in Algeria*, written by Alexandre Dumas, the Three Musketeers man, who travelled here in the 1840s. At one point, Dumas – appalled, he says, by the mess and filth that lies outside the walls of Maghreb cities – goes so far as to complain to a local emir about it. He gets nowhere. The eccentric emir, Dumas tells us, is firmly convinced that keeping a great pile of stench outside a town will protect its inhabitants from disease. But what if Dumas, used to the dirt of Northern European cities of the time, with their open sewers and midden-heaps, simply misunderstood? I wonder whether what the emir really meant was that the town's health was protected by having the dirt outside the walls, and not within?

Guy suspects that this book of Dumas' may have been behind his ancestors' decision to up sticks and start their new life in North Africa. Although, sad to say, no myth or legend has survived in Guy's family to explain their departure from France, his parents and grandparents all agree that the book, an original edition, had stood for long generations on the bookshelf of their Algiers home – though nobody had ever been known to take it down and read it. Guy pulled it from a dusty box in the attic of his Paris home, where it had languished ever since the 1960s when his family joined the panic-stricken French exodus from Algeria – and found it in mint condition. He must, he thinks, have been the first member of the family to open its pages for over a hundred years. And a very disturbing read it was, too!

Dumas' trip here was paid for by the French government, in the hope that a book by such a popular author might conjure up willing volunteers for settlement in the newly conquered North African colonies. At the time, the desperate poor of the French countryside were flooding into the already-overcrowded cities, seeking non-existent work, and causing no end of trouble. The plan was to entice this hungry and disorderly peasantry across the Mediterranean, where they would not only be out of the way, but could usefully be set up to farm the good fertile land sequestered from the vanquished North Africans, and contribute, in return, to supplying the hard-pressed Motherland with grape and grain.

Like Guy, I found it hard to imagine that Dumas' book had attracted anyone at all to this part of the world. Dumas is fascinated, true, but constantly torn between anger and terror, as he tries and fails to control the various bunches of rebellious Maghrebis allocated to him as servants. They will use his horses for unauthorized races, wearing them out behind his back, or refuse to touch the wild boar he's bagged while out hunting – an unclean pig-type animal – so that Dumas and his European companions are forced to lose face and carry it home themselves. Dumas describes in horrified detail the sav-agery of the *bastinado*, the usual punishment for such insubordinate behaviour – a severe beating to the soles of the culprit's feet. But he sits by while it is carried out on his behalf, regardless. His fear of losing the upper hand when outnumbered by natives – which, this being their country, he usually is – naturally outweighs his Christian compunction. Could anyone possibly have seen this book as a reas-suring advertisement for a prosperous new life abroad? It certainly wouldn't have attracted me. But then, who knows how adventurous Guy's forebears may have been? Or, indeed, how hungry and disor-derly?

Among the olives now are cork oak plantations. You can see the great three-foot scars on the sides of their trunks where slabs of bark, destined one day to seal the necks of the wine-bottles of Europe, have been carefully removed. Piles of them lie by the side of the road, waiting to be collected. Must be a strange job, if you're a practising Muslim, to make your livelihood from something so utterly useless in your own culture. Unless perhaps Moroccans are partial to a nice bit of cork tiling? Yazid looks at me as if I'm mad. He's never heard of such a thing.

All this, the olives and the cork too, is certainly organized, commercial production. No sign of the small-time peasant farming I was expecting to see, from all we've heard about the Rif.

Not till after Chefchaouen, says Tobias. We're still in the land of the Arabic-speakers here. Prosperous parts. Another hour or so before we're in the Rif proper and among the Berbers.

We're passing through a small town now, a strange mixture of shacks and isolated houses, with the occasional modern villa standing incongruous among them.

Migrant money, says Yazid, craning round to check the details – comparing and contrasting, I expect, with his own efforts in this sphere. Suddenly, he starts his wheezing chuckle again and, grabbing Tobias' arm, draws his attention to the roofs of the next two villas, just down below the road. They are both – speaking of incongruity – sporting large, shiny colanders, hanging like absurd hats over the TV aerials on their roofs.

Tobias slows down to get a better look. Brave people, he says.

We wait with bated breath to hear what can possibly be brave about hanging a colander from your TV aerial.

The items in question, Yazid explains to us foreigners, are not colanders at all, but *couscoussiers* – steamers for the family couscous. Not long since, the whole of his town was festooned with them, hanging from almost every aerial, until the king got annoyed and decreed that they all had to be taken down. Maybe nobody cares, here in the middle of nowhere? But back home, anyone who still had a *couscoussier* on their roof would be getting a very unfriendly visit from the police. Surreal, yes, but not as inexplicable as it appears at first sight. A while ago, we learn, a rumour went round all the north of Morocco that, if you added a *couscoussier* to your aerial, you would be able to receive the European TV stations that the king, in his wisdom, had banned from the country. It was just an urban myth, but it spread like wildfire.

Tobias laughs: he remembers the day he found himself driving through the inexplicable forests of cookery equipment that had suddenly sprouted from every roof over the border. And of course, says Yazid, once you've bothered to go up on your roof to hang your *couscoussier* on the aerial, you aren't in any hurry to get back up there and take it down, are you, even when it turns out to do nothing at all for your reception? People saw them on one another's roofs and believed the story all the more. By the time everyone had realized they didn't work, the whole skyline was adorned with *couscoussiers*. And though they might not get you any foreign TV stations, they certainly made a fine – and highly visible – sign of his citizens' discontent with their king and his censorship! And nobody could say you were doing anything illegal, either. Here in Morocco, it is forbidden to criticize the king. But how could a *couscoussier* be a criticism? What sort of crime is hanging a saucepan from your roof? So people went on putting them up, even once they knew perfectly well they did nothing at all! Ah, great times! says Yazid. The police came round browbeating people into taking them down, one by one . . . But the point was made. How can the king say he wants to build a modern, educated nation, and then refuse to let people know what's going on in the world? Or, indeed, to let them watch the juicy American soap operas being beamed out of Italy?

As predicted, within the hour we are making our way along ever more steep and winding roads, climbing slowly but surely, the dry, sun-baked earth of the lower hills giving way to green. Rivulets trickle down craggy rock faces, the courses of their streams marked, way below, by lines of wild reeds and oleanders. We're into real hill-country now: hamlets of half a dozen squat, whitewashed houses nestling in protective coppices of fir. We pass a man ploughing a patch of stony, ochre earth with a pair of oxen. Ahead of us, a flock of goats wanders, blocking the road, the usual child with a stick bringing up the rear. We slow down to a crawl to squeeze through, and find, leading the flock, the first women we have seen in all this time.

Berbers, says Tobias. You don't get Arab women out and about like that.

This information hardly seems to cover the questions that spring to mind at the sight of this pair of shepherdesses. Even more striking than the fact that they're female is the fact that they appear to be in fancy dress. Or in the wrong country. They are wearing an outfit that would not look out of place on a Peruvian *indio*: wide-brimmed straw sombreros decorated with bright red pom-poms and trails of multicoloured ribbons, over green-and-white shawl-like headscarves pinned under their chins. They have lengths of bright red fabric knotted round their waists, broad white pin-stripes woven into it, and loose pale leggings below. Grass-green and canary-yellow socks, respectively, complete the picture.

Rif Mountain Berbers, says Yazid. The colours of the stripes in the fabric show which clan they belong to. He thinks these are Ait Ouriagar. Unless they're Ait something-else. These days, only country people who still stick to the old hill-farming lifestyle wear the traditional outfits, though most of Morocco's inhabitants are really of Berber blood. The rest have moved into the towns over the centuries, ended up speaking the Arabic language, as you do in the cities, and dressing in ordinary jellabas: hardly think of themselves as Berbers any more.

And is Yazid one of them?

Half and half, he says, with a grin.

We pull in to allow the goats and their owners to perform a complex sharp-left-turn manoeuvre, which involves a lot of stick-waving, shouting, and chasing of strong-willed escapees. While we wait for this caprine drama to resolve itself, Gérard reveals that he has been looking forward immensely to seeing the Rif. He is, he tells Yazid, a big fan of Abd el-Krim. I am confused. Abdelkrim? As far as I am aware, Abdelkrim is the name of a young protégé of Moustafa's, an occasional False Guide to the city of Tetuan . . .

But of course, interrupts Yazid. Many people are named after Abd el-Krim, who was a very great man indeed, a Berber hero! Abd el-Krim and his Rif shepherd fighters kept the Spanish at bay – if Tobias will excuse his putting it like that! – for a good two decades, when Spain was trying, in the first half of the twentieth century, to occupy the whole Mediterranean coast of Morocco. Thanks to Abd el-Krim, the Rif, and Yazid's own town, only suffered thirty years of colonization and humiliation, unlike the rest of his country – and, indeed, his continent.

Gérard joins in with gusto. Abd el-Krim was a brilliant guerrilla strategist, he says, and a man who had many admirers outside Morocco as well as within. Che Guevara, Ho Chi Minh and Mao Zedong – everyone who was anyone claimed Abd el-Krim as an inspiration in their own fights against colonialism.

Abd el-Krim and his supporters, Yazid says, were fighting for self-rule: they had set up their own Berber Republic of the Rif, wanting no truck with either Moroccan Arabic Royalty or other people's Empires – something that today's Rif Berbers have still not changed their minds about! They even managed, at one point, with guerrilla forces of a mere 3,000, to defeat a Spanish army of 13,000! Later, in his shame at this dishonourable trouncing, the Spanish general in charge of the invading forces committed suicide. His death, as chance would have it, cleared the path for a newcomer with a great future, now promoted to anti-Berber operations: a certain General Francisco Franco.

But the final downfall of the Rif Republic, Gérard tells us, was only brought about by his and Guy's own country stepping in to lend a hand. France had decided it had to crush this rebellion, even if it meant helping the Spanish competition. The flame of Abd el-Krim's successes was spreading fast among France's own colonized peoples – not just to the French sectors of Morocco, but to next-door Algeria, as well, and even to Indochina, where the Vietnamese were starting to rebel. And so a saturation army of a quarter of a million soldiers descended on the towns and villages of the Rif – a massive swamping manoeuvre.

And the mustard gas! Don't forget the poison, says Yazid. Fired into our homes, against our aged parents, our women and children! Nobody could stand up to such an onslaught, not even Abd el-Krim, who was captured now and exiled far from his homeland, to be kept prisoner, incommunicado, on some distant island in the Indian Ocean.

Gérard doesn't know if it was Franco who came up with the idea of testing out chemical weapons on the Berber hill villages, or his French allies. Still, the victory didn't last long, did it? Even the Roman Empire, Gérard tells us, never did manage to subdue the Berbers of the Rif. For centuries now, their homeland has been nicknamed the *Bled es-Siba* by the rest of Morocco: the Land of Dissidence.

Though you could also translate it 'Land of the Argumentative', says Yazid.

And all that, Gérard adds, will be why the Rif Berbers get left alone to grow cannabis if they want to. The Imperial Powers demonstrated only too clearly, long ago, that it takes a quarter of a million armed men to bend a few thousand Berbers to your will!

Yazid says there's more to it than that. He doesn't believe his government really wants to stop the cannabis farming. There is no other crop the Berber farmers could grow on their tiny plots of stony land anyway – nothing that would earn enough, these days, to support them and their families. They would have no choice but to abandon the land altogether and head down from the hills, flooding into the already-overcrowded cities seeking non-existent work and causing no end of trouble . . .

The women have finally got their goats across the road and down a track leading to a small collection of cube-shaped buildings a short way below us, on the side of the valley. You can see chickens scratching about in the yard down there. They wave their thanks, shouting a greeting. I like the look of these Berbers a lot. Very reminiscent of another group of people of whom I am most fond: the pugnacious inhabitants of the Ligurian hills, back in Italy. The Ligurians, too, are known for their dissident traditions, and for their successful resistance, from their mountain fastnesses, both to the home-grown Italian and the invading German Fascists. Also some centuries earlier, to the Romans, whom they allowed to waste much time building a road to Gaul through their tribal lands, only to make passage along it so perilous that the Romans gave up and went by sea instead. Can it be the recalcitrant landscape from which both these hardy peoples make their livelihood that produces the spirit of resistance?

Compared to the tight-headscarf-and-jellaba women in Tetuan, these Berber women also seem very free-and-easy – out and about with the flocks, waving and smiling to people they don't know. And though they are wearing head-coverings aplenty, nobody could call them modest and unostentatious, not with all those colours and bobbles and ribbons – no question but they're aiming at pleasing the eye, rather than at pious modesty.

Tobias says that Europeans like me always misunderstand the situation. Berber countrywomen may look more free to Western eyes, – but to other Moroccans, they just look more poor and less valued and respected by their families. We needn't imagine that other women round here will be looking on enviously at Berber 'freedom'. Just the opposite. The way they see it, Berber women are forced to work – and to show themselves in public while they do it – because their husbands can't afford to keep them decently at home. Or are too shameless to care. Or both.

We pass an orchard of fruit trees now – apricots, by the look of it – where a group of these shameless and argumentative people, sickles in hand, are clearing the ground of spring weeds and grass, men and women working together. The Berbers themselves, it seems, don't give a fig for their compatriots' disapproval. Not a few of them appear to be singing.

5

The countryside is getting more and more spectacular. Down in the valleys are deep green pastures and swathes of arable land, fertile slashes cut through the parched hillsides high above. Ahead of us, forested hills interlock above green river-plains and the occasional mirror-blue lake gleams down in the intricate valleys; great limestone crags loom above us. Rounding a bend we glimpse a hill-town up ahead, a pile of roofs clustered together in the misty distance. Way down below us, on a grassy bank, a tiny group of scattered golden-brown tents is pitched near a meandering river. Nomad Berbers, says Tobias. Or semi-nomads, rather. Their clans wander with their flocks all summer, in search of pasture, and go back to their villages for the winter.

Here we overtake a young boy riding a donkey laden with what look like jerrycans of petrol. At first sight, a bit of a contradiction in terms, but what do we know? Maybe his other beast of burden is a Porsche. Or, indeed, a Mercedes. His mixed bag of animals is straying out across the road: a cow and half a dozen sheep, two lambs prancing around them. He's using the long hood of his jellaba as an improvised shopping-bag. There's a big round loaf peeping out of the top of it, and what looks like a lettuce.

That's how Yazid grew up, he says. The donkey for transport, the cow for milk, the sheep for meat and wool, the lambs for cash in hand. Taking the family fortunes out for a wander to fill their bellies, just like that boy there! And now look – not a single one of his own children would survive a week in the countryside. Everything's changed. Against all the odds, two of his sons are at university. An unexpected spin-off from emigration. The least educated are becoming the most educated, he says. And meanwhile, a poor ignorant man like himself has to go on working an extra decade to pay for it all! Thirty years ago, back in his village, you expected your children to be grown and working by the time they were thirteen or fourteen. If things had stayed the same, Yazid would have been back home and comfortably retired years ago, grandchildren already playing around his knee. Some hope!

The story goes like this. Yazid, like the other migrants of his town, has always made sure his children never lacked for money. Spoilt them, maybe, he confesses. Their father might be a mere unskilled countryman, but that made it all the more important that they should be able to hold their heads high in the town. In his absence, his children grew up on the migrant money he was sending home – and in comfortably off middle-class style. Except that, unlike the parents of their middle-class friends, a migrant father has no family business to set them up in when they leave school. And no connections in the town to help them find a job, either, after a lifetime spent away. What can he do to make it up to them but carry on working – and support them through university so they will, eventually, get a job that will keep them in the style to which they're accustomed?

And keep out of their way when he's home, too, Yazid adds, after a pause for thought. So as not to embarrass them with his uncouth peasant ways! Not one of them could so much as draw a bucket of water from a well, never mind care for a flock of sheep. Or, in his daughter's case, spin the wool for her man's jellaba. And now she wants to join her brothers at college, too. She has applied to a Spanish university to study medicine! When will he ever be able to retire? His parents would turn in their graves!

In a clearing on the tree-lined bend up ahead, a small white-washed dome appears. A mini mosque?

A *marabout*, says Yazid. The tomb of a Sufi saint.

A *marabout*? I remember the Algerian brothers telling me that *marabouts* were wise and holy men who could advise you in times of trouble – and make up amulets to protect you from harm, too. Do they have them here in Morocco as well?

They certainly do have them here. And all through the Maghreb. The tombs are called *marabouts*, as well as the Holy Men themselves, it seems.

And can we stop and have a look?

If you really want to, says Tobias, but the countryside is littered with the things, we'll pass plenty more. He gives in to my whim, though, and pulls over. I climb out to inspect the shrine, blindingly white in the sunshine. Only just repainted, too, by the look of the splashes of fresh whitewash adorning the tufts of grass and clumps of violets around it. The dome is not really round, but four-sided; irregular and home-made looking, as if its mud-plaster and the zig-zag decorations round the deep doorway had been applied by hand, like the icing on a cake. I step down into it, poke my head into the cool darkness within – and discover that the place is already occupied. There is a powerful scent of incense, and three women are kneeling around what must be the actual grave of the *marabout*, a long narrow stone with a green fringed carpet draped over it. They are murmuring prayers, their hands held out, palm-upwards, and their eyes closed. But not entirely closed, evidently, because as I start to reverse back out, not wishing to disturb their devotions, the woman nearest to me stands up, grabs my hand, and starts talking animatedly, doing a lot of that hand-on-the-heart action. Now all of them join in at once – not in any language I can understand, unfortunately, but still, I can tell their intention is friendly. The one who is holding on to me throws up her hands in despair when I try some French on her, says something long and complicated in her own language, laughs at my incomprehension, and gives me a pat on the cheek. She is wearing a complicated arrangement of patterned scarves and shawls over her head, knotted and draped; one of those stripy shawl-like things is tied round her waist. A Berber, I deduce.

Her friend, similarly dressed – no boring pastel jellabas in here –

has a fine tattooed line running from the bottom of her lower lip right down the middle of her chin, as does the older woman with the heavy gold earrings and the hennaed palms and fingertips who is sitting in the corner with one leg outstretched towards the grave. The hennaed fingertips, with their golden-brown tinted nails, give her the look of an extremely committed smoker.

I soon gather that the women want me to crouch down along with them and join in whatever it is they're doing. They are pulling at me and making kind of sweeping movements with their arms, from the tombstone towards the old lady with the outstretched leg. Willing though I am to participate (probably), I don't have the faintest idea what this gesture might mean. The old lady clearly appreciates the absurdity of the situation: she has started giggling behind her hand.

Wait a minute, I say, holding up a finger – a gesture easier to understand, I hope, than the ladies' mysterious sweeping motions – and nip back out to call Yazid. He refuses to come into a *marabout* filled with females – not socially acceptable at all, evidently – but is prepared to go so far as to stick his head round the doorway. And with his help, I discover that the imitation-sweeping is simply the motion they want me to join them in doing, so as to transfer the saint's *baraka* – a mystical power somewhere between good luck and divine grace, it seems – out of the grave of the *marabout* and into the leg of the old lady, whose knee-joint has been swollen and sore for several weeks. Her helpers feel that my presence will confer extra *baraka* upon the scenario, and could make all the difference to the cure.

But why would that be, when I'm not even a Muslim?

Yazid doesn't know. Some things have more *baraka* than others, that's all, he says testily, keen to get away. A soup made with seven vegetables has more *baraka* than one made with six. A white camel has more *baraka* than a brown one. How should he know why?

There being no deeper meaning to the ladies' desire for my presence than if I were a camel or a bowl of soup, it would certainly be curmudgeonly to refuse. And I know how painful a sore knee can be. So, crouching down, I join with a will in the rhythmic sweeping of divine grace across the room and into the leg of our patient, who has turned her golden-red palms upwards and begun quietly chanting again. Now the others join in the chant. The language barrier prevents me from helping with this part of the procedure, so I gaze interestedly around the tiny domed room. There is a kind of shelf around the wall at the bottom, sooty smudges on the whitewash: a few tiny fragrant cones of incense smoking away. Nearby, a saucer with more smouldering burnt-offerings, a tiny piece of lit charcoal heating some chips of brown resin-like stuff, some translucent white pebble-things, a few fragments of what looks like dried seaweed, and another cone of incense. The more I gaze at the contents of this dish, the more I think I've seen them somewhere before. Yes indeed. Never again will I be at such a loss outside that Tetuan perfume-shop.

Back in the car, I find that Guy is trying to get Yazid to show him how to wind a *chèche*. I knew it. Must get to place that bet quickly. Yazid is resisting, though. It's impossible in such a small space, he says: there are a good five metres of cloth in a *chèche*. Later, yes, when we get out. I save him from Guy's importuning by seeking more information on *marabouts*.

People come on mass pilgrimages to these shrines, Yazid tells us, every year on the saint's holy day, to celebrate his miracles. There is drumming all night, music, singing – people keep it up till they've danced themselves into communion with his spirit, into Oneness with Allah. This *marabout* must have had his feast-day recently – the pilgrims always whitewash the shrine as part of the festivities.

But there are still *marabouts* alive today? Not like the Christian tradition, where you have to be respectably dead before you can become a saint?

Of course there are: because a Holy Man's *baraka* is hereditary. At least one of his descendants, sometimes more, will take up his mantle in each generation; has done throughout the centuries.

And how come there was nothing about *marabouts* in any of the stuff we read on Islam? Are they not really Islamic?

Yazid hums and has about this one. There certainly are Muslims who call the *marabout* ways un-Islamic – those bearded boys in the Dutch mosques, for example. But they know nothing, according to Yazid. They are just aping the puritans and the intellectuals, the city *imams*, who want Islam turned into a religion for lawyers, a set of rules and regulations for how to live every detail of your life in the Ways of Allah – and nothing more. Fundamentalists, Wahabis and Salafists. That is another reason why Yazid wouldn't bother going to their prayer-meetings. What sort of religion is that, no fire in its belly, where nothing is miraculous or mystical, and a Muslim can have no personal relation to his God?

We must have got the wrong sort of book, anyway, he says. Did it not mention the Sufi variety of Islam? Those Muslims who withdraw from the world to seek mystical union with God? Yes? Well, a *marabout* is another word for a Sufi saint – the Holy Man whose followers set up a Sufi brotherhood, a *zawiya*, many centuries ago. And if it wasn't for the Sufi brotherhoods, Yazid himself never would have learned to read and write. He got the only schooling he ever had at the local *zawiya*. The Brothers were the kindest and most pious of men, and nobody is going to tell Yazid that they were un-Islamic!

Aptly enough, the midday call to prayer interrupts this conversation. The call is taken up by one muezzin after another, half a dozen invisible mosques in invisible villages up and down the hillsides all weaving together into one plaintive and beautiful chant that echoes across the dry, sun-baked slopes above us, and the luscious green valleys below.

The call to lunch, says Tobias, irreligiously. And he is starving!

Yes. I did read something along those lines. For many centuries the *zawiyas* of the Sufi brotherhoods – kind of Muslim monasteries – ran the only schooling there was in much of the Maghreb, teaching reading, writing and the holy texts, just as the Christian Church did in Europe until pretty recently. And also the historical explanation of the country people's preference for the Sufi version of Islam: that a countryside dotted with the tombs of miracle-working saints, where they could seek Holy Grace and communion with God without having to leave their flocks and herds, suited the nomad lifestyle a lot better than a network of bookish, mosque-bound city *imams*. More importantly still, the Holy Man's living descendant, imbued with the powers and wisdom of his (and even, sometimes, her) ancestor, was essential to peace and social stability. Whenever there were major disagreements between tribes about rights to pasture or to water – which might, unresolved, escalate into warfare and bloody chaos – the Holy Man was called in. Thanks to his innate *baraka*, his decisions would be accepted by both parties as final and binding. Only he could keep the peace.

Does anybody happen to know which kind of Islam the Algerians have just voted for in these cancelled elections, then? Is it the kind with, or without, *marabouts*? The puritans, or the old church?

My French experts think it was unspecified. The Front for Islamic Salvation just talked about respect and decency, an end to government corruption, more justice and equality – things anyone in their right mind would agree with, but couched in Islamic vocabulary.

Well, who is going about shooting policemen?

The Dutch! says Yazid.

Twenty minutes of steepness later, we arrive at Tobias' first stop, a small town whose road-sign is written in Arabic only, with no transliteration beneath it. Help. Where are we? A horrible new experience. We are, all of a sudden, illiterate. Imagine if Tobias and Yazid should up and leave us now! We don't know where we are, and we couldn't even look it up on our map to find out. How useful is the art of reading that we take so much for granted! And how scarily shapeless the world becomes without it. Gérard starts leafing feverishly through *The Little Cunning One* in search of an Arabic alphabet.

Passing a pretty domed mosque with a tall ochre-painted minaret, Tobias turns off the main street through a low archway, into a wide, dirt-paved walled courtyard. A beautiful, if very scruffy-looking, courtyard, with an espaliered pomegranate against one wall and an ancient-looking fig tree in the centre. A slightly depressed and dusty grapevine trails along the balustraded first-floor balcony, which runs round all four walls, supported by columns and arches, barrel-vaulted porticoes sheltering a cobbled area. Threads of smoke are rising from the embers of a bonfire, while a donkey and a mule stand in the opposite corner, under their own private bit of portico, tethered to iron rings in the wall. The donkey is wearing a couple of big sacks of something, flour maybe, while the mule is as nature intended him. There must be twenty or thirty of these tether-rings built into the walls, though, right along the back: how many people do they get in here, on a good day? Is it a mule-park? Or maybe a mule-market?

A fat brown chicken clucks at us; a closer look and I see that it too is tethered, by a piece of string round one of its legs, to an old bit of iron – a ploughshare, is it? On the back wall beneath the porticoes there is a row of rough wooden doors: one of them, a half-door, is open, and two goats rest their chins on the closed lower part, munching and staring us out rudely.

Tobias won't be long, he says, heading for the opposite corner from the donkey, where he opens a door into the heart of the building. There seems to be a quite startling amount of clattering, clanging, crashing, and shouting going on behind it. He heads into the racket regardless, calling out *hola!* in Spanish, and then something in Arabic, as he vanishes inside.

We all clamber out of the car and stretch. Gérard is making an I-told-you-so sort of a face. How come Tobias knows these people deep in cannabis-country, in the middle of nowhere? Guy feints a backhand slap across his chops. Gérard dissolves into laughter. Thank goodness. I don't mind him having a wild fantasy life, as long as he doesn't get all anxious about it. As far as Guy and I can see, if the only viable crop round here is the kif-leaf, and if everybody's doing it, it's hardly going to be associated with gangsters, crime and violence, is it? More with farming folk, you'd think: tractors, wellies and horse-manure, or whatever the Rif mountain equivalent of that may be. Oxen, sandals and donkey-droppings?

I take a seat on the log beside the chicken-plough and now realize that we are not alone in the yard. Across from us, under the shade of the portico, there's an old man in one of those classy white-wool robes, sitting stock-still. He has a very tidy white beard, a white crochet skull-cap under the draped bit of his robe, and is puffing gently on a home-made-looking pipe with a very long reed and a tiny, round bowl.

Kif! says Gérard, nudging me.

I think he's right: there's a certain sweet perfume in the air. Still – a nice, respectable old man, nothing scary about him. If he was in France, he'd be sipping a cheering glass of red wine; here, he's puffing some soothing kif. No hint of the evil gangster about him, for sure.

The old man raises his pipe in a slow, dignified greeting. Gérard and Guy raise their hands back, but without the pipe. Not having yet attained the John-Wayne level of dignity required to share in such manly, silent greetings, I decide to try my first Arabic one, as prescribed by the *Petit futé*.

As-salamu aleikum, I say, Peace be upon you.

The correct answer to this greeting is, the book claims, *Wa aleikum salam*, And upon you be peace. The old man just stares at me, looking positively astounded. After a moment or two of silence, Gérard helpfully repeats the greeting, in case this makes my intention clearer. Or in case respectable old men here are not used to having peace wished upon them, unprovoked, by unknown females. This seems a horribly likely explanation. It's only a decade, after all, since old men in Italy stopped being appalled by unsolicited remarks from unknown females. No – what am I saying? They never did stop being appalled. They just died out.

Gérard's greeting seems to work better than mine, whatever the reason. The old man takes the pipe slowly from his mouth, nods and responds. Alas, whatever he may be saying, it is certainly not the reply prescribed by the guidebook. It sounds like '*labass*'. Probably he's just never got round to reading the *Petit futé*.

Labass, echoes Guy and receives a polite nod in return. A smug look comes over his face. Another thumbs-down for *The Little Cunning One*.

There's someone else in the courtyard too, I now register. A woman, swathed in a black *haik* from head to toe, with only her eyes and the bridge of her nose showing, is sitting a couple of yards behind the old man, in the darkest corner under the portico. Are the two of them together? They're ignoring one another completely, but I suppose that doesn't mean much, in any culture. I decide not to venture another hello. She doesn't look at all as if she's expecting to join in any public greetings. A potential minefield, and I'm already exhausted by the first attempt.

Yazid arrives in the yard to join us now, with a brisk and competent *labass* all round. Surely he can't have been looking for a phone again? A different perfume has begun wafting our way, out through the noisy doorway behind us: a delicious, spicy, savoury one. Guy sticks his head round the door, curious, and comes back out grinning. A restaurant kitchen, he says. We've come in the back way, that's all.

I nip over and look out through the gateway onto the street. Yes, there's even a sign, out on the street side. Chez Ismail, it says, and in an alphabet I can read, too.

Restaurant Ismail, nods the old man from under the portico, looking as if he thinks we're slightly deranged. I suppose it must seem a little odd, a bunch of foreigners coming into a restaurant and then acting all surprised that it is one.

Tobias bounces back out, looking pleased as punch, and introduces us to two cheerful-looking men, both called Mohammed. Mohammed the father and Mohammed the son. Or Mohammed *bin* Mohammed: that's how you say it in Arabic. They are the father and brother, respectively, of one of Tobias' neighbours in Ceuta.

Labass, they both say, shaking our hands. *Labass*, we say back.

It means 'No harm', Yazid tells us. A lovely expression. Even better, you can use it both for hello and for goodbye, simplifying life a lot.

The three of them go over to the car, Mohammed the father

chatting away to Tobias in fluent Spanish. Tobias opens the boot, and the two Mohammeds heave out a large cardboard box, which they carry off into the restaurant. What on earth can be in it? Tobias has sat down next to me on the log, so I ask. He gives me a sidewise look and lays his finger along his nose. OK. None of my business.

Guy can't believe what a nation of linguistic geniuses the Moroccans are. Does everyone speak Spanish and French, as well as their own language? Yazid says they get a good start in this Berber part of Morocco. Once you've learned one new language, especially as a small child, the whole thing becomes simpler. Children who grow up in Berber-speaking homes will start learning Arabic as soon as they set foot outside the house. Moroccans have always had two languages of their own to deal with. Adding a working knowledge of the colonizers' tongues was no trouble at all to bilingual Arabic- and Berber-speakers.

Gérard has heard, he says, that they don't like being called Berbers these days. At least, the Algerian Berbers certainly don't. Not only is 'Berber' not their own word, but it's derogatory too – a rude name given to them by foreigners. The word 'barbarian' is derived from it, and 'barbaric'. They want their own language, Tamazight, officially recognized as a national language. And to be called by their own name for themselves: Amazigh, which means 'the free'.

Yazid says Berbers feel the same way in Morocco, but here it's kept very low-key. The king does not like to see Berbers taking pride in their cultural differences from the country's Arabic-speakers, or demanding that their language be recognized as a national one, even though a good third of the nation grow up speaking Tamazight. The king is afraid he might end up with a Berber separatist movement on his hands. And it's no joke. A good friend of Yazid's back home, a Berber who runs a café, let a foreign academic who was studying Berber culture sit in his bar, collecting Tamazight expressions from his customers. Next morning Yazid's friend was dragged off by the police, who shoved him into a chair and forcibly shaved off his beard.

Nearly ripped his face off. He didn't dare speak his own language with his clients for weeks afterwards.

His beard? Seems a very odd punishment.

But Yazid says it makes perfect sense. Because another group of people the king dislikes a lot are the Islamists, who have a tendency to criticize him for not sharing his multi-millions with the poor of his nation. And these days anyone who has a beard can be presumed to be an Islamist. Absurd, in his friend's case – Berbers are the last people to turn Islamist, as the police very well know. The Islamists want the whole world to speak Arabic, the holy language, as they see it, and naturally enough hold no brief at all for Berbers and their Tamazight tongue! And the feeling is mutual. But shaving Yazid's friend was a clever move: made it look as if he was being punished for extremist religious beliefs, rather than for publicizing Berber language and culture among foreigners, and neatly confused the issue. He never has grown the beard back, though. If there's a next time, it will be obvious what's at stake!

Over in the shadows, one of the goats has started making a weird groaning noise. Or is that what goats always sound like? Can't say I've spent a lot of time at close quarters with the creatures. I decide to ignore it.

What is this place, anyhow? I ask Tobias, hoping for a fuller answer on a less controversial subject than his delivery. Is this yard part of the restaurant? Do they do barbecues out here or something? And why so many beast-parking-spaces? Do so many of their customers come by donkey?

You call it a *funduq*, he says. Most of them are falling to bits nowadays, though. Like this one. *Funduqs* were places for merchants to stay, in the days before lorries. When goods had to be carried on mule-trains – maybe for weeks on end, right across the country – you needed somewhere for the animals and their owners to rest up overnight, with a lock-up to keep all the merchandise safe, too. The rooms upstairs, above the portico, were for the travellers to sleep. Beasts stayed down below, and the goods went into the ground-floor rooms – see the wooden doorways at the back, where the goats are? But there's not a lot of use for a *funduq* now, when lorries can transport ten times the load in half the time, and never need to be unloaded and rested. So Mohammed decided to open the restaurant. The *funduq* still gets used on market day, though, when all the people from the outlying hamlets come into town with their wares.

It's a kind of bed-and-breakfast, then?

Not really. The guests use their own bedding, mule-blankets or whatever, and do their own cooking out here in the yard. The *funduq* just provides bed, water and a brazier, and the guests sort themselves out. If they want a wash, they go to the *hammam*. That's just normal here, though: lots of people don't have an indoor bathroom.

It comes to me now that I have, in fact, been in a *funduq* before. It was in the south of Spain – in Andalusia, naturally enough – during my teenage travels. And it was such an incomprehensible experience that it has stuck in my memory ever since. I'd asked for a cheap hotel and been taken to a courtyard just like this one – a lot bigger, though, and with two balustraded storeys above it rather than just the one. Night-time when we arrived, pitch darkness, a wide dirt yard in the centre, the only light coming from a couple of dim lamps hanging under the porticoes, showing where the stairs led up to the balconies, and three separate bonfires, each with a group of figures hunched round it cross-legged on the ground, muffled up against the cold night air. A perfume of wood-smoke and char-grilled meat, glimmering reflections off pocket-knives and wine-bottles, unshaven faces in the flickering glow. In short, nothing like any hotel I'd ever come across in my life.

I'd been travelling all day with a van-driver who, whenever he fancied stopping for a coffee, a glass of wine or a *tapa*, had paid his way with baby cos lettuces pulled from his load. He just parked, pulled out an armful of them, walked in, plonked them on the bar and got us whatever we fancied in exchange. A strange enough experience already, as far as I was concerned, though the recipients showed no surprise at this unusual form of currency. They would grab a lettuce, slice it in half lengthways, sprinkle it with salt, and munch it up appreciatively, just like that. Until now, thanks to my deprived British upbringing, I'd always imagined that lettuce was not edible without some kind of dressing. Eventually I tried one. It was good, very good. Later, as evening drew on, I asked the driver if he knew of somewhere cheap to stay. He did, and he was going there himself. I might as well come too. And so we arrived in – well, in what I now know was a *funduq*, though its yard was mule- and donkey-free, of course. Spain had given up the long-distance beast of burden some decades before. The most unnerving thing about this Spanish *funduq*, though, was what I found when I finally went off up one of the stairwells in the corners of the yard, seeking my bed on the second floor. The whole staircase had been transformed into a sort of misshapen tunnel, by dint of lining it, right round the walls and across the ceiling, with yards and yards of tacked-on red flannelette. The light being dim, and this being a type of decor I had not so far come across, I gave the cloth above me a prod with my finger as I passed, just to make sure it really was flannelette, and almost choked on the great cloud of dust that flew out of it. Somewhat more unnervingly, I seemed to hear the crunch of small quantities of masonry being dislodged behind the cloth. I was too tired to care, though, and since none of the other guests seemed to fear that the place was about to fall in on their heads, I went on up and climbed into the rickety metal bed I'd been allocated. No sheets or covers, so I just spread my sleeping bag out on it. In the morning, when I stepped out onto the balcony, wondering where you got breakfast round here, I found that the travellers in the yard had rekindled their bonfires, on which they were toasting *bocadillos* and making coffee. I headed down through the filthy red tunnel to join the other guests, hoping they might be disposed to share, and on the first-floor landing, my eye was drawn to an impossibly bright pool of sunlight shining from under an ill-fitting door. Curious, I bent down and looked under the three-inch gap at the bottom. Clouds. Sky. There was nothing at all on the other side of it.

No building, just a disintegrating pile of building rubble down below. Undoubtedly the most peculiar hotel I'd ever been in.

I see now that I must have been in at the long, slow death of one of the very last *funduqs* of el-Andalus.

Tobias heads back indoors. He's asked the Mohammeds to give us infidels a spot of lunch, as long as we eat it out of sight. A plate of soup, or something. They're cooking anyway, for tonight's festivities. I must have a very weak character, because I now feel horribly embarrassed at the thought of eating at all while everyone else is fasting. Even though, until only a few hours ago, I had absolutely no notion of such a thing.

The goat lets out another of those awful groans. I wonder if animals don't get fed until sunset during Ramadan, as well as humans. Steering clear of the goat, which doesn't seem too even-tempered, I go over and pet the mule, scratching its big flicky ears. It gives my hand a hopeful velvety nuzzle. How much I would love to be a merchant trader of old, with an excuse to roam the fascinating Rif hillsides with a whole string of these lovely creatures.

The old man knocks out his pipe, gets up, unties the donkey and, with a polite nod at us, sets off out of the yard, leading the creature by the halter. The woman gets up and follows him out through the archway. The goat does some more gurgling.

Outside in the street, beyond the arch, a small crowd of people is now standing around, their backs turned to us. All of them seem to be staring with great interest at one of the houses opposite. There must be twenty or thirty people there, though when I looked out to check for restaurants ten minutes ago, there was hardly anyone about. The building everyone's suddenly so gripped by looks like a completely normal house: a plain stuccoed front with the usual intricate ironwork at its windows. What can be so fascinating about it? I wander over to the gate but can't see anything at all past so many bodies, wearing so much voluminous drapery. Some of the women must be Berbers; they have those striped cloths tied round them, though nobody is wearing the full straw-hat get-up. The others in pastel jellabas and *khimars* will be Arabs, then, I suppose. Or people who've forgotten they're Berbers, as Yazid puts it. One woman is dressed in another of those all-enveloping *haiks*, though hers is white, not black. You must be able to tell a lot about people from these various outfits, if only you knew what they meant. Indecipherable to me, though. I'm an illiterate not just in language here, but in dress-codes as well.

Curious, I go on over the road, where I attach myself to the fringes of the crowd. A few people have turned to look at me. I try asking a moustachioed man in another of those cunningly wrapped *chèches* what's going on. *S'il vous plaît, qu'est-ce qui se passe*, I say in French, for lack of a better alternative. He just blanks me. Looks right through me, then turns back to the house. Maybe he doesn't speak French? I try Spanish. *Que pasa, por favor*? Same result. These people don't seem anything like as cheery and welcoming as the rest of the Moroccans we've met so far. I try asking the lady in the long stripy kaftan, a draped headscarf and an extra square of flowery cloth for a veil, all but her kohl-lined eyes hidden. She gives me what seems an unnecessarily short, sharp reply. A positively angry reply, you might think, if you were feeling a little paranoid. Probably just the effect of fasting on the temper, as outlined by Moustafa earlier. But I myself am in holiday mood. I may as well edge a little further forward and satisfy my curiosity.

Hardly have I taken two steps more in amongst the biblically flowing garments and fascinating headgear when, at last, wild adventure finally does break out. One woman gives me a sharp shove in the ribs with her elbow; several others, one with that blue tattooed line from lower lip to chin, start to screech right in my face. A score more angry people turn towards me, narrowed eyes under twisted *chèches* and crocheted skull-caps, lowered brows above black kohl. Voices are raised, pointing fingers waved under my nose. I am being jostled and pushed at from all sides now. Suddenly, I'm scared. What have I done? Is it because I'm dressed in Western clothes? Because my head is uncovered? My face is showing? What a terrible irony if I were to be felled and trampled upon, die a Christian martyr's death beneath a tidal wave of billowing Muslim robes, when I was never so much as baptized! Should I try saying I have no religion? No, they'd probably hate a thoroughly unbelieving infidel even more. And anyway, we don't seem to have any language in common. A grey-bearded old man at my side raises a gnarled fist, shakes it menacingly at me. OK, got the message. I am definitely not wanted here.

I back off and turn tail. Angry shouts follow me as I cross the road to safety, lean in the archway to take stock of my situation. Gérard and Guy seem to have vanished, Yazid too. They must have followed Tobias indoors. My heart-rate is just returning to normal when I get another shock. An unexpected arm grabs mine from behind. I swing round, heart thumping – to meet the smiling eyes of a singularly unmenacing-looking young woman in tightly-tied *khimar* and grey jellaba. Am I all right, she asks in perfect French. She saw me in trouble back there – did I not realize what I was pushing my way into?

No, I certainly did not. What on earth, I ask, slightly hysterically, was the matter with those people? Why did they get so insanely angry? Is it something religious? I was only squeezing in to see what they were looking at! Is it because my head's uncovered?

But not at all! she says. They are just the poor people of this town, and they thought you were claiming to be poor too.

Poor? Are they? To my eye, they look the same as everyone else here. The nuances of jellaba and kaftan – not to mention Berber get-ups – that divide rich from poor, are, as I have mentioned, beyond me as yet. Remembering how school uniforms used to work, I check it out at ground level. Yes. Broken-backed plastic sandals, worn-down flip-flops. Poor, OK. But I don't see why that should make them fly into a rage with me, particularly.

My new friend, still holding my arm, is shouting something in Arabic – or possibly Tamazight – to the people across the street. The atmosphere relaxes noticeably. The angry lady in the stripy kaftan even seems to smile – though it's hard to be sure with that veil in the way – and shouts something friendly-sounding back.

What's going on? I ask my Good Samaritan. What did you say?

I told them, she says nonchalantly, that you were not after their money, that you are just a simple foreigner who thought she'd found a tourist attraction.

But why would they think I was after their money? I ask indignantly. Do foreigners often come over here to pick poor Moroccans' pockets?

My new friend, Mariam – who is a schoolteacher from a nearby village, she tells me, just the other side of Chefchaouen, and we must come and visit her if we have time, she's sure we'd find it very interesting – explains that the house everyone finds so fascinating belongs to a rich goldsmith, the richest man in town. And on the last day of Ramadan, the rich of Islam are duty-bound by the law of the Koran to share some of their good fortune with the poor. Nobody should go hungry or ill-clad tomorrow, on the feast of Eid al-Fitr. Soon the goldsmith will open his windows and distribute the customary alms for the end of the fast, the *sadaqa*. Still, Mariam says, gently steering me on into the yard, you would not have been stealing, anyway. The Koran says that *sadaqa* must be given not only to the poor of the area, but also the needy wayfarer.

What? I say, so just anybody who came and stood there today would get cash showered on them? Or gold, or whatever it is?

Yes. Apparently they would. But local people would not dream of standing there asking for charity if they didn't really need it. They would be shamed in the eyes of God, not to mention the eyes of their neighbours. It is a Muslim duty to look after those poorer than yourself; that is the third Pillar of Islam. To take charity you didn't need would amount to publicly stealing from the poor.

So they thought a rich Westerner like me was about to grab herself a share of their paupers' alms! I am hot with shame.

Now Tobias sticks his head out of the restaurant back door.

We're in luck, he shouts. Come on through and eat!

For goodness' sake. As if I hadn't had enough public embarrassment already.

The Mohammeds have plenty of soup, they say, settling us on low padded benches round a knee-high table by a window with its blinds down for good manners. Yazid has decided to wait outside, adding to the guilt-quotient.

Do we want to try some *harira* – that's the classic Ramadan fast-breaker all over Morocco? Or some *baisa*, which is a local Berber version? Or both, maybe, why not?

We hesitate. It seems bad enough eating at all, never mind greedily wanting to try both. Which we undoubtedly do. But we needn't have worried: the Mohammeds are positively encouraging us to eat. We need to keep up our strength for our travels, they say. Of course: the wayfarer waiver. Both it is, then!

The *harira* is meaty and thick, a soup your spoon would almost stand up in, flavoursome mutton and chickpeas, plenty of spices, and a good half-dozen kinds of vegetable. Seven kinds, actually, says Mohammed the father. The Berber fast-breaker is delicious too, if somewhat more restrained in its ingredients, and oddly reminiscent of Uncle Kebir's breakfasts. Is there, maybe, some special Berber affinity with broad beans? Because that's what the *baisa* turns out to be: a broad bean soup pureed with garlic and a large dash of chilli, thickened with a splash of olive oil. A big chunk off a round loaf of fresh sesame-seed bread to dip in it. Lovely.

The Mohammeds soon come to sit with us, plying us with extra bread and chilli sauce. As hospitable and as curious as everyone here – except those you are trying to steal from, that is – they are soon asking where we're bound.

Algeria? Mohammed the father is very unimpressed. A foolish place to go, he says, still speaking Spanish. Why don't we stay here in Morocco? The Algerians are a Godless people, he adds, echoing Moustafa. A nation of Communists and atheists!

Why on earth do people keep saying this, when Algeria is apparently collapsing into chaos, as we speak, because its people tried to elect an Islamist – or at any rate, Islamic – party to government?

Mohammed the father gives a hollow laugh. Islam is just their excuse to fight their government, he says, refilling our plates from the soup-pot. It has nothing to do with piety.

Forgive him, says Mohammed the son in French, which Mohammed the father apparently does not understand. His father is only repeating what his countrymen have been told about Algeria for decades. Morocco is a kingdom in the absolute sense of the word. And any absolute monarch worth his salt, when his next-door neighbours declare a monarch-free democratic republic, will do his best to blacken their name. Cold War propaganda may have gone out of style elsewhere, but here in Morocco it's still going strong.

A newcomer arrives at the table, wanting to speak with Mohammed the father. He is wearing a large bath-towel on his head, for all the world as if he'd been playing at sheikhs in his mother's airing cupboard. Or concealing his identity on a French building site. This is getting ridiculous. We have gone along with the idea of a dishcloth as ordinary everyday Moroccan headgear, but bath-towels, surely, are going beyond a joke?

Mohammed the father soon puts us right. The towel on the head is merely the correct procedure for returning home after a visit to the *hammam*. You should never let your head cool down too quickly – it is dangerous to the health.

All of a sudden there is a commotion from out the back. An agitated youth with an apron over his jellaba rushes in from the kitchens, and Mohammed the son is called away urgently to the court-yard. Towel man goes with him. The goat, it seems, is giving birth. I thought there was something odd about that noise it was making. Why on earth didn't I tell anyone?

Mohammed the father, unfazed, has begun idly tracing out a map of our journey in the breadcrumbs we have somehow managed to spread all over his table. He has decided to show us how easily we can get to the Sahara, and to Timimoun, without passing through more than a small corner of Godless Algeria. We are surprised that Mohammed even knows where Timimoun is. It's a tiny town, several hundred miles away across a large chunk of desert, and in another country.

It may be small, he says, but in a desert, small does not mean unimportant. And in its heyday, this *funduq* was one of the last stops on the trans-Saharan route towards Tangier. Once upon a time merchants and their camel-trains would arrive here from right down in the desert – and sometimes even all the way from distant Mali – telling tales of their travels. The name of Timimoun was often heard within these walls.

The town of Adrar, Mohammed remembers, was the first stop after the desert crossing where you would find drinkable water. But with only one more day's travel northwards, you arrived at the green paradise of Timimoun, the shade of its date-palm oasis. There, the caravans could really rest after the hot sand and the dry thirst: the walled *palmeraies* cool and fresh, the welcome sound of trickling water everywhere, the people friendly and hospitable. And you paid for your lodgings there not with money, not with goods, but with the manure from your animals! Because in Timimoun, manure was as precious as gold. How else could their gardens bloom in all that sand? So of course they would always welcome travellers – and their beasts of burden even more.

But when was this, we ask, perplexed. It must have been long ago, surely?

Of course it was, he says, laughing at our ignorance. But the tales still got told when he was a boy. Things don't get forgotten as fast here in the countryside as they do in the cities. And even when Mohammed was a child, the caravans still came up from the Tafilalet – where the ruins of Sijilmassa lie – and from the Gourara, the string of oases with Timimoun at their head. They would bring delicious fresh dates and strings of dried figs, spices and woollen cloth, camel-hair burnouses, baskets made of palm-leaves and panniers of palm-fibre for your mules. But the nomads' visits, he says, had slowed to a trickle over the last few generations. The nomads' traditional spring and autumn grazing lands straddled both sides of the border; they had always crossed it at will, and combined their trading with the grazing of their flocks. But on the Algerian side the French had taken the best land and covered it with vineyards. The rich grazing had gone: there was little reason to come this way any more. Then in the 1960s the French army captured every nomad it could find – 6,000 of them, people said – and locked them up behind barbed wire in what they called *regroupement* camps. And what was left of their pasture, up on the high plateau, was split in two along the colonists' border with a lethal fence; 200 miles long, 5,000 volts of electricity running through it, flanked by minefields into the bargain. Meant to stop the Algerians getting help from across the border in their war for independence. The French lost Algeria anyway, but they certainly put an end to the nomads' old ways. You'd be hard put to it to find a camel-hair burnous around here these days.

Gérard wonders, he says, why they haven't thought of electrifying the fences and adding a few minefields around Ceuta and Melilla.

Tobias looks most alarmed. He hasn't caught the irony and, worried about what sort of nutters he has taken up with, says nervously that he doesn't think Africans deserve actually to die for trying to get into Europe. I submit a much better idea: why not copy a superbly eco-friendly British fence from a little earlier in the twentieth century, a simple natural barrier of impassably ferocious thorn bushes, fifteen feet high and thirty feet wide, built – or planted, rather – in India. A thousand miles long, I seem to remember. Or was it two? Not designed to stop Indians getting into Britain, of course, but to stop them getting to their own seashore, where they would cunningly evade British taxes, and undermine British authority, by making their own salt.

Tobias gets it now and laughs weakly.

Mohammed the father, meanwhile, has returned to work on his breadcrumb map, over which he soon has Gérard and Guy poring. Instead of heading east along the coast as we're planning, then turning south for the desert after the city of Algiers, he says, cutting a north–south swathe with his fingertip to represent the border, we could avoid the whole Mediterranean part of Algeria, with all those great cities full of troublemakers. Just head south-east inside Morocco and take to the desert right away. A hundred-odd miles to the south of the main Oujda frontier, the one we're heading for, a perfectly good back route crosses the border. Here, he adds, crumbling another fragment of bread to cover the south-east more thoroughly, at Figuig – it's an oasis town, on the old desert trail heading straight for Timimoun. Most of it's asphalted, these days. And the only city you need meet en route is Beni-Abbes, a small and peaceful place.

I've already stopped listening. There's no way Guy is going to want to miss out on Algiers, home of his fathers. And we've got a perfectly good – and, thankfully, inedible – map of our own, anyway, if we change our minds.

Mohammed the son now returns, accompanied by Towel-man and a delighted Yazid, who is positively glowing, bearing in triumph a tiny baby goat wrapped in a bit of sacking. He certainly seems to have enjoyed getting back to his roots out there. They bring the creature over to the table for our admiration.

Just a quick look, says Mohammed. It needs to go straight back to its mother.

It lets out a tiny bleat. Aaaah, isn't it lovely? I say, reaching out a hand to stroke its sweet little nose. Mistaking my finger, understand-ably perhaps, for a source of goat's milk, it bites me. Quite hard. OK, it definitely does need to get back to its mother.

Goatless again, the menfolk get back to their route-planning. I turn to gazing about the room. A gleaming blue-neon fly-killer attracts my attention now, buzzing quietly on one of the far tables, evidently brand new, making a loud hiss and crackle as some passing insect meets its untimely end. Tobias catches my eye, gives a wink and a jerk of his head in its direction, followed by a big grin. Aha!

That's what we brought here! Electronic goods, as predicted. A contraband fly-killer! I don't think I'll bother telling Gérard.

Back to the men's travel conversation. And now I get a terrible urge to giggle. This scenario is absurdly similar to so many I have sat through back in Europe, with one of those numerous travel-fetishist men who insist on going through every detail of some journey you're about to take: exactly which motorway exit you'll need, how bad the traffic is on a Tuesday morning, the good short-cut from the Little Chef, don't miss the bridge at Wyre Piddle, third turning on the left . . . I always stop listening, just as I have now. I won't remember all that stuff, won't recognize landmarks I've never seen before, and I've usually got a perfectly good map of my own.

The only difference here is that Mohammed is wearing a jellaba. And that we're not talking about the intricacies of the A32 but of a trans-Saharan desert trail. I suppose this does prove, against all expectation, that there once was some evolutionary use for middle-aged male travel-fetishism. It probably saved countless lives in the high days of cross-Sahara camel-trade. But just think how many generations of middle-aged merchants must have sat in this very spot, discussing *ad nauseam* the minutiae of their camel- and mule-travels, in order for not just the fame, but the precise location, of Timimoun to have spread this far. I'm glad I wasn't there.

6

Cool, fresh mountain air. We are in a high valley cleft in the hills, where a pair of spectacularly craggy peaks towers above us, rising into a crisp blue sky. We have finally arrived at Chefchaouen, a jumble of buildings nestling into the stony hillside like some precipitation of the rocks themselves, a rough crystal formation of whitewashed cubes. A red-sandstone citadel guards the main square of this bustling market town, where we are now casting about for signs of a hotel. There should be plenty available, Tobias said. Come summertime, this place is always packed with cannabis tourists from Europe and America.

Tobias has left us now, gone on his way with Yazid, without ever giving away the secret of our mysterious delivery to the Restaurant Ismail. Or so Gérard believes. We do know, however, that Tobias' morale has taken a turn for the better. He has vowed to take his courage in both hands, as soon as he gets back to his mother's tonight, and ring Marla again. He is sure, in his heart, that hers was just a momentary panic, only natural in a young girl thinking about her future wedding. She will have come to her senses by now, and all will be well. He will be in Texas by summer, he is sure. A happily married man with a good American job.

Gérard wonders idly about that huge, long frontier between Mexico and the USA. He's sure he's heard that there are many hundreds of miles of fencing along it. Does anyone happen to know if the Texans have some upgrading plans in the pipeline?

This main square here is on the edge of the old medina, just like the one in Tetuan, but this is a much more countrified version.

Chefchaouen doesn't have an extra, colonial city outside the old medina walls, the way Tetuan does. As Yazid pointed out, the colonizers never did get much of a grip here. A mere thirty years, all told. And Chefchaouen has succeeded in staying as it always was, mostly contained within the red-sandstone ramparts built over five centuries ago. It is a big place, too. Somewhere within those walls, says Gérard, there are a whole twenty mosques. *Chaouen*, he adds, means 'peaks', or 'horns', while *chef* means 'see' or 'look'. Isn't that an amazing name for a town? 'Look at the Horns'!

That depends, says Guy warily. You could just as easily translate it 'Peak View', couldn't you? I gather from this dusty response that Guy has certain suspicions concerning the source of Gérard's information.

At the bus stop across the square, a bus-driver waits for a jellaba'd man to persuade a reluctant sheep into the luggage compartment below. A farmers' market is going on at the far end, an open souk. Up there, chaos reigns. Can there always be this many people shopping in Chefchaouen? We've tried doing the tour and have had to retreat. We stumbled between mules and donkeys, were jostled by crowds of shoppers and spectators, tripped over women in those Peruvian Berber outfits sitting cross-legged on their rugs with pyramid piles of fat, round loaves. We squeezed past a queue of women taking their turn to speak to a man who sat inside a wooden box, dressed in gleaming white linen jellaba and massive white *chèche* – a kind of low-slung sentry-box, a stool outside it for the client of the moment. A scribe, the local man of letters. Evidently, here in the wild country, none of Yazid's alternative solutions to the public reading of letters has yet caught on. And no wonder the scribe looked so sleek and prosperous. More than half of the citizens of Morocco can't read or write, according to *The Little Cunning One*. The figure's more like seventy per cent for women, while thousands of their sons and husbands leave home to find work each year. Think how many missives must go to and fro. Past the scribe and into the fruits and vegetables area, works of art in red, yellow, green and gold, gleaming on beautifully arranged stalls, or casually heaped in buckets and boxes, the surplus produce of someone's vegetable garden; the grower lying in wait, cross-legged on the ground, to trip us up again. And broad beans without end – whole stalls piled high with them, bowls, buckets and sacks overflowing, in every possible shade from dark brown through green to almost-white, the stallholders doing a roaring trade. More Berber women passing through the crowd, one bent double under a load of kindling-wood, another with a smiling face and a swaddled baby strapped to her back, who stops to chat with an Arab woman, a white *haik* covering her from head to toe. How could these two groups of people can have lived side by side for centuries, neighbours and friends, and yet have kept their cultures so separate, I wonder? Outside the square, on the way to the mule- and donkey-park, more food: sheep, goats and chickens. Meat on legs, ready to load onto the bus. And butchers standing by, knives sharpened, poised for the kill, in case you prefer your dinner in passive mode. Time for a quick exit.

Turning to skirt back round the crowd, the next woman we passed was – someone we knew! Mariam the schoolteacher, along with her husband, whom we now know as Aytan – an intense-looking young man with a short black beard – accompanied by a much older man, a countryman by the look of his weather-beaten face and rough wool jellaba, whom she presented as her neighbour Mokhtar. She and Aytan had been travelling the hills with Mokhtar all afternoon, on a quest for a new, and inexpensive, mule for his farm, she said. No luck so far. Not a mule to be found. Not at a reasonable price.

Mokhtar shook our hands in the slowest and most ceremonious style, with a long gaze into each of our eyes, and a pause at each hand-on-the-heart. Then he expanded for some time, in a mixture of French and Spanish, upon the price of mules and the dishonesty of their vendors, while Gérard and Guy nodded wisely and sympa-thetically, as if to horse-trading born. Mokhtar was appalled by the day's bargaining. Especially that one up the road from the Restaurant Ismail! Daylight robbery! Gérard agreed that, indeed, in this day and age, the world was full of dealers from whom he himself wouldn't buy so much as a second-hand donkey.

And all of a sudden, we all found ourselves invited to join our new acquaintances tonight for the feast of Eid al-Fitr. Everyone in the whole of Morocco – in the whole of the Islamic world, from here to Indonesia – would be celebrating the end of Ramadan and the Breaking of the Fast tonight, said Mokhtar. We must come and celebrate with them! Plenty of food for everyone! Look for a hotel? He would not hear of such a thing!

Mariam and Aytan backed him up. They would be eating with Mokhtar and his family anyway, they said. There was plenty of room to sleep, if we didn't mind a pile of woollen rugs on the schoolroom floor. The school would be closed for the next three days for Eid, anyway.

Our first taste of the startling hospitality of North African people, which would continue to amaze us throughout our journey. It was agreed, then. No hotel. We would all squeeze into a couple of taxis, they said, as soon as the market was over, and head for open country. Brilliant, we said.

Little did we know just how brilliant. We would end up spending half the night and most of the next day with our hosts, stuffing our faces with as much enthusiasm, I'm ashamed to say, as if we too had spent the last four weeks fasting. I have never seen such an amazing array of food produced with so little in the way of equipment. Or, for that matter, such heroic commitment to educating the young with so little in the way of equipment. But more of that later.

The three of us have now paused to regroup for a moment on the terrace of a bar at the quiet end of the square, shaded by tall, feathery eucalyptus trees. It isn't open, of course, but its chairs and tables have been thoughtfully left out for weary passers-by. A man comes peddling pastries from a tray – some fig-and-honey rolls for later? he asks enticingly, spotting my interest. Almond cakes? Vanilla slices? Cumin biscuits?

I can't resist it. And we need a little something to contribute to the evening's entertainment, after all. I get two huge paper cones, half a dozen of each. I don't bother even trying to barter. It seems ridiculously cheap anyway – why should I quibble over a bit of rich-country-resident tax being added to what a local might pay?

Alas, within minutes of our arrival, our quiet end has stopped being quiet. A lorry-load of wood is being decanted and reloaded onto a train of donkeys, a few feet away from us, to be carted off uphill into the medina. One spirited beast has taken violently against this thankless task and is protesting at the top of its voice.

The wood is for the *hammam*, says a small child who has now attached himself to us. For heating the water. Interesting information, and we reward him with the biro he asks for. Mistake. We are now swamped with infants, squeaking and gibbering, trying to scare us by bouncing out from behind the tree-trunks or creeping out from under our seats, giggling hysterically and asking over and over again for biros and/or dirhams. Now, beside us, a nice, peaceful man who has been sitting quietly smoking in the back of his open van suddenly reveals another, noisier side to his nature. A passer-by approaches him, brandishing a large pair of scissors, and he leaps nimbly down from his vehicle to reveal a knife-grinder's wheel within, coupled to a two-stroke bike engine. He starts the motor, creating a throbbing bass counterpoint to the donkey's roarings and the infants' squealings. So far, so loud. But now he applies the blunt blade of the scissors to the stone wheel. The sound of a thousand fingernails scraping across a blackboard. Every fibre of my being tells me to run.

Time, I think, for a tour of the old town. Thank the Lord for city walls. A marvellous invention. Just a few yards inside them, all is peace.

Moustafa was right: once you're inside the city walls, there is certainly a lot of blue in Chefchaouen. Every doorway, lintel, railing, even the plant-pots sitting outside the front doors on the narrow pavements of the medina – all of them have been painted in many variations on a strong, vibrant, Madonna blue. Nothing I ever saw in

Portugal could compete with this. There is no sign of a blue-paint Hand of Fatima here, though, and little need for such a thing, since half the doorknockers in the town are little brass Hands, palm out and fingers raised – the correct alignment for warding off the Evil Eye.

The inhabitants of Chefchaouen don't stop their blue paint mission at woodwork, metalwork and ceramics, either. They even add a dash of their favourite colour to the lime wash they do their exterior walls with. Every street, wall, house, strikes a slightly different blue-note from its neighbours; the alleyways glow with a surreal, cool light. These are obviously the homes of people whose morale is high. Everything amazingly clean, neat and in good repair. A very prosperous-looking town, whose prosperity, we gather, is based mainly on the marijuana plant.

We walk on uphill through alleys perfumed with frying garlic, coriander, cumin, cinnamon – festive preparations on hand. Above us, two women are silhouetted against the sky, calling out to one another as they hang their washing on high roof terraces. One low doorway stands open; inside it a man is working at a vertical loom. He turns as we pass, and we all wish one another No Harm. The alleys are just wide enough for goods to move freely – for two laden donkeys to pass one another, that is. Which they do rather frequently, causing us to squeeze ourselves into bright blue doorways. Good town planning, this, though, as I know from Italy. The narrower the alley, the more hours of shade it gets in the day, and the more temperate the homes and streets will be. There are lots of steep twists and turns, arches everywhere, and plenty of evidence that this is a town which has grown over the centuries, extra space added on, squeezed in, wherever it could be fitted. Aerial rooms have been suspended just above head-height on beams slung across the streets, filling the space between the houses and forming low shady tunnels, with benches of stone under them so the old folk can rest their bones from the steepness. Off the main drag, a profusion of secretive arches and even narrower alleyways, of nooks and crannies, gates into tiny patios or vegetable plots, sudden dead ends where you find yourself in somebody's wood store or sheep-pen. So many centuries have they been working on these buildings, replastering and rewhitewashing, that there is not a plumb line to be seen anywhere: the whole thing looks organic, created more by the hand of Nature than of Man. Nature in a very azure mood, that is.

I am disappointed, though. Until today, I've always admired the intrepidity of those Moroccans who, leaving their homeland far behind, come to Italy to make their living trekking up and down the steep, narrow alleys of our Ligurian hill villages selling from door to door. They carry huge packs on their backs, from which they sell rugs and household items: dishcloths, oven gloves, sheets, pillowcases . . . Now that I've seen Chefchaouen, though, I realize they're hardly intrepid at all. You could drop a Ligurian hill village in here without anyone even noticing, though you'd need to spruce it up a bit first, or the neighbours would soon be giving you what-for. They must feel completely at home.

Well, not quite, I have to admit. The superior hydraulics of Islam are as evident here as in Granada or Calabria. There are public water-fountains at almost every crossroads, decorated Andalusian style with tiles and brickwork. Andalusian style, because this town too was a place of refuge from Spain. It had not long been founded – by the argumentative Berbers themselves, in 1471 – when seventeen families of refugees, both Muslims and Jews, arrived here from el-Andalus seeking asylum. The Berbers had plenty of Christian trouble on their hands as it was – Chefchaouen had been conceived as a safe base from which to attack the Portuguese, the latest comers to snatch Ceuta. Now, across the water, Granada finally fell to the Christians. Many Andalusian Jews had already arrived seeking safely here. Now came the Muslims. Soon, the Spanish sailed in and seized Melilla. Refugees would go on arriving on Berber shores for the next century, as Spain's policy towards her remaining non-Christian population hardened. Enough was enough. The Jews and Muslims of Chefchaouen decided to ban any members of the troublesome Christian religion from entering their city gates, ever again – on pain of death. The ban on Christians stood firm from now until 1927, when all of a sudden, faced with those quarter-of-a-million armed men dispatched by the aberrant third People of the Book, the local residents had no choice in the matter.

In all the intervening centuries, history records only three intrepid (or mad) Christians succeeding in entering the town. Two Victorian travellers of the nineteenth century, rising to the challenge as only Victorian travellers would, managed to infiltrate Chefchaouen, one disguised as a Jew, the other as a Muslim trader on his way in, and a beggar on his panic-stricken way out. The third was a Christian missionary, who for obvious reasons did not bother with a disguise. He died shortly after his visit, from the effects of the poison administered to him during his stay. Or so the story goes. And in 1927, when the Spanish troops finally entered Chefchaouen, they were stunned to find the town's Jewish community addressing them, with great fluency, in a very odd version of their own language. They still spoke Castilian Spanish, as it had been spoken 400 years earlier.

The blue paint on Chefchaouen's walls, I notice, often doesn't go much above head height. Maybe it serves some useful function? I was once told that, beneath the superstition, the underlying reason for the blue window-surrounds of olden-day Portugal was to do less with discouraging evil spirits than with repelling insects. Apparently a lot of species find blue particularly unappealing. If so, this must be the most insect-free town ever. The children are still doing a good job of replacing them, though: buzzing round and round me like a bunch of manic bees. One of the boldest keeps trying to put her hand in my pockets. *Nazrani*, she keeps saying. No idea what this means, but I can tell from her tone that it's some kind of taunt. *Oy*, I reply eventually, resorting to international sound-effect language as I slap at her wrist. A woman sweeping the street outside her doorstep comes to my aid – calls the infants to order with a shout and a hand-clap. Within seconds, they have all vanished.

Voilà, she says, with a magician's twist of the wrist, making me laugh.

Ah, that's how you do it! I say in English, imitating her hand-clap. Now we're both laughing. Who needs language? And look at that – even her doorstep is painted blue! A little further on, at the dead-end niche of an alley, the cobblestones themselves are blue. And at the next fountain, two young women are rinsing out a paint-bucket with water. No prizes for guessing what colour paint.

Bonjour, Nazrani, says one of them.

As-salamu aleikum, says the other, giggling.

Bonjour! You're painting? I say inanely, flapping an imaginary paint-brush against an imaginary wall, in case *bonjour* is as far as their French goes, and wondering anew about this *Nazrani* word. It surely can't be that rude, can it, if these two friendly-seeming women are saying it too?

Yes, yes, painting! Hard work! they say, pointing out a patch of freshly painted blue, head-high, just down a side-alley.

Finished, they add. Cleaning now!

But you stop this high? I ask, gesturing just above my head, hoping to get some interesting information from them about the low-flying behaviour of evil spirits. Or of insects, at a pinch.

The answer does not concern either insects or spirits, however, but humans. *Los maridos.* We've gone into Spanish now, and I gather that their menfolk don't want them going up ladders. Other men might see things they shouldn't. (Lots of giggling as one of them raises the hem of her jellaba to show me how.) But the men of Chefchaouen are too lazy (or do they mean too stoned on their own hashish? They are imitating a lounging man puffing at a cigarette) so the upper storeys never get done!

Sounds just like home improvements everywhere, then . . .

Er – *Nazrani?* I say now, in a questioning sort of voice, hoping for illumination on this matter too.

They both fall about laughing: I've gone and made it sound as if I'm calling them *Nazrani*, whatever *Nazrani* may be.

La, la, they say, wagging their index fingers: No, no! And now they point at me, nodding emphatically. *Nazrani*, they repeat.

Yesus, one of them adds helpfully, as I go on looking puzzled. I get it at last. Jesus of Nazareth – Jesus the Nazarene! And that's what they're calling me – a Nazarene, a Christian.

I suppose, in a town with a history like this one, that is a kind of an insult.

When I meet up with the boys again, it is to find that they've spent the last half hour in the square fending off an endless stream of horribly tenacious young men who categorically refused to believe that they did not want to buy several kilos of hashish. Or, at the very least, visit a carpet shop. In retaliation, Guy has bought himself a burnous: an enormous ankle-length cloak of white, or rather natural-coloured, wool, a traditional garment in which he thinks he looks less noticeably tourist-like. *Au contraire*, he just looks absurdly melodramatic. He is about a foot taller than any Moroccan we have seen so far, and quite a lot skinnier. Moreover, we've only seen one single ancient countryman wearing a burnous: traditional they may be, but something tells me they are severely out of fashion amongst the locals. Also, Guy's uncovered European head, complete with Ray-Bans, does not suit the ensemble. Nothing to be done, though. Guy is in love with his burnous and will refuse to take it off until the heat forces him out of it, several hundred miles further south.

Meanwhile he has got chatting to a Dutch woman, who was apparently undaunted by the odd figure he now cuts. She's been living here for twenty years, married to a local man, and she tells us that the blue paint of Chefchaouen is actually a fashion that was launched by the town's Jewish community, some time in the 1920s. Sadly, the Jews are all gone now, but their chosen colour remains. The last Jewish artisan, a saddler, she says, went in the 1970s, to Israel. And a few years before him, the last family of jewellers left for France. Apparently particular trades went with particular ethnicities here, once upon a time: Jews always made packsaddles and other rough leather goods, or worked with fine metals. Only Jews could do this last job, because the mixing of two different metals by a Muslim would unleash the supernatural wrath of some particularly awe-inspiring and vengeful djinn.

Chefchaouen's Jews, our new acquaintance tells us, had already been leaving for a couple of decades; ever since the creation of the state of Israel. Not because they wanted to go there – they didn't, and in fact, most of those who left went to France. But every time Israel was seen to commit some act of outrage – first, right at the beginning, driving the Palestinians off their land and out of their homes, then the occupations of more Muslim peoples' lands after the Six Day War, and so on and on – the Jewish community here was doomed to bear the brunt of public outrage at the actions of a land that was not theirs, and to which they had, and desired, no connection. Their lives had become unbearable. Those of the Jewish faith were now seen in the same light as the troublesome Christians before them. Depressingly, it was the existence of Israel, a supposed place of refuge, that turned the Jews of Chefchaouen, after all those centuries, back into refugees.

Meeting up with Mokhtar, Mariam and Aytan again, we learn some more about the town's intriguing relationship with Christians. As we stand waiting for taxis under the red-sandstone citadel, Mokhtar grabs Gérard and Guy by the elbows, and swivels them round to face it.

What do they think of it? Would they be up to building a thing like that, he asks. No? Are they sure? He thinks they could, if they really tried, he says. If they were given no choice! And he gives a sinister cackle of laughter.

He now reveals that it is not entirely true that all Christians have been banned here since the arrival of the Granada refugees. It stands to reason, Mokhtar says with a grin, that you Nazarenes are fine people, as long as you're not at liberty to start causing trouble!

The very last Christians in town were prisoners of war, we now hear, taken some time in the late 1500s, when the bold warriors of Chefchaouen managed to capture a whole invading Portuguese army. They marched them right back here and forced them to build this citadel, in which they were now incarcerated for the rest of their lives. Mokhtar doesn't sound remotely sorry about it, either. The Christians started it all, anyway, he says; and they were not coming here to settle their families peacefully on the land, like true People of the Book, but to pursue profit and warlike aims: whereas the Jews and Muslims they had driven out of el-Andalus had been living quietly in their homes, minding their own business, in a beautiful, fertile land that they themselves had created, over all those eight long centuries. European settlers have been in the Americas only half that time, and how would they feel if they were suddenly told to pack up and leave? El-Andalus was a beloved country, celebrated in song and in verse as an earthly paradise. Here in the Rif, those Andalusian songs are still sung, and over the festival of Eid, Mokhtar promises, he will make sure we hear an Andalus band play the songs of the old homeland.

Memories are certainly long in this part of the world. TV in the Rif being something you go to the bar to watch – king permitting – people are, I suppose, obliged to entertain themselves in the old way, of an evening, by telling and retelling the old stories passed on by their grandparents, and the grandparents' grandparents. Not so long since it was like this in Europe, too, though; before the professional creators of endless streams of new tales moved into our homes. I remember the Scots granny, in her later and more confused years, telling us children a tale of terror – in which she was certain she'd participated herself – wherein our family home was burnt down by rampaging soldiers, but the menfolk had managed to save the roof-timbers, carrying them forty miles across country on their own shoulders, all the way to the sea. The burns were running with blood: she had dipped a hand in the cold, cold water and it had come out as red as if she were bleeding herself . . . We eventually realized that these events belonged to the Highland clearances, when the clans-people of the north of Scotland were driven out of their crofts to make way for the more profitable sheep-runs – well over a hundred years before she was born. There must still have been some fine, vivid story-tellers around in Europe when the Granny was young.

Our taxi grinds its way on along ever narrower mountain roads, winding through green hillsides dotted with wild marigolds, great ochre gashes here and there where the steep land has fallen away in a cascade of rocks. I am squeezed into the back seat with Gérard and Aytan, Mariam travelling in front. Somewhere behind us is a second taxi with Guy, Mokhtar and another two passengers who were going this way. You don't hire the whole taxi in this part of the world, just a seat in it. And it doesn't leave until it's full.

Aytan is intrigued to hear that we're on our way to Algeria. Plenty of trouble there, he says, shaking his head. He's been following the news on Algerian radio. Latest is that the stand-in government – though maybe that really means the army – has banned the Front for Islamic Salvation. They're rounding up thousands of its supporters and putting them under arrest. A stupid move. The FIS were calling for peaceful reforms, but they're being treated as if they stood for an Islamist revolution and an end to democracy, a country run by *imams*.

I am impressed. At last we've met a Moroccan prepared to believe that the Algerians may not be a nation of Godless Communists who merely masquerade as Muslims.

Worrying, says Gérard, who seems to have taken to Aytan right away. Surely that will only push people into the arms of the extremists, convince them that change will never come through the vote, only through violence?

We're going over a high mountain pass now, through a spectacularly narrow sunless gorge. But I'm hardly taking any notice of the landscape. I am busy concentrating on how unafraid I would be of holidaying in Ireland. Where on earth did I pack Samir and Mireille's paper napkin?

We clamber out of the taxi at last, in what seems to be the middle of nowhere, and stand waiting for the others to turn up. The afternoon sunlight on the mountains is beginning to mellow. Birds of prey are soaring and dipping across the wide valleys, shrill angry cries as they compete for air space. Below us, the vibrant green of the spring hillside is interrupted, here and there, by the lighter green of almond trees. Down at the foot of the valley, a silver ribbon of river snakes its way along a rock-strewn bed. In a fold of the hill above the road lies a village of scattered stone houses, terraced fields all around it, and the dome of a small mosque. It all looks idyllic. Maybe we shouldn't bother with Algeria after all?

7

Guy and Mokhtar arrive, laughing and nudging one another, *labass*-ing away at the other people in their cab. They've been at that old price-of-mules bonding again, evidently. Once Guy has disentangled himself and his burnous from the rest of the passengers, Mariam and Aytan lead the way down a narrow dirt track through a sparse olive grove. There are primroses and violets in the grass at its edges, and tiny star anemones under the trees. We're going to stop off at Mokhtar's first, to drop off the stuff Mariam has bought for tonight's dinner. There's a golden-orange pumpkin for the couscous, a tiny twist of saffron for the *pastilla*, and Aytan is carrying a bag filled to the brim with almonds still in their shells. They're for the *pastilla* too: it's a kind of pie filled with chicken – or with pigeon if we're lucky, Mariam says. Sweetened, toasted almonds are always part of the recipe, everywhere in Morocco – except here in the Rif. But for tonight, Khadija, that's Mokhtar's sister, has generously agreed to let Mariam treat the family to her own home-town version. And she's brought the almonds herself, she says, just to make sure there's no backtracking!

Mariam and Aytan, we have discovered, are not from the Rif at all, but from the city of Casablanca, a couple of hundred miles away. When you first qualify as a teacher here in Morocco, you have to take whatever job you're offered for your first four-year stint. Poor villages like this one, Mariam said, would never get any teachers otherwise. It's a catch-22 situation. Hardly any locals have ever had any schooling, so there never will be any local teachers wanting to settle down here to work. These four-year billets are part of the king's literacy campaign, which might one day change all that. When Aytan and Mariam have earned their laurels here, they'll get a chance at jobs nearer to home and family.

It seems a good plan to us foreigners. But Mariam doesn't sound too hopeful. You will see later, she says. Then you will tell me how serious this country is about educating the children of the Rif.

We turn uphill into a sort of smallholding, a jumble of low stone buildings enclosing a wide dirt yard. On the nearest side stands a relatively modern house, its sharp cement angles an odd contrast to the ancient, organic stone-and-mud of the older buildings. They have everything you could possibly need to survive here, Yazid-style: chickens clucking about the yard, a cow tethered by the far building, munching its way through what looks like a pile of dry palm-leaves, rows of vegetables down below the house – tall stands of peas or beans towering over the rest – and citrus trees beside them. The most noticeable feature of the yard, though, is a bread-oven of enormous size, shaped like a great domed beehive, mud-plastered and well over head-high.

Here, on the far side of the bread-oven, we find Khadija herself, the matriarch of this place, wrapped in one of those apron-like striped cloths, hunkered down over a glowing brazier. A beautiful, high-cheekboned face, deeply lined from sun or laughter. And a tattoo, one of those vertical lines in faint indigo running from lower lip to chin. Khadija's has a pattern of little dots on either side, too. It's impossible to tell if she is closer to forty or to sixty. Unlike Mariam's *khimar*, pinned tightly under her chin and religiously covering every last hair, Khadija has a bright blue-and-white headscarf wound loosely round her head, knotted on the top; plenty of hair showing. And another piece of cloth, a smaller version of the stripy hand-woven stuff, draped over it for good measure. Around her shoulders is wrapped a sort of pink-and-white patterned blanket, crossed over at the front shawl-style and tucked in tightly under her armpits. How on earth, I wonder, do women here manage with so many bits of cloth flapping around them, none of them apparently very firmly attached to their bodies? It would drive me mad – they'd be falling off all the time. It must take years to learn to keep them all under control and still move about more or less freely. I see now though that what I'd taken for socks are actually soft leather leggings with lots of little ties down the side. Good plan: one item of clothing at least that will definitely stay on.

Khadija makes a gesture at the hand-on-the-heart salutation, which we return. We can't actually shake hands, because in her right one she is juggling a ball of some kind of extremely sticky-looking, almost liquid dough. Still, Khadija manages to make us unexpected guests feel that she could have wished for nothing better than our presence in her home for Eid al-Fitr.

You are welcome! she says in Spanish, beaming at us, before launching off excitedly to Mariam in Tamazight.

Khadija's making the pastry for this evening, translates Mariam, and she says you've done well to land up here, because hers is the best for miles around!

Pastry? Is that what it is? I've never seen anything like it. With a bowl of that strange, wet-yet-springy dough at her side, she dampens her hand in a small jug of water, gets a new grip on the ball of dough, juggles it some more to the right consistency, then dabs it at the smooth metal hotplate balanced over the brazier. Each dab leaves a paper-thin layer on the hot surface that cooks, almost immediately, into an oval leaf so delicate it's almost transparent. Now she peels it off with her fingertips and adds it to the pile next to her, wrapped in a towel on an upturned pot. It's called *warka*, or *millefeuille* in French. Later you brush each sheet with melted butter, says Mariam, then layer it with the other *pastilla* ingredients.

Behind Khadija, stirring something over another brazier in the wide entrance to the modern part of the homestead, is her daughter-in-law, Nadia, who receives us with the same delight as her mother-in-law. She doesn't speak Spanish, though, or French either. Mariam translates for her. Wayfarers are always welcome, she says, especially today of all days! And there is plenty of food for everyone, God be praised!

From a distance I took this newer building for the actual living quarters, and the others for outbuildings, but evidently I misunderstood. There is no door to its ground floor, which in any case seems more like the entrance to a garage or a shed than a home. Within it is the oddest kitchen I've ever come across. The walls are of modern brick and cement, raw and unplastered; the floor is just earth. The window has no glass. And Nadia, in bright pink headscarf, fuchsia cardigan and red-yellow-and-white striped skirt-cloth, is preparing the meat part of the pie – and half a dozen other items, by the look of it – in here, over a selection of cooking devices all at ground level. In the middle of the room, or possibly shed, a round-bellied, smoke-blackened pot simmers on an iron trivet over a small bonfire. No chimney of any kind. I suppose the smoke just goes out of the doorway and window. No sign of electricity, either, never mind gas. A sooty hurricane lamp hangs from a hook in the ceiling, unlit as yet. Inside the doorway stands a second brazier, with a conical earthenware *tagine* resting on the glowing embers – and a spicy, meaty perfume rising from it that makes my mouth water. Against the back wall is a smaller version of the outdoor bread-oven, built out of the same mud-mortar, stacked with brushwood and ready to light. Over in the corner of this room – can it really be the kitchen? – are a large pile of hay, an even larger one of brushwood – and a mule.

Nadia sees me looking at the mule, laughs and begins to apologize. It isn't their mule, Mariam translates, and it doesn't always live in here. A neighbour has just lent it to them for a few days to bring their firewood home from the mountain.

Ah, well, that explains everything, then.

Back outside, Khadija's pile of pastry leaves is growing. I'd love to try making one. No, maybe not. It'll be one of those things that looks easy but takes years of practice to get right.

Imagine meeting *millefeuille* pastry, though, in these surroundings! I remember once reading that if you drew a line around the parts of Europe where there was a tradition of using that fine layered pastry, you would also have a map of the areas that had been penetrated by Muslim culture: the strudel of Central Europe, where Islam reached the Adriatic from the east, and got almost to Vienna; the *sfogliatelle* and *millefoglie* of Naples and Sicily; and the *millefeuille* of France, whose deep south was once no stranger to Islam. I thought this sounded idiotic. How could ordinary people with simple medieval cooking equipment have taken up something so complicated and used it so regularly that it became a tradition? And what about Spain, then? No *millefeuille* there. Did the Moors just take it away with them wholesale when they left? Maybe they did. Because, against all odds, here is the simple medieval cooking equipment, still going strong, and there is the *millefeuille*. I'm going to have to eat my own words. And I'm looking forward to it.

Pastilla – muy gustoso, says Khadija, confirming this in Spanish.

Khadija speaks very good Spanish, says Mariam. Her father was a soldier in General Franco's army.

Was he? A Moroccan soldier in a Spanish army? This rings a bell. The year was 1936, and along the dusty roads of the Iberian coastline, peasant farmers working their fields saw a strange vision, unseen in Spain for many centuries: a thousand Muslim warriors, bearded and burnoused, weapons at the ready, marching to war. In a thick fog over the Straits of Gibraltar, 4,000 troops, a thousand of them Rif Berber tribesmen, had been smuggled, in fishing boats and tenders, past the Republican blockade to fight for the Generalíssimo Franco. A certain ginger-bearded gentleman living in forced exile on a small island in the Indian Ocean – Abd el-Krim, Rif chieftain – must have given a grim chuckle when he heard that his own men were being rearmed by the very Spanish officers who had destroyed their own republic – now paid four pesetas a day to make war on the elected Spanish government and destroy the Spanish Republic.

Did Khadija's dad actually fight in Spain, then? In the Spanish Civil War?

Khadija, cleaning her hands at a water-butt in the far corner, isn't sure what exactly he did. He never talked about it. But that was the choice men had here, in his day. They could sign up with the Spanish army, a full-time job – with a pension for the family, too. Or go over the border to Algeria for the seasonal work on the farms of the French *pieds-noirs*.

Hear that? says Gérard to Guy, waggling his eyebrows meaningfully. Khadija's father preferred to face death than to work for you and your *pied-noir* colonialists!

Guy sighs. Gérard knows perfectly well that his father was a mere Post Office worker. He didn't employ anyone, Moroccan migrants or otherwise. He just worked in the Algiers sorting office!

Really, asks Aytan. Your family were *pieds-noirs*? In Algeria?

It dawns on me now, for the first time, that Guy may turn out to be a pretty controversial travelling companion once we get to Algeria.

But that wasn't how Khadija meant it, anyway. Her father came back from the army with a pension – and enough money to buy the bricks and cement for the new house, she adds, waving a dismissive hand at the building. Except that it turned out to be no good. The family tried it for a bit, when Khadija was a child, but they soon moved back into the old, stone-and-daub house. That new one is made the European way, she says. You can't live in it. You either bake or freeze.

Now that her hands are clean, Khadija comes to inspect me more closely, pats me maternally on the cheek, and has a feel of my hair. She looks like a Berber, doesn't she, she says to Mariam.

Do I? It doesn't seem too likely to me. But reddish hair, freckles and light-coloured eyes are, it seems, one of the many colour-schemes in which ethnic Amazigh are available. After some debate with Nadia, they decide that I look most like a Kabyle, a Berber from the hill-country beyond Algiers. I'm lucky not really to be a Maghrebi, though, the ladies inform me. My freckles would be considered a major blemish here, when it came to finding myself a husband.

Now that we've got this intimate, Khadija moves from patting my face to patting my bosom. This will be a recurring theme during my North African journey, and I am sorry to have to report that I have absolutely no idea why. My bosom is perfectly ordinary and average. Is there some myth or legend current in these parts, concerning Western women's mammary glands? I don't know, because women are much less likely to speak any language I know than men – and I am almost always alone with women when these bosom-testing events take place. I can never manage to be offended, though – they are always so good-natured about it. Odd, when their breasts hardly seem any different to my own. It doesn't seem to be to do with bras – nobody takes much of an interest in the underwear, though you'd think the western contraption I wear, with its hooks and eyes, would be worth an inspection. No idea. Mystifying.

Khadija is now chucking me happily under the chin – apparently her investigations have proved satisfactory. A venerable old gentleman in grey beard and skull-cap, very frail-looking, emerges from a side entrance of one of the old buildings. He is using a double-barrelled shotgun as a walking stick and is being followed by a small but rowdy flock of children. This is Khadija's husband, Farid, says Aytan, performing the introductions. Three of the boys are his and Khadija's grandsons, Nadia's children: the two smallest girls are her granddaughters. The rest belong to neighbours. Farid shakes our hands cheerily, then says something long to Aytan. The infants bounce around us, pulling at our unfamiliar clothes and stroking my unfamiliar naked hair, giggling naughtily.

Farid is saying, Aytan translates, that he and Mokhtar are going down to the mosque to join his son Abdelkrim (certainly a pretty popular name in these parts!) and the rest of the men. He's asking if we will join him later, after the afternoon prayers. Sure enough, Mokhtar now appears, also armed, a slightly more modern-looking weapon slung over his shoulder. Seeing us, he unslings the weapon and brandishes it wildly, to a round of cheers from the children.

Shooting, he says in Spanish, with another enthusiastic flourish. Boom! Boom, he adds, to more roaring and applause from the children.

Shooting in the mosque? This seems a little excessive, even in a land known for its dissident traditions. But no: he doesn't mean actually in the mosque, but in the square outside it. All the men in the village will be down there, waiting to catch the first sight of the moon: because the moment it appears, Ramadan is officially over. And then, every firearm the village possesses will be fired off, to make sure that nobody, not even the most distant goatherd in the mountains, can miss the good news.

Mariam, Khadija and Nadia are chatting away by the brazier, and I begin to suspect, from the looks and laughter coming my way, that Mariam is telling the tale of our meeting – of my earlier attempt to rob the indigent poor outside the goldsmith's home.

What are they saying? I ask Aytan, who has taken his seat with Gérard and Guy on some rush matting by the bread-oven. But he has no idea: he's only been learning Tamazight since he arrived here, he says. Not like Mariam, who already spoke a southern version of it, thanks to her Berber grandparents, and had a head start. Tamazight is not a dialect of Arabic, as I've imagined, but a completely separate language – over 5,000 years old, and with an ancient alphabet of its own, which I will discover, when I finally get to see an inscription in it, looks remarkably like the Elven script invented by Tolkien. Tamazight is the original language of the Maghreb, of course, and is still spoken wherever Berber cultures have survived. It seems that when the Berbers first encountered the conquering Arabs and their new religion, not all of them were too impressed. Many tribes just removed themselves from the sphere of influence of their new rulers – not hard to do when you live a semi-nomadic life anyway – and went off into mountains or deserts, where they would be left in peace to carry on their lives as they always had done. So the Tuareg nomads right down in the south of the Sahara speak it, as do the Kabyles over to the east, on the coastal hills of Algeria, not to mention the other Moroccan Berbers of the Middle Atlas mountains to the south – Mariam's family's home. And here in the Rif. Then, of course, my first ever Berber acquaintances, the Zenete Berbers, living in the desert oases of Algeria and Morocco.

It's a horribly hard language to learn, anyway, says Aytan. And he can't understand a word once they get going at that speed.

Our hostess is now wiping away tears of laughter with the back of her hand. She takes a quick look in my direction and chortles some more. Yes, they definitely were talking about me.

Khadija says it was the crowd who were in the wrong, not you, translates Mariam. Once upon a time they would have respected that, Muslim or not, you must be in need, or you wouldn't have been there.

But don't worry, adds Khadija, going back into Spanish. You will be fed tonight! Our *sadaqa* will go to the poor hungry Europeans begging at our gates! And she collapses into laughter again.

Nadia has begun beating up some eggs. Mariam is emptying the almonds out into a big plastic bowl, and Khadija, not looking too thrilled by this contribution, has started chopping up something she says is a salted lemon. I try a bit. Ferocious: evidently an acquired taste.

Can I give them a hand with anything? I ask.

No, you certainly cannot, says Khadija, slapping playfully at my leg from her spot on the floor. Guests do not work in this house!

This, frankly, is quite a relief. I'm not too good in other people's kitchens even when all the equipment is perfectly familiar to me. Something tells me I might not acquit myself too well in this unfamiliar low-level stable-type arrangement.

But maybe, says Mariam, we could get the almonds shelled, before we go and settle in at the schoolhouse?

A lovely, simple job. The shelling equipment consists of one large flat stone and one smaller one – find them yourself. While seeking ours over beyond the yard wall, Guy and I stumble upon a mound of freshly plucked pinkish-grey feathers among the grass. Looks like we're in luck: it will be pigeon *pastilla*, as recommended by Mariam.

Khadija confirms this. Much better than chicken – and cheaper too! Her grandsons bagged half a dozen, yesterday and this morning, with Mokhtar's shotgun.

Her grandsons? Lord have mercy. The oldest of them only looks about ten!

Nadia has stirred the eggs into an onions-and-spices concoction and squeezed in the juice of a lemon, which she nipped over and collected off the tree at the far gateway. I've already done a casual spot-check on the tree's health – can't help looking for someone to blame for the tragic state of my Italian one, can I? – and I am pleased to report that it's in fine fettle, not a sign of blight upon it.

Now Nadia's oniony spicy eggs just need to be drained for half-an-hour, and we're ready to go. Oh, and once we've finished shelling the almonds, they'll need to be blanched, skinned, and lightly roasted. Then Mariam will pound them up in the mortar with a few spoonfuls of sugar. Then the *pastilla* just needs to be assembled and gently fried for half an hour in butter, over one of the braziers . . .

Such a lot of work, I say.

That, replies Khadija, is another good reason why people here in the Rif wouldn't bother putting almonds in their *pastilla*. In Casablanca they probably just buy them in a shop, ready-prepared, don't they?

Mariam, not rising to this bait, laughs and carries on bashing away. Nadia goes over to the sooty cauldron to fill a tin bowl with boiling water for the blanching and as she does so, her hand slips. Some of it spills from her dipper. Surprisingly, considering the floor is of earth, this small mishap causes a major disturbance. Khadija shouts something. Nadia backs out into the yard, turns her hands palms up and, eyes shut, recites some kind of prayer at high speed, half under her breath. Now, passing no comment at all on this occurrence, both of them go back to what they were doing, as if nothing at all had happened.

Djinns, says Mariam, seeing my puzzled expression. The earth is their element; if you spill boiling water on it, you annoy them. Nadia was neutralizing the offence.

What kind of revenge might a djinn take, then, if you didn't appease it with prayer?

You could never guess, according to Khadija. Djinns are capricious creatures, of uncertain humour. Depending on their mood they might do anything from just pulling your hair to mischievously burning your dinner, or making the milk go sour, or even making you or your livestock ill, putting the Evil Eye on you. Best say the prayer right away, calling the angels in to take their place. Then you need never find out!

I've always imagined djinns as massive, powerful creatures that burst out of bottles and lamps to offer you three dangerous wishes and change your life. Thank goodness we are in the company of experts. This local underground variety sounds a lot easier to deal with: more like an imp. Or do I mean a sprite? A demon? A pixie? What a lot of varieties djinns did come in, once upon a time, in my own culture.

So here we sit, on our reed mats on the now djinn-safe ground, next to the great dome of the bread-oven, bashing away with our stone-age implements, the pile of sweet brown almonds growing ever higher. Ahead of us, the rolling hills are turning blue and gold in the distance as evening begins to draw in. Down below, the river at the bottom of its deep valley is slowly disappearing into shadow, while high above us, the tips of the rugged mountain peaks are still brightly lit. Now, just to add the finishing touch, the muezzin down in the village starts to call out the evening prayer across the hills: *Allahu Akhbar!* God is Great! A moment's respectful silence follows, but nobody seems as bothered about praying to God as they were to the djinns.

Why, I ask once I'm certain nobody is about to start their evening worship, is it called *pastilla*, anyway? It sounds a very Spanish name for a traditional Moroccan food.

Nobody knows, says Mariam. Some people say that it's really *bestiya*, in Arabic, and *pastilla* is just a Spanish way of spelling the same word. Others that it's a Moorish dish, invented over the sea in the days of Muslim Andalusia, and that's how it got its Spanish name. This last seems pretty likely. I remember reading that pigeon pie was so popular in Granada a few centuries ago that the high towers of the ruined Alhambra were always thronged with pigeon-hunters, who would bait lengths of fishing line to dangle down into the roosts below and catch their dinners for free.

Khadija snorts. That's all nonsense. *Bestila* in her own language is a dish of chicken with saffron. It's a Berber dish. *Bestiya* is just the same stuff made into a pie with a few eggs, and mispronounced by Spaniards and Arabs. And, not content with that, they have added almonds to the recipe – and sugar too, she says, with a sly grin at Mariam. Ingredients that would make her father turn in his grave! But there, what can she do, seeing she has let the wife of an Arab take charge tonight?

Uphill along the grass-bordered path – this time towards a clean, modern oblong of cement plaster up above the village. The school, and Mariam and Aytan's home. We enter the schoolrooms first, to deposit our bags. Two large, bare rooms, each with a blackboard on the wall and neat rows of desks – places for fifty pupils, says Mariam, but they've only managed to raise thirty-three so far. A bucket of chalks and a pile of little slate blackboards for the children: they don't use paper, it's too expensive. A pile of well-thumbed textbooks sits under a window with a huge view across the valley to the misty mountains in the gold-and-blue distance. It all looks fine, if a bit basic, and I wonder what Mariam thinks is so terrible about it.

The teachers' residence is a shock, though. Certainly not the comfortable apartment I was imagining. More of a camp-site: one room, containing a small table and chairs, a divan bed and an alcove cubby-hole for a kitchen. The place was never intended for living in. The education authorities, building it, fantasized local teachers with homes in the village. There's a gas-bottle-powered hob for cooking – at least Mariam and Aytan don't have to borrow mules and wander the hills gathering wood like their neighbours – but that is the end of the mod cons. No fridge, because there is no electricity in the building. No electricity in all the village, in fact. The nearest electricity is at Chefchaouen. There are electric sockets in the walls all right, looking perfectly normal, but they are connected to nothing, and no date has ever been given when they might become operational. Just an optimistic gesture by the builders, says Aytan. Meanwhile, they too have hurricane lamps for the hours of darkness. And a battery-powered cassette radio for information and entertainment, which they'll be bringing down to Khadija's later, for music while we eat.

And what do they use for heating, in the cold mountain nights? A couple of charcoal braziers, of course.

Aytan nips back into the schoolroom and returns with one of the textbooks from the windowsill. Take a look at this, he says, flicking through its pages. You three have actually visited a village home in the Rif – more than most people at the Ministry of Education have ever done – so you'll see how useless it is right away. It's a reading-primer, we can see that: pictures of ordinary, everyday objects with their names in Arabic script below. But none of us can read Arabic script – how are we supposed to tell what's wrong with it?

Never mind the words, says Aytan. Look at the pictures! Any old page! Here: a box of washing powder and a washing machine. What are Rif children supposed to make of that? They've never seen a washing machine, or a packet of soap-powder, in their lives. People here in the country scrub their clothes down at the spring, with a chunk of soap.

He flicks on through pictures of traffic lights and zebra crossings; of fridges and electric cookers; of lace-up shoes and rubber gloves; of supermarkets and pre-packed foodstuffs. Hardly anything, we see now, that a Rif village child would ever have come across. What a strange country Morocco is: how can such extremes coexist, and so close to one another?

So, Aytan says, our village pupils have first to learn the uses of these alien things, then to learn their names, in a foreign language, then, finally, they can get on with learning to read and write.

In a foreign language? What does he mean?

It's not just Arabic script, says Aytan. It's in the Arabic language, too. And the villagers here don't speak Arabic, do they? But since the Berbers' Tamazight is not recognized as a national language, there are no textbooks written in it. The kids have no choice but to learn Arabic in order to learn to read and write.

This seems insane. How can a government just ignore a language that's spoken by so many of its people? Easily done, it seems, when all those people are poor and living in backward, isolated places like this, deep in the countryside. And when anyone who mentions the matter is seen as trying to ethnically divide the nation – and given an unexpected trip to the barber's.

Then, says Mariam, a lot of people involved in education – especially the more devoutly religious ones, from Arabic-speaking backgrounds – sincerely believe that Arabic is somehow morally superior as a language, because it's the language of the Holy Koran. To them, Tamazight is the backward speech of an ignorant country people, unworthy of their attention, hardly even a real language at all, in their eyes.

Things might not be so bad, according to Aytan, if their pupils were being forced to learn the ordinary Moroccan dialect of Arabic. That would be some use to them, at least. You only need to go as far as Chefchaouen to hear Moroccan Arabic being spoken. And if they ever wanted to move to a city, they'd have to learn it. But the Arabic of the schoolbooks is very different. It's literary Arabic, closer to the language of the Koran – the classical Arabic used as a *lingua franca* across the whole of the Arabic-speaking world, the way Latin was once used in Europe, to ease international communication across its many dialects. But how many of these kids will ever need to communicate with an Egyptian or a Saudi? Or even meet one?

Moroccan Arabic, we now gather, is about as different from classical Arabic as modern-day Italian is from classical Latin. Kids from Arabic-speaking families, city kids with TVs, can pick it up pretty quickly – lots of the words are similar, and plenty of TV imports from

Egypt or the Lebanon, soap operas and stuff, as well as the news, are broadcast in it. But not only do people here in the villages of the Rif not speak Arabic to start with, they don't have TVs either, do they, since they don't even have electricity. A TV here is something you might glimpse when you go to market in Chefchaouen. So they have no connection with the language at all. It's utterly useless to them.

I can personally vouch for the difference between Moroccan Arabic and its classical version. Some time after this trip, I found myself showing off my language skills to a Palestinian. I had learned how to say 'bread' in Arabic, I said, and 'water', and 'Look!' – and I could count up to ten . . .

Go on, she said, let's hear you count! So I began: *wahad, zuzh, talata* – and before I'd even got to number four my Palestinian was convulsed with laughter. *Zuzh*, in classical, proper Arabic, means a pair. I had just said 'one, a pair, three,' and I sounded like some old Maghrebi peasant woman! Ha ha ha ha!

Poor children. A veritable Tower of Babel to cope with. And an education system apparently designed by Kafka, or some other aficionado of the bureaucratic nightmare. As if this wasn't enough, once you reach higher education – not that Mariam and Aytan hold out much hope of any of their local pupils making it that far – the teaching is all done in French. (Kind of lucky for us travellers, though, or we wouldn't be sitting here chatting now.)

The last teachers here, Mariam is saying, were a stridently pious Arabic couple, who managed to drive away half the pupils. Harangued them from day one in an incomprehensible tongue and then got angry when they were slow to pick it up. Dished out more and more punishments in their frustration. Some way to teach children a new language! And as for learning one themselves, in the whole time they were here those two didn't trouble to learn a word of the Tamazight tongue. Not even to say hello to the parents, or barter for a kilo of their home-grown vegetables. That's how far beneath them it was!

I turn now to look at Mariam as she speaks and do a double-take.

She has done a Yazid on us, in reverse. She has quietly removed her jellaba now that we're in the house. The religious-looking woman in the tightly tied *khimar* has vanished, transformed into a girl in a T-shirt and trainer-bottoms with a mop of dark, shiny curls. She and Aytan both laugh at my expression, while I quickly readjust my stereotypes. These are her normal Casablanca clothes, she says. She has to look ultra-respectable here, though, in the eyes of village parents, especially if she hopes to convince them to send their daughters to school.

Do people not actually have to send their children to school, then? I ask.

Supposedly, yes. But there's no way the government is going to enforce the law. This is the Rif, the *Bled es-Siba*! We've seen how Mokhtar and Khadija live, and as long as nothing changes, the older generation can't see the use of schooling. There's no work but on the land. Parents need their children's help in the fields. And without running water or electricity, or labour-saving devices of any kind, work on the homestead takes up most of the hours of the day. People can see more point in training their children up in that – especially the girls, since most of it is women's work – than in sending them off to school. The skills that will fill your larder and see the family through the winter are essential: unlike reading and writing.

What an uphill struggle it must be to get and keep those thirty-three pupils! I take off my hat to Mariam and husband. On top of the other disincentives, it seems, parents often fear that this new-fangled government-sponsored kind of education must be somehow irreligious. Traditional schooling here has always been run by the *zawiyas*, the local Sufi brotherhoods. Boys learned to read and write, did some basic maths and studied the Koran. This new national schooling, for both sexes, may be sponsored by the king himself – who is a *sharif*, a direct descendant of the Prophet Mohammed, the best of Muslim pedigrees – but the king's name is not greatly respected round here. The Rif Berbers never wanted him anyway. Some say they're no better off now than they were under the Spanish. And then, there is much talk of his jetsetting lifestyle. People suspect the king of being tainted by Western corruption, or, if they are too loyal to allow of such a thing, believe he is led astray by his Westernized advisors. Which makes his schools only too likely to infect their children with the evil ways of the *Nazrani*.

Depressing. What exactly can we represent in the eyes of Muslims? What sort of corruption is it?

Mention of her king has had an electrifying effect on Mariam. Not greatly respected? I should think not, she says angrily. Have we heard of Sheikh Yassine? No? She is not surprised. He would be called a dangerous fundamentalist by the West, of course, but he's a hero to poor Moroccans. He dared to publicly demand that the king should share his riches with his people, or admit that he was not worthy to call himself a true Muslim ruler. The sheikh is locked up now, of course. But his daughter is carrying on his good works still, in his name – helping out in hospitals, distributing tents, blankets and food after fires in the shanty towns, organizing funerals for destitute people, giving meat to poor families on Muslim holy days. Did we know, she asks, that in this country it is officially a crime to discuss the Royal Purse? She will commit a crime now, and tell us that the king personally owns a whole third of all the farmland in Morocco, as well as the phosphate mines that are practically its only source of hard currency. Thanks to all that, he and his family are multimillionaires. And look at his country!

Come on, enough chat, says Aytan, hastily changing the subject. Time to get our beds ready – and get down to the mosque before someone catches sight of that moon.

The rugs Mariam promised us are rolled up against the wall, serving as cushions on the divan. Beautiful rugs, I see, as I spread my selection out between the desks: fine, thick wool, the warm earth colours of natural dyes, woven by hand into intricate geometric patterns.

All local Berber rugs, Mariam says. She's collecting them to take home to Casablanca. This one must have been woven as a wedding gift. She points out the deliberate mistakes in the symmetry of the design – deliberate, because only Allah is perfect. And look at this diamond shape here – see how it has little extra 'v's for legs? And the two little dots here for eyes? It's a frog, a Berber fertility symbol, but heavily stylised so that nobody could say that it is blasphemous, that it is imitating God's work, and disrespectful to Him. Still, it's perfectly recognizable as a frog once you know, isn't it? People in the village offer her them cheap. They know she loves the old ones most. She shouldn't really take them, but how could you resist? That's why she's got so many. Luckily for her guests!

Beds sorted out, we are introduced to the bathroom facilities. No taps. No running water. Their water supplies are a bucket with a dipper in the kitchen alcove. The school loo is a row of earth closets in a shed outside. Guy would rather go in the bushes, he mutters, horrified, in my ear. How quickly we Europeans do forget our own past! The only loo in my Italian home was, for some years, an earth closet. They may not be ideal, but they are perfectly bearable if you look after them properly – and the best possible solution for not wasting scarce water. Meanwhile, the most repellent earth closet I ever came across in my life was somewhere in the heartlands of Guy's own country, a mere decade or so ago. It was out at the back of a country café-bar, and so vile was it that, though I am not a squeamish person, I actually went straight back in and cancelled my omelette. At least this facility, though it may have no running water, is scrupulously clean.

Where do we get more water from, we ask, if we want to wash? Is there a well or something?

No. Nothing. Just the bucket. Each pupil carries a bucket of water up to the school, once a month, so they get a bucket every day for cleaning and cooking, and a couple extra. Thirty-three children, thirty-three buckets. Otherwise, the nearest public water supply is the field aqueduct, a whole kilometre away.

Some of the people in the village have wells or springs, water good enough for washing and cooking, though not for drinking,

Aytan says, but he and Mariam were warned before they came never to accept any offers of neighbours' water. Access to water is always the biggest source of trouble and strife in the Moroccan countryside, and other neighbours might easily believe the water was being provided in exchange for preferential treatment of their children. Then, if the teachers got embroiled in some local water-controversy, it would just give people another reason not to send their children to the school. So Mariam and Aytan only get a proper wash at the *hammam* when they go into Chefchaouen, and they pay Nadia to do their laundry down at the spring.

I can't believe they've stayed here two years, in these conditions! And another two to go! Awful to admit this, but it seems all the more shocking now that Mariam has transformed herself into – well, into someone who looks just like me.

How do people here really see us Westerners, then? I ask Aytan, as we hurry off downhill towards the mosque, racing against the dusk, skirting round a low rockface with an outcrop of smooth tooth-like rocks before it, three pine trees standing at its heart. What is this terrible Western corruption that is threatening Islam?

I am hardly prepared for the onslaught this question will provoke.

Aytan purses his lips in thought. You are seen, he says eventually, as having no loyalty to your family, or your community, or even your religion. You care for nothing but money. And for display – for ostentation. Your moral world has shrunk to dog-eat-dog. Your grown adults behave like selfish infants, without responsibility or self-control. Husbands and wives leave one another on a whim, and children suffer. You have lost any sense of decency and shame: your families abandon their old people and show them no respect, once they can no longer earn. Women are not respected either, but reduced to sex objects, half-naked images on every street corner. You have no fellow-feeling for your neighbours, or generosity towards those poorer than yourselves – neither individuals, nor nations. Your own prophet, Jesus, turned over the tables of the moneylenders at the temple. But you have turned your backs on him and forgotten the Book.

Sheikh Yassine puts it well, he adds. You have sacrificed yourselves on the altar of desire, as clients addicted to a consumer market. Capitalism is left to run wild, untamed by human values or moral principles.

It's nothing personal, though, says Mariam hastily, looking daggers at her husband. That's just what's said about your culture, not about you as people.

No dispute, anyway, we tell her. We would all love to see capitalism tamed by human values! But how is all that threatening Morocco, anyway?

Aytan laughs. Not just Morocco, he says. Have we not seen that the West has a controlling hand in every Muslim country in the world these days? Every country must base itself on the logic of the market and the rationality of self-interest – or suffer the consequences. Look what's happening in Algeria! But logic and rationality are not the only values humanity needs. Logic and rationality would tell you that Hitlerism was a fine system! And if we in the West don't like that, if we want a return to human values, the answer is obvious – turn to Islam! Islam supports the family and the community; the powerful do not turn their backs on the weak, or the rich on the poor.

Like our good king and his friends, says Mariam.

Her Aytan, she says, turning to us three rational Westerners, looks at the unemployed back home in the shanty towns, at the poverty and ignorance here in the countryside, and dreams of a return to an Islamic tradition of social justice. It's good, of course, to wish for a happier, more just world. But she is not at all sure that this lost paradise ever existed.

Aytan interrupts her sharply, speaking Arabic now. Things are evidently getting too heated for non-Muslims to participate. The argument goes on, still in Arabic, as we stumble on down the hillside.

Suddenly, making us all jump out of our skins, a great salvo of guns shatters the gathering darkness, roaring out from all over the valley, and from the valley beyond, and the one beyond that, the rolling echoes crashing round the mountains. A roar of cheers now from up ahead. Amid more outbursts of sporadic shooting, the women in the courtyards all around take up the call, filling the air with surreal guttural wails: the traditional ululation. A drum starts to beat out a triumphant rhythm.

As we arrive at the courtyard before the mosque, three figures detach themselves from the crowd and come our way, arm in arm, firearms slung over their shoulders, shouting their goodbyes to the rest of the group, very flushed and happy: Mokhtar and Abdelkrim, supporting the frail Farid between them. *Vamos!* says Mokhtar. Time to eat!

As we head off up the hill, the lamp-lit scene before the mosque is one that would not disgrace Abd el-Krim, or any of the other war-like Rifians of the last few centuries. A pall of blue smoke hanging above a jubilant band of white-turbaned warriors; roars of triumph fighting the the wild beat of the drums; and a gleaming forest of brandished rifles, brass accoutrements flashing against the darkening sky. The moon of Eid has been sighted.

8

Out here in the yard the children are banging out an excited rhythm with sticks, stones, and a small drum – a sort of ceramic tambourine. The sporadic firing of guns is still going on across the hillsides, the valleys multiplying the long booming echoes, as the men come back in. Farid insists on Guy, Gérard and Aytan staying outdoors to smoke a manly pipe of kif to improve their appetites. Well timed: the French contingent were secretly bemoaning the fact that there would be no wine at this meal. They're not used to eating a festive dinner without so much as a glass of wine; it just doesn't seem right.

Hopefully the local solution to wine-less-ness will sort them out. Mokhtar is now giving Guy a lesson in burnous-wearing, folding the front sections carefully back, then flipping them over his shoulders into wide, draped wings. Guy looks even more melodramatic than before: positively Dracula. Still, now the sun's gone in and the mountain chill is upon us, Guy's purchase hardly seems foolish at all. I wouldn't mind one myself.

At the sight of us, the little girls have started up another round of that weird ululation in their throats. They grab me, want me to join in. Hopeless. I just sound as if I'm gargling. The children can't believe a grown woman could be so incompetent. Mariam demonstrates again. She can do it perfectly – apparently even city-dwelling women do this at moments of celebration, or when they want to give the alarm. It is called a *you-you*, she says. Try again!

I do, but it's no good. This time it comes out like that strangled *aaah* you do when the doctor has his spatula down your throat. I admit defeat and go indoors.

Inside the old house, the one where the family really lives, two carpets have been spread on the ground for the first meal of Eid al-Fitr, taking up almost the whole of the floor space. In here there is something a bit more like my idea of a kitchen: a sort of food-preparation and storage area with a work-table and a sideboard, buckets and bowls standing in for a sink, sacks of flour, spices and dry goods arranged on broad wooden shelves. I suppose it makes sense to divide your cooking arrangements this way, when you have no running water anyway, and you cook on open fires. Why mix up the clean zone, involving your stores and your buckets of clean water, with the messy, fire-smoke-and-ashes and dirty-water part of your operations?

There is a plastic tablecloth in the centre of the carpets, where the communal platters of food go, and sheepskins and cushions are scattered around the edge against the walls; cushions whose covers look as if they've been thriftily created out of the usable remnants of the last few centuries of family carpets. No pickings for Mariam here. Nine of us adults are soon gathered upon the rugs, women at one end, men at the other. The children have their own corner beyond the female area, in which they are already creating a party atmosphere with an intricate clapping-and-singing game. Mariam and Khadija have put the radio on, promising us some Andalusian music – there is always an Andalusian band for Eid al-Fitr – but for the moment the station is just broadcasting an excited commentary, and even more celebratory explosions.

Farid, Mariam told me once we women were indoors, is not a well man. He has trouble walking, his joints pain him so much, and he seems to be getting thinner by the minute, fading away. She thinks he is out of it most of the time on kif, to relieve the pain. He sits in his room all day, with the door open to the hills, smoking, warming himself on his little brazier and gazing out across the land; potters up to the mosque a few times a week to sit with the other men; and that's that. He's not really functioning as head of the household any more – Mokhtar has had to take over the role, though, truth to tell, Khadija is the real power in the house.

Should I ask about doctors? I think I can already guess what the answer will be.

Nadia and the older granddaughter are doing the serving, and bring out the *bestiya* – I hope that is the politically correct name for it – as the starter course. It really is the *pièce de résistance* it was advertised to be: a startling combination of tastes and textures, sweet and nutty, sharp and lemony, creamy and spicy, voluptuously meaty – sounds improbable but it's wonderful. It's been fried over the brazier in butter, both sides, all golden and crispy on the outside. You just grab an edge of it between fingers and thumb and pull. Burn your fingers, but it's worth it. Mariam is proud that she's managed to convince Khadija to try it with the almonds. It's good, isn't it?

Not bad, says Khadija, answering for me, since my mouth is full. But that's the cunning of it, she adds. You'd hardly know what mistakes were made in the cooking, would you, with all those sweet almonds to cover them up?

Around the pie are a selection of salads, one of them mainly made of slices of orange, another of wild herbs which, Khadija says, shouting against the racket, she gathered this afternoon along with the smaller of the granddaughters, that one there who is bringing round the bread. They are doused in delicious thick olive oil, Khadija's own, freshly made and still creamy with the olive flesh that will later settle and need to be filtered out – just the way you eat it in Liguria when it's newly pressed. The wild herbs are not like anything you'd find on our hillsides, though. A flavour somewhere between rocket and watercress, and I don't recognize the plant at all. But the orange salad is almost exactly like one a Sicilian friend once prepared for me, using those oranges with a very thick rind, most of which you leave on, just peeling off the zest as thin as you can. A speciality of his home town, Catania, he said. Another trace, perhaps, of the long-gone days of the Peoples of the Book? The bread is Khadija's own, naturally: to be used to scoop up the salads. And everything is eaten with our hands, from the communal dishes, just like at Uncle Kebir's. Though I shouldn't say hands, plural, because it's just the one hand, really: the right hand.

You may be rubbish at this eating method, dribble and spill and create a mess all over your part of the carpet that would shame even a two-year-old Maghrebi, and every fibre of your being may be telling you to bring your left hand into play – but never do it! Much worse than any amount of mess. Your left hand is reserved for cleansing and loo-going purposes, and these being shared dishes, it would be like throwing a bit of used toilet-paper into the middle of the dinner. Unthinkable.

I seem to have lost what little skill I ever acquired at dining Maghreb-style. I watch everyone else plunge a thumb and two fingers into the piping-hot pie, pulling off a neat section and raising it tidily to their lips. They even negotiate removing the occasional pigeon bone elegantly from between their lips without using the other hand. None of the above applies when I try. Guy and Gérard are faring no better. Everyone else enjoys the spectacle a lot, though, especially the infants, who are fascinated and delighted by our incompetence. Khadija, in stitches of laughter again, goes off to look for Western-style utensils among her cooking equipment, and comes back with three huge serving spoons.

We eat and eat. Next comes the lamb *tagine* we saw in the making, with pumpkin and chickpeas, piled onto hot buttery couscous. Farid divides up the meat at the men's end, placing a portion in front of each of them. Khadija does the same at our end. Now for the acid test: how to get the couscous into your mouth when you couldn't even manage a piece of pie. All the children's eyes are upon us, agog to see what kind of a mess we'll make of it. We do not disappoint them.

This couscous is strangely unlike the usual couscous, though: much nuttier and crunchier. A Berber speciality, Mariam says, only made in spring when the barley is young, by cracking and steaming the fresh grain, rather than grinding it into flour and then reconstituting it, like ordinary couscous.

Why don't people always do this, then? It's delicious, and must be a lot less trouble to make. But there is a very good reason, says

Khadija. Storing fresh grains of wheat or barley for any length of time is risky. They are living seeds, and may start to sprout or moulder; leaving your family to go hungry till next harvest. Not so with couscous. By grinding up the corn and rerolling it with water, you have turned each grain inside out. The bran is inside the granule now, the flesh on the outside; its own starch coats it in a protective film as you roll. It will stay fresh for years.

A revelation. In all these years in Italy, it has never once occurred to me to wonder why people had bothered to invent pasta. The same principle, of course, applies. A lot of work, but at the end of it you have a year's worth of your basic staple, in an indestructible form.

As Nadia brings round a jug of some kind of sweetened yoghurt or buttermilk for us to drink, an Andalusian band comes onto the radio at last. Mokhtar shushes the children so we can hear.

Moroccan blues, says Abdelkrim. What do we think?

This music of el-Andalus has a good complex drum-beat at its heart, and I'm a sucker for anything with plenty of booming drums. I love it. It doesn't sound at all like the flamenco-influenced music you would hear in Andalusia today, though. If anything, it's more like the Portuguese *fado*, the phrases of song quite separate from the instrumental sections. No doubt, though, the roots of the *fado* will lie in Portugal's Islamic past, too. But what's the singer singing about? Are the songs actually about Andalusia? Everyone listens carefully.

No, says Abdelkrim. Well, yes, in a way. It's about a man who goes to visit his oldest friends, but there's nobody there any more. The beloved buildings of their old home are standing empty and abandoned . He is asking the stones and the mortar what has become of the family, of all the joy and the love, the life that once filled the place . . . Now, it is just an empty shell.

The next song, translated by Mokhtar, is about a Sufi saint, a *marabout*. The true story, he says, of a good and holy man, born in el-Andalus, in Cordoba, who gave up his riches and his high station to come here to the Maghreb and live a humble life of poverty, spreading the wisdom of Islam among the children; respected for his purity of spirit by everyone in the city, right up to the emir. But an evil, jealous courtier accused him of sorcery, had him beheaded, and his body thrown to the dogs. Later, the emir finds the vizier out – listen, that's the bit he's got to now! And metes out the punishment he deserves for wronging a man of such innocence. The emir has him encased in fresh lime mortar. As it shrinks, he dies in slow, excruciating agony . . . and now the people of the town build a beautiful tomb and mosque to the memory of the kind and holy man, who will never be forgotten!

A fine, improving tale, and told with great zest and relish by Mokhtar, though his lively, not to say bloodthirsty, rendering of it hardly matches the musicians' sad and soulful version coming from the radio.

With the fruit course – delicious dates, I've never had them fresh like this, oranges and dried figs, and piles of nuts and toasted seeds – I get my second lesson on djinns.

Khadija is warning me not to let Aytan take us back to the school by that short-cut past the rocky outcrop, the one with the three pine trees. Are we Nazarenes not afraid of djinns? Because in there among the trees is a small spring which is home to a very powerful one. Djinns, it seems, if they don't live underground, like to live in water. And Khadija can't believe how brave – or foolhardy – Mariam is, to pass right close to his lair like that, when darkness is so close. People say the djinns – the *djnun* – can steal your soul if they get hold of you as the light changes. After the afternoon prayers is the most dangerous time.

Djinns are not, as I've imagined, mere creatures of folk tradition. They are officially part of Islam. It says in the Koran, Mariam tells me, that when God created man from clay, He also created the djinn from smokeless fire. Demons, I decide, must be their biblical equivalent.

Khadija says that when men go to sleep, the djinns wake up and carry on the life of the village, growing their own invisible crops, feeding their own invisible beasts. You can hear them in the night, moving about, though you will never see them. God made man and djinn both, to help take care of his beautiful creation of the heavens and the earth, she adds, piously.

Mariam laughs. She doesn't think that part is in the Koran, she says.

The djinn at the rock pool has a good side, too, though, Khadija continues regardless. He will help women who are having trouble getting pregnant. They must say their morning prayers there, seven days in a row, and on the last day leave him an offering of barley and henna leaves. It works, too! Mariam's sister tried it, didn't she, when she came visiting? And next thing we heard she was having a baby! Really? Maybe djinns aren't so much like demons, then. I've never heard of a demon who had a good side – or, for that matter, one who engaged in agriculture.

Mariam giggles and shushes Khadija up, checking the men's end of the room to see if Aytan's listening. He hates her doing that sort of thing! He even got angry when she took her sister to visit the *marabout* shrine back home – said it was superstitious nonsense, and not true Islam at all, and that no good could come of it.

So what, I ask, has Aytan got against djinns, if they're in the Koran? Or against *marabouts*, come to that?

It's not the djinns themselves, or the Holy Men, but the praying to them that he doesn't agree with. He is becoming more and more of a puritan, like so many of their old friends from university, always talking of cleansing and purifying Islam, returning their religion to the fundamentals, getting rid of Sufi country people's heresies and superstitions. Only then will the Islamic world, once the heartland of civilization and enlightenment, be able to return to its former greatness, and gain the strength to fight off Western corruption. He tells people off for being pagans and idolaters, asks how they can repeat the Islamic credo five times a day – that there is only the One God – and then go off and pray to some woodland spirit on the side? He says the same thing about praying to *marabouts*, too. It is the sin of *shirk.* But surely Christians have the same sin – praying to anyone other than the One God himself is wrong?

They certainly do. It is the very first of the Christian Ten Commandments. *Thou shalt have no god but God.* And the next two commandments, dealing with the making of images and the worshipping of them, simply expand upon the theme. You can still see churches in England where, in the days when some members of the faith took these injunctions as literally as do the Islamic purists of today, they went about attacking the shrines of the opposition, smashing the heretical heads off statues of saints for this very reason. Mariam is shocked. Destroying holy shrines? Her Aytan would agree that praying to a saint is wrong – and to a graven image even worse – but he would never dream of such a thing as desecration!

I am sure she is right. Aytan seems the gentlest of men. Still, I am beginning to think that he would have got on like a house on fire with those stern Scots relations of mine. My Calvinist great-great-grandfather, I've been told – another man keen to cleanse and purify his religion – had plenty to say on the pagan tradition of leaving votive offerings at the wishing tree on the wild boundaries of his home town, and the terrible doom that would befall those who kept it up. His Scots campaign against woodland spirits has met with as little success as Aytan's Moroccan one. On my last visit to Cromarty, the boughs of the tree, still crouching windswept over its holy spring, were entirely hidden by the myriad shreds of votive cloth flying from them, tattered pennants bleached and shredded by the sea gales.

Your Aytan can't help being made like that, anyway, Khadija tells Mariam comfortingly. Who could guess what he might take against next, though? He told Khadija off about her tattoo the other day – did Mariam know? He said tattoos are un-Islamic – because they alter God's perfect creation! Perfect creation! Whoever would have guessed that Aytan had such a high opinion of her, she says, letting out a peal of laughter.

Speaking of heresy, I notice, now that the greed has begun to wane and I can take more interest in my surroundings, another of those geometric frogs in the carpet before me, under rather a lot of fragments of food. Would Aytan disapprove of those, too, then? But there is much worse than a mere abstract frog in this room. Mariam draws my attention to a shamelessly figurative image hanging from a nail over on the far wall. Not having been brought up to be shocked by such a thing, I hadn't even noticed it.

It's a picture of a man on horseback – no frame, a bit raggedy round the edges, and vaguely Persian in style, rich deep colours, with the horseman's turban and robes flying out behind him, his curved sword raised, his great white horse rearing up, about to crush underfoot a tangle of supine men in uniform.

Abd el-Krim, crushing the Nazarenes! says Khadija. Mokhtar, sitting beneath the image, raises a clenched fist, giving us a gap-toothed grin. The traditions of the *Bled es-Siba* have not been forgotten. And far from being ashamed of this graven image, or whatever the technical term may be in Islam, Farid the patriarch is so proud of it that he insists on our coming over for a closer look. Gérard is right in there, checking out his hero, while the real Abdelkrim adopts the heroic pose of his namesake, and Mokhtar gives him a round of applause.

The children, whose drumming-and-clapping game has been building up into ever more complex rhythms in the background, have been joined by Aytan, now, on a pair of teaspoons. Can all Moroccans do this? It's very impressive. One of them will change a rhythm or add a different one, and the others will vary theirs to counterpoint it. At first it seemed just a complex game, but now it's become real music. The family percussionists build to a mocking crescendo as Farid draws Gérard's attention to a banknote pinned to the bottom of the picture. Evidently this is an oft-played scenario. Farid unpins it for our inspection. One Riffan, it says. Legal tender once issued by the short-lived Republic of the Rif. Strangely, it seems to be printed mostly in English. 'State Bank of the Riff' it says at the top; and down below, 'equal to ten English pence', above the French version, *'bon pour un franc d'or'*.

Of course it's in English, says Farid. It was designed by Captain Gardiner! Captain Charlos Gardiner! A good man, an arms smuggler, who brought many fine guns, English Enfield rifles and Italian Stati too, to help our republic against the colonizers' armies. And see what fine-quality banknotes he made, too – seventy years on, and it looks as new as the day it was printed!

The granddaughters have been singing little phrases, copying the Andalus singer from the radio, along with their teaspoon rhythm section. But Farid tells them to be quiet. Khadija must sing a song from the Rif War, now, for the guests to hear. The song is chosen, and Khadija launches into it, accompanied by the infant percussionists. A sad, passionate song, and Khadija's performance is only slightly spoilt by Mokhtar's simultaneous translation into Spanish. 'Lalla, oh, Lalla, listen to the sound of the guns across the river . . . Lalla, oh, Lalla, I still keep my pride, even if the colonizer is here . . . The men wear the jellaba, but it is we, the women, who have prepared them and sent them to war . . .' Stirring stuff. Gérard is over the moon.

Dinner being over, Nadia brings in a lit brazier for the tea. Farid and Abdelkrim take charge of making and pouring it. Serving tea to guests is men's work here in the Maghreb. Masses of sugar and a handful of fresh spearmint go into the pot along with the tea, and a sprig of mint into each glass too, for good measure. Abdelkrim makes a fine art of the pouring, raising the teapot almost to head height with each glass, creating a stream of bubbles. It looks beautiful, the bright green leaves against the gold of the tea, the bubbles winking at the brim, though the French contingent are, of course, wistfully dreaming of the fortifying dash of cognac they would be getting back home to aid their digestion.

I settle onto a nice big pile of cushions to drink my tea. I badly needed to stretch my legs out. How do people handle all this sitting cross-legged on the floor, this crouching over their cooking apparatus? My legs don't seem to be designed for it at all. Mariam comes over to sit next to me. And now, the volume being pretty loud in here still, she decides to talk privately about the reason why she argues with Aytan: her experiences with the Islamists in her own home *quartier* of Casablanca. Those boys, she says, had nothing to do with the spirit of community and enlightened generosity her husband and his fellow intellectuals imagine when they talk of a rebirth of Islam. More like hatred and despotism. Their claim to respect on the streets was that they'd gone off to fight against the Soviets in Afghanistan – and won. They came back wearing big beards and Afghan tunics, swaggering with their new macho-Islam credentials, in and out of the mosque, saying their five-times-a-day prayers as ostentatiously as possible and harassing others to join in, scaring young girls like Mariam and her friends over their Western-style clothes, or tormenting small shopkeepers to close up for Friday prayers. Nobody had any respect for them before they left – they were just the usual layabouts – but now they were holier-than-thou heroes who'd been prepared to die for their faith. Who could stand up to them? The moral high ground, Mariam says, is the perfect place to bully people from.

You get just the same kind of thing in Christianity, I say, thinking we're on the same wavelength. You see evangelists calling for tolerance and brotherly love, family values and what-have-you, but then, as often as not, when they go off to live the dream, there is no tolerance for anyone outside their own sects, the brotherly love turns into race-hate or immigrant-bashing, and the support for family values turns out to mean attacking gays and unmarried mothers.

Well said. I have just confirmed everything a respectable Muslim might think about Western degeneracy. Mariam looks deeply alarmed: she certainly does not identify with gays or unmarried mothers. This place really is like Europe forty years back. Plus or minus a few supernatural beings, that is: I suppose you'd need to go back more like eighty to find Europeans in serious fear of evil spirits. Still, henceforth I shall remember never to say anything that wouldn't have gone down well with my granny. Then I'm bound to get it right.

The farming folk are ready to take to their beds nice and early. They'll be up at dawn tomorrow, as usual. And now, we degenerate Westerners discover that alcohol is not so far off the radar as we've imagined. Abdelkrim will join us for a bit, he says, looking slightly furtive, as we collect the radio and get ready to take our leave. As we make our way back up the hill, he produces a bottle of Moroccan red wine, magician style, from the deep pocket of his jellaba. Surprising enough, but we are utterly amazed when, back at the house, Aytan brings out a half-bottle of scotch whisky and a bottle of Coca-Cola. I hardly know whether it's the whisky or the Coke that is the more shocking.

Fortunately, if there's one thing whisky is good for, it's getting over a shock; and once Abdelkrim has found a radio station he likes we party the night away – no longer to the ancient music of Islamic Andalus, but to the East–West fusion of Rai music. It's being broadcast from Oran, says Abdelkrim, where it was first born. Over the border in Algeria. The best music in the Maghreb.

Morning. It's hardly even daybreak. I've been lying awake for ages. Everything's too interesting for sleeping. The radio is lying right by my carpet-nest. Maybe there'll be some news from Algeria? I turn it on.

Stupid idea: they're talking in Arabic, of course. Two announcers are interrupting one another, sounding very agitated. Has something momentous happened?

The door to the teachers' apartment opens. Aytan sticks his head round it to see what's going on. I've woken him up. I apologize profusely.

Not at all, he says. Carry right on! It's fine by him if I want to listen to the Algerian football results.

And he goes back to bed.

The water in the bucket is looking very low. I decide to wander on down to Khadija's. Maybe I can have a splash at their water-butt? I'm not going to be staying here long enough to get embroiled in any water controversies, after all, am I?

I stop off to have a look at the djinn-pond on my way. A beautiful little grotto under the pine trees. You'd have to be blind not to notice the suggestiveness of the forms nature has taken in this welcoming green damp nook. In the dawn light the tall straight rock looks remarkably phallic. And the spring, a tiny mossy crevice in the rockface, ferns sprouting all around it, looks remarkably like the female equivalent. A low boulder by the side of the little pool has been worn smooth by the bottoms of generations of would-be mothers. I have to agree with Aytan. Definitely un-Islamic. I should think this place must have been a focus for fertility-magic since time immemorial.

The dawn muezzin starts to call as I leave the grotto, reminding me, in the nick of time, that there is only One God. I pass a herdsman smoking a pipe and watching his flock, gazing peacefully out across the mountains. Kif at dawn . . . This must be what the stuff is really meant for. Another muezzin starts up in the distance. And another. Like all the shooting last night, you can't tell whether there are really dozens of voices calling, or if they're just echoes and re-echoes thrown back by the hillsides.

I find Khadija and Nadia already out in the yard, busy getting the bread-oven lit. Apart from its enormous size it's identical to the country bread-ovens you still find in Italy, a kind of igloo inside which you make a fire of wood, slapping a horseshoe-shaped iron door over the entrance to keep the heat in. Once the fire has burnt down, you shove the embers aside and add your dough. The accumulated heat within does the baking, imparting a lovely smoky flavour to your bread.

Khadija is very proud of hers: she and Nadia built it themselves. The only thing they paid for was the metal door. The reason for its huge size is so they can make a few pennies doing other villagers' baking for them, and extra loaves to sell on market days. She is so pleased with my appreciation of it, and my genuine interest – born out of certain Italian experiences with an outdoor pizza-oven – in the topic of mud-plaster recipes and the desirability of adding cow dung to them that she decides she'll make me a special treat for breakfast – a *brik*. But don't tell the others!

No risk of that. Firstly, they're still asleep. And secondly, I don't know what a *brik* is.

Nadia is spreading a pair of rush mats over the other side of the yard: time for prayers. Didn't I hear the muezzin? Why don't I join them?

Er, well, to start with, I don't know the words.

The first bit is easy, says Nadia. *As-salamu aleikum*, she begins. Come on, just try!

What, the prayer starts by just saying hello?

Of course it does. You are saying good morning to your two djinns.

News to me. I didn't even know I had two djinns.

But everyone does. The djinns who sit on either shoulder, one of them calling you to do good, the other to do evil: and keep a record of your actions for Judgement Day.

Really? Not news at all, then. I don't think they are exactly Christian, not in the biblical sense – more folklore. But that makes it even stranger to come across the same thing here. I remember from my childhood that, if you spilt salt, you had to throw a pinch of it over your left shoulder, into the eyes of your Bad Spirit, whose perch it was! I am amazed.

Khadija and Nadia just laugh. What's to be surprised about? Of course I know about the djinns: everybody does! Except Aytan, that is. He will give you a big long lecture about how the greeting is not to your guardian djinns at all, but to the *umma*, the rest of the Muslim world community. But then, city people do have their own ways, don't they?

I am beginning to have a theory about all this party-pooping behaviour of Aytan's. I think people here, especially educated people, are so traumatized by a long history of colonial disdain that they've internalized the colonizers' image of their nations as scruffy, superstitious savages. Good luck to Aytan, but I'd say you're shooting yourself in the foot if you get rid of all the magic and mystery in your religion. The Christians have done that in my own country – invented a supposedly rational religion – and look how many people ever go to church in England!

The *brik* turns out to be a brilliant Rif version of the fried egg on toast. Khadija folds a left-over pastry leaf from last night into a sort of cone in her hand, like the paper cornets sweets used to be sold in once upon a time, then cracks an egg into it. She adds salt, pepper and fresh coriander leaves, folds over the top, and sticks it down into a triangular envelope with a bit of the egg-white. Now she fries the whole thing crispy in olive oil and butter mixed. I immediately make plans to breakfast on these things forever, until I remember what a performance it is making the pastry. But then, maybe you could use filo pastry, or the stuff you wrap spring rolls in?

Scenting delicious snack aromas, the grandchildren now appear, demanding the same. Indulgently, Khadija makes them one each – only because it's Eid, now! – and they all run off, dribbling egg-yolk.

Khadija sighs. What is going to become of her grandchildren? She will tell me a secret: the only reason she is glad that they are going to Mariam's school is so that they will be able to leave this place one day. Education is good, because it makes it easier for people to go. There is nothing here but scraping a living from the land, living on a tightrope, wearing your fingers to the bone – always anxious and worried. Nothing will stop her from getting those children reading and writing as well as the *imam* himself!

What about your olive trees, though? I ask. I've been wondering about this since I tried the oil yesterday. Why can't people here make a living from anything but cannabis? There are plenty of olive trees. Surely there's a good market for olive oil? That's certainly what saved our village in Italy, just when it seemed about to die on its feet, with every last son and daughter either leaving for the cities or emigrating. And I know for a fact that Italian wholesalers are buying up more and more hectolitres of North African oil every year.

Khadija says nothing in answer to this, just gets to her feet and leads me off outside the yard. Here, round the back of the house, beyond the yard walls, a single fat millstone stands out in the open, resting in a deep circular enclosure – the pit that holds the olives. There is a wooden bar slotted through the millstone's central hole to rest on a central pivot, also of wood. Khadija leans on the bar, worn smooth and gleaming with the effort of years. The stone creaks round an inch or two in its channel. This, she says, is how they mill their olives here.

I have heard of this very low-tech kind of mill, but I've never actually seen one before. You call it a *frantoio a sangue* in Italian, a blood mill, which may sound barbaric (*pace* my Berber-Amazigh hosts!), but the name is just to distinguish it from a *frantoio ad acqua*, a water-mill: the driving force being not the water flowing through a river, but the blood flowing through a living body.

Well, I say, obviously she and her neighbours would have to take their harvests to a proper commercial mill and pay to get it pressed, but it would be worth it, the price they'd get for the oil would easily cover the cost and make them a nice big profit too.

I am already planning to start ringing people up as soon as I get back to Italy – maybe I could single-handedly save this village from poverty? – when Khadija puts a full stop to the fantasy. There is, she says, no such thing as a commercial olive-mill here. Not anywhere in the region. People here have always made their oil on this small family scale.

I take another look at the mill. Usually, the living body that drives one of these things is a mule or some other beast, not a human. Imagine having to use nothing but your own body-weight to shove that great stone round and round over the olives. I thought I'd gone back to the simple life when I moved to Italy. Little did I know how much simpler it can get! There's a ring of cobbles set in the ground around the millstone to give some purchase as you battle to shift that massive weight. What a terrible job it must be.

You can harness it to a mule, Khadija agrees. That's what they used to do in her father's time, but a mule costs seven or eight hundred pounds, an investment well beyond her family's means.

But wasn't Mokhtar trying to buy one only yesterday, when we met him?

In his dreams, says Khadija. He likes to be out and about, doing the rounds, talking horseflesh and money-making schemes to other men, who are probably in the same boat as him anyway, penniless. So they all end up smoking so much of their home-grown kif that they can't even remember what the scheme was, never mind get hold of the mule!

I find myself wondering whether the river down in the valley might be powerful enough to drive a mill-wheel. No, silly idea: medieval technology can't be the answer. They would have to go for ultra-modernity, to start such a project from scratch and make it profitable. But no, that's no good, is it? First, they would need electricity. I give up. I knew I wasn't cut out for commerce. Not surprising people here end up turning to kif.

Where is the press, then? I ask. How do you extract the oil from the crushed olives?

Khadija points out a large pit a few feet away, in the lee of the house wall. I gaze at it, perplexed. How on earth do you use a hole in the ground to squeeze crushed olives?

No squeezing involved: that is the explanation. You throw the crushed olives into the pit, she explains, and cover them with hot water. The oil rises slowly to the top over the next day or two, and you scoop it off, spoonful by spoonful.

Very ingenious indeed – if you only need to make oil for your own use, and couldn't afford the massive torque of classical oil production anyway. Something tells me that, though Khadija's extra-virgin would certainly qualify as organic, it might well contravene a few modern hygiene rules once it had sat in that hole in the ground for a day or two. What we need is a millionaire philanthropist. Or better still, some government investment. It was European Union money that saved us in Italy – I wonder if they're really planning to let Morocco into the European Union any time soon? Doesn't seem too likely. They're spending a fortune building great high fences to keep them out, aren't they? And if they let Morocco in, I suppose they'd have to build an even longer one right through mountain and desert, round the outside of Morocco instead.

The whole thing is ridiculous. All those fat, healthy olive trees and not a dirham to be made.

Come, says Khadija, leading me on down the path towards something more hopeful – the terraced fields where the winter corn has just been harvested. They always used to plant a second, summer crop of wheat here in April, she says, and still end up hungry by the end of winter. You're safer with a good cash crop, one that will make you enough money to buy the household flour you would have grown, and still to have some left over for necessities.

And what crop is that?

Cannabis, of course. Safer, maybe, but, Khadija says, not completely safe. Because your whole harvest can be rooted up and destroyed any time the forces of law and order, never too friendly with the Berber Amazigh, feel like making a point of their power. Or, of course, whenever the king and his government feel the need to gather a bit of kudos in the eyes of the Nazarenes abroad.

I am happy to report that not long after our visit, a fabulous piece of new technology appeared in the olive lands of the Rif. Some kindly genius has invented a massive mobile olive-mill and press, all combined into one, mounted on a lorry. An Italian organic-olive-oil cooperative, seeking uncontaminated groves, brought this item to Morocco: invented, no doubt, to make use of the wilder and farther-flung olive groves of Italy itself, where harvests are small and the mills distant. They have started a training scheme in modern olive-farming techniques, too, aimed at the women left behind in the villages. Hurrah. Hope at last. Electricity not required.

9

Our bus arrives fresh from Tetuan, pulling in beside the Portuguese-built red-sandstone citadel. We climb aboard. I can hardly believe it's only two days since we were in that city. Though Tetuan seemed so exceedingly strange and foreign on that first day, now, after our brief sojourn in the heartlands of the Rif, I find I'm thinking of it as a positive paragon of cosmopolitan culture.

Guy, meanwhile, is marvelling that we've been staying with cannabis farmers for two whole days without even realizing it. And at how much all the middlemen must be earning from the business – because Khadija's family were certainly not rolling in money, were they? They can't even afford a radio of their own! You'd hardly think anyone would bother breaking the law to earn their living, if they were going to make so little out of it.

Gérard is maintaining that he knew it all along: it was obvious to anyone would who had bothered checking out the guidebook properly . . .

As dusk falls, we are heading eastwards once more, along high hairpin-bending roads through walnut and chestnut forests, a landscape that looks so thoroughly Ligurian that I keep forgetting I'm on the other side of the Mediterranean. This is the main road towards the east, running parallel to the sea, but keeping well away from it, sticking to the hills, just the way the old Roman road does back home in Diano. It may be hard to believe, in our modern beach-obsessed days, but once upon a time, when agriculture was still the staff of everyday life, a sea road was the last thing anyone would bother to build. Roads were needed to connect important market towns, which were up in the hills, naturally enough, where the fertile agricultural land lay, and not down among the meagre pickings of the seashores.

Darkness now, and a bright starry night. The warmth of the day is turning to chill, and our fellow passengers begin pulling up the big hoods of their jellabas and snuggling down into them. All the length of the bus, outlined against the windows, pointed hood after pointed hood now rises to mimic the dark hills beyond. We are heading for Oujda in a busload of sorcerers.

Guy, who is, I now see, a man of impressive foresight, follows suit, pulling up the hood of his burnous and wrapping its yards of woollen folds warm around him. Enviously, Gérard and I pull out our mealy-mouthed European fleeces, fiddling with cold zips and recalcitrant toggles.

An hour or two later, in pitch darkness, Gérard decides he needs a pee. Quite badly. I ask my nearest neighbour, the woman across the aisle, if we're likely to be making a stop any time soon. But the answer is just to hold on – *attendre, faut attendre!* I pass on the sad news to Gérard. The wizard in front of us, with more French at his command than the ladies, turns round to explain that we wouldn't want the driver to stop, not round here in these wild hills. This is a very lawless area. And the bus won't be stopping at Ketama, either, although it's the next official stop. It's too dangerous.

Really? What sort of danger? Gérard's alarm-antennae are out again. The cannabis farmers themselves may be lovely people, as we now know, but the business side of the operation will be another kettle of fish entirely.

The danger, though, our wizard reveals, is not hashish-connected. A bus was hijacked last week just outside Ketama. It's happened several times in recent months.

Really? What, and did the hijackers hold the passengers to ransom? I ask.

But no! The wizard laughs at the very idea. They're not after Western tourists! They know the Tetuan bus is always full of the duty-free goodies its privileged residents have humped across the border, which the enterprising among them will now be transporting for resale further inland. Making this particular bus a sitting target. An unpleasant situation, but nobody here in the Rif would either expect, or want, the forces of the state to step in. They prefer to resolve things in their own way. So the bus-drivers have come up with their own ingenious solution to the problem. They are simply punishing all the inhabitants of Ketama collectively. This will cause them to put pressure, in private, upon the hijackers, who will certainly be well known in the town. In a month or two, the service will resume, by which time the perpetrators will have been thoroughly chastened, brought into line by their own community. The hijackings will stop, with no need at all for the agencies of law enforcement.

An admirable solution, we agree. Simple, yet elegant.

So, on we go, through Ketama and out the other side without stopping. The place looks pretty decrepit, anyhow. I don't think we're missing much. Except, of course, a loo.

Now follows a confusing event involving local methods for dealing with the lack of loo-stops. I have noticed that a thin stream of liquid is now running down the centre aisle of the bus. The woman across the aisle sees me staring, nudges me and giggles. Men! she says. Not wait!

Can the locals really be discreetly relieving themselves from beneath their jellabas as we travel? Maybe so, if stopping really is out of the question. Presumably the bus company would just hose the bus out when it reaches the journey's end? Should I pass this information on to Gérard? Though, without a jellaba, Gérard would have no veil to draw modestly over his business, were he to follow local custom. Unless, I suppose, he borrowed the burnous from our percipient friend Guy? Now, as we lurch round a left-hand bend, the trickle laps at the soles of my shoes. I move my feet squeamishly out of the way. My neighbour across the aisle slaps me on the arm, giggling. The woman sitting next to her, her mother by the looks of it, is hiding her face in her hands, giggling too. She holds up a plastic mineral-water bottle, and mimes emptying it onto the floor. Are they telling me the liquid on the floor is not pee after all, but water? It was just a joke. Thank goodness I found that out in time. Imagine how badly we might have brought Christendom into disrepute.

Some time later Guy wakes me up. Grinding and coughing noises are coming from the engine. Something seems to be horribly wrong with it. The driver is keeping going, but very, very slowly. Other passengers are waking up. Soon a whole cabal of hooded sorcerers is communing down at the front, deep in mechanical debate with the driver. Eventually the bus limps off the main road towards the lights of a town. Is this an official halt or an emergency stop? No idea. But it seems the bus will not be not going anywhere soon. We'll have to wait for a mechanic to show up. And who knows when that may be?

A bad situation, you might think. But not a bit of it. As we pull into the main street of the town, we are met by a fusillade of random gunfire. The feast of Eid al-Fitr is still only on its second day. A short step away, in the town square, heralded by another burst of gunshots so close that I jump out of my skin, festivities are still going on, accompanied by a lot of wild drumming. There is even a roadside kebab place – or two places, rather. We follow our fellow passengers to a butchers' stall, at which you buy your meat, then to the stall next door, which has a glowing barbecue, and two cooks waiting to cook it for you. Impressive. Clearly Moroccans are as fussy as Italians about their meat. They want to see that it's fresh, with their own eyes, before it gets cooked. Copying our friend the wizard, whom we now know as Abdel, I order a toothsome liver brochette. Once it's been grilled, you lay it inside half a baguette, shut the baguette tightly, pull out the long metal skewer and hand it back to the barbecue-men. Bite in. Lovely.

We wander off towards the square, munching, still following the rest of the passengers, to join in the fun. There's no choice but to sleep in the bus – no chance of a mechanic till the morning, not with Eid still going on. Nobody seems too bothered about this, even though every passenger we talk to, down in the square, is hoping to get home to their family celebrations before Eid is over. Not a sign of anger or frustration. Do people here have a much more relaxed attitude to life than us, or does this kind of thing happen so often that you factor it in to your expectations?

A band is playing outside a café – Andalusian music, if I am not mistaken. Outside another, an ancient man in a huge turban stands telling stories, some terrifying, some hilarious, to judge by the reactions of his audience. Abdel and most of the other passengers settle here, completely gripped. Short on simultaneous translators tonight, we foreigners give up on him and make for the musical corner. I am soon stoking up, as you do in an emergency, on plenty of strong sweet tea. The Frenchmen, their delicate digestive systems quailing at the bizarre dietary habits of the English and their Moroccan friends, settle for soothing mineral water.

Around dawn, only minutes, it seems, after we have finally drifted off to sleep, the muezzin starts up. All the men traipse off the bus to pray by the side of the road, and hardly any of the women. When he returns, I ask Abdel why that should be. It is less important, he says, for women to pray than for men.

Why, though? I ask. Is God less interested in women?

He has no idea, he says, looking faintly hunted. Still, I can't resist asking him whether he was saying hello to his two djinns, or to the Muslim *umma*?

The djinns, of course.

Getting on for midday, the bus still behaving pretty oddly despite the lengthy attentions of two mechanics this morning, we pull into another small town at last. So much partying in one small high street! People are playing cards, eating *tagines*, changing buses, playing drums and singing; we even spot a woman with fishnet tights beneath her jellaba. There is a hostelry a short step down the road, still open, and still feasting. They have put on a traditional Eid lunch of *mechoui*, whole roasted sheep. Several of our fellow passengers decide that the only solution is to go and join in. And they lead us down the road to the best restaurant ever, where you sit on long low divans around knee-high tables inside waist-high wooden booths, each one with heavy velvet drapes for you to draw right around you, and dine in total privacy, if you so wish! We don't close ours, of course – we're much too interested to see what's going on around us; though some of the dining areas are already modestly curtained off, people eating behind them, heaped dishes being passed in by the waiters. Is it so that wives and daughters can eat out in relative privacy, maybe? Or something to do with the anti-ostentation principles of Islam? Maybe it saves you seeming to be showing off how much you can afford – or indeed saves face by not revealing how little? There seem to be an awful lot of rules about ostentation. Even, Yazid told us, about the lengths and widths of men's jellabas. The Koran tells you never to try to impress by the length and generosity of your robes. With voluminous fabric swirling wide as you walk, hem swishing along the ground, you may cut a fine figure, but you are risking your place in paradise. A truly devout man will use no more material than he needs to cover himself with comfort and modesty: no extra width just for show, and no miserly skimping, either – which can easily be another form of ostentation. A workmanlike length between knee and ankle. That is the correct path.

This anti-ostentation business isn't unheard of in Christian tradition, either, though. I recall something similar in Granada, at the Easter celebrations, when the city hosts massive parades of saint-effigy carrying men who wear face-covering pointed hoods with eyeholes cut in them, horribly reminiscent of the Ku Klux Klan. What, I asked Pedro, was the point of the hoods? Answer: there is always a risk, when you participate in a great religious display, that you are doing it not out of sincere conviction but from motives of ostentation. Concealing your identity ensures your purity of heart and avoids the Sin of Pride. And there was nothing so unusual about pointed headgear in Spain, after all, when these processions were still young. Somehow, the Moorish hood escaped the close attentions of the Inquisition.

Abdel the wizard, who knows his way about, takes us out to the small garden at the back to see the roasting sheep. There are two smoke-blackened ovens especially for *mechoui*: great open-mouthed tubes, like Khadija's bread-oven with the top sliced off, each with a whole sheep hanging vertically down into it on a hooked spit, and a small boy basting them constantly with some deliciously spicy-smelling stuff. Pure butter and cumin, says our wizard.

Better still than the roasting *mechoui* are the two ready-prepared examples lying on the counter indoors, being carved and served – and we are more than ready to dig in. Meat lovely and buttery, falling off the bone, crispy on the outside and melt-in-the-mouth on the inside . . . and couscous to go with it. You get a given a little bowl of mixed salt and cumin to season it with. The boys decide to be brave and ask for wine. No problem, says the waiter: he doesn't bat an eyelid over the request. The wine is Moroccan, too, when he brings it. Though the Wizard tells us that hardly any ordinary people here would drink wine; if they drink at all, they're much more likely to have a beer. Wine is stuff for the *francisants* – the Frenchifiers – and ordinary people don't feel right drinking it. They feel as if they're letting the side down.

And what is so bad about Frenchification? We gather, once we've decoded the answer – which Abdel delivers over the next half-hour, perched hawk-like on the corner of Gérard's divan – that French culture is a class issue here in Morocco. Unlike the French language, which is public property, its culture – from the drinking of wine to the exposure of naked female arms, legs and hair – is the province of the rich here, of the ruling elite, suspected of being the main bearers of the dreaded Western Corruption. Which goes some way to explaining the odd fact that, while rich Moroccans who would Frenchify the home culture are deeply suspect, ordinary French tourists – of whom many thousands turn up every year, supping their intoxicating beverages and sporting their naked hair and limbs – are perfectly well received in Morocco.

A pot of tea finishes the meal, the waiter pouring from a positively theatrical height into tiny thimble-sized glasses. As lunch draws to a close, more and more people are drawing the curtains around their tables, and we are surprised to see that some of them are actually stretching out on the cushioned benches as if they were planning to take a post-prandial nap here. But that, says Abdel, is exactly what they are expected to do. And, as the waiter removes our plates and heads back towards the kitchens, he gently closes the curtains around us. Amazing! You are actually supposed, once you've finished eating here, to lie back, snooze and quietly digest inside your snug enclosure. The most civilized dining arrangement we've come across in all our lives. Why don't we have such a thing in Europe? Couldn't we open one just like it when we get back? It would be bound to be the most popular dining-place ever!

Alas, we soon work out that in our own hectic lands a restaurant whose tables remained occupied, even if only for an hour or so per sitting, by non-spending nap-takers, would be doomed to speedy failure. We would go bust in no time at all. How right Aytan was. Ours really is a dog-eat-dog world. Profit running wild, untamed by human values.

Among the various unexpected services this restaurant provides, it now turns out, is that of travel agency. After a respectable napping-period has elapsed, a certain Youssouf appears, sticking his head through our curtains. He is heading east, he says, and his turn-off is only a few miles before our destination, Oujda. So if we don't want to bother waiting for the bus, which won't get there till nightfall now, since the mechanic is waiting for a spare part . . . ?

Wonderful, we say. And we follow Youssouf, a tiny lively man with sparkling eyes – another of those ageless Moroccans, could be any age between thirty and fifty – outside into the brilliant sunlight, only pausing to settle our amazingly cheap bill and add a couple of extra bottles of wine, that essential aid to French digestion, to be packed away into Guy's bag against future famine.

Our transport-to-be is a bit of a surprise. Not the car we'd imagined, but a small lorry so fully loaded down with hay that you can hardly see there's a vehicle there at all. We clamber aboard – a bit of a tight squeeze, all four of us on the banquette – and Youssouf starts the engine, battling the gear lever into first. Roaring and vibrating, our travelling haystack sets off at a crawl. Something tells me this is going to take quite a bit longer than the bus would have done. But then, who knows how long we would have had to wait before it left? Or whether it would just have broken down again?

Youssouf seems a lovely man, shy and quiet, with an infectious sidewise smile. Moreover, he says his lorry never will break down. It is of a brand called Gak, he tells us proudly, a vehicle that was once often used for fire engines in Europe, many examples of which have now been recycled for agricultural purposes in the Maghreb.

Hardly anyone will be travelling today, with Eid still on, he tells us, but he himself has no choice. He has staked his whole future on this load. Prices for hay have almost doubled down south, on the fringes of the desert, where his family comes from – near Figuig, though he lives in Fez these days, where there's more chance of work. Last year's harvest was bad, and lots of people have run out of forage just at the moment they need it most, to get their livestock into condition for spring. And with hardly any rain this year so far, there's not enough new pasture coming up yet to save them. So if Youssouf strikes lucky down south, and if he isn't too late, because it's taken him nearly a fortnight to borrow this lorry and get the load together, and maybe lots of others have got there already and the price has gone back down again, and if the lorry runs well, *inshallah*, he should make enough money to put a bit aside. And he will be able to afford the bride-price of a wife at last, to settle down and have some children.

Being Europeans, we can't help taking him up on this. Couldn't he get himself a free wife, a good-looking man like him? Maybe he should try going to Europe first?

Youssouf just gives us the shy smile. No, no. He's never been to Europe – he doesn't like going too far from home. Fez is quite far enough. But we are right. The way things are going in his town, anyone who doesn't go off abroad to work and bring home some European wages may as well give up the idea of getting married altogether. You'll never earn enough here in Morocco. It's always the same way in this country. As the saying goes, the dirham's up the dog's bottom, and the dog's got rabies!

Gérard and Guy being not only Europeans but also men, they now, naturally, have to ask Youssouf how much I would be worth as a bride.

In money, or in livestock? asks Youssouf, taking this in good part.

Camels, say my tormentors.

Youssouf takes a good look at me. About twenty, he says. But it would be twice as many if she didn't all have those freckles.

All right. Enough. Remind me to get myself a *haik* at the very next town.

The boys, who have evidently been studying the how-to-barter section of the *Petit futé*, say they won't take less than forty for me. Youssouf is not playing any more, though. His situation is too serious for joking, he says.

But Guy is serious, too. Why does Youssouf want to pay to get married? Couldn't he keep his money to make his home nice, or bring up his children, or whatever, the way Europeans do? How could he believe his bride really loved him, anyway, if he had to pay?

Youssouf laughs. Among his people, he says, the girl keeps the bride-price; it is essential – it is her insurance in case anything happens to her husband. In case things go wrong. And where he comes from, love is something that grows after you marry, not before! First you must choose the right woman; then respect will deepen into family feeling; then come children and love. He needs someone who knows his family, who will be happy to share a house with him and his mother and help look after her in her old age. She is not well. And he doesn't think any European woman – if one would have him! – would want to do that. He wants a girl who understands, a girl from his own home town, down south. Though he's not sure anyone there will have him there, either, because he's fast getting past marriage-able age. No father wants a man over forty for his daughter – not unless the husband-to-be is already rich, that is – because he fears she will end up raising her children in poverty, looking after a sick old man.

Even if things work out, Youssouf confides after a short pause, he'll probably be getting a black bride, not a white one. He's not both-ered himself, but it will disappoint his mother. Even if he does as well as he's hoping, he doubts he'd be able to afford a white, Arab bride . . .

Youssouf's emotions seem to have got the better of him. As if there wasn't enough noise in this lorry already, he suddenly reaches out and turns on the radio, belting out Arabic music at top volume. We are out on the open road now, the lorry at full throttle on the bass register, the crackling radio howling above it. Impossible to talk; the noise is deafening. Not that I have any idea how I would have responded to those last remarks, anyway. Outside my scope entirely.

So I just sit quietly and watch the road unfurl before us, the hilly landscape drier and harsher now. The road must be passing closer to the sea: a flock of seagulls is picking its way through a patch of newly turned field down below the roadside. I am drifting off to sleep, lulled by the steady, deafening roar of the motor, the wailing of the music. An advertisement comes on, now, in Arabic, naturally enough. Idly I listen, not expecting to understand a word. Sound-effects of a Moroccan party going on indoors; drumming, laughter, the *you-you*-ing of women. Two men step outside, shutting the door against the noise, exchanging a few calm words. A restful moment; the click of a lighter; a close-up sigh, an exhalation of pleasure above the distant *you-you*s. A sultry voice-over addresses us: no mistaking the one word I can understand. Marlboro. They are having a Marlboro Moment, Maghreb style.

Opening my eyes some time later, I find myself gazing at some pictures hanging on the padded panel above Youssouf's windscreen, in the place where you might hang a pair of fluffy dice if you were a British lorry-driver, or your favourite saint if you were an Italian *camionista*. Youssouf's pictures are a set of three cardboard-framed prints just a few inches square – simple bold woodcuts, colour-washed by hand. They remind me of eighteenth-century illustrations, the kind of thing you might have found in some Hogarthian street market. One is a seascape: a chunky-looking boat lies becalmed in a flat sea, while above it a ray of sunlight catches a passing bird. The next has a jellaba'd man standing in a yellow stubble-field, his arms held wide, some odd-looking stooks of corn all around him. In the last, another jellaba'd man, this one on a wild hillside, gazes at a bush that is going up in red-and-yellow flames.

A burning bush! Of course – they're Bible pictures. The story of Moses and the Burning Bush, Noah's ark with the dove bearing its olive branch and . . . I'm not sure what the other one is. But the first two are definitely Christian stories, from the Bible. Is Youssouf a Christian, then? I ask him, shouting over the noise of the engine, pointing at the pictures.

Of course not, he shouts back. Those are stories from the Koran! We are all *Ahl al-Kitab* – Peoples of the Book!

I sit quietly and ponder this one, speech being too much like hard work under present conditions.

All Peoples of the Book! I'd thought this was pretty esoteric knowledge when I learned it in Granada – it certainly isn't something most Christians know today. Apparently it's ordinary run-of-the-mill information here in the Muslim world. It had certainly never dawned on me, though, that we meant one and the same book, with the exact same stories in it. But of course, if the Old Testament stories are really Jewish ones, Talmud tales from before Jesus was born, and Christians have simply added their own Jesus-stories on top, there's no reason why Muslims wouldn't have done the exact same thing when the Prophet Mohammed arrived a few centuries later . . .

But – Islam? I shout. The Koran? Images? How come?

Ah, they are very old, says Youssouf. And that is all he has to say on the matter.

I wonder what Aytan would make of this. Not just imitating God's perfect creation, but the very holiest of his works. There are more intricacies to this world of Islam than even *The Little Cunning One* can tell.

Another loud hour or so has passed, and the road must be drawing ever closer to the coast: there are seagulls everywhere now. Suddenly there is a roar from behind us, so loud it is even audible over the racket in the cab. The seagulls take off, startled. The roar is upon us, starts overtaking. A squadron of huge black Motoguzzis, half a dozen of them, their riders in black too; leather knee-boots and mirrored sunglasses, straps and holsters criss-crossing broad-shouldered black bomber jackets. They whoosh past us in a rush of air and vanish beyond the horizon as suddenly as they appeared. Extraordinary. If I didn't happen to know I was in Morocco, I would be certain that we'd just been overtaken by an oversized squad of Italian traffic cops.

Not a hallucination, but the Special Personal Police of His Moroccan Majesty, Youssouf explains, called to some emergency. Riding off, no doubt, to nip in the bud some heinous crime that threatens to unseat the Royal Person – or to give someone a shave. The king, I gather, has visited Italy at some point in his life, and been well impressed by the Armani-designed police get-ups. Sacrificed himself on the altar of desire, you might say. It looks as if his subjects are only too right to see him as a man easily entrapped by the dubious charms of the Nazarenes.

As dusk begins to fall, Youssouf pulls over to the side of the road, coming gently to a halt on a wide, flat area of beaten earth beside a spreading olive tree. He switches off the engine. The radio dies with it. Wonderful.

Food, he says. *Manger! Venez!* And without more ado he opens his door and jumps down from the cab.

But we haven't brought any food, we say, not liking to mention that we thought we'd be in Oujda by now.

Never mind! There is plenty for everyone! Youssouf always

travels with enough to last him several days, just in case. By the time we have struggled down from the Gak haystack, he is already on all fours, unloading his dinner equipment from somewhere deep beneath its chassis. A rolled-up rug with two thick blankets inside it, half a dozen chunky bits of branch – off the woody, lower limbs of a grapevine, I see, as we go to help – and last of all, a mystery item: an eighteen-inch-high slice off the top of an oil-drum. Youssouf bowls this along the ground towards the tree, indicating to us where to spread the rug, and lies it on the ground nearby, whereupon we see that its top is pierced with three neat, round holes, large, small and medium.

His own invention, he tells us proudly. A friend in Fez, who fixes cars for a living, cut the holes out for him with his angle-grinder. The big hole is for steaming the couscous, the medium one for the stew, and the small one for the teapot afterwards. It saves messing about balancing your pots on trivets or stones, and you use a lot less wood, too. You just light your fire – grapevine wood is the best, burns a good long time and doesn't take up much room to carry – and pop the oil-drum contraption over the top of it. And see, here in the side, an air inlet where you can add more wood or poke in a stick to spread the fire and lower the heat.

We are suitably impressed.

We should get our bedding out of our bags, Youssouf tells us now, unrolling his blankets, and get ourselves settled in.

What, are we going to sleep the night here, then?

Certainly! he says. First eat, then rest! Night has fallen. This hotel has a thousand stars. And better still, it is free!

This seems a little odd, coming from a man who seemed to suggest that we would arrive in Oujda sooner than the bus if we came with him. But maybe he just thought we'd rather travel than sit and wait. Or did he mean we'd be so late we'd have to get a hotel there anyway?

Who cares? This is a lovely spot, the air cool and delicious, the landscape wide and open, the gnarled limbs of the olive tree framing the first few stars in a huge and darkening sky. Silence is all around us. Nothing to hear but the faint trilling of the night cicadas, a honeyed lullaby after the ear-battering lorry and its radio. And who would have missed the patent cooker?

Youssouf has the fire lit in a trice, cooker ready next to it. Now he goes back to the lorry and produces a cardboard box from behind his seat: two round-bellied saucepans sitting neatly one inside the other, holding a bag of couscous granules, two carrots, an onion, several twists of newspaper, a hunk of meat and a two-litre bottle of mineral water. And a round metal tray. Youssouf is clearly a man of many skills. He pulls a clasp knife from his pocket now, and sets to creating a finely chopped onion with no need for a chopping board. A series of vertical slashes with the onion held in the palm of the hand; rotate the onion ninety degrees, do the same again; now hold it on its side over the pan, and slice crosswise; and there's your onion in bits, ready to fry. Just the way Italians do it.

We didn't realize we were going to be eating en route like this, we say apologetically. We really have nothing at all but half a baguette and some wine to share with him, and he probably doesn't even drink wine, does he?

No, he says, but it'll be good for the sauce. With a bit of wine, the camel meat will tender up nice and quickly.

Camel meat . . . none of us has ever tried that, we admit. Nervously, in some cases.

Best meat there is, according to Youssouf. Especially for *steak hâché*. We'll have to try camel *steak hâché* another time, but there's enough meat for a good sauce for the couscous. Nobody will go hungry. He cuts a corner of fat off the meat, throws it into the pan and uses it to fry the onion, along with the contents of one of the twists of paper: two small red chillis. The other holds some kind of deliciously aromatic herb. It's called *za'atar*, he says, but we are none the wiser. Now in goes the meat, the carrots . . . Where is that wine? A big splash of that, too, and the pot sizzles. Now some water. And will we pour the rest of the water into the other pan, please, for steaming the couscous?

So we settle down round the fire with Youssouf, master-chef, and wait for dinner. We pass the wine-bottle round, taking a swig each, and, to our surprise, Youssouf accepts one too. Nobody here to notice this frenchified behaviour, I suppose. We thank him for his generosity, sharing his food with us, cooking our dinner.

But you should always be generous with others, he says, and God will be generous with you.

Of course, those Pillars of Islam again. Which reminds me. Who, I ask now that I have some chance of hearing the reply, is the man in the picture in the lorry, the one standing in the field?

Do we not know that story? Youssouf is amazed. It is a picture of his own namesake! Of Youssouf's dream! The dream that told him that one day his brothers would all bow down before him. Surely we have him in our own Holy Book too? The nine brothers who were all jealous of him, Youssouf goes on, warming to his theme, because he was their father Yacoub's favourite, so one day, while they were out pasturing their flocks, they met some passing Egyptian merchants and sold him into slavery, then went off home and told old Yacoub that he'd been killed by a wild beast.

I've got it now – Youssouf must be the same name as Joseph. And Yacoub is Jacob. Our own Youssouf is too carried away by the story, though, to notice that I'm with him at last. He has got on to Youssouf interpreting the Egyptian king's dream, which told that there would be seven years of plenty and seven years of hunger.

Of course, and he became advisor to Pharaoh, I interrupt, almost as excited as Youssouf himself. He saved Egypt from famine, and his own brothers had to come begging to Egypt for corn, and didn't recognize him as the man in charge.

That's it, says Youssouf. So his dream had come true, and there they were, bowing down before him!

Gérard and Guy are looking mystified. How on earth could Youssouf and I both know this story so well? It is a strange feature of

Catholic countries that they hardly seem to get told any Bible stories when they are children. Italians are the same. The old Church hierarchy may have lost the battle to stop the Bible being translated out of Latin, but still, somehow, it has managed to cling on to the ancient system where only priests knew the Holy Texts, and held the power of interpreting them to the common multitude.

Islam, on the other hand, doesn't have an Establishment. There is no fixed hierarchy of priests, bishops, archbishops, no Head of the Church. An *imam* gets and keeps his position by popular consent of other *imams*, and of his congregation. So unlike the Christian Church, I suppose, Islam never had any incentive to try to restrict access to the Tales of Power. In fact, of course, it does the exact opposite: schoolchildren here spend hours of their lives reciting the Koran aloud.

Be all that as it may, Youssouf and I are enjoying ourselves a lot, taking turns to tell this story we both know. Another of the things people did before television, evidently. This must be the time-honoured equivalent of bumping into someone who's been watching the same TV series as you. The Peoples of the Book club, Holy Writ as shared soap opera.

Our Youssouf may be called after the Youssouf of the Book, he says, but alas, he is not so handsome. And so far, not so rich, either. Still, there's hope yet, maybe, once he's got his hay sold.

Handsome? Was Joseph especially handsome? I don't think I remember that cropping up in the Bible version. Though I do recall his having a very good-looking Coat of Many Colours, I say. A kind of stripy jellaba that his father had made for him, which made his brothers all the more jealous.

Did he? This tickles Youssouf's fancy a lot. Imagine that, he says, chuckling, if it wasn't his looks at all, but his outfit! No, no, there's no coat of many colours in the Koran, but Youssouf certainly was very good-looking. Remember how his slave-master's wife couldn't resist him? Even though she was a married woman, she went after him, but Youssouf was an honourable man and turned her down.

Ah, yes, that rings a bell. Potiphar's wife. And in revenge she lied and got him arrested. She told everyone that it was him, not her, who had tried it on.

Yes! Yes, that's it! But before that, there's the bit where she invites all her women friends round to see how irresistible he is. She's arranged for Youssouf to come in and serve them. He walks in carrying the bowl of fruit, and they choose one each, pick up their knives to begin peeling and eating, but they are so overcome by his beauty that every last one of their blades slips, and all of them cut their hands, blood everywhere! So handsome he was!

No, I'm absolutely certain we don't have that part of the story. How could I forget that image: a room full of women blinded by their lust for a handsome slave, their hands full of cut fruit and flowing blood? The Koran version of the story, as recounted by Youssouf, now shifts from the erotic to what must be the world's first whodunit. The elders of the tribe, called in to judge who is telling the truth over the alleged rape-attempt, consult together a while and ask to have Joseph's garments brought before them. If they are ripped from behind, it will prove that Joseph was trying to get away; if they're torn at the front, though, Potiphar's wife is telling the truth.

Youssouf – our own lorry-driving one, not the koranic, talmudic and biblical one – breaks off his tale to attend to the food. The water has come to the boil. He sets the *couscoussier* over the steam and adds the couscous. A delicious odour is now wafting from the camel stew. Even Guy, who looked a little pale at the concept, is joining in the chorus of *mmmm*s as our chef takes off the lid and gives it a stir, displaying the reality of the dark, wine-laden sauce.

The thousand stars of our hotel have all come out now, set against a black velvety sky. The couscous is ready. Youssouf takes off the pots, hooks his cooker casually off the fire with an olive-branch, and throws on the branch and a couple more bits of vine to keep us warm while we eat. The night is starting to cool down fast. He empties the couscous onto the tray; the sauce goes on top. Youssouf cuts the meat up into bite-sized chunks, and we're ready to go. There turns out to be nothing at all weird about camel meat. You would easily believe it was a rather robust bit of beef. And out here in the open air, under the stars, the hot spicy sauce is heaven.

So here we are, sitting round a North African camp-fire, eating camel with our fingers and swapping Bible stories with a man who looks as if he'd just stepped out of one. Well, two men actually, Guy now looking very convincing in his burnous in the dusk – and minus the sunglasses. The couscous-eating technique I had thought lost is coming back to me now. The trick is to keep your elbow higher than your wrist, so gravity helps the juice stay at the right end of your arm.

Youssouf is still keen to carry on comparing versions of the good old Holy Tales. What, he asks, about the bit where, much later on, when Youssouf is rich and powerful, he meets Potiphar's wife again, and she is is destitute now, widowed and all alone. He sees her in the street, recognizes her, goes over to her, and when their eyes meet, his heart melts. And he ends up marrying her.

No, I don't think we have that part either. The Koran is evidently a lot hotter in the love and romance department than the mealy-mouthed Bible. As well as much more gripping in its plotting.

As the cooker goes back on for the after-dinner mint tea, Youssouf tells us a story which isn't actually in the Koran, but which he says is a holy story anyway, told to him by the Sufi brothers at the *zawiya* school. A story of the time, long, long ago, when all the birds got together, a member of every different species, and set off to find the Tree at the End of the World. They were certain that, when they got there, they would look upon the face of God at last. After many vicissitudes they found the tree, only to come face to face with – a reflection of themselves, a mirror. Because, of course, Allah is every-where – he is within every living being!

Evidently it is up to us to tell the next story. *Blanche Neige*, suggests Gérard. Or *Capuchon Rouge*? No. Snow White and Little Red Riding Hood do not finish on the uplifting moral note we need here. We can't think of anything offhand. So Youssouf moves on to Abra-ham – or Ibrahim, as he's called here – and the time God called upon him to sacrifice his youngest son. What about our version of that, then?

This being one of those camp-fire evenings, and the second bottle of wine well on its way down, I sing him the twangy Bob Dylan version of the Abraham story:

> *God says to Abraham, Kill me your son,*
> *Abe says, Man, you must be putting me on.*
> *God says, No. Abe says, Well.*
> *God says, You can do what you like Abe,*
> *But the next time you see me coming, you better run . . .*

Youssouf enjoys this musical interlude a lot and accompanies me with some of that impressively complicated Moroccan clapping. He has heard of Bob Dylan, he says, although he's never heard any of his songs till just now, because they have a Berber singer here in Morocco, Walid Mimoun, who is always described as the Bob Dylan of the Rif. Or used to be. He was too popular among the Berbers, so his songs were banned, and he wasn't allowed to perform any more. He went off to live in exile in Holland and turned into an alcoholic. Doesn't sing any more now.

But there are ancient Andalusian songs about Ibrahim, too, Youssouf tells us. Abraham is the greatest example of Islam. Because the word *islam* means 'submission' – submission to the will of God – and Abraham submitted to the highest point. He was willing to sacrifice the son of his old age, the apple of his eye, if that was what God wanted.

Will he sing us one, then? Or something by Walid Mimoun? No. Youssouf refuses even to try. He is a terrible singer, he says. We will have to wait until we meet some proper musicians. Which won't be long, because Oujda is famous for them.

It occurs to me later, pondering the evening as I drift off to sleep, that this business of our all having what amounts to exactly the same Book must explain the terrible trouble the Spanish Inquisition had in establishing whether one of their suspects was, or was not, a heretic. I've often wondered why their trials required the presence of such hordes of religious experts. Hard to tell, I see now, whether your suspect was celebrating a Christian, a Jewish or a Muslim holy event. The devil, as usual, was in the detail.

Youssouf drops us off, early next morning, on the outskirts of Oujda. He is last seen beetling off south towards the encroaching edges of the Sahara, a roaring blur of hay and dust. The load looks so lopsided that we can't believe he'll get more than ten miles without losing half of it. But maybe that's what Youssouf secretly wants. Speaking last night of love, romance and the Koran, after a couple more bracing swigs at our wine-bottle, Youssouf returned to the topic of his forthcoming marriage, bride still To Be Arranged.

The truth was, he confided, that he would secretly prefer to marry a black wife. The white girls are too stuck-up, they don't know how to laugh. Back home, though, if you're known to be able to afford the paler variety of bride, it is extremely disrespectful to your people not to get yourself one. But the truth is, he's been pretty keen on a certain dark-skinned girl for a while, and he thinks she likes him too. Of course, they've never actually spoken – how could they, in a small town like his? But a woman can speak volumes with her eyes . . .

10

The university town of Oujda, *The Little Cunning One* informs us, is a sprawling frontier city, much of it modern, with little to detain the traveller. We're finding plenty to detain us in the old part, though. Last stop in Morocco, and we're finally getting to thoroughly investigate a city medina. This is the first market day after Eid al-Fitr, and the chaos outside the medina walls is impressive. We've fought our way through endless stalls of vegetables and fruits, of spices and olives, of Western-style children's clothes, kaftans and jellabas, multi-coloured scarves and shawls; we've skirted round various cross-legged Berber countrywomen, squeezed through a small herd of goats and got caught up in a mule-and-cart traffic-jam outside the medina gates.

Through the gates at last, and inside the medina it's still hard to move. There are fast-food stalls – one selling enormous pancakes two feet across, another sheep's heads neatly halved, so each customer will get a little bit of tongue, of brain, of cheek-meat . . . Gérard and Guy are appalled, but I have already been initiated by southern Italian friends into the sheep's-head snack – you treat it like a salad, add vinegar and oil – and refuse to be disgusted. It is harder not to be disturbed, though, by the *Petit futé*'s revelation that the massive terracotta-coloured medina gate we just came in through is called the Bab el-Wahab, meaning the Gate of the Head, because the medieval rulers of the city had a habit of hanging the heads of people they disliked from it. The combination of visible sheep's heads dissected, and imaginary human ones a-dangling, is too much for Guy, who now sequesters the guidebook, zipping it firmly into his rucksack.

This medina is more airy and spacious than the Tetuan one – or than what I managed to glimpse of it, at any rate. Its alleyways often open out into galleried squares, each one dedicated to its own trade, colonnades arching round all four sides, shading the walkways below from the hot sun. The columns support balustraded balconies above, their inner walls intricately tiled. We weave our way through porters of water, of skins, of wood, of gas-bottles, of sacks of flour and suddenly find ourselves in the square of the makers of those country-style jellabas. A dozen treadle sewing machines sit outside the workshops in the shade of the arches, and four or five members of a family all sit stitching at the rough woollen cloth, some out in the square, some in the tiny shop behind, its wooden doors thrown open to catch the breeze. There are looms in the back of the shops: they actually weave the cloth to size, then, rather than cutting and wasting any. Yes, now I come to consider the matter, the country jellaba certainly is entirely made from plain squares and oblongs, no fitting or curves. Even the pointed hood is just a cleverly folded oblong, one side stitched together. You can still smell the lanolin in the unprocessed wool, too, I discover, when I pick one up to feel the texture, a perfume that takes me off to Scotland and fishermen's jerseys. You leave the natural oils in the wool for extra warmth and waterproofing on a Scots fishing boat. Berber herdsmen, out in the mountains in all weathers, evidently have similar requirements. A young boy passes us, carrying four loaves – or rather, four balls of shaped, risen dough – on his head, resting on a wooden board. On his way to the baker's shop, or the *hammam*, to get it baked, Guy says. Each family makes sure to put its own special mark on the dough, so they can tell their loaf apart from everyone else's when it comes back out, cooked. Essential, or all hell will break loose, as people argue over which is their own, superior, property.

After a square of weavers – rainbow-striped blankets, bright primary colours – we pass through a square filled with piles of shiny-bright silver trays and teapots: the metal-engravers' square, where the twirly designs are added to the tea-ware for that finishing touch of elegance. Through the narrow connecting alley into the next square, we step from the shade to find the most flamboyant trade yet. Out in the centre, blinding in the sunlight, shocking pink and grass-green and sky-blue prevail. Multicoloured sheep's fleeces dangle, dripping, from bamboo frames around a dozen juggernaut vats of dye. Robed figures are poised above the vats, high on rickety wooden scaffolds amid white swirling vapours and great cloudy bales of pale raw wool, straining as they stir their cauldrons with poles as long as ladders, a two-man job to heave the wool back out, heavy and steaming now, luminously bright and colourful, to drain on the racks above, staining the ground below every possible shade of rainbow-and-mud.

In the square at the end of the next alley, the passers-by seem to be stepping, crabwise, over a series of invisible obstacles. We draw closer, to see that there are indeed long skeins of thread stretching right across the centre of the square. A craftsman sits cross-legged on one side, under the shade of the arches, performing tiny complex manoeuvres with handfuls of twisted threads, while right across the square, under the opposite arches, a child – or sometimes various children – holds on to the far ends, mirroring his work to prevent tangles. We stop for a moment to watch. They are braidmakers, making the twisted-and-plaited cord that's used to decorate the borders of jellabas and kaftans; and to get across the square you have to step carefully over the braids-in-progress, one after another, like a slow-motion version of some school skipping game. It is not just the skill that's amazing, though. Equally marvellous is the fact that the craftsmen can count on so much tolerance, not to say loving care, on the part of every last passer-by.

How alienated we are, us Europeans, from our own objects of everyday use, I say to my companions. When do you ever get to see anybody making any of the stuff you buy in the shops back home? Or to marvel at their skill?

And do I know, replies Gérard, why it should be that all these centuries-old medinas of Morocco are so perfectly preserved, with the old crafts going on in them in a way that's hardly changed for centuries?

No, I don't. But I can see I'm about to be told.

It's all down to the French, it seems. And it's not something my companions are proud of. When France invaded Morocco in 1912 and took over running much of the country for the next fifty years, she put an amazing amount of effort into preserving the country's antiquities. Teams of French experts were brought here to catalogue the local artistic and architectural heritage and advise on its conservation. Their conclusions were embodied in law: all new French building was to be done outside the walls of the ancient medinas, and absolutely nothing changed within them. Moreover, a building-free area of 200 metres was always to be left empty, a *cordon sanitaire* separating the crowded Moroccan medina from the wide avenues and boulevards of the new French towns, the *villes nouvelles*. We've just come through one of those spaces on our way from the modern part of town, of course. That's where the street market was being held, on what was once the empty colonial *cordon sanitaire*, now re-occupied by bustling Moroccan life.

The mixed motivation for all this, my French informants tell me, was a paternalistic commitment to saving Morocco's heritage from a nation deemed too ignorant to appreciate its own treasures, and naked self-interest on the part of colonizers and settlers. By the time they decided to take Morocco, the French had under their belts almost a century's experience of colonizing next-door Algeria, which they had been running since they first invaded, in 1830. They had learned many lessons in this time and had concluded that the less noticeable the settler presence was, the less likely the indigenous people were to get annoyed and begin resisting the colonial regime. This was the reason the *pied-noir* farms of Algeria employed Moroccans from the next-door Rif, and even Spanish peasants from Murcia and Andalusia, as seasonal workers, rather than locals. The thing to do was to keep the two communities as separate as possible: an *apartheid* system, with no settler interference in the old Moroccan cities, which would be left to Moroccans, untouched and unchanged, while the settler-French cities developed independently alongside them.

The French settlers began actively forbidding any modernization whatsoever by the local people. In their old home towns, shopkeepers and artisans were not allowed to install glass shopfronts, or replace their old wooden doors with modern ones, or indeed to paint them any colour but brown. They were not allowed any form of street advertising and, most bizarre of all, they were not allowed to install electricity anywhere in the medina. I find this part hard to believe – with thousands of people living in the medinas, and all the tradesmen who might need it for their work! But it was so, although, as the 1940s hove into view, medina shops were finally permitted one electric light bulb each, as long as it was hidden right at the back, out of sight of passers-by.

Since the Moroccan areas of Moroccan cities were thus forcibly prevented from taking up new technologies or developing along normal twentieth-entury lines, all modern commerce and industry soon became concentrated – as luck would have it – in the hands of the French *pied-noir* settlers of the salubrious New Towns. The medinas now became virtual ghettos for Moroccans – overcrowded, insanitary and poor. Causing, naturally enough, frequent uprisings against the French presence: not at all the intended effect. Still, right through the 1940s and 50s, the French settlers went on adamantly preserving the Moroccans' heritage for them. By now, petrol had become a necessity of life, but no petrol stations were allowed anywhere except in the French *villes nouvelles*. And handily, whenever anti-French trouble broke out, the beautifully preserved gates of the medina could simply be closed, locking the indigenous residents in, while the 200 metres of empty space between the two towns made it a simple job for the French troops to round up protesters before they could get anywhere near their French targets.

So there it is. That's what I'm enjoying looking at, here in the medina of Oujda. The results of fifty years of utter vileness. Or not entirely, because the locals did get some plumbing and electricity in the end. In the 1950s, once they had got rid of their French tutors, they ran amok, Guy tells me, gaily despoiling tons of lovely old paving stones in their centuries-old medinas so as to put hygienic new sewers and proper power lines into their homes. They also demolished quite a few ancient buildings to make way for roads wide enough to take motorized vehicles.

One is appalled.

Over in the corner of this square is a narrow, winding staircase that seems to lead to the upper level, above the arches. We can see people up there – are there more stalls and workshops up above? Or is it private? We hesitate, and a gaggle of bold young girls accosts us. Who are we looking for? Do we speak French? Why are we here in Oujda? Do we like it? How come I am travelling with two Frenchmen if I am English? Which one am I married to? Can French people marry English people? Do we know their father, Hamid? He lives in France too. Or their uncle Rashid? This sister is called Zeinab, and that one is Aisha, and they have two little brothers as well, and one big one, but he's in France too, and they all live up there on the balcony above, except the ones who are in France. What are our names? Look, up there on the balcony, that's their mother, Latifa, and the other one's their aunt, Naima.

Mother and aunt look on from above, smiling, waving, nodding.

Would we like to come up and see their house? asks Zeinab, the bravest girl. Aisha translates the invitation into Arabic for the older generation's benefit, exhilarated by the naughtiness of it. Aunt and mother exchange glances for a moment, but why not? Nudging one another, giggling, they beckon us up.

Under the arch we go and up the curving staircase, carried on a tidal wave of excited, chattering children – another half-dozen infants have added themselves to the cavalcade now – to find ourselves out on a wide communal balcony above. There, down at the far end, are the mother and the aunt of our captors, next to one of the ubiquitous braziers of this land. They are still giggling, covering their mouths with their hands, as they head this way to welcome us. Two of the smaller children race up to them, clinging to their legs for security in the face of this unheard-of Europeans-in-the-home situation, while the rest carry on dragging us forward.

Half way along the balcony a venerable old man in white *chèche* and snowy jellaba sits sentinel, cross-legged on the ground outside his door, a knobbly stick across his knees, patriarchal beard flowing. He glowers as the kids dash past him, happily chattering, and shouts at them as they run in at the next door. Now, as I squeeze past in my turn, he gives me a sharp whack on the ankle with his stick. I wheel round, shocked, but he just looks straight ahead, as if nothing had happened. Maybe he's blind? Or did I just imagine it?

We're already overwhelmed, being greeted by the mother and aunt, exchanging names, getting bombarded with another twenty million questions by the youth, some of whom are sent indoors to bring out sheepskins for us to sit on. Yes, put them there, have a seat, make yourselves comfortable. Our new hostesses were just making tea – will we have some?

Yes, of course we will. Never known to refuse.

I would be lying if I said that our Arabic and Tamazight had come on at all noticeably in the last day or two. And neither Naima nor Latifa speaks more than a few words of French. No chance of Spanish, either, since the Spanish Protectorate stopped, for inscrutable imperialist reasons, just short of Oujda, which was left to the French. Still, we hardly notice the language problem among the twittering of the infants and the various French-speaking adolescent girls who are sorting everything out, keeping order, translating, bringing out the tea things. Our hostesses are excited to hear that Gérard and Guy are actual Frenchmen from France. Whereabouts in France, they want to know, and what is it like? Is it very different from here? Both Latifa's and Naima's husbands are there, it's three years now that they only come home for the French national holiday in August and then go straight back off again to work. And Latifa's oldest son Ali is there too this year, even though he's only sixteen, and she hardly recognized him in all his French clothes when he came back in the summer, and he was even talking in a French kind of a way. Would someone who lived there maybe never want to come home to Oujda afterwards? Latifa isn't sure if it's Marseilles or Paris they're working in – are those places very different from one another, then? The three smallest girls are looking on wide-eyed, their gaze moving from us to our translators Zeinab and Aisha, then to Latifa and Naima, as the conversation goes round. They are also clinging onto my hands, taking turns to sit on my lap, and slapping at one another over whose turn it is next. It's quite hard to concentrate on the conversation.

It's definitely Marseilles, says Naima. And how she would love to go too! Neither of them has ever been to France – or even out of Oujda, except for the annual pilgrimage to the *marabout* shrine of Sidi Yahia – but their husbands say that the French government won't allow them to come over, even for a visit. Is that really true? It's probably just an excuse for the boys to run around living it up, all men alone, isn't it?

While Gérard and Guy are breaking it that, alas, it is very likely true that Naima and her sister-in-law would not be allowed to join their husbands in France, even for a holiday, the old neighbour with the beard begins muttering angrily to himself. Nobody turns a hair, though my collection of little girls giggles to one another. He's a bit past his sell-by date, maybe, and always rambles on like that?

It dawns on me that the man-less life this family is leading, just females, small children and the occasional old age pensioner, is the exact counterpart to the Parisian exile of Uncle Kebir and the boys from Timimoun. The other side of the same coin. Was Kebir married? I don't think it ever occurred to me to ask him.

Latifa's and Naima's husbands – two brothers – are butchers, though, they tell us, and not building workers. But there is no skill in it, not in France, says Zeinab, translating for her mother. Here a butcher is a respected man, because knowing how to kill an animal swiftly, neatly, with no suffering and according to the precepts of Islam is an honourable skill. And then you must know how to section up the meats from the carcass afterwards, and clean the skin for the tanners to make the leather. In France Zeinab's uncle and her father – and now Ali too – kill thousands and thousands of cattle a day. But you don't need any skill, that's why her brother could go, even though he was only sixteen and didn't know anything. Her father says Ali never will learn anything, either, not in France, because there they just do the same two moves over and over again, bim, boum, bim, boum. And then they throw half the animal away, too.

It makes her father sad, says Aisha, interrupting, and he wants to come home to Morocco, doesn't he, where he could teach Ali properly, but he can't, because we need the money, and it's the *Nazrani* way, he says, because they have too much and so they always waste half of it. Zeinab, speaking in Arabic, shushes her little sister up and gives us an apologetic grin. I wish everyone here wouldn't always assume that we agree with the way things are done in the West! But then again, why should they suppose we didn't?

Latifa tells Aisha to tell us that we must go to the shrine of Sidi Yahia ourselves before we leave. He is a *marabout* highly regarded by all three Peoples of the Book: Christians, Jews and Muslims all join the pilgrimage to his tomb in the oasis a few miles outside Oujda. His is one of the best *moussems* ever!

Who can he be? we wonder. We've never heard of a Saint Yahia. Sidi Yahia bin Younes! says Latifa encouragingly.

No. Still no idea. Then Zeinab remembers what we Nazarenes call him: *Jean Baptiste*.

John the Baptist! Can this be true? But then, why not – I suppose he has to be buried somewhere, doesn't he? And then, the name 'John' is 'Yannis' in Greek, isn't it? So 'Younes' would certainly be right.

Zeinab vanishes indoors and comes out with a small brass bowl and a jug, which she fills from the tap on the balcony wall. She trickles water over our fingertips, into the bowl, three times each. You must always wash your hands three times, before you touch food or drink. Aisha puts tea, mint and sugar into the pot; her sister adds the water and stirs, slips it back on the side of the brazier to brew. No men here to perform the tea-ceremony, so anything goes. One of the little ones sets the glasses out.

Along the balcony, the aged patriarch's angry muttering continues.

What's he saying? I ask the girls, intrigued.

He probably just wants some tea, says Aisha, an answer that causes her sister to go into fits of laughter. Her mother and aunt join in too, once this exchange is translated to them. Mysterious.

Another couple of neighbours, two middle-aged women, have come along the balcony to join the fun. They squat down next to Latifa, and a lot more giggling goes on. One of them has that Berber tattoo on her chin, the vertical stripe in indigo-blue running down from her lower lip. And two little ones up on her cheekbones, too, like tiny palm-leaves. Once you get used to the idea, they start to look pretty stylish. Even if they are spoiling God's perfect creation.

The tea brewed, Latifa pours out a glass for everyone, slapping away the hands of the two smaller children, who are hoping to muscle in on this grown-up treat in the general confusion. Thank you, we say: *shukran. Shukran!* repeats Zeinab, laughing. *Shukran!* says Aisha too. Another outbreak of giggling. You sound like the *imam*, they say, preaching in the mosque! *Shukran* is the classical Arabic word. Maybe they say that in Egypt or Saudi Arabia, but it sounds stuffy and po-faced to Maghreb ears. Here, you wish people a good dose of *baraka* from God to thank them. *Baraka Allahu fik!* Say it! Try! Go on!

Another sign of the unorthodox Maghreb take on Islam, evidently.

Now Naima sends Aisha along the balcony with a glass of tea for the old man. More laughter as she nips gingerly in to set it at his knee, whereupon he raises his stick at her, roaring something – wish I could understand Arabic – while she darts back out of reach and runs to throw herself into our midst, breathless and laughing. Latifa, peeking through her fingers at this, clutches at Naima's arm, and they both go off into more fits of helpless laughter.

A violently disposed old nutter, then. Maybe he really did whack my ankle on purpose? I suppose they have to look after him anyway – those Pillars of Islam again. I'm starting to feel a bit sorry for him, all on his own down there, with half a dozen women entertaining themselves, apparently, at his expense. I sip away at the hot tea, fending off as best I can the many tiny hands that are busy investigating everything about me – from my hair to my watch to my clothes to my footwear – while Gérard and Guy get involved helping the two slightly older ones, Naima's children, who are trying to halve and stone a bag of apricots into a bowl. They're to go into tonight's chicken *tagine* – why don't we come back later and eat it with them?

I'm doing my best to join my hostesses in completely ignoring the old man with the beard, but it's not easy. The tea seemed to mollify him for a bit, all right, but then he went back to his muttering, which he is now interspersing with a sort of doom-laden chant. Suddenly, banging his stick on the ground, he lets out an almighty roar.

He wants someone to go and help him up, says Zeinab, causing yet more naughty-schoolgirl laughter. He can't do it by himself any more. Not even with the stick.

Ah, I see, I answer, untruthfully, wondering why, in that case, nobody is showing any sign of going to give him a hand. Shall I go and help him up, maybe? I ask.

This idea is so hilarious that it has everyone rocking in the aisles. Our hostesses decide to let us in on the secret. The angry old man is no mere neighbour, but Latifa's and Naima's father-in-law, the children's grandfather. And it is our own presence here that is making him so angry. Women are not supposed to invite unknown strangers into their homes, especially not unknown men, though probably unknown *Nazrani* women come a close second. Grandfather has been ordering his family to remove us from the premises immediately, ever since the moment we arrived. He has now moved on to reciting verses of the Koran that deal with the topic of immodest and insubordinate women, and how badly they will be punished – both by their husbands when they return, and by God in the hereafter. They didn't want to tell us what he was saying, in case it spoilt our visit.

The chivalrous Guy starts getting to his feet. We should leave right away . . . we're really sorry if we've caused any trouble . . .

But Latifa, still laughing, grabs Guy's sleeve and pulls him back down onto his pile of sheepskins.

She doesn't want you to go, translates Aisha. None of us want you to go! Why should we take any notice of him? What harm are we doing?

And what is he going to do about it, anyway? asks Zeinab. He can't even stand up without our help! He's got no other men to back him up – they won't be home for five months! They may shout a bit when they hear that we had foreign guests, but it won't last long, will it, because they miss our mothers too much to be horrible to them, and they'll be off back to France in no time!

Strange. Now that I know exactly what the family patriarch is saying, I find it surprisingly easy to ignore him, just the way his womenfolk do.

Another hour of translation and miming, of children's antics, pandemonium and hilarity goes by: and eventually we stand up to take our leave. The family are starting to get their meal ready – vegetable preparation takes place out here on the balcony, it seems, as well as tea-making – and we need to go and find a hotel before it gets much later. I don't care if it's a waste of precious money, I am going to take a proper shower and sleep in an actual bed, with actual sheets, at last.

A shower? But no, say the girls. I must come to the *hammam* with them! They will all be going this afternoon. It's only round the corner – the women's session goes on till six. Brilliant idea. I will come and meet them there once we've found somewhere to sleep.

Heading off along the balcony, I put on a burst of speed as we pass the bearded-patriarch danger spot. Not fast enough, though. My shin gets another whack anyway, much to everyone's entertainment.

Outrageous that he only goes for me! What about the men? Why doesn't he give Gérard and Guy a good rap on the kneecaps? Surely they're more of a threat to his family's honour than I am? As usual, women are the easy target!

The mirth from the immodest, insubordinate females above is still echoing down the stairwell as we make our crablike way back across the square, high-stepping between the braidmakers' webs.

As we wend our way back to the *ville nouvelle*, Gérard gets very excited about this encounter. Maybe, he says, some small positive thing has come out of all this migrant-worker business – if it's actually allowing Muslim women to stand up to their patriarchal menfolk!

I hope he is right. The man-free life Latifa and family are leading certainly seems to have its liberating side. But I have a horrible feeling that the tearing apart of all these families, women at home, men abroad – especially when it's been going on for generations, the way it has here – could make the Islamists' ideas more attractive, not less. Especially when it seems that it's the power of the uncaring, money-grubbing *Nazrani*, yet again, that has created the situation. I don't find it at all hard to imagine that women, as well as men, might compare the harsh insecurities of modern life with the comforting certainties of a lost Islamic idyll, their men back at home, real husbands once more, taking charge of the duties and responsibilities of family life, caring for wives and children. Latifa and Naima were positively delighting in the thought of how angry their husbands would be over their escapade with us lot, weren't they? They miss normality the way anybody does, even if normality isn't perfect. I suspect they would go happily back to the patriarchal past, just the way English and French women did after the last war, if only they could have their husbands back for good.

And then, looking at the situation from another angle, I'm sure the reactionary old stick-wielding patriarchs are gathering plenty of put-the-women-back-in-their-place ammunition to share with their absent sons when they return, if the sort of disrespectful behaviour we saw today is being repeated all over the country!

The *hammam* is a wonderful place, all dry heat and white steam, blue tiles, vaulted ceilings and deep arches, a combination of steamy gossip-shop – not that I have any idea who we're talking about – Turkish bath and intimate do-it-yourself beauty salon. There must be thirty or forty of us in here, stripped down, every conceivable age and size of woman, all of us giving one another a hand with back-scrubbing and shampooing, much naked giggling. Extraordinary to step from streets where hardly an inch of female flesh is to be seen, and crush into this intimate space crowded with naked curves. My bosom, as usual, is very interesting for those inscrutable North African reasons, even though, as I'd suspected, it doesn't look any different to anyone else's. Somehow, due to the self-consciousness brought on by this unaccustomed amount of public attention being paid to my breasts, and to having to concentrate on the intricacies of the *hammam* ritual itself, I don't notice what their bras, if any, are like. I certainly do notice, though, that many of them depilate their whole bodies – including their pubic hair. First into the changing room, where you undress and collect a pair of buckets. There are a surprising number of children in here, little boys too. They only get banished to the Men's Event when they are drawing close to puberty. What a memory for every young boy in this land to have – a lost paradise of voluptuous female nudity!

Now through to the hottest room, where the water cistern is. Fill your bucket – using the right hand only on the tap, remember – then claim your place in the middle, slightly-less-hot room. Here you splosh a bit of water on the floor where you're planning to sit, which I can't get right at all, much to everyone's entertainment, since I have no notion what I'm trying to achieve, or indeed what I'll be doing in it once I've earmarked my place. The rules, once explained, are perfectly sensible: you just have to make sure not to sit where you'll be in someone else's stream as they wash, or where your used water will go on them, since it all drains down to the plughole at the centre of the tiled floor.

Now, out comes a tub of silky black mud. We butter ourselves and one another all over with this extraordinary stuff – including the hair – then take our seats on the floor and relax. And sweat. And sweat some more. Now my hostesses and I take turns at scrubbing one another down with a giant ball of something that looks like baling twine. An amazing amount of dirt and dead skin comes away. Into the hotter room; another scrub-down. My turn to scrub Naima now – and I'm not doing it hard enough, it's not supposed to be just a tickle! There are some ladies in here doing the hands-and-feet hennaing popular with a lot of older Maghreb women. They must, I think, henna the soles of their feet and the palms of their hands every single time they come to the *hammam*, because they are dyed a deep burnt orange colour, and the tops of their fingers too, right down to the first joints, giving their nails that intriguing sixty-a-day amber colour. Zeinab tells me that everyone is hennaing all at once now, because you can't do it during Ramadan. Henna is for victory and for rejoicing, not for praying and fasting. And it doesn't only colour your skin, it makes it stronger and stops it getting rough when you do a lot of washing, or hard work on the land. Also, contributes Aisha, you put it on newborn babies' heads, so they won't be taken back from you by the envious djinns.

And on the bottoms of your feet, I guess now, because they're the part that comes closest to the djinns' home, down in the earth beneath you?

Of course, say the girls.

Latifa and Naima are melting something in a small saucepan over by the Russian-oven-like device that heats the cistern. It makes your hair lovely and shiny, they say – I must try it too. But what a pity they didn't think to bring a lemon with them, to help me with those freckles!

Bah.

The stuff in the pan looks like fragments of translucent pale-yellow quartz, except that it's melting in the heat, so it can't be. I do know, though, that I saw a whole basketful of this stuff, whatever it may be, in that shop in Tetuan. Yes! Another indecipherable commodity nailed, by use, if not by name. Once it's melted, you smooth it through your wet hair, wait five minutes, and then rinse it off. And the results are amazing. Unfortunately, I've never managed to track it down again. Its Arabic name, unwritable in any alphabet I could read, went in one ear and out the other. Could it have been silicone?

A party of Naima's friends arrives: a bunch of happy, excited women and girls getting ready for a wedding, who have come to do the required elaborate henna traceries to their feet and the palms of their hands. I am so gripped watching the skill of the expert – an extremely old lady wearing masses of kohl in her eyes – as she trickles on the intricate fine designs of henna paste that I completely forget that I'm standing here naked. Mind you, so is the expert. What a brilliant institution the *hammam* is! It must be very good for your mental health, too, constantly seeing such a huge variety of other ordinary women's bodies in a state of undress. It would certainly stop you neurosing about your own. Though, speaking of neurosing, I certainly don't envy them all that depilation. A few feet away from the henna-lady two women are removing the hair from one another's legs by a strange technique involving running bits of thread up and down them. I can't understand how it works, even when they demonstrate it on my own legs. You twiddle two threads together, and somehow they grip on to each hair as they roll past, and rip it out by the follicle. Some women in here have gone a lot further than the Brazilian: not only no hair at all, but the intimate area in question highlighted with an arc of henna instead. If they even so much as mention trying that one on me, I'll be out of here so fast . . .

Now everyone decides that I would look a lot better with some kohl in my eyes, and somebody produces a strange little object like a tiny leather bottle, with an applicator-stick of made of a sliver of smooth bone. Now, lean your head back, shut your eyes – and the stick is whisked between your shut eyelids. *Voilà!* Everyone agrees that I am greatly improved.

Seeing how spellbound I am by the henna-designs, Latifa and Naima convince the henna-lady to stop the intricate stuff for a moment and apply something quick and simple to my hand. Mischievously, they suggest a moon and a star in my palm. Everyone is giggling as she paints it on: but then everyone is always giggling in here, so I suspect nothing. Later this evening I will discover what it signifies: that I've just got engaged. And for the next fortnight, until it starts to wear off, I will have to remember to keep it hidden – or put up with constant cackling enquiries as to when the wedding is.

We leave the *hammam*, all pink and glowing, just as Ladies' Time is coming to an end. I am wearing the towel on my head, as Islamic health theory prescribes. And I have discovered that, if you're female, there is a lot more to it than just your own health. You are wearing it for the sake of men's souls. Apparently the sight of wet hair on a female, implying that she has recently been naked – and possibly having intercourse with her husband, since she may have been doing her ritual post-coital cleansing, as prescribed by the Koran – is enough to inflame the senses of any poor, weak men she passes and drive them beyond the limits of temptation. They might easily *commettre une faute malgré eux* – commit a fault in spite of themselves. Is this 'fault' the same as a sin? Would it be in thought, word or deed? I daren't ask.

I didn't realize, I say, that the theory behind the *hijab* was that men needed protecting from their own weakness. I'd always imagined it was more or less the opposite. But little Aisha and Zeinab assure me that this is so. Women must cover up to help men, because they cannot help themselves.

Gérard and Guy are sitting outside a café down the alley, waiting outside to take their turn as soon as the men's time begins. My towel works brilliantly. Not only do they not commit any faults, but for some perplexed moments they don't recognize me at all, with my enveloping headgear and startling black-lined eyelids.

The attendants will soon signal the changeover from women's to men's *hammam* time by simply removing the bit of cloth that's been hanging over the street door. Cloth means women: no cloth means men. Gérard and Guy wait for the Sign that they may head on into the steam, while I go back with Latifa, Naima and gang to wait for them. With a small detour, that is, to an area of the market we missed previously, which the girls feel I should see because it is full of great bargains in the world of toiletries – an area called the Melilla souk, where all the gear brought over from Spanish Africa by the privileged inhabitants of the border towns or by local smugglers gets sold on. Almost all household items are cheaper on the Spanish side of the border than here – from soap and shampoo to towels and sheets. It is mostly women who do these smuggling-runs, they say; the lady smugglers bind their purchases onto their midriffs with lengths of cloth – often so much stuff that they look absurdly huge around the middle. Then they slip their jellaba on over the top, and off they go. They don't care how obvious it looks, because they know that the frontier guards, men and Muslims, could never manhandle a woman, or insist that she undress before them! The guards do their best to punish the female contrabandists by making them wait hours before they finally let them back through the border. But why should that bother them? They are expecting it, they're used to it, and they know they'll be let through eventually – and make enough profit to feed their families for a month! A fine creative use of Islamic tradition.

Faced with the Grandfather Situation again, I decide that I am certainly not going to scuttle past him like a naughty child this time. I shall greet him properly, holding my head high beneath my towel, and see if I can't make him feel a bit discourteous at the very least. The *labass* greeting, a bit on the friendly-and-casual side, is certainly not good enough for this occasion. I want to greet him ceremoniously, religious-style. So as I walk towards him, I politely announce *As-salamu aleikum*.

Absolutely no response – not even so much as a grunt. He does not wish me peace, he just straightens his back to ramrod stiffness and stares right ahead. He's certainly very convinced of the correctness of his behaviour. But look, maybe it has worked after all. He hasn't raised his stick!

As soon as we've sat down by the brazier, with the *tagine* now simmering upon it, tended by Naima's boys, everyone starts insisting that we must stay for the meal – there is plenty for everyone. Is there no end to the hospitality of Moroccans? I manage to say no, against much protestation from the hostesses. I don't think I can take much more multilingual socializing. And then, of course, there is the lure of the real bed with the real sheets . . . I badly need to let all these experiences settle down in my head, to sit quietly in a room all on my own.

I am ashamed of this thought when I am called inside Latifa and children's home, where the three little girls are now putting on an impromptu dancing display in my honour, while Aisha accompanies them on a sort of double-sided tambourine with a big red henna handprint on the drumskin. Nobody who lives here has the remotest chance of sitting quietly in a room on their own, that's for sure. Their whole home turns out to be just this one room, opening straight off the balcony. I'd imagined it was an entrance, leading into a flat somewhere at the back of the building. But this is all there is: each of the doors along the balcony leads to just one room. There is no furniture in here at all. A tin chest sits in the corner, and there are four neat piles of sheepskins against the walls. The plumbing is the tap on the balcony; the balcony is the kitchen. On the tin chest stand two enamel washing-up bowls, the jug I met earlier, a round-bellied cooking pot and a *couscoussier*. Everything is scrupulously clean and tidy. On a shelf in a wall embrasure sits the tray, holding the neatly washed teapot and glasses, together with some screws of brown paper: the tea, mint and sugar. Nothing else. This is the sum total of the family's possessions. Naima's is next door: it's identical. The boys sometimes sleep in with Grandpa, two doors along, and sometimes here with their mamma. And the beds? The sheepskins are piled up for seats by day, spread out for sleep at night. The sheets are in the chest. Thanks to those paving-stone vandals of the 1960s, there's a single light bulb in the ceiling, at least, and a shared loo in the corner of the stairwell. And you don't need a bathroom because you have the *hammam*.

The girls are now dragging me over to join in the dancing, trying to tie a shawl around my hips. I do my best to copy their hip-waggles. The shawl, knotted at the side, emphasizes the movement so dramatically that you quickly get the hang of the thing, weight on one leg, other knee bent, a quick sideways jerk of the pelvis. Aisha starts speeding up the beat, and all the little girls are jiggling and squeaking along with me, when I suddenly realize that we have a large audience at the door. Not just Latifa and Naima but the neighbour women and plenty more children. The doorway is filled with eyes, at every possible height. And, right at the back, Gérard and Guy, now jubilantly clean. Embarrassed, I try to scuttle off to the side of the room, but no chance. The women all start joining in, dancing their way into the room and doing that *you-you*-ing in their throats, clapping, waggling, banging their hips flirtatiously into mine as they work their way round the room. The little girls are hysterical with joy. Pandemonium. Is this the way they always carry on of an evening? What they need is a nice quiet TV set.

Eventually, as darkness begins to fall, things calm down, and the sheepskins are brought in, this time to play the role of sofas. The men's version of the *hammam*, as told by Gérard, sounds a lot tougher than the ladies' one. You get a ferocious pummelling and stretching from a big fat masseur who seems intent on rending you limb from limb. Guy doesn't believe it's always like that – he's sure they were getting some macho test for foreigners. Either that or all the men here are double-jointed! They feel wonderful now it's over, though, and they are absolutely starving!

Our generous hostesses immediately start offering to share their *tagine* again, and I pinch Gérard's leg hard, from my sheepskin seat, before he starts accepting. We are certainly not going to eat any of their food. They seem a lot worse off even than Khadija's family, in spite of having two husbands sending money back from France. What on earth sort of wages do French abattoirs pay? We agree to come back tomorrow instead and have lunch with them before we leave for the border. Much better – at least if we come tomorrow we'll be able to bring them a bit of shopping, a couple of chickens or whatever, some small gift to balance things out.

We wander off through the town and find a small friendly couscous place for our dinner. I can hardly wait to get it down my neck and be off to that quiet hotel room on my own. Not only am I worn out with foreignness, but even when I'm relaxing I still have to speak French. When I get to the hotel I'm going to talk out loud to myself in English for half an hour, I decide, in case I end up forgetting how to do it. But the evening is destined to be longer than I expected. Suddenly, one of the waiters appears bearing an extra bottle of wine. Compliments of the house, he says, smirking. And which of you is the lucky man?

11

Gérard and Guy must have done some fine networking down at the *hammam* last night. Every man in Oujda seems to be wishing us No Harm as we stroll about the town, trying to find a chicken shop in which to buy our parting gift for Latifa and family. *Labass*, we answer casually, as if to the manner born. Eventually, with the help of a large number of interested bystanders, we track one down, in the medina – a most extraordinary shop, or booth rather, its shopfront embellished with a lurid ten-foot-tall painting of a crowing cockerel, cut out of a bit of hardboard. One in the eye both to the tasteful French and the repressive Islamists. Underneath the cockerel lies – rather contradictorily, you might think – a large pile of eggs in a wide-mouthed basket. Towards the rear of the establishment several rows of nesting boxes are fixed to the wall, while at its centre, on a floor covered in a layer of straw, a dozen or so live chickens are pecking and clucking. At the back sits the owner, who seems to be an intimate friend of every member of the small crowd that has delivered us to his door.

Tentatively, with a picture in mind of a nice ready-plucked clingfilm-wrapped specimen, we ask about chickens for eating: but in our hearts we already know what the answer will be. Yes. Just pick the ones we like the look of. This event suddenly takes on the nature of a test. Does any of us three have the faintest idea how to detect, by looking at a live chicken, how good it will be to eat? No. The two things – obviously rather intimately connected – belong in our addled *Nazrani* minds to completely separate categories. A cosy, feathery creature clucking about a farmyard or a pallid headless-and-legless oven-ready thing in a butcher's shop. (Debating amongst ourselves, we find that we have another *idée fixe*, derived from the intensive chicken-industries of our lands: that the chickens that give you eggs cannot be the same ones you eat. We quickly discard this notion. What an alienated bunch we are.) So, on with the dilemma of choice. Are we going to choose the wrong one, and have the chicken salesman snickering behind our backs? Nothing else for it. Gérard shuts his eyes and selects two at random, complaining that he has never passed the death sentence on a living creature until today. The shop man, looking quizzically on at all this performance over a simple chicken dinner, starts picking up our chosen victims.

But we have reckoned without our cortège: they are having none of it. Two of the boys now demonstrate the correct way of selecting a chicken: you pick it up, ignoring its protests, and you prod and squeeze at breast and thigh, checking for meatiness. Then you argue about the price for quite a long time, telling the owner what pathetic skinny creatures they are, while he tells you that, *au contraire*, they are prime specimens, the like of which you will not find for many miles around. Eventually, two chickens are selected and removed to the back of the booth. A squawk or two later, and our gift is ready. We bear the victims off to Latifa's, tied together unceremoniously by the feet, necks lolling horribly. The children spot us from the balcony as we and our cortège are still threading our way painstakingly through the braid-plaiting, in the style of the Ministry of Silly Walks, and the whole family comes down into the square to receive us. Now they send our chicken-purchasing companions packing, in no uncertain terms. Good. I've been fearing that we might worsen the outraged-Grandpa situation immeasurably if we entered his house yet again – this time accompanied by a large number of local witnesses to his inability to control his womenfolk.

But all is well. The patriarch is indoors, lying down, and we get along the balcony unscathed. They have a huge pot of *harira* ready for lunch, which we eat with great chunks of bread instead of spoons.

Honour is satisfied. An hour or so later, bidding many farewells to everyone, we goose-step our way back across the square.

Algeria, here we come.

Before we have even managed to establish exactly which bus will take us to the frontier, and what its timetable is, one of the boys' new *hammam* friends, passing by in a decrepit Renault, offers to drive us there. He has nothing better to do, he says, and it's not far. He needs to go that way to get himself some petrol anyway. We climb in and off we shoot. Ahmed will take us the unofficial way, he says, which is quicker because you don't have to mess about with all the paperwork. That's the way most people go, from round here, and they do it often, because petrol is an awful lot cheaper over the border, among the Algerian cousins, who have their own oil wells, and are happy to share.

We drive out of Oujda towards a broad, undulating plain, nice and green compared to that last parched stretch of the Rif, streams and their accompanying greenery criss-crossing it. We soon come to an area of very swish mini-mansions, mostly in a somewhat brash 1970s style, complete with suburban-type gardens. Émigrés' houses, says Ahmed. Rich people.

I puzzle over this remark for some time before realizing these are not émigrés from another country, but Moroccan ex-émigrés like Yazid – returnees who have managed to build the fine house they'd always dreamed of. Ahmed tells us that the émigrés have gone a lot further than this to make a good impression in the neighbourhood – they've even built a new mosque on the outskirts of town to show everyone how devout they still are, even after all those years among the faithless Nazarenes. And the funniest part of it is that, after spending all that money to make a good impression, not one of them is ever seen there at prayer-time.

Another five minutes out of town, and we're off the main road, heading along a wide, dusty track across the plain. After a while it begins to make a long curve around the back of a stand of low trees.

All of a sudden we are in a broad, empty field, deeply rutted with many dried-up tyre-tracks, with something of the aspect of a very lumpy parking lot. There are various cars dotted about the place: and a largish lorry is parked tight up against the vegetation.

That is the *bombardier*, says Ahmed, the lorry that brings over clandestine supplies for people who need more than just a tankful of petrol. We'll carry on another couple of kilometres and get back on the main road again, Algerian side.

Fortunately it now strikes Gérard that an unstamped passport could cause all sorts of problems for us Europeans if we happen to get stopped and asked for our papers as we travel through Algeria. Especially if there are going to be lots of extra patrols on the roads, with all the trouble going on. Taking this back way in, just to save half an hour, could be a bad mistake.

It's all the same to him, says Ahmed. He'll fill his tank here, from the *bombardier*, and we'll set back off the way we came.

Twenty minutes later, he drops us off in view of the Algerian frontier post, does a slaloming U-turn, and vanishes back towards Oujda in a cloud of dust.

This little deviation from our official route would hardly be worth mentioning, were it not for the role that this unofficial back door into Algeria will play in a few years' time. Once the new millennium has got under way, many Black Africans will begin to turn up in Oujda, heading for the Melilla fence – if you can call a solid metal construction, now twenty feet high, a fence – to seek asylum or work in Europe. There are plenty of black students at the university here, so they don't stand out as much in Oujda as they might elsewhere in Morocco, and much of the local population is sympathetic to their situation.

Not so the Moroccan police, though. Morocco, still keen to curry economic favour with Europe, has agreed to join the battle to keep its borders secure. The royal forces of law and order will begin raiding immigrant communities as far away as the city of Rabat, rounding people up at random, throwing them at gunpoint into convoys of buses and driving them through the night to Oujda, crossing the border secretly, at this very spot, and dumping their prisoners many miles inside Algeria, on the fringes of the desert. On Christmas Eve 2006, at least 450 men, women and children were driven across this field and on illegally into Algeria, where they were abandoned in the wilderness without food or water.

The good citizens of Oujda had been horrified on various earlier occasions to find numbers of starving, badly dehydrated victims of this treatment coming stumbling into their city, but this was the worst case so far. There had already been an unknown number of deaths on the Ceuta frontier: shooting sprees by both Spanish and Moroccan forces. Unknown numbers, because the victims' bodies can so easily slip into the Mediterranean, never to be seen again. Their families and friends back home won't be raising any hue and cry, either: they weren't expecting to hear from them any time soon.

There has been a massive outcry among Moroccans who do not wish to see their country doing Europe's dirty work. How could the victimless crime of trying to cross a border deserve the death penalty? And in the Oujda case, a long, slow death penalty, by thirst and starvation in the desert. With the help of Médecins sans Frontières, international opinion was aroused – for a while, at any rate – over these Oujda events, and hopefully the cruel dumping has stopped.

Meanwhile, the Ceuta authorities have recently begun digging some sort of massive trench around their city. Who knows what the future will hold? If they dig deep enough, they may perhaps manage to detach Ceuta from its African moorings and drag it right off across the Mediterranean to safety.

At the Algerian frontier, we fill in rather a lot of forms asking all sorts of insanely irrelevant questions. I am already nervous about crossing this border, what with all the rumours about violence and tales of Islamist guerrillas attacking border posts. Nervous and bored at the same time is, as I may have mentioned, a bad combination for me. Finally, when I am asked the full names of both my parents, I become seriously exasperated. What on earth has that got to do with anything?

But Gérard and Guy don't seem to think it's particularly odd. You often get asked that in France, too, on official documents, they say.

Well, you can certainly tell whose colony Algeria used to be, then.

Escaping from the form-filling bureaucrats in their booths at long last, we take in a good, long, deep breath of fresh Algerian air. But the freedom is not to last. I am now selected by a young female border guard in immaculately tailored uniform, very modern and Western-looking compared to any female outfits I've seen since we got off the ferry, to be taken off and searched.

She's obviously not an Islamist, at any rate. But what if the opposition launches an attack at this very moment? I have gone from nervous to extremely nervous now. Why on earth didn't we take Ahmed's advice? Once we reach the privacy of the shiny steel cabin in which the search is to take place, though, I discover that the true object of my captor's interest is not the putative drugs, arms, or wads of illicit money that I may be trying to smuggle into her country; not religion or politics; but the contents of my toilet bag. In fact, she is about the only person we will meet in the whole of Algeria who says not a word about suspended elections, armies or arrests.

Instead, together we go minutely through my every toiletry, examining and testing my deodorant and my cleansing wipes, my tinted lip salve and my almost-dried-up mascara. We admire my stripy toothpaste, squeeze a bit out to make sure it really does come out in stripes, and – intimates by now – discuss the use of interdental floss and its *raison d'être*.

There is nothing like this to be had in Algeria, she says eventually, wistfully caressing the double-ended two-shades-of-metallic-green eye pencil she's found right down at the bottom of the bag, while I stand there twitching, fearing that we are about to move on to a full-body search.

Nothing here, she adds, but boring old traditional kohl! How she would love to own such a beautiful thing!

I have never, ever used this eye-pencil since the day I bought it. It was a terrible mistake, and I didn't even know I had it with me. What can I do but make it a gift? I wonder for a moment whether to add the toothpaste, which was clearly a big hit, but then I would have to find some Algerian toothpaste before tonight. Can I bear to make my life that complicated? I needn't have worried. We're about to go through the rest of my luggage, anyway. Plenty of time to discover that there are no stretch lace bras to be had in Algeria, nor matching knickers either . . .

Twenty minutes later, having thoroughly corrupted this flower of Algerian womanhood with my degenerate Western trinkets, and without having removed so much as a stitch of clothing – though I have, naturally enough, been given a friendly prod in the bosom area – I emerge, blinking, into the sunlight, arm in arm with my new best mate. Gérard and Guy, who have been biting their nails and fearing the worst all this time, are flabbergasted.

Soon we are waiting for the bus towards the city of Tlemcen – first stop on the road towards Algiers. A bus which everyone at the border post agrees definitely exists, but about whose exact timetable very little, it seems, is known.

Guy, uttering a cry of joy, pulls the now dog-eared *Little Cunning* guide to Morocco from Gérard's back pocket and hurls it into a handy bush to biodegrade. Its day is done. Time for our first Algerian travel lesson.

We stand here in the warm spring sunshine for about three-quarters of an hour, during which time less than a dozen vehicles pass – this is obviously not a nation of car-owners – but every single one of them pulls in to see if we need a lift. Most of them are only going a few miles, so we just thank them and pass the time of day – where are we from, where are we going, nice weather, yes, but what a pity it didn't rain more this spring. Obviously Algerians just have more time to take an interest in one another than most people in Europe, with the possible exception of Ireland, where I recall having experienced something very similar.

Now comes a car so tightly packed with passengers that nobody else could possibly fit in. The driver stops anyway, to apologize for not being able to give us a lift. A granny in the back seat is wearing a small triangular half-a-hanky veil over her nose and mouth, an item so ferociously starched and folded that it sticks out like a strange white lace-edged beak. I do my best not to stare, but it's hard work.

Gérard, meanwhile, seizes this great opportunity to do some research into Algerian public opinion, asking everyone who stops – once we have covered such essentials as our destinations, our provenance, and recent local weather conditions – what they think about the cancelled elections and the Islamist arrests. At last, he says, he is free to collect his own news reports – which nobody at all can make him throw in a bin!

He has been very heartened to hear that a certain Mohammed Boudiaf is about to take over the leadership of the emergency government. Boudiaf, he says, really is a man of principle, and one of the old heroes of the war against the French, too, which might do something to reunite the country. He left Algeria – and the Front for National Liberation – in disgust, not long after it had won the war. He said that the organization should be disbanded right away, that their country needed a freely elected government to run it now, not an unelected revolutionary army and its political wing. Boudiaf has certainly been proven right about the corruption that would overtake his country if that was not done. He's lived in exile ever since. The FLN and their army must be pretty desperate to have asked him to come back, since he's always argued for their destruction! But if he's really agreed to come, he may be the saving of Algeria.

Gérard's roadside opinion poll has come up with four people who voted for the Islamic Front, four who don't want to say, and three who voted loyally for the FLN, which has run the country for the last thirty years. Not one of the passing car-loads agrees with the arrests of the Islamists, and Gérard finds this very cheering, too.

Personally, I don't know why he cares if they're locked up. They sound like a horrible lot. Why are they so obsessed with women, anyway? No schools for women, no jobs for women, no divorce for women unless the man wants it, no property rights for women, go around in a big black bag or a daft white beak of you're a woman . . . is there no other content to their politics? There doesn't seem to be.

Gérard doesn't think it's really about women, though. It's about family life. The only part of people's identity that the colonizers didn't manage to mess about with. The only vestige of self-respect they managed to keep. That, and their religion. That's why the two things are so inextricably linked, whenever people here talk of resisting the encroachments of the West.

I don't know why Gérard thinks their family lives haven't been messed about with. Look at Latifa and Naima not seeing their husbands from one year to the next. Or Youssouf's town, where you can't afford to get married unless you emigrate first. But I suppose he'll just tell me that that's post-colonial.

Anyway, I say, it all comes down to picking on women in the end – whatever the motives behind it.

Well, all right, maybe they are horrible, says Gérard, but you still don't want to just arrest them and lock them up. That turns them into martyrs. A terrible mistake. You want to beat them in open, democratic debate.

Really? I think my preferred method of beating them would be round the head with a large cast-iron frying-pan.

No wonder nobody's too bothered about the details of the bus timetable round here. The point of standing at a bus stop here in Algeria, we finally grasp, is not necessarily to catch a bus at all. You are just signalling to any passer-by, in any vehicle, that you are trying to go somewhere and need some transport. So there's no point fussily waiting for an actual bus when we'll obviously get to Tlemcen, only sixty-odd miles away, with or without one – though maybe in a lot of small steps. We accept the next offer of a lift. Ali will drop us at a crossroads further on, he says, where another Tlemcen-bound bus joins this road, thus doubling our chances of coming across one.

Sounds good. We climb in, Guy at the front, Gérard in the back with me. As we travel, Gérard begins fishing around in his rucksack; with a conspiratorial nod in Guy's direction, he sneaks something out of it, which he holds low on his lap for my inspection, giving me a surreptitious wink. Oh, no. *The Little Cunning* guide to Algeria.

The Sahara may start only sixty-odd miles to the south, but heading east towards Tlemcen, still running parallel to the Mediterranean, we are soon driving through tree-lined country roads, across a broad and fertile plain of undulating fields and endless serried vineyards. Surely we are back in some region of southern France? Have we fallen through some hole in the space-time continuum? Long, straight highways are shaded by trees evenly spaced along their verges, boles painted white, *midi*-style; out beyond the avenues of trees stretch the endless rows of vines coming into leaf; there are small country towns of ochre-and-yellow French provincial architecture, with leafy squares and pavement cafés at their centres. The stone-built farms and big vineyard estates all look weirdly familiar, amid fields of potatoes and beans, orchards of apples, pears and apricots. We even pass a shuttered and lost-looking French-provincial church. It is tragically obvious that the builders and owners of all this bucolic charm had no notion that one day they would suddenly have to up sticks and leave it all behind, abandon their whole lives and start over . . .

I sneak a look at Guy. If it's making me feel nostalgic on their behalf, what effect can all this *pied-noir* legacy be having on him?

What we need are a few bracing statistics. Here goes. In 1960, after 130 years of French rule, two-thirds of Algerians – six million of them – no longer owned the traditional crops and livestock with which they had once fed themselves. When the French arrived, literacy levels in Algeria had been similar to those of France itself. By now, only four per cent of Algerians could read and write. And French social-scientists had come up with the perfect technical term to describe the effects of their nation's policies on the Algerian people:

clochardisation. Beggar-ization. Down-and-out-ization. How had this come about?

Guy says that when his nation arrived here, most of Algeria, beyond its few sophisticated merchant cities, was a land of self-governing tribes, with a complex and ecologically balanced economy, developed over the millennia. The settled, farming clans of the fertile lowlands grew the grain, fruit and vegetables the country needed. Meanwhile the nomads, wandering the highlands with their flocks and herds, produced the country's wool, meat and dairy goods, and brought their livestock down to graze upon, and fertilize, the grain-lands at fallow times of year. Their camel- and mule-trains provided the country's transport system. Any surplus went to fund the mosques and *zawiyas* which provided for education and spiritual needs, and trained the country's lawyers and teachers.

But to the European colonizers, this low-key economy of mutual exchange appeared as: no economy at all. To businesslike French eyes, the Algerian lowlands, ripe for intensive commercial exploit-ation, were being used in an insanely lackadaisical manner. Clearly, they must be taken in hand. According to the prevalent European world-view – horribly similar to the received wisdom of our own era – a free market was the solution to all evils. Land, like everything else, must have a commercial value. But if land was owned collectively, by a whole clan, who could buy or sell it? Nobody. *Ergo*, tribal lands must be privatized – into competent French hands. Guy's compatriots simply sequestered vast swathes of Algeria's best farmland, destroy-ing at a stroke the delicate balance between nomad and settlement, and, combining force and cunning, dismantled the traditional sys-tems of land tenure, along with the Islamic legal framework that safeguarded them.

Naturally, this involved seizing all property owned by Islamic institutions. No more schooling for Algerians, and no more lawyers to protect their rights. Guy says the Algerians were declared French subjects, like it or not, but they could claim no legal rights as French citizens – unless they abandoned their religion.

The Christian persecution, begun so long ago in el-Andalus, had moved on inland from the Mediterranean coastal strip, it seemed, and arrived, victorious, in the heartlands of the Maghreb, which were soon covered in good, profitable vineyards and modern, mechanized wheatfields – no nomad grazing allowed here, thank you – while Algerian peasant families were left to scrape a living from the marginal lands of no interest to commercial developers.

Ironically enough, by the time France decided to provide some education for Algerians – an educated elite, they now hoped, would replace the old clan leaders they had destroyed, and form a soothing bridge between colonizers and colonized, while a chance to better themselves might calm the rebellious masses – it was too late. The new French-educated Algerians simply took the lessons of the French Revolution to heart, turned on the hand that fed them, and joined the fight for Liberty and Equality along with the illiterate and the dispossessed of the villages.

And now, Guy says, things got even worse. His country began emptying out, at gunpoint, every village suspected of sheltering the rebels. Three million country people were driven from their homes. You can even see film of it, too, he says, because, as they burnt the roofs off thatched cottages throughout the land, the French army proudly recorded its progress on camera. Now for the finishing touch: herding the peasant farmers into the *regroupement* camps, where those thousands of nomads already languished pasture-less, amid the barbed wire, no longer in any position to supply our friend Mohammed the father with the customary cargoes of figs, dates and camel-hair burnouses.

No wonder Guy described Algeria under French tutelage as a hell on earth.

The south of France mirage is soon broken, anyway. Here come two straw-hatted shepherds in hooded jellabas, leading a flock of sheep and new-born lambs: much more Joseph of Arimathea than Jean de Florette. Amidst orchards of apple, pear, and cherry, the domed, whitewashed tomb of a *marabout* appears. Outlined against the rolling green acres, a huge stork's nest balances atop the minaret of a mosque. The old men lounging companionably in the street cafés in the next Place de la Mairie, shaded by tightly pollarded plane trees, are not dressed in berets and *bleus de travail*, but in burnous and *chèche*.

Further on, the early fruits of this generous countryside's abundance are being sold by the side of the road. Ali stops the car to buy a sack of potatoes; other vendors are hawking loaves of freshly baked bread, strings of red onions, huge bags of freshly caught snails – at a bargain price, too, according to Gérard and Guy. What a pity we have nowhere to cook them, *n'est-ce pas?*

Back in the car, we're soon on the hot topic of the constitutional crisis and the Islamic Front. Ali says that the arrests of the leaders and the real troublemakers, the city mobs, was right. But arresting properly elected representatives – the Islamic Front candidates who were voted in to the town halls last year – is absurd. There may be a few bad apples among them, but many of them are good, pious men. The *Pouvoir*, the powers-that-be, have foisted their own men on the local authorities to replace them. Some of these new town hall usurpers have already been shot at. The Mouvement Islamique Armée is re-forming. And Ali is sure they won't have much trouble recruiting. What do the *Pouvoir* expect? Anyone would think they were doing it on purpose. Why set up a multi-party system, go on about democracy and choice and then laugh in everyone's face? This country has a tradition of fighting back when it has no other outlet.

I don't like to seem selfish, I say, but is there any chance that these armed Islamists will have it in for European travellers like ourselves?

Ali laughs at the very idea. Of course not. This is between Algerians, he says, echoing Samir back in Italy. Nothing to do with foreign tourists.

Soon, true to his word, Ali drops us off, with much well-wishing, at a crossroads bus stop twenty or thirty miles down the road.

Baraka Allahu fik, we say, in correct Moroccan-Maghreb style. Will it be the right thing to say here, too? Yes: a triumph. Ali, naturally enough, answers with yet another unfamiliar expression, but at least he doesn't laugh.

Here at the crossroads, exactly the same thing happens as at our last bus stop. We enjoy the spring greenery, the almond trees to one side of us, the olive groves to the other, the warm sunshine, and the company of plenty of nice people who wish they had enough room to give us a lift and have no idea when the next bus is coming. I'm hardly bothered anyway. I've found a rather comfortable rock to sit on, next to a clover patch with a lot of bees buzzing around it, and asked to borrow Gérard's new *Little Cunning One* for my entertainment and enlightenment, causing controversy to break out between him and Guy. Gérard is now scowling at me as if it was my fault. Surely he didn't seriously intend to try and conceal his sins right the way through Algeria? Once we reach Algiers and turn south, he and Guy still have another 2,000 kilometres of Algeria to cross before they reach the Malian frontier and throw it away. I know this for a fact, because it says so, under '*Géographie*', right here at the front of the book.

After a while, I find that the bees have begun to focus their attentions less on the clover than on my T-shirt. It is, indeed, a sort of cloverish pink but, I would imagine, a lot less nutritious than the plant itself. Still, man does not live by bread alone – and I daresay something similar applies to bees.

Our bucolic how-do-you-do-to-every-passer-by scenario reaches a climax of oddity when a small, wiry-looking man on a motorbike pulls in beside us. The fact that he is riding the bike in a jellaba, with an orange *chèche* wound doughnut-style round his head in place of a helmet, does not decrease the oddness quotient. We chat for some minutes of this and that, thoroughly covering the classical topics: our provenance, our destination, the weather conditions, along with a new addition – the unfortunate laws of physics that prevent four people and three bags fitting onto a motorbike. Now, friendship having developed thus far, our interlocutor decides that obviously we need to come and see his home before we travel any further.

Do we?

Yes, we certainly do. We are here to see Algeria, are we not? His is an historic house. He will go back there now and get his cousin Hamid, who has a car. Hamid will bring us to the house; we will all have some coffee; and then he will take us back onto the bus route, but several kilometres further on. Yes? *D'accord?*

Yes indeed! It seems possible that the Algerians may even outdo the Moroccans for hospitality. And we haven't had any coffee for days.

The man on the motorbike shakes all of our hands with a grip of steel, announcing that his name is Khaled, before taking off in style, *chèche*-tail and jellaba flying in the slipstream, to fetch the cousin. Within five minutes, our friend is back, riding in cavalcade with the cousin behind him in an old black Citroën, the fish-faced kind of Citroën that hisses and rises up alarmingly by several inches when you turn on the ignition.

Hamid is altogether a much larger and more expansive man than his cousin, with an impressively curling moustache. Flanked by our motorbike outrider, we set off down a long, straight tree-lined side-road. Soon we are driving through another perfect vineyard, heading for a stand of taller trees. Rounding the trees, we come face to face with the house, and stand amazed. We are in the gravel forecourt of a massive French-colonial villa, all plaster curlicues and colonnaded front doors, high windows with intricate mouldings and green-slatted shutters, narrow pagoda-roofed verandas. No wonder they want to show the place off to every passer-by they come across! Major surprise, all the more so since neither of the cousins gives the impression of being especially well-heeled.

We don't go in through the main door, though, but round the side of the building, passing through a beautifully kept kitchen garden between the main building and a row of outhouses, and in through a smaller, side door. Do our hosts just work here, maybe? Along a low corridor with lots of doorways in it now. These must be the servants' quarters, where the kitchens and suchlike will be – but no, we are ushered straight on, to stop at a pair of gleaming brass-handled mahogany double doors. Hamid opens them with a flourish, and we step into so much light and space that I can hardly make sense of it at all. An absolutely enormous room with a high ornate ceiling from which four great glass chandeliers hang, the sunlight sparkling off them, while four massive French windows give onto a terrace with a broad and beautiful view across vineyards, fruit trees, rolling fields, cypress trees, and yet more vineyards stretching right off into the distance. The floor in here is of polished wooden parquet; the glass in the French windows is bevelled; the walls are mirrored and intricately moulded-and-corniced. Surely this must once have been a ballroom?

The furnishing somewhat confuses the issue, though. In each corner there are two or three sofas, set at right angles to one another and dwarfed by their majestic surroundings. In the huge space in the centre, half a dozen small children are playing, while two slightly older ones race around them, skidding across the parquet on a sheepskin.

We all take our seats on the brown velour suite in the nearest corner. The one opposite us, fifteen yards away, is a peculiarly vibrant shade of purple. There is a rather antique-looking TV set beside us, a long, low coffee table and – naturally – a brazier to one side, where the water already simmers for our coffee. From here, we can see two youths out on the terrace, tools spread around them, fixing a Vélosolex bike under the shade of a vine-leaf pergola. It gives me a momentary pang of homesickness.

What do we think of the house, then? ask the cousins gleefully, though certainly they have already seen that we're gratifyingly gobsmacked.

This ballroom, they explain, is now a living room, or rather, four living rooms – a corner each for four families, hence the many three-piece suites. Each corner has its own TV, too, I now see, and its own brazier. The room is so enormous I don't suppose they ever get annoyed by one another's choice of TV programme. There is still ample space in the centre for the communal nursery area, where another four children have now joined the others to sit observing, wide-eyed, the fascinating foreigners.

The place is amazing, we all agree. *Incroyable!* What luxury! And do the fields and the vineyards go with the house?

They certainly do, and the flour-mill and winery round at the side, too. We'll go and inspect the premises after our coffee. Khaled's and Hamid's families moved in here once the French owners had run off. No point leaving it lying empty, was there? Six families live in here now, where once there was only one. Two more in the outbuildings we passed on the way in, since the next generation has started to grow up and marry. All of them, all the estate's employees, used to live in the cottages to the side of the mansion, but this is much better! A beautiful place, isn't it?

It certainly is. And it's touching to see how pleased and proud the new proprietors still are, thirty years after the French exodus. I can't help but wonder what the old owners of the estate would make of their ballroom being put to such a use, though. Imagine if they could see it now, full of farmers in jellabas, tangles of playing children and smoking charcoal braziers. Not to mention a bunch of scruffy European travellers. I'd love to be a fly on the wall.

12

Hamid's and Khaled's families had worked on the vineyards, they tell us, for four whole generations – and the other two families who ran the flour-mill as well. So when the *patrons* vanished, and the manager too – just upped and left without so much as a goodbye and fare-well to the Algerian staff they had lived amongst all their lives – the families took the estate over themselves. And believe it or not, no Frenchman has ever set foot in here since then – until today!

This last remark has, to my mind, rather worrying undertones of Chefchaouen and its Christian visitors. I fear that the first Frenchmen to view these premises since independence aren't necessarily going to have an easy ride of it. But Gérard and Guy, apparently unperturbed, politely thank our hosts for the honour that has been accorded them. And Guy says, very formally, that he hopes to behave better than the last members of his nation to occupy this room.

Well, as long as you say goodbye when you're leaving, says Hamid jovially, and don't sneak out as if you thought we were planning to cut your throats!

Ouch!

Ah, says the quiet Khaled, the *patrons*, the owners, were good enough people at heart, which is more than can be said for the estate manager. But a lot of water has passed under the bridge since then. Nowadays, instead of just supporting four families, one of them in luxury, the estate supports ten families sharing equally – and they still live better than ever they did in the old days!

It took their parents months to even think of moving in here after the *patrons* had gone, Khaled tells us, passing us our glasses of coffee.

Their mothers and sisters went on respectfully cleaning the place from top to bottom every week. For the benefit of nobody. It was Khaled and Hamid, just teenagers at the time, who suggested it. Their fathers were still in shock for the whole first year, it was all so sudden. Even though they were running the business themselves now, they still couldn't believe they had a right actually to use the bosses' old homes!

It's true, says Hamid. Almost a year to learn that we truly were our own masters. But we've become a lot quicker-witted since then!

I take a sip of my coffee now, and it's extraordinary. It tastes absolutely nothing like the coffee I've been expecting, and looking forward to immensely, after the last few tea-loaded days, but even so, I love it. Which is a serious accolade. It's perfumed and spicy, with a flavour that is strangely familiar, although I can't pin it down.

Delicious, I say, taking another large swig. What is the extra ingredient?

A kind of seed-pod, ground up – but Khaled only knows the name in Arabic. He passes me a little wooden container, beautifully carved, to sniff at.

Cardamom! That's what it is. I've never heard of mixing cardamom in coffee, but it is an inspiration. Another recipe to remember. Wonder how it would go down with the fried-egg *brik*? A whole breakfast menu to take home with me already!

Two women have followed the last wave of children into the room, one of them veiled with one of those little white triangles, the other with a *khimar* draped to hide most of her face. They don't say hello, but go and sit in the farthest corner of the room, calling the children over to them. Aren't we going to be introduced? Nobody's taking any notice of them at all. Is this Islamic good manners? Or is it just the etiquette of a multiple living room: you pretend you can't see one another? Dare I ask who the ladies are? Best not. For all I know, since you aren't allowed to ask how people's wives are, there may be some other unimaginable rule where you have to pretend they are invisible if you haven't been introduced.

Still, they must have put the veils on because of us lot. People don't go around veiled in their own homes, do they? This is terrible – we're inconveniencing them in their own living room, and ignoring them into the bargain. But then, maybe it's normal to them? What a ridiculous amount of thinking you have to do, in a culture where you have hardly any bearings at all.

Khaled is pouring out our second glass of coffee now – do coffees come in threes as well? – while Hamid tells us the tale of the vanishing French owners. Nobody knew what was meant to happen next, he says. Then, just as their fathers were wondering how on earth they were supposed to pay the extra hands they would need for the *vendange*, or whether they would have to leave the grapes to rot on the vines, word finally came through from the new Algerian government, the Front for National Liberation, that all property abandoned by French proprietors now belonged to the state. And that all Algerian patriots should do their best to keep the ex-French businesses running if they possibly could, to keep their new nation functioning and solvent.

So here they were, employees in a state collective all of a sudden, and this house a state building too, running the whole show themselves, without a single Frenchman to order them about!

Joy and exhilaration at first, says Khaled, and then the nightmare began! Because it was not just their own *patrons* here that had left, it was all of them. Every last Frenchman was off: 800,000 of them. All the management of every business in Algeria! And most of the technicians, too. There was nobody there any more. All gone.

And, says Hamid the ebullient, his and Khaled's families could keep the fields and vineyards going, no problem, but they knew nothing about what happened to the produce they grew. Their fathers could hardly read and write, never mind their mothers. And when they finally realized they'd better break into the office to get some information – dared smash a window to get into the house of Masselier, the estate manager – he turned out to have burnt all the books!

Orders, receipts, accounts, everything – nothing left to work from but a pile of ashes in the fireplace.

It may be hard to imagine, says Khaled, but none of their parents had ever touched a telephone in their lives. He and Hamid, a pair of teenagers, had to pick up the phones – not that they'd ever used one before, either, but they had the courage of youth on their side! – and try to find out about wine wholesalers, transport, shipping. Whereupon they discovered that, all over Algeria, there was hardly anybody left trying to keep everything going, but other ignoramuses like themselves.

We had office workers, porters, cleaners even, says Khaled, trying to keep whole businesses running – people with no training, and hardly any education. The management everywhere had been French alone, for over a hundred years! Nobody knew if they were coming or going, or had any more experience of running their companies than Khaled's and Hamid's families did. Worse still, a lot of the *patrons* had destroyed whatever they could as they left, just to make the job harder. Like the estate manager here, an evil man.

The *pieds-noirs* didn't just wreck their own businesses, either, but schools, libraries, hospitals, all over the country. Their parting shot. In spite of the fact that their own General de Gaulle had agreed that everything would be left in good order. France had admitted that the situation was her own fault, anyway, and agreed to help the country rebuild. What was the point in making it harder for Algeria to get back on its feet?

But the *pieds-noirs* hated their own government almost as much as they hated the Algerians, says Hamid. Maybe more. They wanted their army to stay here and go on fighting till every last one of us was destroyed. Who knows who they thought was going to do the dirty work in this country if they succeeded! Anyhow, if this estate hadn't had the flour-mill to keep it going that first autumn – because at least everybody needs bread and couscous, and a sack of flour is easy to sell! – they and their families would all have gone very hungry indeed.

Something tells me that Guy is not going to bother mentioning his family's Algerian connections just now. I certainly wouldn't, in his place. I wonder, did his relations go around vandalizing as they left? Would they have told Guy if they had?

As Khaled passes us our third coffee, the two women in the corner get up, calling a selection of children to them, and head for the door. Still no salutations as they pass us on their way out – not even to Khaled and Hamid – though several of the children, trailing behind, come and hide behind the sofa to get a better look at us, and one daring little boy jumps onto Hamid's lap.

Khaled gives us a conspiratorial grin as the women leave. Those are his and Hamid's mothers, he says. They were too shy to say hello – they hardly speak any French – but they certainly got a good long look, didn't they?

They certainly did. Evidently there is more than one use to a veil.

Now, the two grandmothers having left, Khaled's wife comes into the room in their place. A childcare shift system? Or just curiosity? This time we are introduced. The wife, not veiled, shakes all our hands, but no names are exchanged. And now, disappointingly, she goes off to sit alone in the far corner, like the grannies did. If this is proper Maghreb social etiquette, I can certainly see why my bearded enemy back in Oujda was so exercised about his womenfolk's free and easy behaviour. They were breaking every rule in the book.

But then, if women don't mix socially with men here, what does that make me, sitting here among them? Do I not count as a woman? Would I be allowed to go over and sit with Khaled's wife instead, maybe? But no; she might be horrified. Embarrassed. And not speak French anyway. Best stay put.

Another two children have come to clamber on Hamid. It's certainly starting to get overcrowded in here these days, he says, ruffling the hair of one, while the other whacks at him with a vine-twig. Who knows where all these grandchildren will fit in, once they start growing up?

Your ballrooms, says Gérard, are overflowing! Is this what people mean when they talk about the housing crisis in Algeria?

Khaled laughs, as he is meant to, but Hamid doesn't think it's funny. We should wait till we see the big cities here, *bidonvilles* sprouting up everywhere, people sleeping in shifts because there's nowhere for them to go – and the government cutting back on its building programme, too – before we make such jokes, he says, disapprovingly. Obviously there isn't enough work here on the estate for all the next generation – and what will happen then?

We head off to check out the vineyards now the coffee drinking's over. Nobody acknowledges Khaled's wife as we leave. I try giving her a friendly wave as I go. She looks positively alarmed, and makes no response at all. Oh well.

Out of the side door again, and in among the vines. The motor-bike-repairing boys have vanished from the terrace, though we can hear roaring engine-noises somewhere among the vegetation.

Most of their wine goes to France in bulk, to boost up the strength and body of French wines, Khaled tells us as we skirt round the small plot of vines beyond the house. Because with the good climate here, the wines always come out fine and strong, thirteen per cent alcohol at least. So a bad vintage year for France, where the grapes don't sweeten enough to bring French wines up to strength, is always a good one for Algeria!

We are surprised, though, that there is no problem with producing wine here – doesn't it clash with Islamic principles?

They've had a bit of trouble, off and on, says Hamid, with idiots trying to tell them that theirs was an un-Islamic business. But nobody with enough power to actually put a spoke in their wheels – not so far, *inshallah!* It would be a terrible thing to see all these vineyards destroyed, after so many generations of loving care and hard work.

Khaled wouldn't be surprised, he says, if that starts up all over again now, since the *Pouvoir* seem set on arresting so many Islamists that they're making heroes of them.

Hamid agrees. All the young rebels, every last youth who can't find a job and feels hard-done-by, will be rushing into the arms of the extremist hardcore. There's a new radical *imam* preaching round here, very hot on Western decadence and corruption. He only needs to add the demon alcohol to his list of depravities and give the congregation a nudge and a wink in this direction, and there'll be angry mobs at the gate again.

Their worst moment here, though, Khaled says, was nothing to do with Islamic principle. It seemed the new Algerian government was about to decree that all the thousands of hectares of grapevines in the country must be grubbed up. Not for religion's sake, but because Algeria would never be free of French influence, they said, as long as so much of her agriculture depended on selling to the old colonial power.

Hamid laughs. A terrible time! France boycotted Algerian wine, because the FLN had told her to remove her nuclear testing facility down in the Sahara, and her naval bases on the Mediterranean. So in retaliation Algeria was left with millions of litres of unsold wine on her hands! Luckily the French soon realized that their own wine was worthless, in a bad year, without the southern Mediterranean contribution. The bases went, and, fortunately for both parties, Algeria is still keeping French wine up to strength to this day!

The vines here certainly seem well ahead of the ones I just left in Italy, where the buds were only just opening. Here they are nearly in full leaf. The grapes will get plenty of time to sweeten. These vines just outside the house are Cinsault, says Hamid, giving us the guided tour; a breed brought here by the French. Up ahead are the Mataro and Grenache, bred in el-Andalus, and brought back by the Moorish refugees. The further vineyard is divided up into small plots separated by rows of beautifully pruned fruit trees still in pink-and-white blossom. These ones are Syrah, full-blooded Algerian vines, though people say the cultivar was developed in Persia originally, Iran, that is, back in the dawn of time. Our hosts have had visitors from Italy recently, from some university, cataloguing their ancient local breeds – a project to save the old cultivars hardly used in commercial production any more, in case some new disease comes and decimates all the weaker, more inbred modern varieties, like the phylloxera that caused havoc in the vineyards of Europe forty years ago. Luckily phylloxera can't get a hold in the sandy soil here, and Algeria was safe.

The Italians took a great interest in the vineyard round the front, Hamid says, which was here even before the house was built – and how right they were! Those are the grapes he and Khaled use, along with the Andalusian breeds, to make their own private blend of wine, which we'll all have a little taste of when we get back inside! That is the only thing, he says, that tempts him about this new free-market-economy business. The *Pouvoir* has abolished the state collectives now – they always start their mad experiments on agriculture first! – and by next year there will be a market in land again. You just need to have run your agribusiness for five years, and it's your own private property. How he would love to get into competition with Europe, bottle his own proper vintage wines, show them what Algeria can do.

Khaled makes a sucked-a-lemon face. How likely is that to happen? Once they are drawn into the global market, who knows what new pressures will be upon them? They are just as likely to find they can only sell their grapes as raw material to the wholesalers. One of the big French wine companies has already been sniffing around, interested in buying up vineyards in the area when the privatization date comes, next year. So many lives lost to get rid of the colonists, Khaled says, and now they're looking to come back in through the rear entrance – and give it to us *dans le cul* again.

Another loud roaring noise from between the rows of vines announces the arrival of the two motorbike boys, testing out their repair.

Hamid's sons, he says, as we all shake hands.

What was wrong with the bike, asks Guy. Did you get it fixed? The boys don't understand what he's said and ask him to repeat it.

Bah! Don't bother trying to talk French to those two, says their father. They hardly speak it at all, because of this stupid *hukumat miki*!

Emotion having got the better of him, he leaves Khaled to translate this remark. It turns out to mean 'Mickey Mouse government'.

Yes, that's it, Mickey Mouse! Hamid confirms. But nobody is listening. Guy is already off in the motorbike-repair zone, deep in socket-sets, oil, and mechanical conversation with the two sons who, by the look of it, aren't so badly handicapped in French as their father thinks – not when it comes to motorbike parts, at any rate.

Leaving Guy and the boys to it, the rest of us go off to see the *caves*, impressive barrel-vaulted cellars beneath the terrace, entered through a steep, narrow stone stairwell cut right into the earth. We select a couple of bottles of wine from the *réserve privé des cousins* and go off to see the flour-mill, which is tiny and turns out once to have been a water-mill – there's a small river rushing through rocks only a hundred yards from the house, hidden in a deep bed, which once drove the massive water-wheel that still sits rusting on the outside of the wall. This strikes me as oddly ancient technology for a colonial enterprise, until I remember that the French got here in 1830. The grain hoppers and all the accoutrements are hand-made of wood, too – they must be the original ones, still going strong. The present owners grind their own corn in it and hire it out to other farmers for their harvests. The flour is all for local use, though, not a commercial enterprise like the wine.

Heading for the house again, we spot Hamid's sons and Guy still out among the vines. The taller of the sons seems to be trying on Guy's burnous, his younger brother looking on while Guy drapes its folds becomingly, Farid-style, over his shoulders. The son is looking very pleased with himself. Interesting: could Guy's cosmopolitan charisma succeed in relaunching the burnous as a fashion item once more, in its native land?

Arriving at the house bearing our wine-booty, Guy following, we discover that the women are expecting us to eat with the family. They have already made extra lunch for us.

I knew it. We're never going to get away.

But we'll try the wine first, says Hamid, turning off the narrow corridor into one of the tiny rooms in the old servants' quarters – the wine-tasting room, he says with a wink. More of a drinking den, we soon gather, as Khaled settles down into what is clearly his usual place on the piles of rugs and cushions on the floor, while Hamid produces a washing-up bowl full of peanuts in their shells. The peanuts come out of something I took for a freezer against the back wall; now, gazing abstractedly at the thing as I sip, it dawns on me that it's not a fridge at all, but an ancient top-loading washing machine, just like the one my mother used to have, in brand-new condition. How come they use it for peanut-storage?

Because that's all it ever has been used for, according to Khaled. It's good and mouse-proof and has always come in handy for storing dry goods the vermin would go after! The machine was brought here, it seems, when the *patronne* first arrived – the *patron* having married a Frenchwoman from France. She didn't realize that here there was no use for such a thing, that two poor widow women in the village depended upon the money they earned here doing the laundry by hand, in the concrete vat in the yard.

Once Khaled's mother had explained this carefully to her, he says the *patronne* never even got the thing plumbed in. Some French people, even though they were not Muslims, could understand that they had a duty to look after the poor.

We polish off the two bottles of wine in a trice; a light, dry pale-red wine, cool and refreshing – and with a kick like a mule. Khaled and Hamid enjoy the Frenchmen's reactions immensely. Aha! Now you're tasting proper wine from a proper wine country! None of your French weaklings' brew!

More wine comes out from a second reserve in a larder in the corner, to go with the lunch: even stronger, says Hamid gleefully. Wait till you taste this!

The sons join us back in the ballroom, along with a much older man – their grandfather, who does the Moroccan hand-on-the-heart handshake, unlike everyone we've met in Algeria so far. Hamid's wife, whom we now know as Fatima, brings in the lunch, served on the low table by the sofas: the usual giant communal platter of couscous, this time with a deliciously savoury sauce of lamb and artichokes, peas and onions – oddly similar to one of my favourite Ligurian pasta sauces, give or take a pinch of cumin.

Fatima does speak French, if not as fluently as her menfolk, but she is certainly not coming to sit down and eat with us! No indeed! She laughs in an amazed-and-horrified way at the very suggestion, and nips off like a startled faun to eat in the kitchen with the rest of the women. Next time Fatima comes out, it is with Khaled's wife, Lamia – already giggling at the mere thought that we may ask her, too, to join us. She won't meet our eye when we're introduced, hiding her face in the folds of her headscarf.

Looks as if my bold and simple cast-iron-frying-pan-to-the-head solution might not be the answer after all. You'd need to aim a few whacks at the women, too. Or even, who knows, come up with a more subtle approach.

Fatima and Lamia clear away the platter and the bones, and bring in the fruit, a pile of absolutely enormous oranges and a plate of dried figs, dates and nuts. Now Lamia returns with the tea-making accoutrements. This time she is actually holding the edge of her headscarf in her teeth to make an impromptu half-veil, which I'm sorry to say makes me think she's slightly mad, though I will soon learn that this is a normal thing for a woman to do here, when she's feeling shy.

Hamid is not making the tea yet, though. He opens a third bottle of wine and insists we drink more. His sons haven't touched a drop so far. Now he starts insisting they take a glass, too. They refuse. He insists some more. They refuse some more.

A short silence ensues. Now, having lost the battle on the alcohol front, their father starts having another go at them about their rubbish French.

Another brilliant idea from the *Pouvoir*, he tells us. Stop teaching the children to speak French: that will make our nation more independent of the West! What foolishness! Why would only being able to speak one language make you more independent? Why turn a bilingual nation, where almost everyone speaks French, into one that only speaks Arabic? Anyone who trades abroad, like Hamid himself, needs a European language. Anyone who wants to keep up with science and technology, too – because where is the Iraqi research into vine cultivars? Where are the Saudi Arabian advances in viticulture?

Hamid says that the *Pouvoir* were all educated in French-speaking schools anyway, they're all bilingual, and he doesn't believe for a moment that any of them sent their own kids off into their pointless Arabic-only education system! No, their children go to French *lycées* in Algiers. And to French-speaking university in liberal Tunis! They've foisted this Arabization business onto places where there was no decent schooling anyway, and this is their come-uppance – Islamist violence! They've made the Kabyle Berbers rise up against them, too, by ignoring their Tamazight language. The *Pouvoir* have created a stick for their own backs, because Hamid actually had to argue with his own son – that one there, he says, pointing at the taller son, the one who was trying on the burnous earlier and is now looking deeply mortified – to stop him voting for the Islamic Front!

We don't get the connection: is it the wine slowing down our already-overloaded brains?

The *Pouvoir*, Khaled explains, had to import a lot of teachers from the eastern Arabic countries, the Mashriq, where the more puritanical and warlike versions of Islam are strong, to get its Arabic-speaking education launched. Algeria's own teachers had all studied in the French language – they could hardly name an Arabic text on their own subject, never mind teach it in Arabic.

And what happened? interrupts the irascible Hamid. He will tell us what! Big surprise – students who'd done their schooling in Arabic alone could hardly find a job! Nobody wanted them: French-speakers were more useful. The Arabized students had a great career ahead of them – as *haitistes*, as wall-proppers!

The influence of those puritanical teachers, it seems, along with the lack of opportunities for Arabic-only graduates, has turned out an explosive combination.

So you didn't vote for the Islamic Front yourself, says Gérard, continuing his researches despite the wine.

Hamid launches off again. Not only did he not vote for the Islamists, he is disgusted that theirs was recognized as a party at all and allowed to stand. Because, according to the Algerian constitution, parties based solely on religion are barred. It's obvious – they're supposed to be political parties, aren't they, so they should be based on politics!

Khaled takes his arm soothingly and begins giving his back a gentle, circular rub. The Islamists are so ignorant, Hamid is saying angrily, that they think wine was brought here by the French, that it's some colonial imposition on their traditional teetotal culture! But Algerians have been making wine – in this very region – since before the Roman Empire! The very word 'alcohol' is Arabic – did we know that? *Al-kohl*: it means the pure substance, the sublimate, the essence. And even the Prophet Mohammed himself, peace be upon him, speaks of the wine of paradise, which will make you happy, but never inebriated! (This is certainly not the case with our hosts' wine: my French is coming out all blurry. In fact, I may stop trying to speak at all.)

Does this mean our hosts agree with the arrests, then?

Khaled certainly does not. He thinks these first-ever multi-party elections were just a smoke-screen imposed by the foreign powers – especially your country, he says, fixing Gérard and Guy with a gimlet stare – who are blackmailing Algeria into giving up on socialism. It was the French economic advisors who encouraged the multi-party elections, and suggested legalizing the Front for Islamic Salvation so it could stand, too, just to confuse the issue. Everyone here's a Muslim, after all, and any voter might hope that, if the government couldn't solve the country's problems, Allah would make a better job of it!

Hamid agrees. They meant to divide the opposition, while they quietly sold off the country's assets to the highest bidder. Unluckily for them, they succeeded beyond their wildest dreams – the Islamist party has turned and bitten the hand that fed it!

Khaled is disgusted at the West's silence over the suspension of the elections, too. Of course they didn't like the look of the probable winners. But why shouldn't democracy be as binding here as in their own countries? If France, at least, had pressured the *Pouvoir* to accept the results, there could have been dialogue with the moderate Islamists – a lot of them are reasonable men. The extremists would have been left in limbo.

And why would they do that? asks Hamid. Anything that weakens Algeria is good news to foreign investors. France's love of democracy is only as deep as her businessmen's pockets!

The wives reappear now, expecting to remove the tea equipment, only to find that we haven't even begun the tea course yet. Fatima begins berating Hamid in her own language – about his wine-drinking, I guess from the way she snatches up the empty bottles. The sons seize the chance to make their getaway, still on the moral high ground, not having touched a drop.

I am confused, I say to Khaled, as we do our best to ignore the *sotto voce* tongue-lashing his friend is now receiving. The Front for National Liberation, when I first heard of them all those years ago, were great heroes, about to build a new Algeria with the nation's oil money. But now they seem to be called the *Pouvoir*, and accused of everything from corruption and incompetence to being in cahoots with the country's enemies?

Simple, says Hamid, waving a dismissive hand at his wife, who now exits with a flounce, carrying the empty bottles. They listened to their French advisors!

Khaled says they used the oil money to build massive factories: steelworks and stuff. Industrializing industries, they called them. Smaller factories were meant to grow up to supply them, farming would expand to feed their workers, well paid now; a generation with a good, state-run education would appear – and the economy would take off.

French ideas! chips in Hamid. Did they put any money into agriculture? No! Now Algeria is importing food – where once she fed half of France!

But the factories, Khaled continues, stoically ignoring Hamid, were white elephants – ran at half capacity, cost a fortune, and the only thing that took off was mass unemployment! While the bureaucrats who organized it all – or said they did! – paid themselves handsomely. Like the army, which still oversaw everything from behind the scenes. Both clans grew good and fat. And there you have it – the *Pouvoir*. Squabbling among themselves, snuggling up to their superior French experts, military or economic, and looking down their noses at the rest of us!

Which isn't to say, he adds, after a pause, that there aren't still some good people in the FLN. But will their voices ever be heard?

No, they won't, says Hamid. Of course not! Why worry? Have some more wine! And he pours out another round.

I'm certainly not going to touch another drop. Another bottle is opened anyway; Gérard and Guy go for it too. Some glasses later, Guy begins confessing the secret of his family's *pied-noir* past. Our hosts take it blithely in their stride. How would they blame him, a young man, for his father's misdeeds? He need not bother mentioning it.

Now, though, Guy wants to exonerate his father. He was by no means an evil destroyer of hospitals and schools, but did all he could to stop other Post Office employees sabotaging the place, and voluntarily gave the keys of his family home, on the day they left, to an Algerian workmate and his family.

Guy obviously feels much better having got all that off his chest. And now, humankind being a many-splendoured thing, Khaled and Hamid remember that their old *patronne* was a kind and motherly woman, who baked a mean *madeleine*, took tea under the pergola with their own mothers, and always helped Khaled and Hamid out with their French spelling.

I suddenly feel horribly drunk. The wine is full-blooded Algerian, not watered down by any of that namby-pamby French stuff: fourteen per cent alcohol. Those extra percentage points make some difference indeed, with a full stomach and the North African sun, windows wide open to the sleepy vineyard without.

Luckily the after-lunch nap traditions of Morocco apply here in Algeria too. Soon we are all stretched out on sofas, rugs and cushions and zzzzzzzzzzzzzz.

13

Finally we are on a bus. They do really exist. This one is taking us eastwards still, across a broad plain of yet more olives, vineyards and orchards. The city ahead of us, just visible through the heat-haze, is Tlemcen. Gérard's new *Little Cunning One*, consulted with Guy's grudging approval, tells us that Tlemcen – whose name was also written 'Tilemsen' in earlier times, when its inhabitants were fonder of vowels than they are today – means 'springs' in Berber Tamazight. It was also once known as Agadir, which is Arabic for 'fortress', and before that the ancient Romans called it Pomaria, meaning 'orchards'. Guy and I agree with Gérard: there is plenty of back-up for all three names in the surrounding landscape. Springs-orchards-fortress-town. But we're finding it hard to take much of an interest. We wish we hadn't drunk all that wine.

We were planning to look up the first relative on Samir's list, his cousin Hocine, tonight. But I've gone off the idea. I don't want to talk to more people I don't know and worry about whether I've missed some essential point of Islamic etiquette and probably have to eat a lot of food for hours. I want to sit quietly and not be assaulted by all sorts of strange new stuff. The boys feel the same. Cultural exhaustion. What we need is a nice quiet evening of nothing at all. As soon as we get off the bus, we'll start asking around for hotels.

Tlemcen looks very promising as we ride in: an ancient and noble walled city, not an upstart frontier town like Oujda, set in a jewel-green landscape with a background of pine forests and deep-red cliffs. Within its walls are small, friendly streets with plenty of greenery. Its architecture, ancient, modern and French-colonial, all harmonizes sweetly.

No hope for peace and quiet, though. The first person we ask about hotels when we get off the bus, a curly-headed young man whom we soon know as Liamine, turns out to be a professional guide. It was obvious, really. Why else would he be hanging about a bus station, waiting for new arrivals to ask him silly questions? Liamine is not any old guide, either, but a personage of great liveliness, not to say effervescence, and full of enthusiasm for his subject: the historical treasures of Tlemcen. Which we need to come and check out immediately. Of course we do! What could be a better time than the present?

None of us is in any state to withstand a charm offensive. And we certainly couldn't claim that the cost of Liamine's services was prohibitive – he's asking so little it's positively embarrassing. Within minutes we have been loaded up into his friend Ismail's small yellow taxi, and we're off on the grand tour of the town. Of course they'll take us to a hotel – soon, soon! They know just the place, a lovely, clean, tidy, cheap hotel, right here in the centre. But first we must relax, sit back in our seats, stop worrying, and let them show us around!

Liamine and friend now take us and our hangovers on a bewildering switchback ride through a world of mosques and holy tombs, of bizarre histories and irrational tales, weirdly interwoven with histories of science and logic, of intellect and rationality. But then, in the high days of Tlemcen's might, as a great university city of the thirteenth and fourteenth centuries, that was one of the hot topics of philosophical debate: the question of the separation, if any, between faith and logic, religion and reason. Come to think of it, history seems to be repeating itself at this very time here in Algeria – hopefully not as tragedy.

First we go off towards the centre of town. Compared to anywhere we have been so far, Tlemcen's streets seem surprisingly free of women in veils. We pass a good half-dozen women without so much as a scarf over their hair. But of course! say our guides proudly. Lots of women in Tlemcen go around *en cheveux* – 'in hair'! This is a cosmopolitan city, not a backwards peasant town!

Strange to note that, after just a couple of days of no-visible-hair at all, the sight of bare female heads actually strikes me as strange and faintly shocking. How horribly easy it must be to launch and perpetuate a tradition of prudery.

Our first stop is the town's Jewish cemetery, and the tomb of Rabbi Ephraim, a charismatic Andalusian doctor and scientist who arrived here from Toledo in 1442, fleeing the persecution of the Jews and, as legend has it, riding on the back of a lion, using a serpent as a rein. Be that as it may, says Liamine, the Rabbi, a very erudite man, cured the Sultan's family of its ailments so well that he was rewarded with a large plot of land in the city, on which to build homes for all the Jews of the area, collecting them together in safety within its stout walls.

Every one of the tombs in here – big slabs of rough stone laid flat on the ground – has been liberally splashed and dribbled with whitewash, just like our first *marabout* tomb. White, Ismail says, is a lucky colour here in the Maghreb, a symbol of happiness and plenty. And we've just missed the February mass pilgrimage to his tomb, we hear, as we throw the obligatory coin into Rabbi Ephraim's fountain. Everyone participates in his *moussem*, a two-day event of wild drumming and frenzied dancing. Being Jewish is no bar to being venerated by Muslims of the Sufi persuasion, any more than being Christian. A last remnant, hanging on by the skin of its teeth, of the great days of the Peoples of the Book.

And are there Jews and Christians still living here in Tlemcen, then?

Hardly any, alas, say our guides. As we may imagine, most Christians left with the French: there was a lot of bad feeling. Most of them had sided with the colonizers. A handful stayed on – those few who had made some close connection to local people and their culture. The story of the Jewish exodus, though, is more complicated.

There are still some Jews left here, but nothing compared to the days before the French. The Christian colonizers of the nineteenth century came up with the perfect scheme to drive a wedge between the other two Peoples of the Book – a divide-and-rule strategy that worked its mischief to the very end. Although they refused Muslims citizenship rights unless they were prepared to renounce their religion, a special case was made of the Jews. They were offered preferential treatment, says Ismail, and they accepted it. Maybe there wasn't much else they could have done. But still, as the nationalist movement grew, Muslim Algerians saw the Jews as traitors, or, at best, lackeys of the oppressors.

Towards the end of the French regime, though, Liamine tells us, things started to look more hopeful. Once Vichy France had started collaborating with the Fascists of Europe, setting up concentration camps here in Algeria, filling them with European Jews – and any other despised groups – not a few Jews joined the ranks of the Algerian nationalists against the colonists. The nationalist movement was not supposed to be about religion, anyway, but about liberation for the whole country. That is why the constitution here forbade political parties based on religion. Still, maybe it was too late for reconciliation: there was too much prejudice and mistrust already. Then, once the war against Hitler was over, there was Israel, and its maltreatment of the Palestinians. When Algeria got its independence, the Jews were not given automatic citizenship: they would have to ask for it individually. A tit-for-tat move. Well over 100,000 Jews left for France along with the *pieds-noirs*. A few thousand went to Israel. Hardly any are left. Less than one per cent of the population.

But let us go back into the past, say our guides cheeringly, to happier times when the last two Peoples of the Book, at least, were still united. Next stop will be the mosque of the *marabout* El Halaoui, whose name means 'The Sweetmaker' or 'The Confectioner'.

We leave the car and head off into the maze of narrow streets that lead into the medina. Interesting to note that there is no separate French *ville nouvelle* here in Tlemcen. This must be one of the places where the settlers got too close to the colonized, then, and those macabre lessons were learned that would later deprive Moroccan Muslims of electricity and sewage systems.

The Holy Confectioner's is a sweet little mosque, set into the side of a hill and built in 1354, when – according to Liamine – the Andalusian style would have been the height of fashion here. The great architects of el-Andalus were very influential on this side of the water, he says: the Grand Mosque down in the centre of town was actually copied from one of their triumphs, the Grand Mosque of Cordoba, which still stands in Spain to this day, now transformed into a Grand Cathedral, its Islamic minaret reworked into a Christian bell-tower.

We don't actually go inside. Although here in Algeria, unlike Morocco, Christians are allowed to visit mosques, I am not dressed correctly. I can't go in with my hair uncovered. The boys stay out in solidarity. All for one and one for all, as Dumas might have said. From the doorway you can see a simple little prayer room; beyond it a courtyard with a pagoda-like shelter supported on a dozen slim columns. Oddly enough, it is roofed with tiles identical to a type I have often admired on certain English Art-Deco buildings: clay tiles glazed in a light pea-green. I have always thought these were a home-grown invention, and they strike me as oddly out of place here in Moorish North Africa. But of course, in the days of Art-Deco, people went around naming their dance-halls 'Alhambra' and their entertainment corporations 'Granada', didn't they? The green glazed roof-tile must have been Orientalist in inspiration. What odd things you do learn when you travel.

The Confectioner's tale, as told by Liamine, is certainly worthy of *The Thousand and One Nights*.

El Halaoui was another Andalusian. Some say he was Cadi of Seville until it fell to the Christians and he fled to take refuge here. Others (Ismail is representing this point of view with some vigour at present) say he gave up the post voluntarily. Willingly or not, he now decided to give up the riches and vanities of this world; he would devote himself to a plain hermit's life and the Sufi search for transcendental Oneness with God. Checking the facts as I write, I see that Seville fell to the Christians in 1248, and El Halaoui arrived here in 1266, so whoever is correct, he certainly made a long slow journey of it to Tlemcen. Once here, El Halaoui lived a life of poverty and simplicity, teaching the children of the city, as they sat at his feet muching his homemade goodies, lessons in the godly ways of justice, mercy and charity. Eventually his reputation for piety and wisdom, and his way with children, came to the ears of the ruler of the city, who invited him into his court to become teacher and guide to his very own sons. But now the grand vizier became jealous at El Halaoui's preferment – as grand viziers will – and began secretly plotting his downfall. One fine day, the Confectioner found himself accused of using witchcraft – of planning to make his pupils love him more than they loved their own father. The vizier had set the worm of doubt in his patron's heart. El Halaoui was beheaded and his body thrown over the city walls to the dogs, as was the custom in those days.

Hang on a moment! I recognize this story. We've heard a song about it. An Andalusian song. Didn't something very nasty happen the vizier, involving lime mortar?

It certainly did. Ismail knows the song, too, and starts quietly singing it as we walk, tapping out the rhythm with his taxi-keys.

Liamine goes on with the story. As darkness fell that night, when the watchmen of the city went to close its gates, a wavering voice from without called to them, saying, 'Rest easy. The town is safe. All is well. There is no one out here but the sweet-maker.' This went on for seven nights, until the ruler and citizens of Tlemcen concluded that El Halaoui hadn't been a sorcerer after all, but a holy man, as they had originally thought. So they built him a nice *marabout*-tomb and this pretty little mosque to make up for it. And then, of course, the vizier, as we know, got his just rewards.

There is something about the way Liamine tells this story that does not resonate with faith and piety. Does he actually believe in these *marabouts*? Would he or Ismail come and pray at their shrines?

No, they certainly would not. Nobody their age – no young educated people – care for all that *marabout*-cult stuff. But many of the *marabouts* really were great scholars and interpreters of Islam, scientists and philosophers who contributed greatly to the sum of human knowledge. It is the worshipping of them that is mistaken. The supernatural stuff was added later, by a people who knew they had been great men but no longer had any understanding – education having been eliminated from this country by the colonial powers – of their true importance. Rabbi Ephraim, for example, not only studied medicine at the University of Toledo, but also devoted many years of his life to studying the commentaries of the Christian Thomas Aquinas on Aristotelian philosophy. And most daringly for his time, the Rabbi argued that the holy texts of the three Peoples of the Book should not be taken as literal truth, but as metaphor. And what do the worshippers at his shrine admire him for today? Using a snake to harness a lion! That is their memorial to a man who was a fervent rationalist! It's stuff for the old folk, or for superstitious country bumpkins. And not really Islam at all.

It is wrong, anyway, contributes Ismail, to believe that other beings than Allah can share his sacredness, or grant you his *baraka*.

Liamine laughs at his friend, and a heated debate ensues, in a mixture of French and Arabic. Liamine's conclusion: Ismail is a superstitious country bumpkin himself. The very concept of *baraka* is a Maghrebi deformation of true classical Islam.

Extraordinary to find yourself in a country where young men engage in animated theological discussion in the streets! How many centuries is it since that would have happened in Britain? Not since Cromwell's time. Another extraordinary thing is the amount of French Ismail and Liamine mix in with their Arabic when they're speaking to one another – do they always do that, or is it meant as a courtesy to us? Because if it is, I say, it's not working. There's a lot too much Arabic in it for us to get more than the faintest idea what they're on about!

But no, says Liamine. That's the way everyone talks here in Algeria. In the cities, at any rate. You swap between the two languages as the fancy takes you.

The French language is our *bottin de guerre*, our war booty, says Ismail with a grin at Gérard and Guy. The spoils of war. We can do what we like with it! Mix and match! Bend it to our will!

But anyway, the answer is that young people prefer the mosques downtown, where you get a good *imam* who has something to say about changing the world for the better – that's what religion ought to be about. Who wants a load of old farmers' mumbo-jumbo?

Back to the car and we are soon skirting a big oval park of oleanders and palm trees, created, our guides say, by draining the ancient lake in which Barbarossa, who took control of Tlemcen in 1518, drowned a dozen of its ruler's sons. What a ferocious man Barbarossa seems to have been – and how far and wide he travelled. When he wasn't raiding small towns on the Ligurian coast, he was drowning princes in Algeria. There was a lot more to him, though, Liamine tells us, than unbridled ferocity. Barbarossa may have been a murderous privateer as far as Ligurians were concerned, and pretty unpleasant if you were an emir of Tlemcen, but he was a saint in the eyes of the beleaguered Moors trapped in the south of Spain. Their forcible conversion to Christianity had been decreed; they were threatened with having their children taken from them 'for the good of their souls'. Now they were forbidden to leave the country. The name Barbarossa, the story goes, is a European corruption of *Baba Aruj* – Father Aruj: the name bestowed upon him by the hundreds of grateful Muslims he rescued, between 1504 and 1510, from the coasts of now-hostile Andalusia, and carried to safety in Algiers. So in 1508, when he plundered Diano Marina, he must have been en route to a mercy mission over in Spain. I must remember to tell my neighbours that when I get home. I'm sure it'll make them feel a lot better.

We roar on uphill now, along an elegantly curving road through the high and leafy hinterland of Tlemcen, towards the mosque and tomb of its patron saint – the *marabout* Sidi Boumedienne. Another Andalusian, it seems, also born in Seville, but a hundred years before the Confectioner: before the persecution began, in the days of bold intellectual enquiry, when the Peoples of the Book were at the height of their cooperative powers.

Do they not have any home-grown *marabouts*, then? How come this town is so full of Andalusians?

Simple, says Liamine. This town has Andalusian connections going right back to the very beginning of the story, and to its bitter end. Boabdil, the last king of Islamic Granada, came here to die. And seven centuries earlier Tariq ibn Zayid – Tariq of Gibraltar fame – was here in Tlemcen when he received the request to lead the invasion of Spain, to re-establish order there. (This seems perhaps an excessively euphemistic description of Tariq's goal in invading Iberia, but hey, it's Liamine's story.) Sidi Boumedienne himself, though, Liamine says, belongs to the high point of Moorish civilization, and the flowering of the culture of the Peoples of the Book: the days of bold intellectual enquiry, when there was a constant to-ing and fro-ing between the Maghreb and el-Andalus.

In Sidi Boumedienne's day the cities of the Maghreb were booming from the trans-Saharan trade, overflowing with wealthy merchants making fortunes from the precious goods pouring in from Ghana and the Sudan, Niger and Mali. The coffers of the emirs, too, were overflowing with the taxes they earned from the traders and merchants. And the universities of Tlemcen and of Bejaia benefited from the riches of their cities, and the new thirst for knowledge. Theoreticians, researchers, manuscripts, new ideas, especially in science and medicine, were in constant circulation between here and the Islamic universities of el-Andalus – of Toledo, Valencia, Cordoba, Seville – and to the east as well, to Cairo and Baghdad, even as far as Asia and distant Samarkand. Not just Muslims, but Jews and Christians of enquiring mind would come here to study philosophy, law, medicine, and above all mathematics, under Muslim masters. Christian and Jewish education was still, Liamine says, hamstrung by theology. But here in the Muslim world, ideas were allowed to flow freely, untrammelled by doctrine. So when the Christian king of Sicily launched the massive project of making a reliable map of the whole of the known world, who did he call in? Ten Muslim geographers. He did not trust his fellow Christians, whose scientific spirit might still be dulled by myth and superstition.

Ismail wonders gloomily what can have gone wrong. Would you believe it was the same place? Liamine says that the great men of that time were truly following the precepts of the Prophet Mohammed, peace be upon him, who told his followers that the ink of the scholar was more precious than the blood of the martyr. Seek learning, he said, though it be in China.

The Arabic language was recognized, he says, from the tenth century on, as the main vehicle of learning. The Jewish scholar Maimonides, born in Cordoba, even wrote his *Guide to the Perplexed* – a handbook of Hebrew law – in Arabic. This *Guide* contained a summary of rationalist critiques of religion so powerful that, the story goes, the rabbis of the time sought to ban it. They said that a man who unexpectedly died while reading that section was bound to go to hell: he would indubitably meet his Maker as an atheist! Meanwhile, the universities of many European cities had begun teaching Arabic, among them Paris, Bologna and Naples. It was thanks to the Italian connection that our European Copernicus came across the works of the astronomist Nasir al-Din al-Tusi, who had died in 1274, already well on his way to proving that the earth went round the sun, and not vice versa.

The list of the illustrious names that flocked to this area of intellectual and cultural ferment in Sidi Boumedienne's day and beyond is enormous. The finest minds of el-Andalus and of Arabia, and the earliest of the Renaissance men of Europe all came together here, often engaging, it seems, in fiery public debate: the culture of the Peoples of the Book was now in full flood. There was the historian

Ibn Khaldun, nowadays credited as a founding father of sociology; the Catalan philosopher Raymond Lulle, the Pope's envoy; Ibn Arabi of Andalusia, metaphysician; Ibn Hamdis, renowned Sicilian poet; various distinguished North African travellers, including Ibn Battuta – who gave us the first written account of the riches of Sijilmassa, and is reputed to have travelled three times as far as Marco Polo. Also my favourite, Averroes, real name Ibn Rushd – another Andalusian and a committed rationalist – whose commentaries on Aristotle were translated from his own Arabic into Hebrew and Latin around 1230, so they were accessible once more to European thought, and to such men as Thomas Aquinas. Even more impressively – considering present times – he wrote a treatise arguing that any society which oppresses its women is bound, eventually, to degenerate and collapse. Lovely man.

Liamine's list goes on and on. The mind boggles. And the hangover does not help. Or the fact that, to my shame, many of the renowned Arabic names he cites are unknown to me. One that does stick in my mind, though, is Ibn Tufail, a philosopher and physician who died in 1185 and whose works, according to our guide, were the inspiration for Rudyard Kipling's Mowgli tales. Ibn Tufail's story of a child brought up by a wolf-mother, alone on a jungle island, was written with much more serious intent than that of his imitator, though: it was an investigation into the possibility of a 'pure' philosophy, unadulterated by social preconception. So there you have it. Walt Disney, we now know, owes a debt to twelfth-century Islamic philosophy.

Sidi Boumedienne's remains lie in a jewel-like complex of small buildings with central courtyards – guest houses for visiting students, the meeting rooms of the *zawiya*, where Ibn Khaldun himself once taught, and a little *hammam* for them, too – on this grassy promontory high above the town, looking out across the lovely plain to the city with its scattered orchards, vineyards and olive groves. The Alhambra style is much in evidence here too: the same forests of slim, graceful pillars and enclosed courtyards, calm rectangular pools at their centres, honeycombs of vaulted ceilings. And a kind of air-vent roofed in those pale green glazed tiles, too. Sidi Boumedienne's mosque itself, built a couple of hundred years after his death, owns a pair of massive cedar doors that are miracles in themselves. They were made in Spain, it seems, and came sailing spontaneously across the sea from el-Andalus. Or so the story goes . . .

While we ooh and aah over the view, Liamine gives us the low-down on Sidi Boumedienne. He began life in el-Andalus as the son of a lowly weaver, but soon worked his way up in the world of religion and philosophy, crossing the sea to study first in Fez, then in Mecca, where he chose the path of the Sufi mystics, renouncing the riches of this world and all its vanities, and went on to teach in the universities of Cordoba, Fez and Baghdad before coming on down to the Maghreb. Here, as well as popularizing Sufi mysticism – till now the religious philosophy of a small literary elite – over the whole area, he also converted the sultan of Bejaia, up on the coast near Algiers, to his point of view. Hold on tight for this bit of the story. Sidi Boumedienne, invited to an evening party at the sultan's palace, sat silent amid the displays of wealth and excess, listening to the flatterers and fawners who surrounded the sultan, inflating his pride and ego beyond all reasonable bounds. Disgusted, our hero called for silence, walked up to the sultan and spread out his burnous before the monarch's eyes. Whereupon, in the cloak's folds, the sultan saw a terrible vision of his city and all its earthly delights reduced to dust and ashes, causing him to realize how vain and fleeting were the things of this world. So now, thanks to Sidi Boumedienne's cloak of persuasive powers, the sultan became a Sufi mystic too, and went off to live as a hermit on a small rocky island just off his city's shores – an island that belonged to the Republic of Pisa.

Is Liamine certain of this? I can swallow the magic-cloak part all right, but what was an Italian city-state doing owning a North African island in the year eleven-seventy-something?

Liamine is extremely sure. Not for nothing does he have a university degree, he says, challengingly. The merchants of Italy had a great interest in the Maghreb at the time: her city-states, of course, were after a share in the rich commerce of Africa. The Republic of Genoa, too – my own regional capital, back home in Italy – had claimed itself an island off Algiers for trading purposes.

So, back to the Italian connection. Have we not heard of Fibonacci, the Italian mathematician who discovered the mathematical sequence of the same name, and who is credited with introducing the Arabic numerals we use to this day into Europe? Well, he studied here alongside Sidi Boumedienne the Andalusian. Fibonacci's interest in maths was a supremely practical one to start with, according to Liamine. His father was a merchant, the Maghreb representative of the merchants of Pisa. Fibonacci junior, growing up on the coast at Bejaia, was sent to study with the mathematicians of the Maghreb simply to improve his accounting skills and boost the family business. He soon appreciated the superiority of the streamlined Arabic system, with its all-important zero, over the cumbersome Roman numerals still used in Europe – and in 1202 published his book *Liber Abaci*, introducing this marvellous invention to his homeland.

Those Arabic numerals may be in worldwide use today, but at the time they got a lot of bad press – so much so that, in 1280, the Christian Church took the view that these strange foreign symbols, with their magical powers of increasing wealth out of all proportion, were without doubt some Islamic mystic code with dangerous heretical implications. Fibonacci's book was banned, and the astute bankers of Florence, who had taken to the new system like ducks to water, were now forbidden to use it. But there was no way to halt the flood of progress. The word *ciffra* – 'cipher' – used by the Church at the time to condemn the Arabic numerals is nowadays the ordinary Italian word for 'number'.

We arrive now at the whitewashed tomb of Sidi Boumedienne which has survived here intact ever since the thirteenth century, only to find, to our horror and amazement, that the last few days of our own century have been its undoing. It has been desecrated. Someone has thrown green paint all over it and bashed at it with what must have been a sledgehammer. Liamine can't believe it. He was up here a week ago. This has happened since then! He and Ismail stand and gaze at it in appalled silence.

It must have been attacked, they tell us, once the power of speech has returned to them, by *intégristes* – the local word for Islamists. Green, Liamine adds gloomily, still informative as ever, is the colour of Islam.

Liamine is distraught; Ismail is just angry. They may disapprove of the *marabout* cults, but that doesn't mean they agree with people going around desecrating their tombs. You must have respect for the believers, says Ismail, who are devout Muslims, even if mistaken. And for the *marabouts* themselves – as great men, if not as holy objects.

Listen to this, says Liamine. '*En louant ce qu'il croit, le croyant loue sa propre âme: c'est pourquoi il condamne les croyances étrangères à la sienne. S'il était juste, il ne le ferait pas.*' ('Praising what he believes in, the believer is praising his own soul: and that is why he condemns beliefs that are not his own. A just man would not do this.')

Do we know who wrote that? Sidi Boumedienne! Who died in 1197. And still people have learned nothing.

14

Back in the taxi, much excited conversation is going on in the front seat about the desecration. The proportion of French to Arabic is just enough to tantalize, but not enough for us to guess what Ismail and Liamine are saying. Eventually we get the distilled version.

This is what comes of cancelling the elections. Of course it wasn't the Front for Islamic Salvation who did this: Liamine himself voted for them. So did Ismail. So did lots of good people – to show that they'd had enough. The only other choice was to vote for the *Pouvoir*. Most of the other parties had withdrawn – or called for a boycott because of the gerrymandering. But this was certainly not what our guides had in mind: senseless destruction.

Being Europeans, the first thing that occurs to us in this emergency is to suggest a soothing glass of *al-kohl* in some nearby hostelry. Probably not the correct move in Islamic circles, though. So we sit quietly in the back of the taxi and say nothing. Ismail drives on, silent now.

Eventually, downtown again, we pull up on a broad main road before a massive mosque which Liamine, now on remote control, tells us is the one modelled on the Grand Mosque of Cordoba. Sidi Boumedienne himself will have prayed here. It was brand new when he was alive. Do we want to go in? They will wait for us in the car.

It seems only polite to leave them alone for a bit. By now I have lost whatever will-power I once possessed, anyway. If I can't just sit quietly somewhere, without being told about bizarre and surreal miracles or witnessing bizarre and senseless vandalism –and two nice boys being very upset by it – I may as well go and look at a mosque.

I clamber out of the taxi. Gérard, who has evidently become a Boumedienne groupie on the spot, is making a beeline for the keyhole-arched doorway. Guy is following hotfoot, burnous flying. So much for the three musketeers. They have forgotten all about my handicapped female status.

Liamine calls through the window. Am I going in too? If so, I need to go round to the side entrance, not the main one – there's a place just inside the door there where I can borrow a *haik*.

And so, a few minutes later, I find myself standing inside the atrium of the side entrance, trying to put on a *haik* for the first time in my life. Fortunately, there are no witnesses, no doorman or woman, just a row of these big white lengths of cloth hanging from a series of hooks. Not garments at all, but great, unwieldy strips of material several yards long and two yards wide. Somehow you have to get this stuff wrapped around yourself in a way that covers your whole body and head, yet leaves your arms and legs free to move. Tricky. My first attempt meets the first criterion, but certainly not the second. I've trussed myself up like a chicken: can't even take a step. I wish I'd bothered to examine the *haik*-clad women we've met more closely. Some *haiks* certainly look as if they're actually sewn up into a sort of bell-shape. Couldn't I have got one of those? I sincerely hope nobody is going to walk in and catch me at this. At last I come up with a functioning solution. Right round the body under the armpits, across the front first, leaving the arms free. Now wrap right round again, over the shoulder and covering the head. Yes! The last length flips triumphantly forward over the other shoulder, leaving an end I can cling on to from the inside, under my chin, to stop the whole she-bang falling off. It certainly feels right. My legs are covered to the ground, but I can still walk. And I seem to have created that authentic drapey-shawl effect at the back without even trying. Hurrah. I've cracked it. Sandals off now. I can go in at last. Little do men know what an easy life they have of it.

Once I've settled in to my *haik*, it turns out to be exactly the right garment for my state of mind. Very comforting, like being in bed under your sheets, yet walking about at the same time. I can look out at everything, but nothing can look in at me. I don't have to interact with anyone: I am invisible. Perfect. Through the open courtyard beyond, the late-afternoon sunlight is flooding into this cool and shadowy place; more light slants in through coloured glass. Small groups of men of all ages are dotted here and there, leaning against the wide pillars or sitting on patterned kelims, listening to the *imam*. Some are meditating, some quietly praying. A wonderfully tranquil atmosphere, and a pleasing sense of energy and purpose in the quiet discussions taking place in among the niches and pillars around this spacious, airy prayer-hall.

Maybe I am having an epiphany? Inside a big white bag, inside a mosque: can this be my true destiny?

No. Not really. For all I know, one half of them may be discussing their next green-paint-and-hatchet assault on the precious relics of the other half. I wouldn't know which side to take. Calvin, or the Old Church? I love the stories of demon lovers and wishing trees, of djinns and Holy Confectioners and the magical uses of henna. Drumming and dancing yourself into a frenzy at a *moussem* sounds very appealing, too. But I can certainly see why young people here would want their religion to be an active one, committed to changing things for the better in the here and now, and not a fatalistic *baraka*-seeking pie-in-the-sky-when-you-die opium sop. Religion may not, in my book, be the best way to get political change, but then, evidently, there's not much alternative in this country. Would I go along with the ones who wanted to get rid of the superstitious *marabout*-djinn angle on Islam, clean it up and make it more rational? I suppose, if I was an Algerian and a Muslim, the answer would be yes. Strip the magic cloak from Sidi Boumedienne, and return him to the enlightened world of science and intellect that was once his.

Well, this is great. Put on a *haik* and discover you're a closet puritan. That your great-great-grandfather would be proud of you, after all. Whatever next?

*

Gérard and Guy, as you'd expect from people who hadn't been obliged to take a DIY drapery course before they entered, are already out of the mosque and back in the car by the time I reappear. They tell me that the boys don't want to go on with the tour. They can't face it. They don't want paying, either, not after what we've been through together. We're going to buy them a quiet restful dinner instead. Good. That was quite enough *baraka* in one dose for a weakling like me.

Off up another warren of back streets, we order a fish dinner in a tiny, crowded restaurant that looks like something you would have found in Paris in the 1940s, complete with lacy, hand-crocheted half-curtains at the windows. And a big fat bouncy woman taking our orders, in a very relaxed headscarf, loosely knotted on the top of her head, plenty of curls escaping. How fast I'm learning to notice things that would normally mean nothing to me.

Within seconds she has spotted my henna moon-and-star, which have so far escaped our guides' notice. What a very unusual *ménage* I seem to be setting up for myself, she says. How many of them are my fiancés? Do I need all of them? Don't I have a spare one for her? And she goes off cackling back to the kitchens.

Do we fancy a beer? asks Liamine. Because he does.

We surely do. Aha! Not such different reactions to trauma as we imagined, then.

Or maybe, says Guy, a bottle of white wine to go with the fish?

But no. This place doesn't stock wine, only beer. Must be more of that anti-*francisant* business. They certainly aren't short of wine in the area, we know that. We're still suffering the consequences.

Still, the beer is good. Hair of the dog, I say, taking my first cool, frothy sip. *Poil du chien*.

Ismail seems startled, not to say horrified, by this remark.

It's an English expression, I explain. Hair of the dog that bit you. It means a hangover cure.

Ismail is greatly relieved. The phrase 'The Dog' has been used locally for a century or so, it seems, to describe the French settlers and their hated colonial culture. It seemed to him that I was making some obscure criticism of their beer drinking.

Gérard is asking about Liamine's degree. Did he study here in Tlemcen? In French or in Arabic?

He did Exact Sciences. In French. At the University of Tlemcen, they've come up with a cunning way of getting around the political problem with the French language – you get to choose between 'Arabic' and 'Latin' for your courses! They're making out it's the two great classical cultures that are in question. And French is a Latin language, after all, so nobody can disagree! But he hasn't got a job out of it anyhow. He is a *haitiste* just like everybody else here – a wall-propper. A waste of time, Liamine says. Nobody can be bothered going to college any more. Except girls – over half the students at the university these days are girls. They're happy to study, even if there is no job at the end of it. It's about the only way they'll get allowed to spend whole days at a time away from the parental home!

Gérard laughs. Do we remember hearing about Yazid's daughter, who wanted to go and study medicine in Spain? He's sure that must be why. To get away from her father's incessant telephone surveillance!

Yes, indeed. And also, who knows, to continue the long and honourable tradition of liberal scientific exchange between the Maghreb and the Iberian peninsula?

A big pile of mixed golden-fried whitebait, squid rings, little tiny flatfish and fresh prawns arrives. It looks delicious. It smells delicious. And I'm told it tastes delicious. But alas, I can hardly eat more than a few morsels of mine. Following my fellow diners' example, I have liberally sprinkled a tablespoon of some vaguely tomato-looking sauce all over it – stuff that sits on the table in a little glass bowl. And it was not tomato at all, but pure red-hot chilli. After a couple of mouthfuls, I am in agony. I have never been any good with chilli, however hard I try. And this stuff is lethal. Why on earth didn't anyone warn me? How could anything possibly be this hot?

But it's harissa, says everyone, including the French component of the dinner party. What else would it be but harissa, in an Algerian restaurant?

Nobody, it seems, could have imagined that I didn't know. Everyone's heard of harissa!

Not, I say crossly, still trying to catch my breath, if they happen to come from an Algerian-restaurant-free zone like I do. There may be millions of Algerians in France, but they are pretty few and far between in England. And in Italy too. Do Gérard and Guy know what an onion bhaji is?

No, they say, puzzled. Why? What is it?

I rest my case. It's all down to who you colonize. And now, thanks to Britain having chosen the wrong part of the world to oppress, leaving my nation in darkest ignorance in the matter of harissa, I can only pick at the few bits of fish round the edge of my plate – and occasionally other people's plates – that happened to escape the drenching. As I begin filling up with bread, *faute de mieux*, the serving woman reappears at our table and enquires why I'm not eating.

I offer her a choice of any one of my fiancés she fancies, if she will just give me a few more of the lovely prawns, chilli-free. No luck. She thinks they've just about run out. But she'll see what she can do.

While we eat – or, in some cases, don't – Gérard busies himself with more news-gathering: as usual, about the Front for Islamic Salvation. What, if any, is its connection with the green-paint attack on the shrine of Sidi Boumedienne? And what made Ismail and Liamine vote for it?

He would once have supported the Front for National Liberation, Liamine says, for all its defects. After all, it's thanks to them that Algeria is a free nation at last. But what clinched it for him was when the hypocrite West and its United Nations launched their attack on Iraq. The Islamic Front responded by calling for mass demonstrations against Western intervention in Arab affairs, while the FLN government not only did not protest, but sent in the forces of law and order to drive the 100,000 angry demonstrators off the streets!

It wasn't that Algerians had any time for Saddam himself, Ismail says. This country was the very first to condemn his invading Kuwait. Here in Algeria he was nicknamed *Khaddam* – which means 'lackey'. That's how popular he was!

Or else *Haddam*, says Liamine, which means 'destroyer', and not in a good way! But then, for an Algerian government not to speak out when the West rode roughshod over the Arab nations, and gave them no chance to solve the problem among themselves, without the pointless massacre of thousands of Iraqis! When Algeria itself had been the prime mover in trying to set up peace talks, too! It's pathetic. If it was left to the *Pouvoir*, Algeria would end up a banana Islamic republic like Saudi Arabia, grovelling to the two-faced United Nations – who claim to stand for impartial international justice, when they've never bothered – since 1967! – about Israel occupying lands the UN itself agrees rightly belong to three sovereign Arab nations. What else could you do, if you had any self-respect, but vote for the Islamic Front?

And in the end, says the optimistic Ismail, the result is still a good one. Who has the *Pouvoir* had to call in, in its desperation to give some legitimacy to this emergency government, but Mohammed Boudiaf! A good man, from the old, honourable guard of the FLN, who has already spoken out straight against corruption and promises to do something serious about it. You can tell his heart's in the right place, because, when he addresses the nation, he doesn't do it either in French or in highbrow classical Arabic, but in ordinary everyday Algerian Arabic.

The green-paint attack on Sidi Boumedienne's shrine is another matter altogether, they say. There are rumours of a new Groupe Islamique Armée: real hardcore *intégristes* who believe that the only way to restore the Caliphate – the true Islamic government, or at least, their version of it – is to take over the state first, with violence and force of arms, and to impose shari'a institutions from above. People like the so-called Afghans, or the Takfir wa l'Hijra, who think that anyone who does not support them deserves to die, because they have broken with Islam, excommunicated themselves. They didn't stand in the elections, of course, because they don't agree with what they call alien Western democracy. They want the country run by some sort of traditional-style *djema'a,* the olden-day Councils of Elders from before the French. This latest fiasco will have strengthened the anti-democracy lot, too. What credibility does that give to democracy, calling elections and then bringing in the army when you don't like the results! Liamine fears the ranks of the *intégristes* will be swelling by the minute.

The lovely serving lady now reappears with something on a plate, which she slips onto the table in front of me. It's certainly not prawns, though. A pair of sizzling kebabs on metal skewers. They smell delicious.

Some white kidneys for you, she says, with a conspiratorial wink.

Fantastic. I take a little bite. No idea what a white kidney may be, but it's going down well. Tender, tasty meat, and not so much as a hint of chilli. I grab more bread and get tucked in.

She gives me a kindly pat on the shoulder. That should keep your strength up for the wedding party, she says.

Grrrr.

Some time later, it is revealed to me that the phrase 'white kidneys' is a polite euphemism for testicles.

Mid-morning next day, and we are at the foot of some beautiful rocky cascades a few miles outside the city, admiring the limpid pools below and the impressive iron bridge away above us, crossing the high ravine, designed and built by a certain Monsieur Eiffel. It looks rather a lot like his tower, too, but tipped over sideways. Apparently he built another bridge, way down in the Sahara. I'm looking forward.

We're at the little shack of a café-bar that serves the picnickers and swimmers who frequent this spot, the Cascades of El Ourit, along with Ismail and Liamine, and three of Ismail's cousins, who are over visiting from France. Two of the cousins, teenage girls in jeans – and 'in hair' – startled us when we arrived here by leaping from their seats, throwing their arms around us, and thanking us in the most heartfelt manner for existing. If it wasn't for foreigners and tourists coming to this town, they said, life here would be completely impossible. The only places a woman can sit out in public are those frequented by enough foreigners to make it unremarkable.

The girls, born here, but now used to the ways of Paris, are disgusted with their home town. They love Tlemcen, they say, and have looked forward to coming home for years, but still they are threatening never to return. This is their first visit back as young adults – and teenage girls here have no life at all! Everyone has it in for you, and you're criticized left, right and centre for having forgotten your roots, for not being Algerian enough! In fact, they say, all these nostalgic old French people who've started coming back to visit the happy haunts of their youth get a lot better reception in this town – in spite of what France did to this country – than do real Algerians like themselves, who were brought up in France!

(I check Guy out: he does not seem to have taken that remark about the old nostalgics to heart.)

The cafés of Tlemcen town, it appears, are not at all female-friendly. They actually refuse to serve you at all if there's no man with you, or, if you do have a man with you, still insist on your going upstairs to sit in a special family room! When the whole point of sitting at a café, as everyone knows, is to be out on the street watching the world go by! But not here in Tlemcen! Only men are allowed to do that! And foreigners!

Worse still, when the girls gave in yesterday and went upstairs to this so-called family room, it turned out to be the haunt of a couple of local prostitutes, who didn't want them there either! So, they say, any woman who goes out for a coffee must be a prostitute, and if you're not a prostitute, don't even dream of going to a café! Even this place, here at the Cascades, has a bit of a louche reputation – too many underdressed bodies by day, and by night the clientèle is certainly not of the most respectable or pious! They wouldn't want their aunt to know they'd been here, no way!

Gérard and Guy sympathize deeply, huffing and puffing about

how awful it all is, as if nothing like that had ever been heard of in their own country. Another example of that short-European-memory syndrome! What are they on about? It certainly isn't very long, I say, since respectable females wouldn't dream of going into English pubs – or French bars, either. Men were still staring and muttering at the sight of unaccompanied women in my very own living memory! Probably still are in small country places. Accompanied women – just like here in Tlemcen – had a special separate bar. I don't recall hearing anybody citing Christianity as a reason for our exclusion in my own lifetime – we've emptied the religion out of it now, call it sexism and disapprove of it – but in the granny's Good Old Days, it was certainly Christian morality that was invoked against the fallen women and shameless hussies who brazenly frequented public hostelries.

The girls are not interested in ancient history, though – or in other people's religions. They want to tell us about their cousin Jamila, and how even more vile it is for people who actually have to live here full time. Jamila couldn't even come here today in case somebody saw her and told her mother! And listen to this! She was grabbed a couple of weeks ago, walking down the street *en cheveux* – the way she always has done, all her life – by a man who stuck his face right up to hers and grabbed her arm, really hurt her too, she had a big bruise on it, and hissed that it would be the worse for her if he saw her out again in such an immodest state of undress. He seemed like the classic neighbourhood *barbu*, the girls says, a 'bearded one', which is slang for a fundamentalist. But then, when Jamila took a second look at him, she realized it was her old physics teacher from school, who had turned *intégriste*! Imagine that! Your own teacher threatening you with violence – and he used to be such a nice man, too, Jamila said.

We all wander off among the rock pools, trailing greenery, warm sun, toes in water. There are level areas of cherry orchards and apricot trees further down, beside the river. What we're seeing is nothing, our hosts tell us, compared to the seven massive waterfalls that once roared down the rockfaces below the Eiffel bridge, before Tlemcen built a dam to save the water for the city. Still, it's perfectly beautiful enough for us, with the warm sun and golden rocks, the babbling brooks and tufts of tiny pink flowers in the crevices. A corner of paradise.

Except that now, distracting us completely from the beauties of nature, Liamine, Ismail and the cousins launch a major campaign to convince us to convert to Islam. I think this is actually some sort of accolade: when religious people get fond of you, they start to worry about your soul, and want to save you. I have had many brushes with concerned Italians trying to save me by converting me to Catholicism over the years. Never make the mistake of admitting to having no religion at all. Your evangelist will go into overdrive, desperate to save you from burning in hellfire for all eternity.

Liamine and Ismail's great hope, naturally enough, is that an Islamic Algeria might return to the tolerance and greatness of the dynamic days of Sidi Boumedienne, not head off into the darkness of the benighted *intégristes*, while the girl cousins launch into an Aytan-type critique of the West and its materialism; the famous freedom of the West is great, yes, but at bottom it's only a freedom to get something better than your neighbour has! They know all about it, because they've seen both sides of the coin! The West is no paradise on earth. What about community, charity, and social justice?

What, though, I ask, about the violent bearded moralists they've just been complaining about, and the women-in-cafés veto?

But all that has nothing to do with true Islamic values, says everyone in chorus.

Do I know about Khadija, wife of the Prophet Mohammed, peace be upon him? Mohammed's own example, say the girls, proves that the *intégristes* are completely wrong in their interpretation of the Koran.

Mohammed's love story, now told by our hosts and their teenagers while I quietly dabble my toes in the water, really is a revelation to an ignoramus like me. For a start, I had no idea how fully documented his life was. There is none of the vagueness and mystery that surrounds the life of Jesus. That, I suppose, is the advantage of being born 700 years later, and into a much more literate society.

So, to the strains of sweet music . . .

When the couple first set eyes on one another, Khadija was an independent woman: a wealthy merchant in her own right, twice married and twice widowed, and a good ten years older than Mohammed. A brilliant businesswoman, by all accounts, whose acumen in matters of trade was evident from the fact that her camel-trains of merchandise were twice as long as most of the others leaving Mecca. Khadija needed someone trustworthy to accompany one of her caravans to distant Syria, so she put the word out among her family. Mohammed, some sort of distant cousin, though she did not know him personally, was recommended. She offered him the job. And so utterly fabulous was the powerful Khadija that it never entered Mohammed's head that she could be interested in a mere penniless stripling like himself: it was Khadija herself who made the first move, through a mutual cousin. Moreover, it was she who supported him financially, and not vice versa, for most of their life together. And though he later married several more wives, he never thought of another woman while she was alive – not until after she died, aged sixty-five.

And in case all that isn't enough to convince me that sexism is not an obligatory part of Islam, one of Mohammed's later wives, Aisha, is the recognized source of at least half the sayings in the Hadith, the book of interpretations of the Koran which is the second Muslim holy text.

Voilà! says Liamine. How can anyone think that Mohammed, peace be upon him, wanted women to be shut up in the house, powerless and illiterate? It makes no sense at all!

True. As far as I can see, Islam is like all the great religions of the world: it can mean almost anything to almost anybody, and its scriptures can be interpreted in a thousand and one different ways. That, I imagine, is how any religion stays great.

Where on earth, Guy wants to know, do the back-to-the-veil people get their ideas from, then?

Just old customs from before Islam was even born, it seems, ancient traditions that have got mixed up with the religion, like the one about women not going into pubs, which nobody sees as part of Christianity any more. Or nobody but a few mad fundamentalists.

Gérard has heard that the custom came from the East, where the veil was used by the privileged classes alone. An invisible wife, with no need to go out and about, or dirty her hands with work, was the sign of a rich man, as Yazid and Tobias told us back in Morocco. Soon everyone was aping their betters, as we humans so often will.

And a few generations later, I suppose, people were stuck with it. A woman didn't look decent unveiled; she looked shameless and argumentative. A tradition was born.

15

The city of Algiers sits on a magnificent Mediterranean bay ringed by hills; it looks like a giant's version of Nice. All along the seafront is a showcase city of broad ex-colonial boulevards, imposing Beaux-Arts arcaded buildings, brilliant white apartment blocks with blue slatted shutters and wrought-iron balconies. We are downtown, having breakfast at a boulevard street café, just like any you'd find in Nice, though there are certainly a lot more women in those beaky white half-kerchiefs than you'd normally find on the Côte d'Azur. My French companions need fear no famine here in Algiers, where the cafés provide not just croissants, but also *pains au chocolat* and *pains aux raisins* – the whole gamut of French breakfast pastries; though I'm sorry to say that things in Algiers have gone too far along the road to modernity for there to be any sign of Momma's old-style breakfast bowls.

Our ways are to part for a few hours. Gérard is off to pay a call on some friend-of-a-friend who is teaching here in Algiers. Jean-Pierre used to teach as a *co-opérant* down in the south of the country, and in Mali too, and has advice, addresses and contacts for the boys' onward trip towards the River Niger.

Guy wants to go alone to look at his old family home. He isn't sure, he says, what his reaction will be. Or maybe he just won't have a reaction? We have already checked out his father's ex-work-place, just up the road from here: the central post office, a massive white edifice in a rotund Franco-Muslim-medieval style, three huge, tall archways filling almost the whole of its monumental façade. Guy stood and stared at it, mesmerized. It seemed, er, improbable, he said . . .

So were Ismail's cousins right? I ask now, as I sip my *café-crème*. Are there really a lot of old nostalgics coming back to look at the Algeria of their youth?

Guy doesn't think there can be many. Not to judge by the vile racist publications his father receives from various organizations of ex-*pieds-noirs*. Half of them are still convinced that the Algerians have no right to this country, that if the French army had stood firm, if the settlers hadn't been sold down the river, they would still be living a life of luxury here in their very own Promised Land. And decent people like his parents are too ashamed of the past behaviour of that lot to return, even for a visit.

And were they really sold down the river? Did they never think of just staying here and sharing the country with the Algerians, as equals?

Guy can't believe my ignorance. The French state collapsed over the loss of Algeria; not just the government, the state itself. All Paris was watching for the skies to darken with planes and paratroopers: the pro-settler generals were threatening a military coup. De Gaulle, retired since World War II, had to be wheeled in to save the country – like Boudiaf here today. And people in England know nothing of all this?

I apologize. But no, we don't. Or I don't, at any rate.

Well, it was the settlers' own fault that they lost everything, Guy says. The Algerians had promised, signing the cease-fire, that all French property honestly come by would be safe, and the settlers could stay on if they wished – under majority rule. Maybe it was the words 'honestly come by' that bothered the *pieds-noirs*? Or was it 'majority rule'? Once the French army was set to withdraw, the hard-liners set up an Organisation Armée Secrète, made up of moon-lighting pro-settler soldiers.

To give me a flavour of the thing, Guy says, it may be enough to mention that Jean-Marie le Pen was involved. The OAS faked

Algerian 'outrages', trying to force the regular army to stay and fight on. There was no hope after that. The *pieds-noirs* had broken the peace agreement themselves. And when their plan failed, there was nothing left for them but to run.

I can't say I envy Guy going to meet the Algerian residents of his old family home. Rather him than me. I've decided not to go with Gérard to visit his school teacher, either. It's a beautiful sunny day, I'm not going on to Mali anyway, and I fancy a walk through this beautiful city on its immense blue bay. Truth to tell, I also fancy being on my own for a few hours. I'll buy myself a picnic, I say, and go and eat it on the port.

Somewhere behind and above us are the high walls and narrow alleys of the ancient casbah, the old fortress city. The Algiers population had overflowed from here well before the French left, and many miles of *quartiers populaires* – working-class areas, I suppose, is the best translation for this phrase – stretch out beyond the city centre today. A couple of hours from now, through a series of mishaps, I will find myself in the heart of one of these run-down ghettoes – a grimy, rubbish-strewn area of grey blocks of flats, of unemployed youths leaning against graffiti'd walls, of dust blowing through empty streets. In short, in exactly the kind of place Samir was so sure I would never have any reason to visit.

I potter off through a street market full of beaky-handkerchief ladies, buy myself some camembert, a baguette, and a bag of luscious-looking oranges, and set off, humming happily, all alone. Thinking private thoughts to myself, in lovely limpid English. No hunting about for not-quite-the-right-word. That, I am sure, is the cause of my present tangles-in-the-brain sensation. When you're constantly speaking a foreign language, you're constantly bumping into things you don't quite know how to say, half way through a sentence: you have to quickly come up with a circumlocution. If it's a tricky sub-ject, you may find you're doing a circumlocution off a circumlocution off a circumlocution – and now you can't remember what you were trying to say in the first place. Tangled brain. But not today! Just me, all alone. Liberation!

Somehow or other, in my joyful abstraction, far from ending up down on the main port in the centre of town, I follow signs to what I realize, some time later, is actually the industrial port: not what I was aiming for at all. I start guessing something is amiss when I find myself on an endless and featureless four-lane boulevard. It is horribly hot, not a hint of a cooling breeze, my head is already at boiling point, and there is no sign of any shade for what looks like miles up ahead. Should I turn back? But I've already walked for fifteen minutes. There has to be a turn-off down to the water soon . . .

Eventually, here it is. A grey, dusty, industrial-looking road with a welcome sea-breeze blowing up it – a road which turns out to lead, not to the pretty harbour of my imagination, nice place for a picnic, full of picturesque fishing boats, triremes of Nineveh, apes and ivory, but to an even greyer industrial zone of oil-slicked flotsam and rusting jetties. And of endless, leering propositions from groups of jellaba'd men. Dockers waiting for work, maybe, though some of them seem to have given up the idea and are trying to catch fish off the end of one of the piers, chatting to some other men in a small rowing boat, bobbing down below them. But I shouldn't have looked at them. More catcalls and suggestive muttering. It is a shock to realize, all of a sudden, how dependent I am on Gérard and Guy's presence for safety – or at least for comfort and normal friendly relations with other people. Not such a liberation to be without them after all. If they'd been here, the leerers certainly wouldn't leer. They would get chatting, let us catch fish from the pier with them, give us a ride in the row-boat, whatever . . . And probably be nice people, too.

You don't get the camaraderie if you're a lone female, but you don't get to sit down in peace and eat your picnic, either. I can't face walking all that way back in defeat, away from the breeze, under that blazing sun. I veer off towards another pier, well away from the men. There must be somewhere quiet to sit down and dangle my feet over the water, even if it is rather unappetizing-looking water. No.

Another bunch of men, climbing up a ladder from some boat down below. It dawns on me that this is a pretty unlikely place for a tourist to be walking about. It isn't too surprising, is it, if all these men think I've come here on purpose to tantalize them? To make them commit faults in spite of themselves, even . . . ?

An idiotic situation. I am hot and tired and hungry, and there is an enormous amount of open space here, but I can't use any of it. Eventually I spot a sort of rusting-dead-end jetty, nobody about. Walk right to the end, sit down facing the water with my back to any chance passers-by – not that there should be any, on a dead end – and get out my bread and cheese. Within minutes, voices are heading my way. Never mind, I'm not going anywhere. I shall just sit here and ignore them. Or explain in a polite, friendly manner that I'm lost, that I'm just having a quiet sandwich.

Minutes later, four men appear and stand right by me, saying things I can't understand – which are obviously not any kind of normal friendly overture. Angrily, I tell them I don't want any company, thank you. Either they don't speak French, or they don't care. At the next knowing grin and suggestive mutter, I lose my rag completely, jump to my feet, sandwich going straight into the water, and roar at the perpetrator in English to go away and leave me alone. He and his friends find this hilarious; they leer and mutter even more. Suddenly I burst into tears. I am so terrified and so angry – with myself, with them, with everything – that I don't care what happens next. I hurl the rest of my bread into the nearest man's face, follow it up with the bag of oranges, aimed randomly at all of them, and shout some more.

My victims, luckily for me, do not retaliate in kind. They merely throw up their hands in perplexity – what did I expect, a woman alone, coming down here? – and go off, sniggering, to join a group of yet more men at the landward end. Now I can't even leave without having to walk right past the whole crowd of them. I stand facing out to sea, sobbing with rage and self-pity, for a few moments; then brace myself and set off back the way I came. Surely they wouldn't harass a woman with tears streaming down her face?

Yes, they would. Jeers and sniggers. But at least they don't try to physically stop me. Safely past them, I wander off back towards the main road, feeling suicidal, fearing footsteps behind me, not daring to look. It seems I've come miles though this wasteland; there is no sign of any other human presence. Another access of rage comes over me: now I have several hours to kill till I'm due downtown to meet up with my travelling companions. Maybe I should go and sit on my own in the hotel room till then? But that would be admitting utter defeat. Voluntarily imprisoning myself! Exactly what the Islamists want!

No, I'm being idiotic. This doesn't have anything to do with Islam. The same thing could happen to, say, some foreign tourist woman lost on the industrial docks of Portsmouth. Come to think of it, Muslim women, unlike us Westerners, have a solution to this problem: hide yourself in a *haik*. Maybe I should just walk back into town and buy myself one?

I am walking miserably on, snivelling as I go, when all of a sudden, a small hand slips into mine from behind.

I take you my aunt, says a child's voice, in halting French. Not cry. I am Mohammed.

I have noticed the boy shadowing me for some time, flitting behind lorries and concrete posts and chickenwire fences. And imagined he was enjoying witnessing my discomfiture. Maybe he was, at that . . . Does he really have an aunt, even? Is he infant outrider for a gang of murderers, kidnappers or *intégristes*? I couldn't care less. At least he isn't leering. And he cares whether I cry or not. Or pretends to, which is better than nothing.

I don't even answer, just let him lead me on, out of the docks and into a maze of narrow back-streets. Where are we going? No point asking: I don't know anywhere in Algiers, do I? And he hardly speaks any French anyway. And I have no energy left to worry about it.

Half an hour and later we are God-only-knows where, a place that seems nothing but one huge grim council estate after another, hardly anyone about in the streets, though we do pass a group of young men I take for fierce tribesmen in from some wild part of the country, in short tunics over loose baggy trousers, wide canvas belts slung round their hips, straggly black beards and scarily piercing eyes. As they draw level with us, I realize they are wearing kohl. That's why their eyes look like that. Mohammed holds my hand more tightly. Not wild tribesmen at all, but city boys dressed up in full *intégriste* regalia. The so-called Afghans.

At last we turn into a narrow side-street. Then into the entrance of a decrepit grey block of flats. Ten long flights of stairs later – lift from Russia, not possible mend, Mohammed explains – we are at Hamida's front door, which she opens with a lovely, welcoming smile. Then, listening appalled to her nephew's excited account, in Arabic, of the circumstances of our meeting, she throws her arms around me, causing me to burst into tears again, and rushes me into her living room, where she cossets me with fig cakes, sweet mint tea, and perfect French, till at last I think maybe it's not so bad being a woman after all, and am in a fit state to speak without sniffling.

Mohammed, too, has eaten his fill of fig cakes. His aunt is extremely proud of his presence of mind in bringing me here. Little Mohammed has seen so many crying women here at her home, she says, that he automatically assumes, clever boy that he is, that if he finds a woman in tears, this is the logical place to bring her. Though I am certainly the first crying European to cross her threshold!

This flat, she explains – where she lives with her father and her own aunt and uncle, as well as a couple of cousins – has become, over the years, an impromptu help-and-advice centre for women in distress. Hamida and her aunt have turned their home into a safe haven for women fleeing violent husbands, or left alone through widowhood or divorce. They are able to do this, she says, because they are protected, in the neighbourhood, by the reputations of the men of the house. Her father and uncle are both well-known local heroes of the War of Liberation, and with state pensions to prove it!

I am surprised to hear that helping widows, divorcees and victims of violence could be bad for a household's reputation, but it is so. In the eyes of the Islamists, it is tantamount to encouraging the breakdown of the family. A woman living alone, without male protection, becomes what they call a source of discord. That is the sin of *fitna*: intentionally creating discord in the community. She is tempting men to commit faults in spite of themselves. And if they do, the *fitna* – and the fault – is hers. If her husband has left her, or died, she should return to her father's protection, or that of her brothers or uncles. Failing that, to her husband's family. The Islamists refuse to see that this may not always be possible – or desirable. That a woman may not want to uproot her children and leave her home, or to throw herself on the mercy of relatives she may never have met – or who may live hundreds of miles from everything she knows. A few months ago a fundamentalist commando set fire to a woman's house because she was living alone with her seven children. One of her sons was burnt to death. She was a danger to the community, a source of discord. Some weeks later, she turned up here – with the remaining six children.

Hamida, unlike almost everyone we've talked to so far, does not agree that the Front for Islamic Salvation are innocent, that only a few mad extremists are to blame for the growing violence. The FIS have been active round here in the *quartiers populaires* for a good five years, she says, and the atmosphere of terror has been growing all that time. The Sons of Hatred, she calls them: *Fils de la Haine*. They chose the acronym FIS, she says, because it sounds identical to the word *fils* – son – in French. They wanted to suggest, by this, that they were the true inheritors of the Algerian Revolution, the legitimate sons of the old and honourable FLN. But they are no such thing, according to Hamida. The legitimate heirs are people like her father, her aunt and uncle: good people who are open to reason and debate – and able to put themselves in other people's shoes! It is hopeless to try and discuss the situations of the women they help with the local Islamists. All they do is parrot verses from the Koran – and when anyone suggests that these words are open to interpretation, they simply close their ears and recite another.

Sounds just like those Christians who come banging at your door on a Sunday. Come to think of it, Christians have their own Army of Salvation, too, don't they? Funny how innocuous the word seems in that context: the Salvation Army. It has such a positively cuddly brass-band ring to it that I've not even noticed the connection till now.

Why, though, I ask, do so many men find this fundamentalism so irresistible? What on earth attracts them so to oppressing and harassing other people?

Because, says Hamida, suddenly looking me fiercely in the eye, an unemployed young Algerian – which means most young Algerians! – feels oppressed and harassed himself. Not just powerless and despised like any unemployed person; on top of that he has an internalized French *colon* sneering at him from the mirror. Independence or not, she says, every young Algerian aspires to the culture of France – the lifestyle, the fashions, not to mention the wages! But he knows in his heart that France has no regard for him. All the more so if he actually goes there – and how many millions of Algerians had that experience, before this country sank so low in France's esteem that she stopped the flow? So, she says, first imagine that despised *boug-noule* of an immigrant – that's what the French racists call us North Africans – then contrast it to the image of the Holy Islamic Warrior, a man with a self-respect based on values that have nothing to do with the West. An image with the power to scare the West – to turn the tables! Now our *haitiste*, our wall-propper, can put on a romantic street-fighter's tunic – instead of yearning for a pair of designer jeans he can't afford that will be two years out of date in French eyes, anyway, by the time he gets them – and be looked up to by his fellow men. Moreover, he's a man of religion now, and if by any chance they don't treat him with respect, he has every right to terrorize them – in the name of God! Of course, it's very seductive, very addictive. And it really is like a drug: they goad one another on, lose all sense of pity or compunction. Last month, sweet, harmless old Aziz, who sat every afternoon at a little table outside his home, taking the sun, drinking his half-bottle of wine, and playing cards with any of his cronies who happened to pass by, was killed. A drive-by shooting. Two crimes: alcohol and gambling. Now he is dead.

Mohammed has crept closer to her on the divan and slipped his arm through hers. She laughs, apologizes for getting carried away. But she is so sick of them. You can never get away from them. Women are arriving here at this flat, in the last couple of months, from as far away as the small farming towns of the Mitidja plains south of Algiers, where intolerance is growing by the day. The Islamists scare them out, and they make a beeline for Algiers, hoping to find a home and some work. But Algiers is running out of places for them. Every home is full to bursting.

These days the FIS *de la Haine*, she tells me, have loudspeakers up on the roofs of every block in the area, a sort of extra *muezzin*, from which they harangue people at every prayer time, with long, rambling moral lessons and exhortations not to fall into evil ways: ordering women to be modest, and men to be firm and manly – they might as well just tell them straight out to beat up their wives, daughters and sisters if they don't wear the *hijab*, she says. These days even the smallest little boy who passes you in the street thinks he has the right to ask you what you're doing out and about, why you're not back home in the kitchen! Not like her little Mohammed, she says, giving him a squeeze. He has been properly brought up, and has a mind of his own!

Mohammed says something to Hamida in Arabic. He wants her to tell me about the boy who was beaten up because of the speakers. It was a young neighbour of Hamida's, a couple of blocks away, only a few days after the system had been put up. He had just worked a night shift at the bakery, he was trying to get some sleep, and the dawn harangue about how much better it was to pray than to sleep was driving him mad! He got out of bed and went up to the roof, fought his way bleary-eyed through the washing lines, found the speaker, pulled the wires out, and went back to bed in peace and quiet. They gave him a pair of broken ribs next day – for disrespecting God. Told him he should thank Allah's mercy that they'd let him live – he wouldn't be so lucky next time. That's how sure they are of themselves – they can't tell the difference between disrespecting them and disrespecting Allah!

Hamida and Mohammed will walk me to the bus-stop, they say, where I can catch a bus back to the centre. Her father's bakery is right opposite: we can stop in and say hello. And tomorrow we must meet up in town, in her lunch hour, if I'd like to come and meet the girls she works with?

Her broken lift, she says as we wind our way around it on the long trek down the stairs, is a symbol of the new world order. Once there was space for a Third World country to manoeuvre: play off one superpower against another, survive in the interstices – even to have modern homes with working lifts. Not any more. The Soviet Union has died, the lift manufacturers exist no longer – asset-stripped, no doubt, by some Russian free-marketeer. No spare parts. There will be no working lift here again – until Algeria is back on her feet. If that ever happens. The jury is still out. Will the Islamists win, and send her country back to the dark ages? Will its present leaders succeed in selling it off piecemeal? Please God there is some chance of Algerians standing up to both, owning their own democratic country and running it for themselves, with full rights for all citizens – including women. And functioning lifts!

Before we leave the building, Hamida stops to tie one of those white beaky kerchiefs over the lovely smile. These days, she says, you're not safe round here without it. I walk out onto the street with a new Hamida, one who has become invisible, just like all the other invisible women in this place.

How fortunate I am to come from a continent where beards are a matter of indifference! In Morocco, people who grow them come under attack. Here in Algeria, on the other hand, it is those who would remove them that get a hard time. Opposite the bus-stop, three workmen are fitting steel blinds to the window of the barber's shop a few doors along from Hamida's father's bakery. The barber's windows have already been broken three times, Mohammed tells me excitedly. The Islamists do not take kindly to a man making his living from the removal of facial hair.

Hamida's father, Zayed, is busy indoors, wearing a white apron and an interesting hat made of folded newspaper, oddly similar to the paper boats I used to fold as a child. No idea whether this is an eccentricity of his own, or normal baker's wear here in Algiers. He is supervising the making of tomorrow morning's croissants, and his three floury young assistants stand rolling up the little triangles of dough, broad end first; a quick bend to give it the moon-shape – its name means 'crescent moon' – and set it on the tray. Now it can sit and rise till morning. Obvious though it is once you've seen it done, I had no idea till this moment that a croissant started life as a triangle.

Zayed, a vibrant bundle of grey-moustachioed energy, shoves a bun into his grandson's hand and takes us all to sit outside the shop, chatting nineteen to the dozen. In the twenty minutes it takes for my bus to arrive, he manages to give me his opinion upon almost every topic under the sun – as well as acting out for my benefit the knock-about comedy version of his famous role in the Algerian Revolution: a tale in which he and his comrades thoroughly outsmarted the French army, who were recruiting what they believed was a fifth column of Algerians sympathetic to their cause – natives they would train up as commandos and use to infiltrate the enemy. So self-delusional were these French officers that they had no notion that almost every member of the group was in fact a supporter of National Liberation. And the few who weren't, says Zayed, were merely ignorant. It didn't take five minutes to show them that they had no possible interest in keeping Algeria French. So, after a period of intensive training, the entire commando absconded one fine night, well fed, well trained, twice as muscular as before, privy to the plans of the enemy, and bearing with them the precious weapons and ammunition, of which their own nationalist side was extremely short! Great days! he adds enthusiastically – to a reproving look from his daughter. No, well, terrible days really, of course . . . he says, toning it down for the sake of the children.

Zayed has also shared with his daughter and me the theory of a friend of his, first expounded to him last night, according to which today's Islamism springs from the same sources as the right-wing Christian movements that overtook Italy and Spain in the 1930s. He races indoors to find the typed sheets the friend left for him, riffling through the chaos of papers around his ancient brass till, eventually returning triumphant. Here! Look, he says, brandishing the document at Hamida. See this bit: '. . . preoccupation with community decline, humiliation and victimhood . . . compensatory cults of unity, energy and purity . . .' It fits, doesn't it! And this bit about 'pursuing with redemptive violence goals of internal cleansing'. Eh? He's right, isn't he? And look here: 'abandoning democratic liberties, seeking charismatic leaders, strong men to lead the nation to its true destiny'! That's like the Islamists wanting to bring back the *djema'a* – chosen by other wise men, supposed to heal the rifts in the nation! Do we not see it? It's identical, says Zayed excitably. Both nations were only too aware of their former greatness – the mighty Spanish Empire, the glorious Republic of Rome – but reduced, like the Islamic world today, to humiliating poverty and backwardness, to licking the boots of the rich . . .

On the bus at last, riding back through the grey suburbs towards the brilliant white of the centre, I certainly have plenty to mull over: Franco, Mussolini, my old friend Salazar . . . It is true that their supporters were seeking a return to a fantasized world of moral order and social harmony. The modern evil of individualism, they believed, could be stamped out by eliminating democracy, exalting the family, and putting women back under male tutelage. Salazar's new constitution of 1933, I recall, proclaimed everyone in Portugal equal before the law 'except for women, due to their nature and for the good of the family'. Sections of the educated middle classes in Europe, as here in the Maghreb, sought to heal the social breakdown of the 1930s depression by imposing their notion of a contented past where everyone knew their place.

Does the parallel hold any further? Alas, I have little energy left for mulling purposes. I can't decide. I am exhausted. So far, the day has been the exact opposite of the peaceful battery-charging one I had envisaged.

Back in the centre of town, at our pavement café, things start to look up. Guy has arrived before me, and is sitting quietly engrossed in a newspaper. I collapse onto the chair next to him and order a tea. Bad mistake: I should have said an Algerian tea. I have been taken for a Frenchwoman, and the waiter now delivers me a cup of lukewarm water wherein a weak teabag-on-a-string lies, floating limply. The ghastly French version of my – and, of course the Algerians' – national beverage.

Guy has been back here for hours, he says. And he hasn't managed to see the inside of his parents' old home. He lost his nerve. He stood outside, walked past it, walked back the other way, stood outside again. He realized that part of him had never really believed it existed. He could hardly take on board how identical it was to the photos that have been hanging on his parents' walls all his life, to the reels of old eight-mil film his father pulls out at Christmas for family get-togethers. It's just a little apartment house with internal balconies round a courtyard in the centre, four flats around it. His grandparents lived in one of them, his parents in another, the third one had a dentist, Monsieur Gaillard, and the fourth, he can't remember. They did the laundry outside in the courtyard. There's a bit of film with them posing there, all laughing, the washing line behind them, and a huge banana palm in a pot. Today there seemed to be dozens of people going in and out – the housing crisis here must really be serious if that many people are living in one small building! He saw only women and children there, though, and he wasn't sure about the protocol for approaching an unknown woman, who maybe didn't speak French and wouldn't know why he was accosting her. He might end up getting lynched, he thought. The banana tree was still there, and so big now that he could spot it down the hallway as people came and went. He wondered whether to ring a doorbell, but in the end he just went and sat in the café over the road – a café that used to be run by a certain Pierre le Moche, who also stars in the family's film archive, an inveterate card-player with huge moustache and jowls – and drank a beer and stared. Of course, there was no Pierre le Moche there either – he must have left along with everyone else. Maybe it's a bad idea to go there, anyway? Does he really want to overlay his own phantom memories with some other family's reality? Assuming they would let him in at all, that is. It seemed impossible that he should think it had anything to do with him, when all those people so obviously had their own busy lives going on in it. Then he started worrying how they might see him. They might think he'd come because he imagined he had some rights over the place. Anyway, it was all too much. He decided to come back here, have another beer while he thought it all over. Maybe he'll try again tomorrow . . . ?

A coffee or two later, a flashy little car pulls up before us with a squeal of brakes, and who should step out of it but Gérard, looking very pleased with himself. The driver climbs out too: a young woman dressed in ultra-European style, skin-tight jeans with tons of make-up and even more tons of jewellery. From the back seat appears a slightly harassed-looking Frenchman – who must be the teacher, Jean-Pierre. They join us, and we are introduced. The young woman, Farida, is the daughter of the headmaster, and one of Jean-Pierre's pupils at the *lycée*. She was coming to this very bar to meet some friends, so she insisted on dropping them off. Farida is quite alarmingly full-on; she is *en cheveux* with a vengeance, masses of curls flowing down her back, and an amount of cleavage on view that would be make her an object of some interest even in liberal Europe. Within minutes Farida has adopted us and is planning our evening's itinerary. As soon as her friends arrive, we'll go for a tour round the casbah. She'll show us the palace where the dey of Algiers slapped the French ambassador with his fan, the famous *Coup d'Eventail* that gave France its excuse to invade in 1830, she says, with a twinkle at Gérard and Guy. Then we'll have dinner at the pizzeria something-or-other. Then we'll go to a club: she knows a place where they have live *cha'abi* music, the popular music of Algiers; of course we must go there! Before the *intégristes* close the place down! If there's one thing they hate more than *Rai*, it's *cha'abi*!

Our visit to the walled town is quite bizarre. We leave the car behind and set off on foot up the steep, narrow streets of the casbah, famous for its poverty, overcrowding and – naturally – fundamentalism. But Farida and her friends – another girl, Lamia, also a pupil of Jean-Pierre's, and a young man, Kamal, who seems to be quite openly gay, dressed in a floppy floral shirt, gold medallion, and jeans – appear to have no fear whatsoever of the *intégristes* and their works. And with reason, it seems: the group of young *barbus* hanging out on the steps of a mosque at an alleyway crossroads, far from spitting at them as I'm expecting, or indeed expressing disapproval or outraged morality in any way, seem terrified of her and her two friends. They turn away, muttering amongst themselves, and make no comment. Everywhere jellaba'd men shrink back into doorways as we pass up the narrow streets in our loud, golden, perfect-French-speaking aura. And when Farida decides that we absolutely must stop at a sweet stall and buy some candy-floss, the salesman keeps his eyes on the floor, and answers her cheerful sallies with a nervous whisper. It is obvious to all and sundry, we gather, that Farida and Lamia are daughters of the *Pouvoir* class. Even without the car, their behaviour, their perfect, accentless French and their Western dress proclaim it from the rooftops. Farida has all the self-confidence, charm and lack of self-awareness of some spoilt American prom queen. My respect for the *intégristes* – in so far as I had any – has sunk well below zero after this experience. And I am certainly getting a clearer idea of where the common folks' hatred of *francisants* may come from.

At the top of the casbah we pause as promised to investigate the palace of the dey – home to Barbarossa in the days of his splendour. Did he set out from this very spot to rescue his beleaguered fellow Muslims from the hostile shores of Spain, and torment the Genoese vassals of Diano Marina? Nowadays the palace is a series of crumbling buildings and courtyards showing hardly a sign of their former elegance: just a patch of blue-and-white tiles with Arabic calligraphy here and there, or a set of slim, elegant pillars with intricately carved capitals supporting a fragile balcony. The dey's *hammam* is dilapidated, half in ruins, like the rest of the area, though people seem to be living here anyway. Washing hangs from windows, or is strung out across bits of flat roof. There is the sound of children everywhere. A door into one of the internal courtyards hangs off its hinges. We step inside to inspect what must be an empty ruin, only to find that we are being inspected ourselves. There are children crowding every one of the four storeys of unstable and chimney-like internal balconies; there are women cooking in the courtyard amongst the debris of fallen masonry. This has only happened in the last few months, says Jean-Pierre, since people began coming in from the Mitidja, fleeing the violence. The only empty space they can find is in buildings like this – places considered too dangerous to live in by everyone else.

Farida leads us on into one of the main palace courtyards to see the plaque put up by the French, to commemorate the famous fan-slapping moment of 1827, and gives us the story of the *Coup d'Eventail*. The French government, she says, owed a huge debt to two Jewish merchants of Algiers, men of Moorish extraction. The Jews had loaned the French government the money to buy grain and save its skin, when the French nation was on the very brink of revolt – in 1799, wasn't it? And the debt had still not been repaid. The French ambassador at the time was a disreputable little businessman who, when the dey mentioned this matter on behalf of his citizen subjects, showed no intention whatsoever of paying up. The dey slapped him in the face, naturally enough, and then the French demanded he apologize. He refused. And so, the French had found their excuse to invade!

Is that not right, Monsieur le Professeur? she says, turning to Jean-Pierre, who gulps and agrees that indeed it was something like that, though there are various accounts of how the situation actually developed . . .

And here you still are among us, after all this time! she interrupts gaily, opening her arms wide to encompass the French contingent.

16

The golden youth of Algiers goes everywhere by car, even if it's only a couple of streets away. Farida seems to love nothing more than roaring at top speed through the traffic of the city centre, racing Kamal in his equally nippy little number. Perhaps that explains her lack of fear of *intégristes*. Hard to intimidate a woman when she's inside a speeding metal box.

They drive us out to see the beach now, where they inveigh against the hypocrisy of the Islamists: we can't even imagine how many dirty little *barbus* come to the beach all holy in their white jellabas, and minutes later there they are in a pair of floral Bermudas, ogling every bikini for miles! Then, when they come here with their children and their wives, it's comical, they make them wear that great white *haik* even when they get in the water! And of course it's ridiculous, you should see how a wet *haik* clings to a woman's body, nothing at all is left to the imagination, Farida can promise us that!

In the pizzeria – jam-packed with other members of this privileged tribe – Western music is playing in the background. Prince, by the sound of it. There is not a hint of *khimar* or jellaba – much less of a veil. It's hard to believe we're in North Africa at all. Except for the conversation of Farida and friends. Kamal is now telling us the tale of a road-block he was stopped at the other day, along with his mother. The military police only got as far as her handbag, which contained a packet of cigarettes. And that was enough for them: they just waved the car on – no checking the boot for explosives or weapons as they should have done. To their minds, a woman who smoked – or at any rate, owned a packet of cigarettes – could not be an Islamist. The Algerian military is supposedly trained according to superior French techniques, he says, with a sly glance at the French guests. But obviously the French have a much less subtle grasp of bluff and double-bluff than one might have imagined.

Back into the cars again, and off to the *cha'abi* night. A crowded upstairs bar, lots of young people, plenty of alcohol on view. Farida and Lamia seem to know everybody in here, and while they do the rounds, we get to talk to Jean-Pierre at last. He has been working in Algeria for well over a decade, he tells us, and first came here with the *co-opérant* movement: once the Algerians got their independence, many thousands of French students committed their first three post-degree years to helping them rebuild their country. It seemed only fair: French public opinion was reeling at the revelations coming out of Algeria. The military had made the bad mistake of torturing a Frenchman to death – a young university professor sympathetic to the Algerian cause. And the worse mistake of letting another French victim survive to tell of their systematic torture of ordinary Algerians – a tale soon corroborated by hundreds of young conscript soldiers from the small towns of France, who, lacking the racist training of the standing army in Algeria, were horrified by what they saw.

Nowadays, though, far from helping the poor, he says ruefully, he is reduced to teaching the privileged! Once the Arabization policy started, the services of French teachers were hardly in demand – unless they could teach their subject in Arabic. Jean-Pierre went off to work in Mali for a bit; but alas, he had left his heart here in Algiers. The country may be a mess, he says, but its people are the salt of the earth.

Jean-Pierre has given Gérard some useful names and addresses, friends to call in on – not only in Mali, but in the south of Algeria, too. Even, as luck would have it, one in Timimoun itself. Hadj Mouloud is a prominent citizen there, he says, a most hospitable and well-informed man, who loves to put up passing Europeans. Jean-Pierre stayed with him a couple of summers ago, and he's already sent him a note warning of our imminent arrival. He's sure we will be more than welcome. Timimoun is the most beautiful of the oasis towns, he says. And the area is more or less untouched by all the religious-political trouble going on up here in the north. That, unfortunately, is why the *Pouvoir* is sending all its Islamist prisoners down there! Timimoun's *palmeraie*, its palm grove, is massive: nearly half a million palm trees on it, and green and beautiful in spring, as we'll soon see. It stretches a whole thirty kilometres along the bed of what was once a river, though not even the archaeologists can say when there was last visible, surface water there: it vanished long before written history began, and maybe even before the oases were first inhabited. We must make sure not to miss the *fouggaras* – the amazing system of underground channels, a thousand kilometres of them and more, that stretch out across the desert. They carry water to the palm groves using gravity alone – from places miles away beneath the sand dunes, where the water table is higher. Keep an eye out, Jean-Pierre tells us, for lines of what look like wells stretching across the desert: they're the openings for inspecting and repairing the tunnels. Hadj Mouloud has diagrams of how they work, done by some team of scientists who came investigating the system – don't forget to ask for a look. There is absolutely nothing natural about the existence of Timimoun and its companion oases: they are entirely, one hundred per cent, a feat of human ingenuity. Archaeologists say the *fouggaras* were built well over a thousand years ago, probably by some of the earliest known inhabitants, who – strange though it may seem – were Berbers of the Jewish faith.

Naturally we request more information. Jewish Berbers?

We're out of luck. The band starts up now, with a scream of strings and a roll of drums: no more conversation. *Cha'abi* turns out (to my ignorant ears, at any rate) to be a close relation of *Raï* – Arabic–Western fusion. Lots of heartfelt balladry to pounding oriental drum rhythms, punctuated by tinkling lutes, wailing violas – and saxophones. Here in the *cha'abi* repertory at least, Algeria's multicultural identity is being celebrated to the full: the first song was written by an Algerian Jew, Lili Boniche (a man, says Jean-Pierre, in spite of this feminine-sounding name, and definitely nothing to do with the Berbers of Timimoun! They all converted to Islam some centuries ago.) The next is by a certain Matoub, a Berber from Kabylia, sung in a mixture of Tamazight and French – and now for a song in Arabic, which I insist on having translated, because the name Bob Marley keeps cropping up in it, along with a hint of reggae in the percussion section. It turns out to be a sort of lament addressed to Marley, tongue in cheek, chastizing him for smoking cannabis, for inducing young men to rip their jeans, and young women to do much worse, and recommending that Marley take a trip round the *marabouts* of Algeria to cure him of his bad behaviour. Can this music, with its pleasingly bizarre patchwork of languages, cultures and religions, be the modern Algerian manifestation of the Peoples of the Book: united and productive once more?

Farida and Kamal now decide, over a round of double-strength gin-fizzes – we try not to boggle – to give us an exposé of the endemic corruption in this country – how you need a *connaissance*, a connection, just to do the simplest thing. You can't even get a parking permit, or a copy of your birth certificate from the town hall, much less a passport, unless you know someone who knows someone.

Sounds just like Italy, then, I say.

But I am very wrong, according to Kamal. Algeria is not like Italy, because Italians know how to work: they know what capitalism is. Algerians don't. They have been spoilt by the state, got into bad habits. Because until recently everything was free, or almost free, here – medicines, schooling, housing. They expect to get everything for nothing. But if they want to get rich, all they have to do is work. That's what a free-market economy means!

Farida and Lamia both find this sally completely hilarious and start calling their friend 'Kamal la Science': Kamal the Science. Fortunately we have Jean-Pierre on hand to explain that this insider joke is a reference to a minister in the now-defunct Algerian government, a certain Abdelhamid Brahimi, an obsessive free-market supporter who constantly appeared on TV, as unemployment burgeoned around him, claiming that what the Algerian economy needed was more 'science'. Earning himself, naturally enough, the ironic nickname 'Abdelhamid la Science'.

Nice to see that, privileged though they may be, the girls don't go along with Kamal's nonsense. I decide to share my favourite free-market quote with them: from an Egyptian prime minister, aptly enough, of the mid-nineteenth century. The freedom of the market, he said – unless all participants were equal, which in the real world was never the case – amounted to nothing more than the freedom of the fox in the chicken run.

Good, eh? He knew this from bitter experience. The Egyptians had had the effrontery to start building a cotton-mill in Cairo, and Britain, defending her freedom to buy raw cotton from Egypt for the Lancashire cotton-mills – whose cloth she would then re-export to the Egyptian market at a fine profit – sent in gunships to bombard the city. The Egyptians, trapped in their chicken run, had no choice but to give in. And go on buying British cloth.

'Only faith in God can allow us to escape the vicious cycle of under-development and neo-colonialism: to achieve global social reform,' says Hamida.

She is translating the Arabic words on the huge poster in the Islamists' window for me. The FIS offices are just a couple of blocks up the road from where she works: you can see the place from here. Each of the eight women sitting at the sewing machines in this dress-making co-op has a little bottle of vinegar and a twist of rag next to her. With the Islamists' offices so near, they have to be ready for the *gas lachrymogène*, the tear gas, they say. Last week there was a car-bomb: they threw bundles of offcuts down from the window, to help tie the wounds of the injured. Meanwhile they make bright kaftans on their machines, and sober jellabas: not exactly high-tech industry, says Hamida, but safe, because however bad things get, people still need to cover their bodies!

And, looking on the bright side, adds Latifa, the stronger the

Islamists get, the more metres of covering a woman needs – and the better for this all-female workplace. Worse luck for them!

I'm relieved, I say, to see that the Islamists do actually talk of something other than women. That poster gives me some idea, at last, of why Algerians might want to vote for them. Since we arrived in the Maghreb, all I've ever heard about is their attitude to women: no hint of what else they stood for – if anything.

The Islamic duty of rulers to consult with the ruled, says Latifa. Their duty to be honest and straightforward in their dealings, and to provide social justice. All of which, she explains, is an Islamist way of talking about putting an end to corruption, and to the privileged elite that runs this country. The irony, though, is that the only success they've had is on women. Because the *Pouvoir*, sucking up to the FIS – or trying to steal their thunder, depending on how you look at it! – has kowtowed to them on women, but nothing else. Obviously, that's the only part of the Islamists' programme the government can possibly steal. They can't shout about vicious cycles of neo-colonialism when they're practically snuggled up in bed with France. And they can't do anything about the privileged, corrupt elite, either, can they? They would be cutting their own throats!

That's how this country has ended up with both its main parties supporting the new Puritanism, says Hamida. In fact, she adds, what she and the girls should really have done is open a cinema in this building, not a clothing enterprise. The cinema is the only boom industry in Algiers at the moment! Thanks to the government's bring-back-Islamic-morality campaign, it's the only place couples can spend some time together in the whole of the city. With the housing shortage, every home is packed to bursting: there's no chance of privacy there. Bars, cafés and restaurants are no longer woman-friendly, let alone courting-couple-friendly! And now there's no more canoodling in the park, either. God forbid the police should see you so much as holding hands in public, never mind kissing! You'll get bundled straight into the back of the black van.

Hamida's fellow workers are all in their twenties and thirties.

Amina is a widow; the others say they couldn't dream of marrying. Marrying here involves your whole family: it isn't something you go off and organize all by yourself. And their families are organizing nothing. Where are the men who could afford the dowry – and provide the home? They would have to live with their parents or parents-in-law; available apartments are virtually non-existent, or unaffordable. Then what when the children came along?

They all live at home with their parents, and all are suffering badly in the new climate of intolerance. Still, they refuse to wear the veil, or even the *khimar*, except for Khalida, who says she wears the headscarf for personal reasons, and Hamida, whose area is too dangerous. But it is scary just travelling to work every morning, putting up with remarks, holding your head high, fearing violence. And as for the evenings, they hardly go out any more. There are no public places open to women. Where can you go these days? And why risk your life to do it? They could afford a flat together, they agree when I ask. But have I forgotten? A woman has to live under the protection of some male relative. One woman living alone through no fault of her own is committing *fitna*, becoming a source of discord. A group of women who had intentionally chosen to live like that would be a red rag to a bull.

And first, says Hamida, they would have to find a responsible male to give them permission to do it! A woman's legal status here is the same as a child's, since the *Pouvoir* rejigged the constitution to make itself seem as *shari'a*-friendly as the Islamist opposition. You need a responsible male's permission to do anything – get a passport, marry, leave the country, even to visit your own parents, once you're married. They were actually trying to allow a man to cast the vote on his wife's behalf at one point, though luckily they lost on that one! There are still a few men of principle in the FLN. But look at Zorah, over there, on the machine by the window – she's twenty-eight years old, and whenever she goes out with her fiancé, she has to carry a letter from her father, to say that he has given his permission!

Zorah nods and smiles her agreement. But it's partly because she refuses to wear the veil, she says. That's why she gets stopped so often by the forces of law and order and needs the letter. And meanwhile, busy harassing lovers to enforce the laws on public decorum, the police leave the *trabendos*, the contrabandists who are making vast fortunes from smuggled goods in these days of private enterprise, in peace to do what they like, no hassle at all.

And there are more *trabendos* every day, says Latifa, who works at a hairdresser's on her day off. Once upon a time all their clients were *francisants*, wealthy ladies from the educated classes, but nowadays you get many loud newly rich clients, *trabendo* wives of flamboyant taste, filling up the place and ordering you about. Meanwhile, the manageress has had to take all the signs off the façade and move the salon to the upstairs rooms at the back, because hairdressers here are as badly out of favour as barbers. There have been threats to declare a *fatwa* on beauty salons. Women aren't supposed to wear make-up, or do their hair, according to the *barbus*. That just entices men to commit a fault in spite of themselves.

What a very odd idea these Islamists do have of themselves and their sexuality, I say. But nobody else thinks it's odd. Latifa explains, like little Aisha and Zeinab did back in Oujda, that men can't help themselves; they're not like us.

Time for lunch. They eat in here, they say: it's cheaper – and anyway, why run extra risks? They are getting the food together as we talk, onto a big brass tray: sesame-seed flatbreads, a chunk of sharp-flavoured white cheese speckled with red chilli, a pile of olives, slivers of roasted red pepper doused with oil and thyme, some stuffed vine-leaves. There's a lovely secret courtyard in the heart of this building, benches round its green-and-blue tiled walls, pots of ferns and aspidistras around a central well, to sit in while we eat. No plates, just a knife each. The bread is your plate: you tear it open and use fragments of it to pick up the garnishes. We have a beautiful big bowl of fruits for dessert, another bowl to fill from the courtyard tap to rinse them.

As we eat, my new friends regale me with more tales of horror.

Amina first. She is a Kabyle, and so was her husband, who passed away a few months ago from cancer. In the hospital where he was waiting to die, the Islamists did their best to drive her away from his bedside. She sat with him a few hours every day, doing her best to comfort him, chatting away in Tamazight and in French – the languages they had always spoken together – but after a while the orderlies began saying she was in their way, she shouldn't stay so long, her visits weren't good for her husband. And when she still kept coming, and staying, finally they brought in the hospital *imam* to tell her that if she couldn't speak Holy Arabic to her man, she had best be gone. Her heathen languages, he said, were burning her dying husband's soul . . .

Latifa has a fifteen-year-old sister, a brilliant singer, who has been playing with a *cha'abi* band since they were all kids, but now she doesn't dare sing in public any more. First, she's a girl, and second, they disapprove of all music, except chanting the Koran. They stopped her and threatened her. The Koran is God's perfect work, and that is all we need.

Zorah tells me of a local stallholder near her home who sold women's clothes, stocked tight stretch jeans. They warned him once, but he didn't take it seriously. The next time they cut his throat.

Next horror: a kindly taxi-driver, Dalila's best friend's uncle, who always used to drive them to the beach at weekends, ever since they were children. They would have such a laugh in his car, music turned up loud, lots of jokes and horseplay. Then suddenly he stopped looking them in the eye, started lowering his head whenever there were women about, wouldn't have music on the radio any more, and finally, he categorically refused to take them to the beach at all. In January he was arrested as the ringleader of a whole gang of *intégristes*. It makes her skin crawl. She was so fond of him!

Now we go back to the *Pouvoir*. They talked of outlawing the taking of second and third wives, says Amina, and then did nothing. Your husband doesn't have to consult you, or even inform you, if he's taking another wife. It happened to her elder sister, he just appeared at the house one day with a new woman, a good twenty years younger than her, and relegated Samira to the back room. She asked him to divorce her, but he wouldn't – he didn't want their grown-up children to think badly of him, he said! A man can divorce at will, no explanation necessary, but there are hardly any legal grounds for a woman to divorce her husband. Ill-treatment and violence don't count. She should practise Islam: submission, in the literal sense. But impotence does! Samira could hardly claim that, though, since the new wife had a baby on the way in no time! So now she's stuck in the back babysitting, while her husband and his new wife whisper sweet nothings in the other room. Amina can hardly bear to go round any more. Who knows what it's like for Samira, having to live there?

Hamida doesn't think the FLN has any principles at all any more. They don't stand for anything – certainly not for Independence, now they're ready to sell half the country up to the first comer. All they care about is staying in power. Except maybe Mohammed Boudiaf. He has dared talk about corruption – and has even actually begun charging people! High-up people, too, not just petty officials! Who knows, maybe he'll do something for women as well?

But Boudiaf or not, the government is still pandering to Islamism. On the news it always calls the killers maniacs or criminals, never Islamists – as if their violence was nothing to do with their religious beliefs. But it is. They are *drogués de la religion* – religion-addicts.

And the women who support them, then? I ask. Brainwashed? Or just dragooned into agreeing with their husbands and fathers?

Heated debate in Arabic as the fruit bowl is handed round. Nothing so straightforward, is their conclusion. Women join the FIS because they can, says Dalila. A girl's family can refuse to allow her to get a job, go to college, get married, but they can't forbid her to throw herself wholeheartedly into her religion. Now she has a role, recognition, status; she can participate, respected, in the debates at the mosque. And at any sign of opposition from the family, a whole mosque-full of honourable men of religion is ready to take her side!

More than that, says Latifa. There's another kind of fulfilment involved, too, if we won't think the worse of her for mentioning it! Join the FIS and all the biggest obstacles to sexual fulfilment in this country are gone at a stroke. It may be impossible for ordinary young women to flout their parents and marry, or have any kind of love-life, in this country, but it's another thing entirely among fellow fundamentalists. Islamists argue for women to submit to their families in everything else, but it's fine to rebel against them to join the FIS. And once the two families are out of the equation, so is parental permission for marriage – and the need for a dowry. They don't even need a home to set up in. Their *imam* will give them his blessing regardless.

Hang on! I say. So in a country where men and women can't even get to know one another unless they're close relations, and where marriage is a horribly complicated thing involving business negotiations between two sets of parents, all young people have to do to break free is to become supporters of radical religion?

Hamida laughs at me. It's not quite that simple, or she and her workmates would all go and join! It may be a kind of liberation, but think of the downside: being married to a *barbu* for the rest of your life!

Dalilah says that lots of women silently go along with the Islamists because women are so vulnerable here. It's a matter of life and death to remain respected and respectable. They can't allow themselves to take the side of anyone who breaks ranks, in case it reflects on them. She herself has heard a pair of ordinary middle-aged housewives talking about a woman who'd been raped: it was her own fault, she had committed *fitna*, created discord, by allowing a man into the house when she was alone. The Islamists' promise is simple: a bigger, better and stronger version of the traditional family. It's hard to imagine any other source of livelihood and security, if all you've ever known is the family. How could an abstraction like 'rights' keep you safe? Women are told – and maybe believe – that people like my present company of seamstresses, women who talk of women's rights, are nothing but deluded mouthpieces of the West. Western 'rights' will turn them into degraded and defenceless sex-objects, shunned and scorned, make them lose the only protection they know, their male relations, and put nothing at all in its place.

Who would take the side of a bunch of hussies like us, anyway? asks Zorah, laughing.

Speak for yourself, says Latifa. We know how much time you and your fiancé spend up at the cinema!

Shrieks of laughter, and suddenly, as we start on our fruit course, everyone falls to discussing love and men, like a bunch of sex-starved teenagers in a school playground. Soon we are covering the charms of various film stars, singers, actors, mostly unknown to me, and even the occasional boy they have dated in real life, as well as times they've managed to hold hands in public, a hidden corner of a certain green and leafy park where you can steal a quick kiss if you're lucky. We're all peeling our fruit now, sitting in a giggling circle, knives in hand. Dangerous stuff. Let's hope no handsome Egyptian slave walks in.

Gérard and Guy have returned from Guy's second nostalgia-at-one-remove mission. They have met Mohammed – yet another Mohammed – Guy's father's friend from the Post Office. Mohammed, once he realized who Guy was, leapt upon him and embraced him so hard he squeaked. Then Guy burst into tears, and Mohammed did too. They went into the house and were made much of, and Mohammed kept telling Guy to thank his father, he had made them so happy, they loved the house so much, it had changed their lives . . . Which Gérard thought was insane, he says, because Guy's father hadn't really done anything, had he, since they could just have taken the house next day anyway? Terrible state of affairs when a man doesn't realize that things have changed for the better thanks to the efforts of his own people, but believes it's down to the charity of a *pied-noir*!

Guy says Gérard is an old cynic, and it makes a huge difference if somebody gave you something willingly or unwillingly.

And anyway, says Gérard, interrupting, they were taken into the house and made much of, and Mohammed still has an old armchair that Guy's family left behind, weird because they sit on rugs and cushions round it so the chair looks like some strange fetish they're worshipping. They made Guy sit in it – you should have seen his face, says Gérard, with everyone sitting at his feet: just what he was hoping for! – and they made a huge fuss of him and brought out tea and cakes, and they are certainly not *intégristes* because Madame Mohammed came and sat with them too, and invited them to stay in the house as long as they wanted. A very mad idea, according to Gérard, because the place seemed to be packed to the limit already with members of the family. Still, now Gérard sees what Ismail's girl cousins meant about visiting ex-colonials. Guy and he were outrageously well treated. You would never believe anything bad had ever happened between the French and the Algerians. But then obviously it didn't, he says hastily, seeing that Guy is about to protest. Not between Guy's dad and Mohammed, at any rate. And then he and Guy left and went for a wander round the *quartier* and found a little park that was exactly the same as in one of Guy's family's films. Except that nowadays there is a monument right in the middle of it to the million dead of the War of Independence.

Before we have even reached Timimoun, we will begin to hear of street fighting in the *quartiers populaires* of Algiers. Within the year, Europeans will be warned not to go anywhere near the area. The Islamists are in full control there. I will write three times to Hamida and only receive an answer to the first. I pray that she and her friends and family may still be safe and sound. There is still hope, even at the darkest hour, when the Groupe Islamique Armée declares a nationwide *fatwa* on all unveiled women. I have saved the testimony of one woman from that morning. She has always refused to wear the veil, and has brought her daughter up likewise, but should she abandon her principles now, and force her teenager against her will to cover herself when they walk to school today? Does she have the right to risk her daughter's life, as well as her own, to fight what she calls 'barbarity and obscurantism'? Her neighbour steps in from the court-yard, dressed to the nines, hair beautifully coiffed. If she is going to meet her death this morning, she says, she wants to do it in style. With daughter and neighbour behind her, our heroine opens the street door, heart in mouth, legs trembling. They are going to be the only females unveiled in the *quartier*, in the city, in the whole country: they are going to die.

But now she looks up the street, and there they are! Everywhere! Bareheaded women – brown hair, black hair, hazel, henna-red. They have not been intimidated, they are at her side! As she steps across her threshold, she hears, she says, mingled with the *you-you*s of all the generations of her women ancestors, the low roar of the walls of intolerance crumbling.

17

Before we head southwards for the desert and Timimoun, we can't resist a quick detour along the coast, curious to see the Rif Berbers' Algerian cousins, the Kabyles. It's a short ride eastwards to Tizi Ouzou, the Berber capital, only an hour from Algiers, but we've paused on the way to take in the atmospheric Roman ruins of Tipasa, right at the water's edge; a favourite spot of Albert Camus in his youth, and of Guy's parents when they were courting.

Here the salt-white ruins stand eroded and gap-toothed among wild shrubs and long grass, outlined against a purple-blue sea, with not a fence or a signpost anywhere. Magically wild; we feel as if we've just discovered them ourselves. Guy clambers onto a rock to declaim his favourite quote from Camus. 'Life can only be understood looking backwards,' he says 'but alas, it must be lived looking forwards.' We pass an amphitheatre, two temples and a villa, to find, right by the water's side, the ruins of what *The Little Cunning One* says was once a factory for garum, that mysterious sauce or seasoning to which the Romans were so addicted that they felt food was virtually inedible without it. It was made by fermenting salted fish, a process so stinky that under the Byzantines its manufacture was banned from inhabited areas. Even the experts know little about the exact recipe for the stuff. Intrigued, I inspect the factory's ruins minutely, but alas, an unable to add anything at all to the sum of human knowledge on this topic. Gérard wonders whether the positioning of a famously odoriferous factory here, right on the path the townsfolk would have had to take to get to the fourth-century Christian basilica, might, in its time, have had some political significance.

After the splendours of Ancient Rome and its mysteriously smelly condiments, purposely sited to annoy the Christians or not, and a quick tour round what was once the Phoenician trading port, now reduced to a few local fishing boats, we jump onto the next cranky bus. Onwards to Tizi Ouzou. A friendly city, but certainly not splendid. Kabyles may have the same reputation for stubborn resistance here in Algeria as the Rif Berbers do in Morocco, but, unlike Chefchaouen, their major city has certainly not fought off the depredations of modern architecture. Naturally, enough, say my companions. Tizi Ouzou, unlike Chefchaouen, is a colonial creation. It was set up by France in the 1870s, conceived as a new home for some of the hundred thousand refugees from Alsace-Lorraine, who had recently arrived in France, fleeing the Franco-Prussian war.

From Alsace to Algeria! That must have been some culture shock. Still, I'm not sure this excuses their terrible taste in architecture – or that of the Kabyles, who took over from them.

We get ourselves a delicious walkabout lunch of *merguez frites* here, a dish I am so used to meeting at roadside snack-stops in France that I genuinely had no idea that the *merguez* was an Algerian beef sausage, and not a French pork one at all. I am well up to speed on the topic now, after a lengthy lecture from the horrified proprietor of the stall – *French* sausages? Are you mad? – backed by polyphonic harmonies of *Mais non!* from Gérard and Guy.

And is the place really full of fair-skinned freckled people with reddish hair who look just like me? No. But the colouring here is certainly on the light side for North Africa, and we spot several sandy-brown-haired individuals, plenty of freckles and even a few pairs of greeny-blue eyes, black-lashed and startling in golden-brown faces.

Gérard has heard, he says – speaking of blue eyes – that there is, or once was, a statue to Adolf Hitler somewhere here in Tizi-Ouzou. The Nazi leader, apparently, was once viewed by some of the city's inhabitants in a positive light. According to Gérard's informant, Hitler planned – once he had achieved World Domination – to take North Africa out of the hands of the upstart Arabic peoples and return it to its original rulers, the Aryan Berbers. Gérard is dying to ask someone if this statue really exists, but when it comes down to it, none of us has the nerve to ask such a thing. What if the story is a complete calumny? It certainly doesn't fit with the image of the Kabyles today: the most liberal and progressive group in Algeria, who don't just fight like their Moroccan cousins to get their language recognized as a national one, in which their children have a right to be educated, but also refuse to have any truck with the *intégristes* of Islam, and are known for demanding equal rights for Algerian women. Moreover, they carry quite a bit of clout in the country, especially since their uprising of 1980 – the 'Kabyle Spring' as they call it – which threatened to topple the government. A ray of hope, maybe . . .

We wander with our unFrench sausages into a street lined with market stalls: lots of Kabyle countrywomen here, in outfits even better than the Rif ones. Layer upon layer of bright flowered chintz – so much for not copying the perfect designs of Allah! – with loads of contrasting ric-rac braid, hung about with all manner of brightly coloured belts, shawls, scarves, twisted silk cords, all contrasting and clashing and looking wild and fabulous, topped off with chunky ethnic jewellery in amber and silver. Wound around their heads are scarves with long dramatic fringes – hot pink interwoven with silky yellow strands is the fashion of the moment, it seems – arranged so that the fringes fall about their faces in a most becomingly coquettish manner.

These Kabyles take my fancy so much that, once we bump into the chintz dresses on a stall at a market, and regardless of anything rude I may have said to Guy on the topic of his burnous, I am unable to resist buying one – in a pale pink with big green, blue and yellow chrysanthemums. And so bold have I become that I offer the salesman a mere half of what he asks without batting an eyelid. Gratifyingly, we eventually arrive at a price half way between the two prices first named. I could easily get a taste for bargaining: an exhilarating sport, involving much subtlety of expression. You need to look as if you know everything there is to be known about the range of commodities in question, whilst also looking meek enough to deserve a bargain. So proud am I of this new-found skill that, minutes later, I also have to buy the pink-and-yellow shawl. Not such a bargain, sad to say; it turns out not to be made of loose-woven cotton, as I'd imagined, but of acrylic. From Taiwan. Still, if that doesn't bother the seductive Kabyles, why should it bother me? Further on is a stall of what I now recognize as make-up accoutrements – how far I have come since Tetuan! – where I also buy one of those tiny leather kohl-bottles. I say leather, but I think the stuff is really some sort of internal organ tissue: hard and semi-transparent. Mine, the stall-holder said, is the Tuareg nomads' version: it is decorated with tiny appliqué stripes of some sort of short, smooth black-and-brown fur. They also come in black wood ornamented with tiny strips of brass and copper. A hard decision. I manage to apply the kohl right away, no mirror, but luckily I can't quite work how to put on the fringed scarf without looking, and tie it round my waist, rather than my head.

I say luckily because, when I finally do come across a mirror, a day later, and try it on, the effect is appalling. I have never, ever owned a single hot-pink-and-golden-yellow garment until now; I should have known that there was some good reason for this. Worse still, after seeing nothing but brown eyes all this time, my own light-coloured ones, outlined in their black kohl, far from being the attractive feature I've imagined, are the exact opposite. Positively terrifying. Like a pair of scary white holes in my head. Off with the kohl.

Next most irresistible item on those Tizi-Ouzou market stalls: door-locks made out of wood. A big square block of beautiful, satiny olive wood, with a sliding tongue within, and a key made of – wood! A kind of giant wooden toothbrush with half a dozen wooden bristles, each one corresponding, as the lock-maker demonstrates – though we have no language in common – to a reciprocal hole somewhere in the innards of the block. Amazing workmanship! I love it, I want it, and even without haggling the price is minuscule. But good sense prevails. I don't need it for anything, and I would have to lug it right down to the Sahara and back again. I resist the temptation. Idiotically. Where or when will I ever see one of those again? I have regretted it ever since.

Checking out the Kabyle countryside, camouflaged in my pink Berber chintz, I discover that the heartlands of Kabylia own even more spectacularly green mountain roads than does the Rif, some of them sliced right into the sides of cliffs, with a sheer and unprotected drop to seaward. And that the village houses out here in the Djurdjura mountains, unlike the town ones, are close relations of Khadija's drystone village in the Rif. Many of the villages are suffering, by the looks of things, from serious depopulation, with half the housing biodegrading back into the hillsides, and only old people left. Sadly reminiscent of many isolated mountain villages in Italy: several dozen houses and only three old ladies still in residence, stoically hoeing away at their vegetable patches.

But then, I suppose this depopulation must mean, looking on the bright side, that there are more opportunities in Algeria than in Morocco to find an easier life than subsistence farming up a recalcitrant mountain. Does it?

Even Gérard doesn't know. It might be that, or it might be a result of the destruction of all traditional ways of life under his countrymen. He's read that less than half of those three million villagers who were trucked off to the camps ever went home, once they were released from their eight-year-long imprisonment. Conditions of life in the countryside here must have been worse than anything we saw in Khadija's village: there was no viable life to return to. Then, if you uproot people from their land, even only for half a generation, so much knowledge about how to survive on it will be lost that maybe it's not recoverable. The villagers just headed for the cities, it seems, seeking work. Algeria began its new life doubly handicapped – with no technicians and managers to keep the country running, and its cities flooded with hundreds of thousands of bewildered peasant farmers, uprooted and illiterate.

But more of that later. At the moment we are in a state of shock. We have just been chased out of a tiny hamlet in the hills by its inhabitants, for no reason at all that we could determine. And they didn't just chase us, they actually hurled stones at our retreating backs to hasten our departure.

We had been dropped off by yet another kindly car-owner at a crossroads in the middle of nowhere – a very dry, stony, dusty and rocky nowhere too, with not a spring leaf to be seen anywhere on the broad scree slopes all around us. This, he told us, was part of the once heavily forested area napalmed by the French to eliminate the hidden bases of the Algerian fighters. The vegetation has come back in some places, though nothing you could call a forest, of course. But some parts have just stayed like this.

It certainly was moonscape-like here. We could see for miles in every direction. But ironically enough, an entire village can still lurk undetected, even in these barren surroundings. Gradually, as our eyes became accustomed to the grey-brown emptiness – a depressing contrast to the luxuriant green of the foothills further north, through which we'd been travelling all morning – it dawned on us that half way up the dusty slope opposite us was a series of rectilinear arrangements of the rocks and stones that could not be accidental. Buildings. A village, as dry and leafless as its surroundings.

I suppose the point of the napalm was not to destroy the buildings, though. As long as succour and support were gone, the guerrillas would have had to move on. Taking the water away from the fish – that's what the French military called it. There is certainly no hint here of plant or animal life on which the villagers could possibly have continued living, never mind feeding and sheltering a guerrilla army.

The place was obviously uninhabited. No sign of any modern amenities, no glass in the windows, no electricity pylons. Had the villagers just left, their livelihoods destroyed along with the local ecosystem? Or been trucked off to the camps, never to return? Intrigued, we set off to investigate their abandoned homes, scrambling up the stony slopes towards the buildings.

Guy had arrived at the first house, somewhat isolated from the others, and actually stuck his head in through the window, when, all of a sudden, faces began to appear in doorways further uphill: women's faces in bright, fringed headdresses. Now an old man and two younger ones, their robes and *chèches* as dusty as the narrow pathway between the decrepit buildings, came from nowhere to stand stock still, staring. A bunch of small children began gathering, shouting and gesticulating. Taking this for a welcome, we continued towards them, until several more men appeared, and we began to realize that the shouting was not intended amicably at all. They were warning us off. Almost eye to eye with them by now, hot and breathless, we stopped and stared, open-mouthed. We had met with nothing but friendly welcomes in this country so far; we could hardly take it in. It was Gérard who registered the bad situation first. Turn around, he said. Leave! Quick! We're not wanted here.

No sooner had he spoken than a hail of stones began to rain down upon us. Only the children were throwing, and only small stones – considerate of them, with much larger ammunition lying all around. But still extremely scary. They might easily move on to a bigger gauge. And there was nothing to prevent the adults, who were clearly making no move to stop them, from joining in.

Worse still, there was nobody around for miles to help, or to witness whatever the village might decide to do next. Suddenly terrified, we raced the last few yards back onto the road. And sat for the next hour waiting for a vehicle – any vehicle – to appear, while doing our best not to direct so much as a glance in the direction of the hostile village.

What on earth had happened? How could anyone live in this moonscape? Did they dislike Europeans particularly, or just anybody who noticed the existence of their homes in this unlikely spot? Being Kabyles, they were extremely unlikely to be any sort of *intégriste*. The

Islamists' insistence on the superiority of the language of the Koran was enough to guarantee that. Were they intentionally trying to conceal their village? They must be. Otherwise surely there would be some sign of human presence – washing hung out to dry, a chicken or two, an attempt at planting some sort of food crop?

Unless, said Guy facetiously, they were living examples of those villagers who had lost all their traditional knowledge, as described by Gérard. They had given up trying to wrest a living from the soil, and these days commuted to work in the nearest town?

Impossible, said Gérard. Where are their donkeys?

We decided that the most likely explanation was that they were a village of djinns – or of *djnun*, rather, which I believe is the correct plural – whose works are, as we know, invisible. That would cover everything, including their bad tempers.

The driver of the sheep lorry that eventually appeared and got us out of this sinister place could not enlighten us. He had never noticed the village at all, he said, though he was often up and down this road. He was not remotely entertained by our *djnun* theory. I fear that disrespecting the djinns is not good form in these parts.

Maybe they had only just arrived, he said, on the run from something? Unless they had some sort of hidden valley behind the village where they grew their food and kept their animals? No, really, he had no idea. But didn't we say that Guy had his head inside the window of one of their outbuildings when the trouble started? Are we sure they didn't just take us for thieves?

Duh . . .

Still, that only explains half the story. The rest will remain for ever a mystery.

Habib the lorry-driver is going all the way to Bou Saâda, next stop southwards on the road to the desert, and beyond it, to the high plateaux of the Saharan Atlas – still in our direction, if we want to carry on. He has a share in a flock of sheep up there: he's taking the lorry up to move them to pastures new. He will probably stop the night in Bou Saâda, his home town, though, and head on at dawn, he says, rather than try to track down men, tents and sheep at dead of night, up on that wild land.

The landscape changes amazingly rapidly in this part of the country. Out of the Kabyle hills, we are soon in another area of fertile plains. Now the vegetation starts to change. The land is much drier, the plant life sparser, nothing around us but an endless desiccated-looking plain of stones, our road a long grey snake through infinite flatness. Within the hour, the Atlas mountains are already visible, outlined against a shimmering sky. Reach them, and we are at Bou Saâda and the high plateaux: last bastion before the desert proper begins.

For now, apart from the distant mountains, there is nothing at all to be seen but 360 degrees of endless nothingness stretching to a level horizon all around. Disconcerting, frightening almost, such utter featurelessness, something you hardly ever experience in life. An hour later, although there is a hint of rising ground, the landscape looks identical. Is this desert of stones never going to end?

Habib is going to stop for a break, he says, pulling in next to a small boulder that stands out from the rest. Funny: just the spot I would have chosen myself. As long as it is not Nothingness, any feature will do as a landmark. Amazingly, within minutes of our clambering down from the lorry, a shepherd with his flock of sheep has appeared in the middle distance. But where from? It seems impossible . . .

Not at all, says Habib. We are already on the fringes of the high plateau, and there is plenty of grazing here if you know where to look. The land is nothing like as flat as it seems.

Habib gets out his tea-tackle – a trivet and a bundle of twigs – and starts to make tea, crouching on his haunches. Everyone here seems to be able to do this: they hunker down, rest their elbows on their knees and relax totally, as if they were actually seated – and in a comfortable armchair, at that. I can't manage it for more than a few minutes, and nor can my companions. We shift and we shuffle, we stand up, we crouch down again, and after a few minutes we give in and sit down properly, inelegantly, bums on the ground. Not clever: if you can manage to hunker down like Habib, your clothes don't get dirty, you don't end up covered in dust, and your legs don't get in the way of whatever you're trying to do: in this case, drink your tea. We put our legs to one side, get uncomfortable again, shift them to the other, juggling the tea-glass. We try the crouch again, get pins and needles in minutes. Bums in the dust again. The shepherd has turned up by now, and Habib gets up to greet him. They give one another a big bear-hug, and plenty of air-kisses. They know one another from up on the plains, says Habib, and the shepherd now hunkers down beside us in just the same nonchalant way. How on earth do they do it? Habib has lit the fire, boiled the water, made the tea, without needing to shift once. Now, in perfect balance, elbow on one knee, glass held elegantly in the fingertips, he and the shepherd are sipping nonchalantly away and exchanging what I guess must be sheep news.

My theory about this crouching business is that, since everyone here starts training for it as tiny children, they develop a network of alternative veins that allows the circulation to flow even when the knees are tightly bent for ages. As well as more stretchy hamstrings. Why on earth don't we Westerners use this amazing ability at all? Think how much furniture we wouldn't need to buy.

The flock has now come to investigate what we humans are up to, and a brown-faced sheep has begun determinedly nibbling at my hair. What a lot of reasons there are for keeping your head covered in this country. I do my best to fight the over-familiar creature off. It hardly looks like a sheep at all, with those big long floppy ears, not if you're used to the dominant breeds of Europe. I give it a shove; it shoves right back, upper lip raised in a let-me-get-at-that-tasty-hair-again kind of way.

The shepherd, having enjoyed the hair-and-sheep spectacle for a moment or two, hurls a handful of pebbles at the offending beast, which gives a muffled *maaaa* and shuffles off, looking most dejected. Poor sheep! It wasn't really doing any harm. Now I want to call it back.

Habib will tell us later, in tones of deepest scorn, that this brown-faced flop-eared type of sheep is a rubbish breed, anyway. It comes from the grasslands of Mali, on the other side of the Sahara, and is only good for meat. The wool is so short it's almost impossible to spin, so no use for weaving; the yield in milk is low; and he personally wouldn't touch a flock of them with a bargepole. Some people just enjoy wasting their time!

Never pick up the stones, Habib says all of a sudden, switching back to French and grabbing at Guy's outstretched hand as he's about to do so. There is a scorpion beneath every one!

And, relaxing back into his comfortable hunker, switching to and fro between French and Arabic, he tells us and the shepherd the story, or perhaps legend, of a French *pied-noir* farmer whose land lay somewhere back along the road, who excavated a deep hole seeking water supplies for his crops and struck, not water, but oil. He quickly bought up some kind of purifying equipment, began selling the stuff on the side to passing lorries, tax free, and made his fortune.

Can this be true? Is it even possible? No idea.

The bit about the scorpions is certainly true, as Habib now demonstrates for our entertainment, gingerly picking up a few stones, holding them by the top. There really are scorpions under every one – or every fifth or sixth one, at least, which is quite enough for me. They're not the small black scorpions I'm used to in Italy, either, which have a sting no worse than a bee's. These are big pale horrible-looking things that, according to Habib, can make you very sick.

Nothing to worry about if you don't bother them, though, says Habib. It's no use to them, stinging you, is it? They would much rather conserve their strength!

Cheering news, but still, I decide to give that crouching position another try.

Back in the lorry we hear another strange tale – of the town of In Salah, which the boys will visit after Timimoun, if they take the Tamanrasset route across the desert. There is a massive sand dune creeping slowly right through the centre of the town, covering over the inhabitants' homes as it goes, filling them with sand, pushing out the people. There is nothing to be done about it but wait: it is unstoppable. It has been moving for many decades now, and can take a generation or even two to clear a group of houses in its inexorable onwards march. But careful records are kept, and when the dune passes on, and the old family homes reappear, their inheritors – who have never seen them in their lives – are ready to take over again, clear out the sand, and move in.

Habib thinks, though, that it's probably best not to take the In Salah route just at the moment. He's heard the army's moving the thousands of arrested FIS activists down that way. There are bound to be road blocks, convoys, lots of red tape . . .

Some hours later we spot, at last, nestling deep green among barren, flat-topped hills, the palm groves of Bou Saâda – 'the Oasis of Happiness'. Well before we arrive at the town, though, we come across another type of habitation altogether – a nomad encampment out on the plain. Three broad tents of woven wool, striped black and dusty red, supported on bentwood poles, side panels raised to form shady awnings, children playing around them.

People of the Ouled Naïl, says Habib, a confederation of tribes who are mostly only nomads part of the year, when the grazing is good. The rest of the time they return to their villages. The range of hills up ahead – where his own sheep are grazing at this moment – is called after them: the Ouled Naïl hills. The High Plateaux have always been the realm of nomads, Berber and Arab, who have roamed here with their flocks for millennia. The French may have stolen half their pasture and ruined their trade routes, but the tribes themselves have survived. Some have even prospered. In fact, Habib's present business partners are Ouled Naïl themselves, though his associates are much more modern-minded than those tent-dwellers, who will barely be scraping a living from their sheep. You need a lorry nowadays, like Habib. Then when the fitful rains of this area fall – if at all, *inshallah!* – you can quickly move your flocks, on wheels, to take advantage of the first flush of pasture. A much better system than walking your sheep over great long distances, only to find, as you often do these days, that someone else's flocks have already passed, and there is not a blade of grass left on what remains of your traditional pasture grounds!

Surprisingly, given how arid everything around us looks, we find that we are crossing a deep river gorge as we arrive in Bou Saâda. Down below us the river is lined with terraces of fruit and date-palms. Here they grow the luscious Deglet Nour dates, says Habib, which means 'Fingers of Light'. Oddly enough, though, it was not dates, but the wool trade, according to Habib, that brought the oasis of Bou Saâda into being. A strange juxtaposition, to my mind, a palm-tree oasis and wool, but then what do I know? Clearly a lot less than Habib, who was born here, and has chosen to follow the town's oldest tradition.

Bou Saâda, though, was once famous for another, much more intriguing industry than either dates or wool. It was, for seventy-odd years, a centre for sex tourism, a trade that flourished from what we British would call the late Victorian period up to the arrival of Algerian Independence, when it was swiftly abolished.

In the late 1800s the erotic dancers of the Ouled Naïl had attracted the attention of a select group of cultured European 'orientalists', including a whole array of painters, one of whom, Etienne Dinet, actually moved here to Bou Saâda and converted to Islam, scandalizing the French art establishment and ruining his artistic career. But the orientalist fashion launched by these artists' sultry images of North African women spread like wildfire, and soon the dancing girls of the Ouled Naïl were being transported across the seas to feature in the Universal Exhibitions and World Fairs of which Imperial nations were so fond at the time.

It was the Chicago World Fair of 1893, and a certain Sol Bloom, entrepreneur, that really made the name of the Ouled Naïl. Bloom, seeking publicity for his exotic dancers, had invented the titillating epithet 'belly dancing' to describe the performances of his Algerian girls. At this time in Western culture, of course, any public display of the body was considered positively scandalous; and so thoroughly covered up were the Christian women of the time that even a glimpse of ankle was erotically charged. 'Natives' of inferior races, on the other hand, were known to be given to primitive and reprehensible displays of flesh. The charm of these North Africans seems to have been that they were not 'savages' by any means, but representatives of a sophisticated and ancient culture that was yet utterly alien to the West. And, of course, comfortingly subjugated. Vast numbers of prurient citizens flocked to the World Fair to witness the dance of the Ouled Naïl. All the more so since rumour had it that, back in their homeland, the girls' favours were available to the highest bidder.

The reputation of the Ouled Naïl was made. And so, through the combined skills of the Académie Française and a Chicago showman, was born the Western image of the oriental seductress, a dangerous creature of great sophistication but wild primitive emotion, whose diaphanous veils revealed as much as they hid, and whose deepest desire, behind those boldly flashing eyes, was (naturally) to be conquered. And also a new, bowdlerized dance, hitherto unknown in the Maghreb, involving the display of the navel area.

For the next seven decades, the punters would pour in to Bou Saâda, seeking steamy encounters with fascinating oriental females. And the young ladies who entertained them would quickly learn what was expected of them, adjusting their dance, and their attire, accordingly. By 1912, Bou Saâda and the Ouled Naïl were so well known that they featured in Edgar Rice Burroughs' *Return of Tarzan*. And so powerful was this colonial stereotype that it could still be recycled in my own lifetime, albeit tongue-in-cheek, in a television advertisement for Turkish Delight: Full of Eastern Promise.

And what was the truth behind all this? Several of the tribes of the Ouled Naïl did indeed have a tradition of sending their young women out to earn their dowries by dancing – and by taking wealthy admirers as lovers. Their dance was known here in Algeria by the innocent name of *Raks Bladi* – *blad* being your country or village, and *raks* meaning to dance or rejoice. It involved no display of body parts whatsoever, being a dance mainly of sinuous and fluttering movements of the hands and arms, performed fully clothed. Within several of the Ouled Naïl tribes, neither the public dancing nor the taking of paying lovers was regarded as shameful. Indeed, the men of the tribes would travel with the girls, accompanying them on drum and flute; and any children born of their unions were kept and cherished. Earning a dowry in this way might not be in strict accord with the precepts of Islam, but the girls were devout – their dances had such names as 'the doves of Mecca' – and they could later repent. Hopefully, they would save up enough to make the Hadj pilgrimage to Mecca, the fifth of the Pillars of Islam, and become cleansed of their past misdeeds. Now they would return to the bosom of their people, who, unusually for most cultures at the time or since, had no problem with their past, and settle down to make a respectable marriage with one of their own, in financial security. Meanwhile, as far as other local people were concerned, the disturbing position occupied by the Ouled Naïl dancers, balancing between the licit and the illicit, made them objects of some superstition and veneration. They were always invited to dance at weddings, where their presence would bestow extra *baraka* on the proceedings.

World fame soon changed all that. Bou Saâda became a boom town for prostitutes, all now known by the generic name of Ouled Naïl, whether they had ever seen the inside of a black-and-red striped tent or not. There were plenty of young women available for the role; the long, slow process of national beggarization had seen to that. Soon a whole area down beside the river and the palm groves was known as the 'Street of the Ouled Naïl', complete with compulsory weekly medical examinations run by the French military, who controlled the trade tightly, issuing identity cards to any girls involved. The women's services were soon reserved, two days a week, for the occupying soldiers' use alone. From now on there was a dividing line between 'decent' women and card-carrying *filles publiques* which had never before existed. By the 1930s, the first wave of Islamic puritanism was hitting the respectable sector among the local population. High walls had to be built along all the access roads to the area, screening the depraved partying from modest Muslim eyes. Another colonial imposition: having your town turned into a brothel. More fuel for the spreading fire of Algerian nationalism.

Habib parks the lorry on the edge of town, so he's ready to leave the moment the first call to prayer sounds tomorrow. There are plenty of people about here wearing the burnous, I note, now that we're in the Land of Wool, and Guy is, at last, blending rather well into his surroundings.

When Habib was growing up here in the 1950s, he tells us as we walk towards the centre, Bou Saâda was a favourite weekend resort for *pieds-noirs* from Algiers. The place would fill up with French families, who would go off to frolic by day at the Ferrero mineral springs a couple of kilometres outside town. Habib would rather not guess what the fathers of those families got up to by night! Though by then, he says, their choice was starting to get a bit restricted. A lot of the girls had taken the nationalist side and refused to have any truck with Frenchmen – however much they were willing to pay.

The street of ill fame is only just down the road. Come, says Habib. Before we go to eat, he will show us the house of Fatima el Coptana – Fatima the Captain – one of the greatest madams of the town in the old days, who recruited almost every one of the girls in her village to the trade, and died a rich woman!

A few yards on, we are among those high-walled streets. Down by the river stands a row of houses that look – well – like ordinary Algerian town houses. Certainly not my idea of a rich madam's place, though I suppose, compared to a drystone village or a stripey tent, they are the height of luxury. Habib's eyes have lit up at the memory of the scenes he and his playfellows witnessed, peeping round corners, in this part of town. They would always be spotted and chased off, he says – but they would be back soon enough, by hook or by crook! Some of the girls would throw sweets or coins out of the windows to you if you were lucky. You might witness a thrilling drunken brawl, or a woman running out into the street in her house-clothes, her naked hair flying!

Something about the way Habib now bites his tongue tells me Gérard and Guy would be hearing some good scurrilous tales if I wasn't here to poop the party. I forge on ahead to give them a sporting chance.

Further along the road is the house of Yamina, who, rather than turning to her neighbours for new apprentices, got her sisters and nieces into the game instead. And every last one of them did well, Habib says, bought houses and palm groves for their families, while Yamina's two sons administered the family fortunes. Yamina and Fatima were both widows: that is how they came to have the independence to engage in their nefarious activities. And they were hardly bothered at all when the French were thrown out of the country, and their old trade was banned. Their finances were in fine shape; they could afford to retire. When Yamina died, at a great old age, she left instructions that she should be buried on a bed of henna leaves and rose petals, and have powdered amber sprinkled on her grave. She had lived as a flower of Allah, she said, and now she wanted to die as one.

We set off to find a bed for the night, pondering the weird role reversal that has taken place over the last seventy years. The once-prudish West has become eroticized beyond measure; only a few tiny corners of the body still taboo. Meanwhile, the once-tolerant Maghreb – partly, it seems, in protest against Western impositions of every kind – has taken to a Victorian-style morality of its own.

As we take our bags upstairs, I hear from the boys that Habib did manage to pass on a small piece of scurrilous information in my absence: it seems that, while Muslim punters did not wish to encounter bodily fluff of any kind, Europeans were disappointed if they did not find a full head (as it were) of pubic hair during their amorous encounters. Many of the girls, not wishing to lose the patronage of either group, resorted to pubic wigs. Can this be true? How on earth would they have kept them on? The mind boggles.

The hotel has a beautiful overgrown courtyard garden, but apart from that, there is not a lot to be said in its favour. In the lobby hangs a fly-blown print of an Etienne Dinet painting – a line of beturbaned men outside a mosque entitled *The Day after Ramadan* which reminds me of a high-class Boys' Own Stories illustration: though chicken or egg, who can say? The name Etienne has been replaced by 'Noureddine', the artist's Islamic-convert name, glued over the original on a scrap of paper. The map of Bou Saâda hanging next to it is a 1942 French military one. And I would say that it must have been about this date that the bathrooms in this place were last cleaned. Old hands now, we decide it doesn't matter – we can use the *hammam*. Maybe that's why they don't care about cleaning the bathrooms – people here would hardly bother with the low-level cleanliness attainable without lashings of steam and a good strong bell of baling twine?

No women's session till tomorrow morning, though, says Habib, and we'll be leaving too early for that. He will take us to wash in the mineral-water pools of Ferrero in the morning, instead. So we all go for a scruffy walk out towards the palm groves and are much consoled by how beautiful the place looks at sunset, the hills violet in the evening light, the almond trees trailing over the river, the dark green mass of feathery palms behind their golden mud-brick walls . . .

Things are a lot less peaceful as we head back into town. The streets are suddenly full of flags, drums, firecrackers, roaring jam-packed cars, jubilant men of every age. Bou Saâda has won a football match against some nearby town, and the whole town is in ecstasy. We take to the back streets, following our local expert, and end up in a *gargotier*, an Algerian greasy spoon restaurant, encountering, on our way, a faded remnant of Bou Saâda's erstwhile tourist industry: a fly-blown sign in a tailor's window offering made-to-measure Ouled Naïl costumes, ready to wear in twenty-four hours.

The *gargotier* is the perfect way, we discover, to get around the problem of my being female. It is all very well deciding to boldly face out the glowering old men and the staring younger ones in the men-only tea-shops of this land, striking a blow – I hope – for Algerian womanhood; but in the end it is extremely unrelaxing. In a cheap eatery like this, low on the scale of respectability, nobody seems much bothered about a woman's presence. The poorer people are, here in Algeria, the more likely they are to have travelled abroad to find work – maybe it is thanks to this that they aren't too perturbed at finding a female in a public place?

No sooner have we eaten and moved on to the three-glasses-of-tea course, than Gérard, Guy and Habib are nobbled by local fans and made to talk about football all night. Every man in Bou Saâda seems to possess an encyclopaedic knowledge of French football teams, and especially of any players of Maghreb origin, so there is a lot to be said. The name of a certain Zinedine Zidane crops up a lot: a local boy, they say, a Kabyle – his family originally from some godforsaken hamlet up in the Djurdjura hills. So brilliant that the president of his Cannes club made him a present of a brand-new car for his first competitive goal!

Shortly after dawn, here we are at the Ferrero springs, splashing gingerly about in the mineral-water pools among the rocks, which would certainly be a great pleasure to bathe in if only they'd had a little more time to warm up under the morning sun. Habib stays up on the road while we wash, sitting in his lorry and smoking, in order to preserve my modesty. A ridiculously picturesque spot, with a waterfall running down a rugged cliff face, a half-ruined building clinging to the rocks at its side. A water-mill once, it looks impossibly romantic in its riverside setting, scattered palm trees above and below it, vegetation sprouting from its ruined façade, its windows blind and empty. The mill was built by one Antonio Ferrero of Turin, who arrived in Bou Saâda in 1867 – attracted here, who knows, by the charms of the Ouled Naïl? – and came up with a wizard money-making scheme of his own, Italian-style. The first ever pasta factories had recently been set up in Italy, saving Italian housewives many hours of laborious *impasto*-making. It would be the work of a moment, Antonio realized, to switch the new technology to producing, not long thin sticks, but little round granules. Soon, here it was – the first ever mass-produced couscous! And over the next century, many generations of Ferreros grew up here in Algeria, mingling so closely with their Algerian hosts that they had no need at all to do a runner in 1962, along with the French settlers. Antonio's descendants still live in the area. And, thanks to his ground-breaking work, these days we can all buy our couscous ready-made in packets, and no longer have to wear our fingers to the bone rolling all those little bobbles from scratch.

18

Next stop, where Habib's way and ours must part, is a town called Djelfa. It lies high on the eastern end of the Saharan Atlas, the range of mountains that runs parallel to the Mediterranean, separating fertile land from desert, all the way back to the Moroccan border. Here it mellows into gentler hills, allowing Mohammed the father's alternative trail to Timimoun to pass across the plains of the Tafilalet, heading south-east through the southern Moroccan oases and the ruins of Sijilmassa. But whether you travel towards Timimoun from the Moroccan north-west or, as we are doing now, from the Algerian north-east, your road will start by heading due south for a couple of hundred miles. It has to skirt the massive oval sea of sand dunes, uninhabited and impassable, that presses all along the southern flank of the Saharan Atlas: the thousands of square miles of the Grand Erg Occidental.

So from Djelfa our road heads south, keeping the sand-sea to our right. Then it will curve back towards Morocco along the Grand Erg's southern edge, the plains of the Gourara, a long narrow east–west strip, marking the bed of the long-dead water course, described by Jean-Pierre, that divides the Grand Erg from the main body of the Sahara. Here, sandwiched between the two great sand deserts, lies the string of oases we're aiming for, at the head of which sits Timimoun.

Djelfa is on our map all right, but there is no mention of its existence in the *Petit futé*. Guy is not surprised. Djelfa's only claim to fame, as far as he knows, is that it housed one of the first European concentration camps on African soil. Vichy France, collaborating with Hitler, imprisoned hundreds of Jews, Poles and Czechs in this unlikely spot, along with many Republican refugees from the Spanish Civil War. A strange parallel with Algeria's situation today, that of the Spanish Republicans: another elected government that did not meet the approval of the Great Powers. This one was too left-wing, though, rather than too Islamic. Britain and France debated the matter, and decided not to lift a finger to help when Franco launched his anti-democracy coup from Morocco. And, it seems, those Republicans desperate or foolhardy enough to flee across the French border seeking safety ended up – bizarrely – here instead, imprisoned in Saharan concentration camps. There was even some crazy plan, Guy says, to use their inmates as forced labour to build a railway across the Sahara: an ancient French dream resurrected. That's what Monsieur Eiffel had been doing down here in the desert, long ago. Having finished building the Statue of Liberty for the Americans, he was now testing out sand-bridges for an Imperial fantasy railway: one that would link all the French colonies of Africa to the Motherland.

Here in Djelfa we say farewell to Habib, who is now heading for the high sheeplands, and go off to hunt down some lunch. The local inhabitants having, alas, no habit of dining out, there is nowhere to eat in town but a horribly expensive hotel, in whose echoing restaurant we bump into two other travellers, the only other customers here, with whom, naturally enough, we soon get talking. They are François and Abdelwahab, who have driven here all the way from Paris with a small convoy of three Land Rovers, to be sold, on the other side of the Sahara, at vast profit. Or at any rate, at the bearded François' vast profit. Abdelwahab, not long out of his teens by the look of him, is just a hitch-hiker, he tells us, temporarily promoted to trans-Saharan driver.

This, François says, is his own special method for recruiting drivers for his Afro-European second-hand car business. He simply drives around the ring-roads of Paris, stopping for every hitch-hiker he sees, and asking if they have a driving licence – and a job. If he gets a yes to the first, and a no to the second, then *voilà*! He simply offers them, in place of their intended destination, an all-expenses-paid trip across the Sahara. It has never, he says, taken him more than a day to assemble the team he requires. Abdelwahab, for example, was only going to Marseilles to visit his family, and now look where he's ended up – checking out his Algerian roots, for the first time ever! The third member of their team, and the third Land Rover, are miles ahead, but our dining companions have got stuck here, waiting to get a tyre fixed.

Naturally, within minutes we are agreeing to travel on with them. Soon we are riding in style – classical British style, at that – towards our first true desert town, Ghardaïa. A few miles on, a convoy of army lorries overtakes us, klaxons blaring: five of them, headed south. Abdelwahab, in whose car Guy and I are travelling, suspects that they are carrying some of the army's FIS prisoners to the new prison camps near In Salah. He doesn't think we're being told the half of what's going on. As he was leaving France two days ago, there were reports of the army firing on the police somewhere near Oran. Or was it vice versa? There's some kind of power struggle going on within the ruling elite, probably between the pro- and the anti-free-marketeers. The Islamists, ferocious though they may be on their own account, are being manipulated. Abdelwahab thinks there may well be a blood-bath. Worse still, *fatwas* have been proclaimed from the *muezzins*, along with the call to prayer, on a good dozen writers, journalists, musicians, women in public positions – and any number of ordinary people not newsworthy enough to mention by name. They are now fair game to any mad *intégriste* who wants to go for them.

The road rolls on, and our first real dunes appear, far to the west. Closer by, perched on rocky outcrops against a glaring sky, among endless plains of stone, stand the remains of ancient red-earth *ksars*, fortresses and grain-stores, some built as defence against nomads, a safe retreat in times of war, others by the nomads themselves, to stock merchandise or supplies for their travels. Some have been abandoned for centuries, others for just a few decades, maybe. There's no way to tell.

Abdelwahab is getting desperate for something to drink. Nothing all around for miles, though, but stones, emptiness, the occasional tormented thorn-bush. At long last we see a sign of human activity: low cubes of buildings by the dusty road, and some kind of market going on, goats on sale, sheep, chickens, carpets – and camels! Our first ever Saharan camels – and Abdelwahab's too. There's bound to be something to drink here. We pull in, François and Gérard behind us, and buy some freshly squeezed orange juice from a roadside stall-holder who has set up in the shade of a handy palm tree. Double rations each go straight down our parched throats – much better! – and we head off to check out the camels. Ridiculously long baby-doll eyelashes on otherwise ridiculously uncuddly creatures. The cameleers fold back one of their front legs at the knee and slip a rope round it to keep it bent up, so they won't suddenly take off on those great long lolloping legs. They hobble gently about, three-legged, looking extremely foolish and absent-minded. There are people – or men, rather: I'm getting so used to the absence of women by now that I hardly notice it any more – sitting and standing all round the square to the back of the buildings, an auctioneer on a wooden-box dais, robes flying, roaring away, intent, intense expressions around us. He is selling carpets, but the auction is not as gripping to us three as it is to the rest of the audience. How could it be? We don't know any numbers beyond ten. I start inspecting the wares, complimenting one of the owners on his lovely white camel. Beautiful! I say. Is it waiting to go on sale? Are all the camels his, or just this one? He seems oddly reluctant to answer, and François suddenly drags me away, sharpish.

Never compliment anyone down here in the desert, he says, on any of their possessions, nor ask them a question whose answer might involve their making a display of their wealth or good fortune – such as how many camels they own! Or, indeed, how many date palms, or how many children they have. People here are great believers in the Evil Eye, and anything that could provoke envy, anything that might seem like publicly showing off their skill or good fortune, may attract it. François doesn't know, he says, if it's the envy of other humans, the jealous rays emitted by their eyes, that puts the Evil Eye on you, or the malevolent envy of the djinns, the *djnun*, provoked into making you laugh out of the other side of your face. But that is irrelevant. Just don't do it!

All right. I won't. Fascinating information, though, especially to one who has spent much time in Italy. Italians, too, are very preoccupied by the Evil Eye, the *malocchio*, and my neighbours there, especially those of southern Italian origin, will often visit mysterious persons in the hills who possess the ability to remove it, with the help of a beaker of olive oil and other such objects of power. But, whilst Italians hotly deny my own argument that, logically, it must be these same mysterious practitioners who put the Evil Eye on them in the first place, none of them has any alternative explanation of where the Evil Eye really does come from, and how. This North African answer certainly fits the bill: especially when I recall that a certain aged southern Italian gentleman of my acquaintance keeps a large mirror on the side of his farmhouse, reflecting out across the valley, which he claims is to keep the Evil Eye off his crops. Of course – because it reflects back any envious thoughts an onlooker may be having about the volume of Salvatore's grape harvest, or the fecundity of his olive trees! The Italians, though they still remember – and follow – the correct procedures, have somehow have lost this important information in the mists of history.

Abdelwahab has spotted a new delight over among the camels: a mother camel with a frolicking baby camel, teetering around its mamma on absurdly unstable and gangly legs that make it look as if it's on tiptoe and fluttering its eyelashes coquettishly. I am charmed, and so is Abdelwahab, who pulls a camera out of his bag and takes a photo of the cameleer and his beasts.

Wrong move. The camel-man goes mad, first demanding the film, then demanding payment for the portrait. A large crowd gathers, enjoying the spectacle. The cameleer, between lengthy speeches to the gallery, keeps raising his eyes to the sky and making a noise like a child imitating a police car: *lee-lah lee-lah lah-lah*. I have noticed quite a few people doing this, in moments of stress. Habib, for example, did it whenever his gearbox gave him trouble. François goes over to try and sort the problem out. Abdelwahab has gone into a fit of depression about his supposed country, sulking and muttering to himself.

Gérard tells him not to worry: he is in good company. The great Auguste Renoir, Gérard says, also complained bitterly about the vast fees demanded by locals to sit for portraits in this part of the world. They had been spoilt by European patronage, Renoir said, ever since the Ouled Naïl fashion caught on. So, says Gérard, people round here naturally have great expectations from the world of Art: they have over a century of posing under their belts!

Money seems to have changed hands now, and all is well. Or somewhat better, at any rate. The cameleer is still glowering and doing the occasional police-car imitation. Abdelwahab is going on being mortified. He wishes he could speak Arabic properly. He can understand a lot of it, all right, from listening to his parents at home, but none of his generation has ever bothered speaking it. They've always just answered their parents in French. He would love to be able to give the camel-man a piece of his mind, but he would sound like a stammering idiot. He is going to start learning Arabic immediately, as soon as he gets back to France.

A sympathetic bystander, detaching himself from the crowd, comes over to apologize for the bad behaviour of the camel vendor. He is not usually so irascible, but he has been driven to distraction by the loss of not one, but three baby camels from his herd. Since privatization, foreign prospectors have, it seems, taken to roaming the countryside drilling unexpected test wells on public pastures. The abandoned crater fills with oil, creating a perilous, sticky quicksand: a *bourbier*. And baby camels, being curious little creatures, cannot resist going much too close to these black morasses of camel traps. We can imagine the rest! And it is easy, alas, to blame all foreigners, whether connected to the oil industry or not, for your sufferings. Abdelwahab does not find this explanation, casting him as it does in the role of foreigner, much of a comfort. The camel-man is still *lee-lah*-ing. Does anyone know what it means? Is he actually saying something?

Abdelwahab does. And yes, he is. He is saying '*ashhadu an la ilah ila Allah*'. There is no god but God. The declaration of faith: the First Pillar of Islam. He doesn't mean anything by it, it's just an exclamation. Abdelwahab is so entertained by my police-car-imitation theory that he gets over his cameleer-outrage at last. He can't help looking at it all through European eyes, though, he says, and being embarrassed for his fellow countrymen. Gérard points out that we Europeans are enjoying every minute of it, and that Abdelwahab's eyes, too, are European. What else could they be, when he has never before set foot in this country?

There may be no god but God, Abdelwahab says, but he has a hundred names. Did we know that? Every Muslim who is called Abd el-something, like himself, is really called 'son of God' – under one of the deity's many aliases. Abd el-Kebir is son of the Great, Abd el-Wahab son of the Head, and so on. If you're called Abd-Allah, though, plain 'Son of God', you don't need the 'el' word, which just means 'the'.

That's one mystery solved at last, then. Uncle Kebir's name must be short for Abd el-Kebir. He really is called Uncle Great.

On our way back to the Land Rovers a boy goat-herd is heading down the street towards us. He must be in charge of grazing the animals for the whole village, because his charges are dropping off from the herd one by one, under their own steam, as they arrive at the various doors and gates in the street. Some householders are evidently waiting eagerly for their goats, and let them in straight away. Others, more nonchalant, leave them waiting on the doorstep. The herd-boy, taking up the rear, is carrying a new-born baby goat in his arms. I steer well clear: once bitten, twice shy. But the innocent Abdelwahab goes right up and strokes it. It does not bite him. Evidently Algerian blood does count for something, after all.

As dusk is falling, we pass through El Golea, the last town before our road starts to curve westwards along the southern border of the Erg and into the uninhabited zone. Real, sand-dune desert from now on, all the way to Timimoun. Soon we are rolling through an eerily empty moonlit landscape. I check the map under the dashboard light. No humans at all live between here and Timimoun: the map shows three places in the middle of nothingness where, if we really need it, we will find water at between twelve and fourteen metres below ground. The fourth, a place called Fort Mac Mahon, has a well. The water is *bonne, abondante, légèrement salée* – slightly salty. That, François says, is where we'll be camping tonight. But don't get excited: it's not much of a fort.

I stare at the map, wondering why anyone would bother to mark those other water-places on it. How likely is anyone to start digging twelve metres in the desert heat? Idiotic thought. If you were on foot, lost, car broken down, you would have nothing better to do, would you – and no other way to save your life – than to dig all those metres. That's why. We roll on through the night, the car vibrating horribly. On a desert road, the sand forms itself into corrugations, just the way it does under the sea. You must never drive at less than sixty kilometres an hour for any length of time, François says. The frequency of the vibrations, at low speeds, will shake loose every nut and bolt in the engine.

Unfortunately, at that speed, you don't have time to spot upcoming patches of loose sand, which send you veering wildly, and may well conceal rocks that will smash your undercarriage as the wheels sink in. Our convoy comes to a halt half a dozen times, while we drag out one or other of the Land Rovers whose wheels are hopelessly stuck in sand. The prospect of digging for water starts to seem a lot less unlikely.

Fort Mac Mahon in the darkness is scary and deserted. A ruin: not a romantic red-mud-brick *ksar*, though, but a French-colonial concrete bunker, its front wall collapsed, bent and rusting girders exposed, slab of roof leaning crazily; around it skeletons are strewn, bones gleaming white in the moonlight. Not as sinister as they appear, though: only the bones of sheep and camels that have died in transit, crossing the desert from the grasslands of Mali – or have been slaughtered and eaten by their drivers. We get a fire lit among the ashes of many others and settle down among the scattered skeletons to tins of sardines, smoky toasted baguette and cans of warm beer. Skeletons never go away here, in this dry air, says François; and he tells us, sitting round the camp-fire, of a caravan that vanished in the desert, somewhere south of Timimoun, in eighteen-hundred-and-something – a thousand men and as many loaded camels – to be found a whole century later, everything intact, except, of course, for the flesh on their bones.

The air, unlike the beer, is freezing cold. The stars are stunning in a huge pitch-black sky. Once you've sat by a fire all night on the edge of the desert you realize that there is nothing surprising in the fact that the desert nations should have been the first to chart the movements of the planets. That is all there is to look at once darkness has fallen, as you eat, drink and rest. There is nothing else. No lights, no buildings, no trees, no people. Nothing but the red glow of your camp-fire, tiny and insignificant, dwarfed by brilliant stars in a massive black velvet sky, filling 360 degrees of skyline.

In the morning I discover an unexpected inconvenience of that 360-degree skyline. How are you supposed to get a bit of privacy for a pee? It's impossible. You could walk for miles, and when you finally crouched down, it would still be plain as a pikestaff what you were at. Thank the Lord I'm wearing a skirt.

I return to the camp, if you can call it that, to find that a pair of vultures has come visiting. Enormous, horrible, bald-headed creatures as big as dogs that spread their wings when they see me, but are so sure of themselves that they can't be bothered to fly off. They just lumber along the ground, wings outspread, till they're out of reach, flapping half-heartedly. Their wingspan must be double the span of my arms, their beaks are pointed flesh-ripping tools. My hair stands on end. I'm glad I know they only want dead things, or they would be utterly terrifying. They're just hoping we'll throw them another dead sheep, I suppose. Suddenly I can't stand their beadily staring presence. I take a run at them. They still don't fly away, but stump a few lurching feet off on their scaly talons, flapping in slow motion. I try shouting and running combined. Several times. Same effect. Now I am hot and sweaty; the vultures, on the other hand, still look cool and sleek, taking it all in their stride. Oh well. At least they're a good way off now.

I crouch down to get the fire lit. Out of the corner of my eye, I can see them waddling slowly back my way, beady eyes gleaming evilly. I give in. I'll just have to learn to put up with them. I want my coffee.

19

It's a hundred miles and more since we left behind the last few gnarled and worried-looking shrubs. Earlier the shadows were sharp on every tiny fold of the terrain. Midday now, and the heat is crushing, the shadows gone, the glare magnifying the flatness all around us. With the endless dunes of the Erg to the north now, the road runs on south-west through an iridescent plain of gravel, polished and black-ened by millennia of oxidation under this harsh sun. There is still nothing to take your bearings from, no inkling that we could be nearing any such unlikely thing as an inhabited place, when, all of a sudden, a battered road-sign stands pointing in absolute emptiness. A large, hand-painted road-sign of sand-blasted metal, announcing the capital city of distant Mali: 'BAMAKO 2685 kilometres'. And for Timimoun, take a right turn. But where on earth is Timimoun? Surely, in all this flatness, we should be able to see it?

But, as Habib told us, the desert is never as flat as it seems. Tim-imoun is set on a gentle dip that falls away to a massive *sebkha*, a low-lying plain that was, some millennia ago, the bed of a salt lake. And you come upon it by surprise. A small, dusty petrol station, a wide, dusty right turn, and the endless grey-brown gravel suddenly gives way to bare red earth. Ahead of us is more red earth – but in vertical mode, fashioned astonishingly into crenellated city walls with tall, tapered buttresses rising above them, dark green palms beyond, red minarets dominating the scene. The portal of the town is a great archway, also of red daub, chunky and square, massively ornamented. The Sudan gate, says François.

Past the gateway, the luscious green of palm trees, lining the road;

and more red. The ground is compacted red earth, the buildings are red earth, and, up ahead, behind more palm trees, are red walls within walls: the ramparts of the old town, the *ksar*. They look as if they were moulded from the red clay by some giant child's hand, roughly smoothed and irregular. A small market is going on among all this terracotta as we pull in and park, a market attended by a most amazing array of inhabitants. A crush of people in every conceivable combination of skin tone and dress style, swathes of brilliant white and bright colour, going about the business of life. There are the pale *haiks* and the fringed Berber headgear, the white jellabas and twisted *chèches*. The *chèche* here, though, is tied with a long tail to one side, to be draped over the neck or the lower face, depending on taste and weather conditions, while the men's jellaba often gives way to the sleeveless gandoura. Among the now-familiar Maghreb faces are tall, thin men of narrow features and hawk-noses with dark *chèches* and the blackest of skin, or broad-featured afro-haired men in the bright robes of Black Africa. There are, most striking of all, the exuberant bare-faced smiles of the first black women we have seen since we started our travels, their hair braided and beaded in a way that wouldn't look out of place on a music video, and about as far from the modest *khimar* as you could possibly get. After so many hours of empty, dead land, of stony beige nothingness, the effect is overwhelming. Timimoun seems impossibly busy and impossibly colourful. And positively cosmopolitan.

Wait here, says François imperiously, heading off into the small market round the side of the post office, also of red mud-brick, though it must be French-colonial. So we sit down on the post office steps, also a popular spot with the local inhabitants, and gaze around us gobsmacked until François comes back with paper cups of flavoured buttermilk – one gold-coloured, mixed with pureed dates, he says, and the other, a pale pistachio, with fresh green barley and honey. So welcome and refreshing that we have to have another one right away before we decide what to do next. Naturally we have already drawn a small crowd and soon we are chatting to two teenagers who have won the battle to take ownership of the fascinating foreigners – they are Moussa and Moulay, two open-faced, afro-haired youths with infectious grins. Moussa is soon leading Gérard and Guy off to find Jean-Pierre's friend with whom we are supposed to be staying, Hadj Mouloud, while Abdelwahab and I sit on the steps with François, Moulay and our luggage, taking in the amazing ethnic mix around us.

What a relief! I feel more at home in this multicultural haven than I have anywhere else in the trip so far, I say. Abdelwahab agrees: he is gazing happily around him, a broad grin on his face. It's just like being back in Paris! Except that, unlike Paris, there's no traffic, the air is amazingly clean, the sun is shining, and nobody looks in much of a rush.

François and Moulay start giving us the who's who of the Timimoun population. Much too much information to take in at one go; my head is soon spinning. Those dark-skinned men over there are Haratine, and that's a Cha'amba Bedouin, the one with the black headdress; those two fairer women are Berbers, and that other one in the pale *haik* is an Arab, of the *shurfa*: direct descendants of the Prophet Mohammed. The black men in colourful gandouras are just passing through, they'll be migrants from Mali or Niger; now two more Haratine – of course they look different from the Black Africans, what do we mean? The two tall, elegant men holding hands, or rather, fingertips, are Tuareg, or maybe Ait Atta – Berber nomads, anyway, not like the Cha'amba, who are an Arab people, though most Cha'amba are not nomads any more these days, but merchants. That scruffy man with the hoe is another Haratine, on his way back from work in the palm groves. The turbaned man leading a donkey, its panniers filled with three-foot-long spears of spectacular fluffy dried flower-heads, is a Berber farmer, a rich *m'rabtin* landowner, bringing date-palm flowers to sell at the market from his own palm groves.

I give up. So does Abdelwahab. How many tribes can you fit in to one small town? So which variety, we ask, are Moussa and Moulay? Moulay is certain we must be able to tell by looking at him. He and Moussa are Haratine, he says. Right from the bottom of the pile. The labouring classes. Isn't it obvious?

Abdelwahab and I soon put him right. It's going to take a lot more than one quick outline before we start to get the hang of Timimoun and its many-splendoured inhabitants. And dressed in Western-style pants and T-shirts like that, Moulay and Moussa aren't giving us a lot to go on, are they?

But, speaking of Berbers, does Moulay know anybody called Kebir? A Berber, with nephews called Mohammed, Sayid, Karim, Rashid, Hassan, who were all away working in Paris, once upon a time?

Moulay laughs. There are over 20,000 inhabitants in this town – more if you include all the outlying villages – and those are not exactly the most unusual names! Moulay will go and make enquiries for me, he says, in the café up the road – the only one in town, we'll soon discover. We follow in his wake, passing a butcher's shop outside which is displayed, on a piece of matting by the doorway, the severed head of a camel: four long, thin camel shins lean against the door like meaty walking-sticks. On a hook in the doorway hangs a very odd-looking cut of meat, which François identifies as a section of sheep's pelvis, carefully cut to include a single testicle. A butcher will only slaughter a couple of animals at a time, here in the heat of the Sahara: meat won't last more than a day. And he sets an identifying section out as an advertisement. Ram stew today, then, or camel kebabs.

Moulay soon reappears, unsuccessful so far in the hunt for my old friends. But he's put the word about for us – there's bound to be some news by tomorrow. Though we might bump into them tonight, if we're lucky – there's a big wedding on all week, and there'll be an *Ahellil*, a night of singing, up in the old market square later; almost everyone in town is bound to pass through there at some point.

Now here comes Moussa, with Gérard and Guy following behind, talking animatedly with a man about their own age, bare-headed in a snowy white gandoura: Abdallah, son of Hadj Mouloud, come to escort us to the family home. Moussa and Moulay now disappear pretty sharpish, but we make little of this, busy making our adieux to François and Abdelwahab, who are off now to join the third member of their convoy at Reggane.

Abdallah leads us off towards the *ksar*, the old town within its high walls. It is blissful to dive into this labyrinth of cool shady passageways and out of the dry heat. Inside the *ksar*, the buildings are not just close together, but built right on top of one another, red clay interlocking with red clay, angle on angle, the flat roof of one house the terrace of the next; the alleyways below almost entirely covered. So powerful is the desert light that there is no need to let the sky in: a few dusty rays from the entrance are enough to illuminate the whole street. We step along the deep alleyways, floors of beaten red earth, loose golden sand around the doorsteps blown in off the desert, and I feel my eyes begin to relax and open wide for the first time in days. I must have been squinting against the brightness all this time. Further on into the *ksar*, the streets open out. There are head-high walls around little gardens, more palm trees rising above them; a narrow stone channel along the alley's side trickles water to them. Back into narrow alleys again, and Abdallah stops at an unassuming wooden doorway in the red walls, roughly outlined with whitewash. We step into a hallway that is floored with cool, soft sand.

Abdallah has been bidden to show us straight to our quarters, he says, leading us into a room whose floor is also of sand, then out through a central courtyard of sand with a single palm tree at its centre. Up a step into another room – more sand – out again and up a narrow exterior staircase tightly enclosed between more red-mud walls. The place seems extraordinarily complicated, all the more so because the thick layer of sand leads me – unused to such a flooring material – to believe for some time that we haven't actually arrived in the house proper yet. Suddenly we are out on a flat roof with a view right across the town, palm trees and walled gardens everywhere, narrow alleys running between them, more flat roofs below us – some decorated with piles of dates, others with chickens, and one

with a small flop-eared sheep, of the brown-face desert breed Habib
so despised. Here on the roof is a free-standing guest apartment, an
extra mud-brick room built on the flat roof. Abdallah throws the door
open. Thick, bright rugs all over the floor. No furniture. No sand
either. Good.

We all traipse inside, and Abdallah, perfect host, leaves us to settle
in. We will be eating in an hour or so, if we'd like to repose ourselves,
though we're welcome to come down earlier to take some refreshment. Would we like tea?

He vanishes off into the labyrinth, and we settle ourselves and our
stuff in. Speedily done, in a furniture-less room. Back out on the roof
we stand and stare, turning hither and thither, stunned. A strange
pink evening light; a view that goes on for ever. On the edge of the
town, the deep green strip of *palmeraie*, its edges blending into a
broad plain – not sand, not stones; it has a strange white bloom to it,
a crystal luminescence. The salt of the *sebkha*. Tall outcrops of red
rock, the colour of the town, are all that's left of the lake's prehistoric
banks; they look like ancient fortresses standing over the plain. One
of them is topped with a real ruined fortress, a *ksar* as red as the rock,
hardly distinguishable from it. Straight ahead, in the distance, way
beyond the salt plain, lie the curving pale masses of the desert dunes:
the Grand Erg. An endless ocean of cream-coloured sand, huge
rolling waves of it, pitted and shadowed, sensuous yet sterile, stretching on right to the sharp line of the horizon. The Sahara. It seems
impossible that this view can be real, that we could just walk straight
out there and . . . die.

Back downstairs – but which of the rooms, if any, is the sitting
room? It is strange how disorienting the lack of furniture can be, our
need to identify a specific function to a room. Here we are lost.
Nobody in the first room. We cross the courtyard into the second. In
here, a huge and beautiful rug of pale greens and golds has been
spread over the sand, and Abdallah and three older men are hunkered
elegantly down on it. And this must be Hadj Mouloud, now rising to
greet us gravely, dressed all in noble and voluminous white, his *chèche*

pristine white too, and so complicatedly entwined that there must be yards of fabric in it.

We all introduce ourselves. Hadj Mouloud enfolds Gérard in his voluminous white embrace, does some air-kissing, then gives Guy the same treatment. I step towards him, start to raise my arms – and quickly lower them. Whoops. *Faux pas*. I am only to be accorded a handshake, of course. I am a woman. An untouchable, almost.

More hand-shaking with the other guests: Monsieur Brahim is a teacher, and the other man whose name I don't catch is an official from the Daira, the town hall. We are welcomed some more, hands on hearts, and invited to take our seats. We do our best to follow our hosts' lead and settle into a neat crouch rather than collapsing higgledy-piggledy onto the carpet. Everyone is behaving very formally, treating Hadj Mouloud with immense respect, as he takes charge of the tea-tackle which is now brought in by a veiled woman – to whom we are not introduced. How hard it is to reverse your usual norms of politeness. Good manners here, we have now understood, dictate that we should steadfastly ignore her – or at least, that Gérard and Guy should. I'm not sure what I'm supposed to do, but since our hostess – if that is who she is – steadfastly refuses to catch my eye, I don't have much of a decision to make.

The tea hasn't even finished brewing before I give up on the crouching and collapse inelegantly onto the carpet. Much better. The rug is lovely and soft, the sand pristine. Gérard, with a gesture of resignation, does likewise, and our hosts all laugh happily, as at a great joke. They have been waiting for this to happen all along. This inability to sit normally is a European failing well known to the residents of Timimoun, which they find most entertaining. I, for one, am beginning to suspect that we've actually got a completely different design of leg-bone, and the thing is physically impossible. Guy, still doing as the Romans do, stiff-upper-lipped, realizes the game's not worth the candle and takes a seat too, to a round of applause.

Now that we've all done our trick, Hadj Mouloud, guffawing, says he will get some cushions brought in for us – we look much too

uncomfortable to eat like that! The tea is ready now: Hadj Mouloud
has added the water to the pot. But it cannot be served yet. A younger
woman, unveiled but also not introduced, appears with a pitcher
of water, stands by Gérard and waits expectantly. Abdallah mimes
washing his hands. Gérard holds his hands out, and she pours a few
splashes of water onto them – and onto the floor, naturally enough.
Took me by surprise, but it doesn't matter, of course, if your floor is
made of nice absorbent sand. Evidently djinns don't live indoors. Or
do they just not like sand?

Gérard rinses his hands, shakes off the water. Still the woman
waits. Of course: three times. Gérard completes the course; the
unnamed female member of Hadj Mouloud's household goes on to
Guy, who follows suit. Now she pauses. Who is next? Should I hold
out my hands? Or will I be making another *faux pas*, looking as if I
consider myself to rank above our host and his friends?

And what are your first impressions of our town? the teacher is
asking politely, apparently unaware of the silent drama going on.

The pitcher girl – a daughter? a servant? – is in the same quandary
as me. Hadj Mouloud has to give her a nod of his head to show that
I am, indeed, next in rank. Clearly a woman eating with the men
is an unheard-of situation. I am neither fowl, flesh nor good red
herring.

Stunning, the boys are saying. Timimoun is beautiful! Unbeliev-
able! And then the people – there are so many different ethnicities, so
many styles of dress, that it's impossible for a newcomer to make
head or tail of them!

I wonder now whether I should have offered to go and sit with
the women, wherever it is that they sit? I don't want everyone being
ill-at-ease, if my presence is a problem. It can't do any harm to ask.
So I do. The gentlemen are most amused. No need at all, they say.
There is, in fact, a system in place for dealing with anomalies like me.
European women, explains Hadj Mouloud, count as honorary men.
It is just that his womenfolk are unfamiliar with the protocol. Hadj

Mouloud has welcomed many foreign guests into his home, but I am the first woman he has had the honour to lodge.

In fact, as it turns out, my presence in Hadj Mouloud's home will present him with various insurmountable problems. However, as yet, I am blissfully unaware of this – and so is Hadj Mouloud.

The first woman returns with our starters. Two sorts of flatbread, piping hot, one stuffed with onions and spices, the other with a kind of cinnamon-and-date compote, whose sweet perfume suddenly brings flooding back the memory of my days as an Undesirable Alien, and a certain Spanish train journey. Abdallah leads the way, ripping a section neatly out of one, using just the fingers and thumb of his right hand the way the Moroccans did with that *bestiya*. I think I'll wait till everyone else has had some. It will look like good manners, and hope-fully there'll be a bit just the right size left, so I won't need to show myself up.

Conversation turns to the rest of Gérard's and Guy's trip. And mine. Everyone is horrified to hear that I am even thinking of return-ing through the north alone. Hadj Mouloud says it is impossible. Things are getting serious up there – the forces of law and order admit to having arrested 6,000 people, but the word is that it's more like 15,000. The extremists are reacting. There is talk of a *fatwa* on all non-Muslims. These people may be deranged, but that does not mean they can't harm you. And a woman travelling alone! Unless, of course, I was to wear the full *hijab*? But even so, my eyes are the wrong colour – and if I were to be challenged, and had to speak, I would be sunk. The Daira man says there's usually a weekly plane leaving El Golea for Algiers – maybe I could catch that? If it's still run-ning? And get straight out of Algiers again, obviously. The Daira man has a telephone in his office, he says. He will find out tomorrow.

As dinner is served, by yet another woman, I try again to make eye contact. She won't look at me at all. But then, why am I expect-ing her to? A decent woman should not make eye contact with unknown men – and that's what I am, if I'm sitting here. An honorary unknown man. I've been an honorary man all through this trip, I suppose. Strictly speaking, apart from the very occasional foreigner – and maybe women selling in the market – men here would never ever speak to any woman at all except ones they were related to, either by blood or marriage. Depressing thought. The very idea makes me feel claustrophobic. Still, at least they have good big families. Imagine if you tried that in England.

As if to the manner born, we three make our little dents in the piled golden couscous on the communal platter and receive our share of the meat and vegetables – smells delicious – being distributed by Hadj Mouloud. As we start to eat – tastes delicious too, tender mutton (perhaps the ram whose private parts we met earlier?), lots of spices, and I think there are dates in there somewhere – we discover that the teacher and the town hall man are not really here for us after all, but to discuss some business with our host. Hadj Mouloud apologizes deeply. He did not know exactly when we would be arriving. But he has delegated his son to entertain us for tonight, he says, and he hopes we will not be offended. Thank goodness: we were afraid Jean-Pierre had built us up as visiting dignitaries of some kind. Hadj Mouloud is having some legal problems over a piece of land he donated to the poor some years ago, he explains. It has not been used in the way he expected: he has been bitterly disappointed. After dinner he will be consulting with his two other guests about this matter.

Over dinner we discover all sorts of interesting things. The first is that the more you move about on a carpet resting on deep sand, the more the sand ends up on top of the carpet rather than underneath. Hadj Mouloud seems to have forgotten about the cushions, and even sitting in the lotus position – or my best approximation of it – does not bring me close enough to the communal couscous-dish to eat without dropping a worrying amount on the beautiful carpet, which I suspect is of silk. Then there is the matter of the cross-legged position being almost as uncomfortable as the crouch. I try putting my legs to one side, then to the other. They either get in the way, or tangle scandalously with my male fellow guests' equally dysfunctional lower limbs. With the three of us squirming about like this – while our hosts eat peacefully from their elegant squatting positions as if nothing was more natural – the sand is soon not only all over the carpet, but creeping inside my clothes, and even more annoyingly, into my food. I soon have to give up chewing the couscous at all; grains of sand are skreeking horribly between my teeth. Luckily, you don't actually need to chew couscous. It could have been designed with just this situation in mind. And maybe, indeed, it was.

The people of Timimoun, we learn, bring all this sand into their houses on purpose, each spring, to keep the floors cool for the summer. It must take years of training, is all I can say, to learn not to get it mixed up with everything. Or do you eventually get used to sand in hair and eyelashes, between fingers and toes, and even creeping into much more intimate areas? I never will find out how on earth they get all this sand back out of the house again, and what the floor beneath it actually consists of – I keep missing my chance to slip this question in to the conversation. While we eat, and Teacher Brahim fills us in on two-thousand years of Timimoun history, I try casually poking my finger down into the sand as far as it will go; but meet no resistance. Just more sand. And you can't really start digging an inspection pit in your hosts' floor over dinner to see what's beneath it, can you?

Meanwhile, Monsieur Brahim is having a go at explaining the complex ethnic situation here in Timimoun. The place is not at all the modern city full of new immigrant populations that we have imagined. Three of the different ethnic groups have been here for centuries – the Haratine and the Berbers getting on for two millennia, the Arabs not much less. The Haratine are the ones who look more like black Africans – they are the very oldest inhabitants. The Zenete Berbers started heading this way – from somewhere in the area of Babylon, though nobody's really sure – around the time of Jesus, well before the birth of Islam. And yes, they really were believers in the old Jewish faith. Archaeologists think it was probably the Jewish Berbers who built the *fouggaras*, the water system that kept life going here once the desert had started closing in. Later, after the birth of Islam, came more Zenete Berber Jews fleeing the advance of the conquering Muslims; then newly converted Muslim Berbers and Arabs; and somehow the Judaism got lost. But there are ancient documents in local *zawiya* libraries, and even in the homes of some of the *marabouts*, dating right back to the ninth century – the desert air preserves parchment better than any museum – many of which are written in Hebrew. The Jewish Berber culture once stretched from here to the Tafilalet and Sijilmassa – and from there, of course, on into el-Andalus. This is known, says Monsieur Brahim, thanks to the survival of an agitated letter, written in about the year 800, by the head of Babylonian Judaism, which is addressed to the Jews of the Sahara and of Andalusia, and pleads with them to abandon their Palestinian heresies.

Gérard asks how it is possible, if all these groups have been here so long, that they have preserved their ethnic differences so thoroughly – do they never intermarry? Nobody is answering this. Trust Gérard to ask uncomfortable questions at the dinner table. Dinner rug, that is.

The man from the Daira leaps into the breach. Each group has always had a different role to play, he says. The town always had a complex relationship with the desert nomad tribes, who had constantly to be negotiated and bargained with: they were essential to the existence of the Gourara oases, both as clients, merchants and transporters for local produce – the dates, cloth, basketwork, spices and so on – and as suppliers of necessities like meat, grain, raw wool and salt. But they were also a threat to the oases' survival, especially in times of war, when one tribe might decide to 'protect' an oasis town – in the Mafia sense of the word – to ensure its supplies, thus making it a sitting target for the opposition. And so it was that the Haratine got on with the farming of the palm groves, to which they were best suited, while the religious *zawiyas*, and the landowning and merchant classes of Timimoun – all Arabs or Berbers – provided the negotiating skills vital for survival. They were in any case closely related to the nomad tribes, by language and by blood. And the nomads also appreciated the skills of the holy men of the *zawiyas*, the local *marabouts*, in resolving their own inter-tribal disputes. And so was harmony achieved.

But they didn't intermarry? Gérard repeats, tenaciously.

No, they didn't.

Speaking of Berbers, this seems a good moment to introduce the topic of a certain Berber friend of mine, who spent some time abroad, working with his nephews in Paris . . .

All this emigration is a bad business! It brings nothing but trouble, interrupts Hadj Mouloud. Nothing but disrespect and shamelessness!

Something in Abdallah's expression leads me to believe that this is a tried-and-tested theme of his father's, which he is hoping we won't pursue. But it is too late. Mouloud, who seems to have a somewhat irascible character, is pursuing it anyway. He is very annoyed about this modern habit of emigrating. It is ruining his town, and all the other oases along the Gourara. Leaving your land and your people to work overseas – or in far-off cities – is not honourable behaviour. Only people who have nothing, or don't own a foot of land, would do such a thing. Irresponsible people, who have never learned the duties of property. Especially the Haratine, but there are some Berbers who are no better. And then the Haratine return with more money than they have sense, all sorts of foolish ideas in their heads: they've got rights to this, and rights to that . . . And when they haven't gone all pious and puritanical, and started denigrating the status of the local *marabouts*, they bring back suitcases full of worthless trinkets that turn the heads of others. Music machines, radios, cameras . . . They have no interest in working the way they once did, here in their own land, and following the old, decent ways. Young people leave and never return to look after their parents; there is no shame and no respect. The place is not safe any more, and theft is rampant! You can't even trust your own palm-grove workers not to rob you, these days. They even sink so low as to steal from your vegetable plot! And from the waste land on the borders of the palm groves, too – because how else do these new jumped-up Haratine manage to keep livestock when they own no land? Obviously they must be stealing the forage! They will lie about the date-crop, too; every year it shrinks, if a man is to believe what his sharecroppers say. Nowadays they don't want to pay the landowner his fair share when the harvest's in, and when you insist on your rights, they threaten to leave! Once upon a time here in the Gourara, there was no leaving! And it was the people with responsibilities who made the decisions for the good of the whole town, not the propertyless and the land-less, who only care for their own personal matters. If you have no stake in the place, what kind of decisions will you make? Of course they won't be for the general good!

Strange. I'm sitting in an Algerian oasis listening to an old landowner coming up with the exact same arguments that were used by old landowners in Britain a hundred years ago, when the lower orders began to demand a say in running their country. *Plus ça change* . . .

Monsieur Brahim has now managed, amazingly enough, to find me an English connection in amongst all his Saharan history – a tiny fragment, but still, gripping. Four English cannons, purchased from Queen Elizabeth the First, once came through this place – in 1591, on their way to Gao, the Malian city that lies directly across the desert from here, on the shores of the river Niger. The Moroccan sultan of the time, it seems, was suffering from the same gold fever that had gripped the Europeans and sent them off to pillage the Incas and the Aztecs. He decided to go for the African gold on his own doorstep. He would invade Mali and take the cities of Timbuktu and Gao, for centuries the source of most of the gold transported northwards by the nomads' Saharan caravans. Six thousand camels and three thousand men came through these oases, dragging the English cannons with them, heading for Gao. Alas, like the Europeans in the Americas, the sultan was doomed to disappointment. There were no fabulous riches to be grabbed, no bottomless mines to be exploited.

Just enough gold was mined in Mali to keep a small, steady trickle coming across the desert.

But the sultan was not to know that. And he was in a precarious position at home. He was not well loved among his subjects, and, worse still, his kingdom had become over-populated with men of fighting age, refugees from Andalusia. The well-heeled Muslims had mostly got out of Spain two or three generations previously: these newest arrivals were restless and rootless, hard up and hungry for opportunities. The situation was bad for his nerves. What better than to send the lot of them off across the Sahara to win his new kingdom? So of the 3,000 men who left Morocco on this mission, 2,500 were refugees from el-Andalus. If the Andalusians succeeded, they could colonize the place for him; if they failed, they were out of his hair for a while, at least – and either way, their troublesome numbers would certainly be reduced.

And so the convoy set off. The English cannons, once the cameleers had got them across the desert – perhaps using the technique recently invented by Barbarossa, of attaching sails to them to help the beasts of burden in their heavy task? – were a great success. The Malians' preferred battle strategy at this time was to bring every available head of sheep and cattle into the field, the livestock both serving as mobile cover and to confuse the aim of their attackers. And, I imagine, providing the celebration dinner ready slaughtered, post-battle. Brilliant plan altogether, if you have never met a cannon. One blast, and their cover was blown.

No great colony grew up from this exploit. But in the environs of Gao there is, to this day, a small group of people known as the Arma, a sad tribal remnant who these days keep themselves to themselves, but who claim that once upon a time they were a powerful military aristocracy and identify themselves – although there is no visual evidence of this – as white. They are, according to Monsieur Brahim, all that is left of the sultan's Andalusian army. Nobody knows what became of the English cannons.

Andalusia to Mali, Alsace to Tizi Ouzou. What distances the

unwanted populations of the world have been constrained to travel! Those Highland ancestors of mine were onto a cushy number, I now see, getting to settle a mere 500 miles from their roots.

Over the salad course, once we have dutifully inspected Hadj Mouloud's diagrams of the *fouggara* system and its workings, given to him by the grateful team of Italian hydrologists who came here to investigate and learn from it, we find out that there is a whole class system to be read from the long white robes people wear here. Guy has asked for some clues to help him decode the multifarious outfits of the town, and we have begun with the basics. You can have a straight white robe, like Monsieur Brahim's, or one that gets much wider towards the bottom, like Hadj Mouloud's. This extra width, Hadj Mouloud explains, is so that he can ride a horse, or a camel: the ordinary narrow ones would get in the way.

Does that mean he has a horse, then? Or is it a camel? I ask excitedly.

He smiles at the thought. Certainly not! He has a Toyota pick-up. He is just explaining the principle behind the garment.

I get it now: his outfit says he's a gentleman, or even an aristocrat, maybe. The same applied in Europe once, didn't it: to call yourself a chevalier, literally just the French for 'horseman', was to distinguish yourself from a commoner. He is being pretty reticent about it, but then, what with all the Islamic injunctions against ostentation, and the Evil Eye that might get you if you were to awaken envy in the hearts of those around you, he has good reason to be. And then, you need to find a good reason for adding those several extra yards of vainglorious fabric to your robe, or risk your entrance to Paradise. My theory about his superior social standing is confirmed when our host gets badly offended by Gérard's assuming that he works in his *palmeraies* himself. He certainly does not engage in manual work. He has sharecroppers to do that. He himself is kept more than busy looking after the business side of his groves.

Hadj Mouloud now turns to converse with his other two guests in their own language. The debate quickly gets very heated. Abdallah, making sure to talk well below the volume of his father's conversation, gives us some low-down. His father doesn't understand the modern world, he says, and it doesn't understand him, either. He's turning into an oasis Don Quixote. (Why am I surprised that Abdallah should know of Don Quixote? Cervantes actually began his great work here: he spent five years in Algiers – captured by pirate corsairs and held as a slave until his friends and family raised the ransom to get him back.)

Abdallah explains that some years ago Hadj Mouloud donated a small palm grove he owned, beside a small village up in the dunes of the Erg, to the inhabitants. A lot of the young and strong had emigrated from the place: the family has distant connections there. The village is out beyond the reach of the *fouggaras* – the land too high, the sand too deep – and the *palmeraie* in question has a small well in it. Hadj Mouloud's was an act of kindness. Quite a few families didn't need to walk so far for their water; and everyone could grow more food.

But at the back of Hadj Mouloud's mind was the notion that he would earn much respect from the émigré men of the village who, when they returned for their month's holidays each year, would appear at his home bearing gifts, and praising him to the skies for his generosity to their old folks left at home. That's how people would have behaved in his father's youth. But not any more: there's an air of democracy abroad, and the recipients of his charity have paid him no homage at all, in all this time. He has been getting more and more offended, year upon year, and now he's asking for his property back, thinking to punish them for their lack of respect! But he's operating by rules only the old even recognize. They are not going to understand the message he's sending them. He'll get himself a name for being a miserly old skinflint – the exact opposite of his original intention!

Monsieur Brahim has promised to try and talk him out of it. But Mouloud has got a lot more stubborn since he's heard that an ex-émigré from the village is actually trying to buy up a palm grove, here in Timimoun, with his French savings. It will be hard for us to understand, says Abdallah, but till recently only Arabs and Berbers ever owned land here – and this man is a Haratine. His father sees it as another sign that the end of the world is at hand!

20

Brilliant moonlight is shining down into the courtyard: at last the heat of the day has died down. Abdallah is off now, but he's going to take a walk round town before he goes home. Do we fancy coming along?

Once we're out of the house, and out of earshot of his father, Abdallah makes us promise to come round for a meal with him and his wife, Amina. She was dying to meet us tonight, but of course he couldn't bring her round – pointless, she would have had to eat in the other room with the rest of the women. Abdallah reveals that he has no intention of going home yet; he is coming to the *Ahellil*. He didn't want to mention it in front of his father. We would all have got a lecture about the fall in artistic standards in the town. Hadj Mouloud would prefer his guests not to see an *Ahellil* at all than to see it in a less-than-perfect form, all the more so since a group of French musicologists came to town and spent an evening with him, lamenting its popularization and consequent loss of purity.

We head ever deeper into the *ksar*, winding through covered streets of earthen walls, following the sound of the drums. Soon we see the flicker of warm light from the square, hear the murmur of a big crowd. We find a bonfire in the square as predicted and the music coming from the flat roof of a nearby house – flutes and percussion, a stringed instrument, some kind of massed chanting. Abdallah tells us that the word *Ahellil* – just in case we have any doubts about the Jewish past of this place – is from the same Hebrew root as 'Halleluia', meaning praise and celebration. It is such an ancient musical form that nobody really knows its origins – a strange mixture of the sacred and the profane, of Berber Tamazight and Bedouin Arabic combined with couplets from the Koran in classical Arabic. It drives anthropologists and musicologists mad. And this town, as we may have gathered, is under constant assault from every kind of -ologist!

Up a narrow enclosed stairway onto the wide roof to find thirty or forty people here under the stars. Edging gently through the packed bodies, we find two musicians, one playing a flute and the other a red clay drum, and one main singer who raises his voice into a strange, harsh sound. He is the caller, and the other singers respond, all in polyphonic harmonies. He stands in the centre of a circle of white robes and white turbans, fifteen-odd men all clapping and singing, or tapping out the rhythm on some kind of metal castanets, standing shoulder to shoulder around the soloist, who improvises a few verses, then the rest repeat a chanted refrain. The words now are Berber, Abdallah says, a mixture of tales of ancient glories and comments on recent events – some humorous, I gather from the audience's reactions. Slowly the rhythm builds up, and every now and then they break into Arabic chanting, verses of the Koran: the lessons to be drawn from the tale, says Abdallah. The circle of swaying white robes is not static but circling around the soloist very, very slowly. Every now and then they do a little double-step-and-knee-bend all in unison, as if they were making obeisance to him. The voices begin to overlap, the rhythm gets tighter and tighter, faster and faster, the dancing kicks in harder . . . After an hour of this, you are totally gripped, and a serious frenzy is building up. Now the soloist improvises a long something that brings a smile to the faces of his chorus, and guffaws from the crowd. A couple of the chorus break ranks, improvise a long response – to more laughter.

It's a good job his father isn't here, says Abdallah. Hadj Mouloud won't even come to an *Ahellil* any more, not when it's a disorganized, family thing like this, and the rules are bent for entertainment's sake. The *Ahellil* is a competitive sport: how skilful is the soloist at improvising around the couplets of the ancient Berber poetry, how stylish the telling of the stories, how brilliant the connections made with the couplets from the Koran that anchor the section and draw out the chorus to improvise in its turn. This is the early part of the event – people will slowly drop out until only the masters of the genre are left. An *Ahellil* won't finish till dawn.

The ignoramuses seem to be having a good time, Hadj Mouloud's opinion regardless. There are even, I am shocked to report, women actually speaking to men in public. This is the first time I've seen men and women socialize together at all, except for our afternoon with Ismail's cousins and our night out with Farida in Algiers – neither of which was exactly typical of ordinary everyday Maghreb life. There are plenty of women here, though, clapping away to the rhythm, clacking with the castanet-things. A pair of middle-aged women next to me, joining in with a will, are accompanying themselves on pairs of pebbles.

Downstairs in a back room, though, is a private women-only party for the bride and close relatives, and suddenly I am dragged away by my pebble-playing neighbour, and taken down to be presented to the bride. I find myself in a room sparkling with bright dresses, golden earrings, tinkling bracelets and anklets – and plenty of semi-naked hair, in every shade of henna. Some are dancing and *you-you*-ing and banging those ceramic tambourine-things, while one seated woman uses the two halves of a quern, a grindstone, for a percussion instrument. I am never going to get any coherent picture of women in this country. One minute they are silent and repressed, trudging the streets wrapped in a big sheet, eyes downcast, the next they are whirlwinds of bright colour, music, dancing, laughter and chaos. They all go wild at the sight of me, double *you-yous*, screams and laughter, manhandling me over to meet the bride, who is all veiled up, sitting on a little dais in the corner. They lift her veil so she can have a proper look at me – or so that I can see her properly? My presence will bring extra *baraka* for the marriage, they say. Like the women of the Ouled Naïl, I guess, my weird neither-man-nor-woman status has the extra *baraka*-power.

Back upstairs, the crowd is settling in to the event, the rhythm slower and more heartfelt. There is still no sign, alas, of Kebir or any of his nephews. The ladies who took me downstairs are beside me, singing along ecstatically. A couple of youths behind Gérard launch into the next response at maximum volume. We look round: they are Moussa and Moulay. And they don't seem to be taking the event as seriously as they should. In fact, they are definitely, if subtly, taking the mickey. Moussa bounces over to me. He thinks he's got a lead on the Kebir I'm looking for, but he will say no more. He waggles his index finger from side to side. No, no. He will tell me when he is sure.

Another bonfire: this time on the edge of the *palmeraie*, where the trees meet the moonlit glow from the *sebkha*. Moussa and Moulay have enticed us away from the *Ahellil* – it's boring and old-fashioned, and anyway, it'll be on all night – to join a bunch of people whom they call the *moksirin* – which means, they say, the 'night-shorteners'.

We have headed out along a red-earth road that slopes gently down through the *palmeraies*, discovering by ghostly moonlight that, tucked in beneath the palm trees, is an amazing array of other crops, whole fields of moonlit barley, of onions, carrots, chilli-peppers, even tomatoes. Once you have the palm trees to protect more tender plants from the violent Saharan sun, you can grow anything here, says Moulay. You can't go outwards – the desert stops you doing that – so you go upwards instead! Three storeys of cultivation: the tall palms up above, vegetables and grain down below, and fruit trees, gourds, pumpkins, and henna bushes inbetween. That's how you make the best use of your land here.

As we draw closer to the *sebkha* these bountiful gardens give way to plain palms, wall-less and unprotected, sown by the hopeful landless on the dry limits of irrigation. Here the *palmeraie* meets the desert, trailing sadly off through a little grove of half-dead palm trees on the very edge of sand and salt plain. The trees down here are sick, Moulay says, not from lack of water – for once – but from too much of it. Torrential rainstorms, unheard of in the past, have hit the town three times in the last few years. They have destroyed a lot of homes – Timimoun's flat roofs of mud supported on palm trunks are not designed to stand up to that sort of treatment – and have brought the strong salts in the deeper levels of the ground up to the surface, poisoning the trees. There is no help for them, says Moussa, nothing to be done. The trees out here on the limits are doomed to die.

Now we hear the sound of voices, of laughter, of *Rai* music from a tinny transistor. The bonfire is red-hot, and it needs to be – it is very nippy indeed, out here on the edge of town, now that the sun is off the land, and the night wind blowing in off the desert. Everyone has dug themselves a protective seat right into the sand, a ground-level nest of an armchair, and a couple of boys jump up to help us do the same, making sure we avoid the shifting smoke-path. Long pipes are doing the rounds, thin skeins of paler smoke drifting between crouching figures and moonlit sky. We're in the Timimoun equivalent of the local pub, we decide. All the more so when we are offered a swig of a very strange and noticeably alcoholic drink called, I think, *deffi*. Brewed from forty different plants, they tell us, and only used at Ramadan. They just happen to have some left over . . . I'm not sure if they're just pulling our leg, though. The stuff tastes remarkably like one of those herbal preparations, sweet yet bitter, that Italians drink after dinner to aid their digestion.

Moussa introduces us to everyone and explains where we are staying. The *moksirin* are intrigued: how do we come to know a *shurfa* family?

We don't know what *shurfa* means. Is it the tribe Hadj Mouloud belongs to?

Shurfa, Moussa explains, is not the name of a tribe, but the plural of *sharif*, meaning a legitimate descendant of the prophet Mohammed. The permanent inhabitants of the towns – unlike the passing nomad populations – have been settled for so many centuries that they have lost whatever tribal identities they once had: they only think of themselves as Arab, Berber or Haratine. The *shurfa* of the oasis towns, though, have become an aristocratic clan. They are the propertied class down here, vying for power and influence with the other powerful clan, the *m'rabtin*, which is just the plural of *marabout*: the inheritors and descendants of the holy men of the area. You can have Berber-speaking *shurfa* or Arabic-speaking *shurfa*: the same goes for *m'rabtin*. The *shurfa* and *m'rabtin* are the educated and literary classes of Timimoun, the merchants and *djema'a* men: they are the people born with *baraka*, thanks to their holy origins, and the owners of most of the palm groves, into the bargain.

A few of the people around this camp-fire, we discover as the bottle and the pipe pass on around our circle, are Berbers and Arabs, but most are Haratine. Almost all of them are sharecroppers, which means, they explain, that they rent a palm grove from its owner by the year and pay him come harvest-time with a share of the crops. This is, traditionally, a whole four-fifths of the produce they have grown – by their own hard work!

This seems, we say, taking our cue, a most excessive proportion!

Everyone congratulates us on our insight. Daylight robbery! But in the old days the proprietors made the rules. According to them, since they provided four of the five necessities – the land, water, seed and manure – and the sharecropper only one – his labour – he only deserved one-fifth of the crop. You couldn't get out of it: the share-cropper families had debts with their landlords that went back generations and grew rather than shrank, always augmented by fines from the *djema'a* for not having paid off enough, in years of bad harvest, or by loans when a plough broke or a donkey died . . . There was no escaping the debt, or, indeed, escaping the town. The only transport out of here was with the nomads, and they were the landowners' own trading partners, with no reason to start helping a criminal to default on his debts. You paid your four-fifths or you got no land to work at all, next year. And then how would your family eat?

But then, says Moussa, when the French left, the new government stepped in and forced the landowners to write off the ancient debts. They said it was serfdom, and it's illegal now. Released the Haratine from their bondage. So now they are free men. They can simply refuse the terms of the landlords – and leave to work elsewhere!

One daring *moksirin* claims to have heard it said that the *shurfa* of Timimoun are not truly descendants of the Prophet Mohammed, anyway. Of course they have more *baraka* – but that's because they're rich! Anyone with more money has more luck in life – *c'est évident!*

They are all stomachs of sin, says one of the smokers, a certain Ali, who oddly enough is wearing a T-shirt with a Guinness logo. Another older man repeats this remark, nodding his agreement. Stomachs of sin! That, he explains, is how you describe rich people here!

Bad rich people, really, says Moussa, diplomatically. Not Hadj Mouloud, necessarily, who he has always heard was an honourable *sharif . . .*

Still, emboldened now, the night-shorteners all plunge in at once, telling us how Haratine have always done all the work here – along with the poorer Berbers and Arabs – while *shurfa* and *m'rabtin* sat on their bums on silken carpets writing poetry, or long involved commentaries on the Koran!

But, says Moulay, the Old Rich are getting their come-uppance now, because plenty of them are worse off than their former serfs, these days – all because they were too noble to leave their fiefdoms and become lowlife migrant workers! Plenty are having to sell up their lands – sometimes even to their old employees!

A quiet older man who has hardly spoken so far says that they haven't stopped their bad old ways, though. His brother, back from France with his life savings, is trying to buy a *palmeraie* of his own, here in Timimoun, and the Stomachs of Sin are pulling out all the stops to prevent it.

A boy in a stripey jellaba and a baseball cap wants to tell us another of the tricks of the Stomachs of Sin. The *shurfa* and *m'rabtin* of these oases, he says, were the only people in the whole of Algeria who actually made a profit out of the French being here! They had always collected the levy off the whole town, in crops or money, that paid the nomads' share – their taxes, as they liked to call them, for protecting the town. Both *shurfa* and *m'rabtin* being respected religious mediators in disputes, and having the *baraka* of their birth-lines, that was their traditional job. But once the French army's presence had ended the nomads' power, and there were no more warring Tuareg or Ait Atta to worry about, the aristos went right on collecting the same taxes as always – which they just kept for them-selves! And got richer than ever, as a result!

We now hear that, when the new government tried to redistrib-ute the oasis land more fairly, the Stomachs of Sin simply hid their holdings. Anyone with more than 1,000 palm trees was supposed to relinquish the rest, to be shared out among the landless and destitute. Of course they just gave shares away to their brothers and wives. And, surprise! When it came to counting, hardly anybody at all had more than 1,000 trees. The few that did get redistributed were right on the sickly edges of the *palmeraie*, or without irrigation. The government were too stupid to realize that land here in the desert is no use with-out access to water, or that the old nobility owned almost all the rights to it! Lots of people had no choice but to sell their plots right back to the old owners. The *Pouvoir* would have done better to redis-tribute the water than the land – that would really have given people a chance. But what do you expect? They would rather consult some expert in Paris than their own people.

The thought of Paris inspires the night-shorteners to start shar-ing tales of their derring-do in Oran and Algiers, in France and Germany, of the heroic sufferings of immigrant life, and of their steadfast courage or deepest cunning in the face of hostile Christians – whose main pleasure in life is in thinking up clever new reasons to throw you out of their country.

Those few swigs of *deffi* seem to have had the most extraordinary effect on me. Can it be down to the fact that one of the forty herbal ingredients, as Moulay now reveals, was the seed-head of the opium poppy?

An hour or two later, as the bottle empties and the smoke from the kif rises thicker and faster around us, we hear the tale of a pair of djinns, seen fighting one another with swords of flame down in the heart of this very *palmeraie*. The hero of the story tells us that, with great presence of mind, he snatched up seven pebbles, quick as a flash, and hurled them into the nearby water-course that must be their home, shouting, 'Djinns begone, and angels enter!' And they vanished, that very moment, in a crash of thunder and a puff of orange smoke.

Out on Hadj Mouloud's roof again, I stand and admire the early-morning sand dunes, now in bold relief with the sharp shadow of the early sun and coloured a very unlikely lemon-yellow. Below the town, the dark plumes of the palm grove keeping the desert at bay; the outcrops of red cliff standing guard beyond, glowing pink in the morning sunlight. Now I turn my attentions inward, to the courtyard below me.

Leaning on the parapet, I watch, unseen, the two women from last night, and two more female household members as yet unknown, going about the business of Saharan housework. One of them is doing something on a brazier over in the corner, a fine wisp of smoke rising from it. Another is sweeping the sand – really! – with a sort of palm-leaf rake. Two of the older ones are busy making what I soon realize is couscous, sitting cross-legged on goatskin mats spread out on the sand, intent on their work and oblivious to my presence.

One is using a prehistoric quern to grind the corn into flour, just like the one we saw used as a musical instrument last night – two chunky stones, the bottom one round and flat, the top one a big doughnut with a wooden noggin set in its side to turn it. She is unveiled now, and her hair is showing, red-gold with henna, beneath a scarf looped at the nape of her neck. She trickles a fistful of grain into the central hole of the hand-mill, then turns the top stone. The flour begins to pile up on the bottom plate-stone, to overflow. The other woman collects it up with a ladle made from half a gourd, pours it into a wooden bowl, dampens a handful with water, dextrously rolls it over a big, shield-like reed mat held between lap and shoulder, the tiny couscous bobbles falling away onto the basket-work bowl at her side, ready for drying: just the way Uncle Kebir described it, back in Paris. It looks amazingly easy. Something tells me it probably isn't.

Fascinating to watch: and I see that my sandy couscous of last night was not entirely my own fault for fidgeting. Created under these sandy conditions, the stuff is actually incorporated into the raw material of the dish.

Gérard steps out of our apartment now, yawning and stretching, and wanders over to join me leaning on the parapet. He finishes rubbing his eyes, and now he too deciphers the activity. Couscous! he announces triumphantly. The women look up at the sound of his voice; we both wave and say good morning. They make no response, just turn their backs resolutely upon us. What can we have done to annoy them so?

Minutes later, Abdallah appears on the roof. In our excitement, we had forgotten that men are not supposed to look at women, at all, ever, unless they are related to them.

His father has forgiven us, says Abdallah, since we are newcomers and obviously didn't do it on purpose – but please remember not to do it again. It has upset the women badly.

This is the first of our offences against the honour of Hadj Mouloud's family. Or at any rate, the first we know of, because hanging out with Haratine and the *moksirin* is not considered good form either. Just about acceptable from men, who must be allowed their little adventures, but impossible to handle when done by a woman. Especially one who is the guest of a *sharif*. Honorary manhood being, as I've already noticed, a pretty unstable category, my sins will multiply over the week we are here, until eventually they produce dramatic results. For now, though, we know nothing. We are off for a stroll around town.

Moussa makes us buy a *chèche* each before he takes us walking. He doesn't want to be responsible for our getting sunstroke. They are enormous – yards of cloth, more even than in that Tlemcen *haik*. Much entertainment now as Gérard and Guy try to put them on. Moussa does his in a couple of nimble twists – but he can't do someone else's, he says, it's impossible. It must be like trying to tie some-one else's tie. I've never been able to do that, either.

I am not supposed to wind mine around my head like the men, but drape it like a stole, according to Moussa. This doesn't seem fair. Rolled up, it gives you a lot more layers of protection from the sun. And aren't I supposed to be an honorary man, anyhow? Moussa says I can do it like a man if I really want to, but not here in the market. He will be embarrassed.

Guy has certainly got the hang of it. Doesn't his look great? Has he been practising in secret? He's even got the nonchalantly trailing side-bit hanging right, I say.

Moussa says that, on the contrary, they've both made pigs' ears of them. Still, as long as they're good enough to please another Euro-pean! Every beetle is a gazelle in the eyes of his mother!

I do a double-take. What, I ask, did he just say?

He repeats it. It's nothing – just a saying.

But is it a saying from here? From Algeria?

Of course it is! Where else would it be from?

Italy! I say. That's why I'm looking so flabbergasted. It's a saying I've heard loads of times from my southern Italian friends back in Diano Marina. *Ogni scarafaggio e gazello a mamma sua!*

Well, probably everyone says it, everywhere, says Moussa.

Not in France, say the boys. They've never heard such a peculiar expression!

And not in England, either, I say. I think we've just found another trace of your erstwhile presence across the Mediterranean.

Moussa is vastly entertained to hear that we're staying in Hadj Mouloud's roof apartment. Those rooms are for storing the precious stuff of the house, and more especially, he says, for new brides, for the first year of their marriage! Didn't we know that? So Moussa is out and about with Hadj Mouloud's three new brides! Moussa finds this hysterically funny, and will repeat it to everyone we meet for days.

Down another of the myriad pathways through the *palmeraie* we set off into the *sebkha*, the bed of the dead salt lake. A lake that was once enormous – and navigable, too, according to Monsieur Brahim, or so the experts think, because some of the names of the villages round here have meanings such as 'port' or 'harbour'. But they have no idea when there was last any surface water here. It was well before recorded history.

If I were to say that the *sebkha* is flooded with sunlight, I would not be giving a sense of the true grandeur of the thing. From here it looks like a white-hot griddle; and stepping out onto it gives you little reason to change your mind about this notion. The sun is not just beating down, but upwards, too. I get my *chèche* wrapped sharpish, regardless of Moussa's feelings.

We skirt along the edge of the salt plain, heading towards the red cliffs to eastward, and cross an abandoned graveyard – the cemetery of the now-defunct *ksar* perched on high, away along the valley. An extraordinary sight. Graves here are marked with ceramic ewers, big dark-glazed jugs that match the iridescent stones around them, their open mouths gaping skywards to catch any drop of water the heavens may dispense: the most precious gift you could give anyone, living or dead, in these parts. A plain shard of stone stands at the head of each grave among this desolation – no names or engravings, just a jagged tip a couple of feet high, pointing into infinity. They could have been made any time in the last two millennia. Or more.

Everything empty and lifeless for miles, it seems. But it is not so. Nearing the recently whitewashed tomb of the *marabout* Sidi Abderrahman (are these the original whited sepulchres, as advertised in the Bible?), we see a man crouching way out on the *sebkha*; he is holding one of those clay ewers used to mark the graves, pouring water from it into a hole in the ground. Why on earth . . . ? Can he be trying to grow something in this unlikely spot?

That is how you make saltpetre, for gunpowder, Moussa tells us. The salts from the ground will melt into the water, then later dry into harvestable crystals. Once upon a time there was a whole saltpetre industry here. The nomads' caravans would make their way out onto the *sebkha* to collect it. Nowadays people just do it for the *barud* – for weddings and festivals, when you make the gunpowder speak. We'll see that on the last day of the wedding celebrations, five days from now.

Past the graveyard and we're heading for the red cliffs, clambering up the gentle side of the rise; soon we're up high and walking on the level. Moussa is taking us to look over the cliff's edge. I creep forward and lie down gingerly next to the others. Down below is a string of villages, clinging to the ground, each one surrounded by its carefully nurtured palm groves, the walled gardens drawn out like an architect's plan. Moussa points out the line of the *fouggaras* that feed these lower villages: a row of tiny black dots in the ground, leading away into the dunes. There are 3,000 kilometres of *fouggara* tunnels in this area, though nowadays many are in disrepair. They don't just carry water from points where the water table is higher, we now know. By day, the cool tunnels suck in the warm, humid air of the *palmeraie*, which condenses on their cool underground walls, depositing precious water back in the channels; then, by night, with the naked desert losing heat at a much faster rate than the mini-climate inside the walled groves, its air, now cool and humid, is sucked back the other way, down into the *fouggaras* to condense yet again. Even though you'd hardly believe there was any water in the atmosphere down here in the Sahara, they pick up something like four litres of water a night from every square metre of desert above them.

Sad to say, only half of them are still in good repair and working to capacity. People are taking to petrol-driven pumps in their stead, which will drain the subterranean veins of water much faster, having none of the sophisticated recycling system of the *fouggaras*. But there's a hope they may be saved. Hadj Mouloud's researching hydrologists were from Puglia, an Italian region which itself owns ancient water systems based on similar principles, also of unknown origin. Puglia is paying for the study and may help finance the repairs the Gourara can no longer afford these days, since the Haratine, traditional caretakers of the system, escaped their serfdom, and have to be paid properly.

Fingers crossed.

*

We press on, downhill now, three-quarters of an hour of blazing sun, and we're back to sand level. These villages are at the farthest extent of the *fouggaras*. Many of their water-courses have died, either from disrepair of because the vein of water has run out. This is the reason there are so many abandoned *ksars* dotted about the desert here: water runs out, sand moves, there is nothing to be done but move on. Archaeologists have never found any domestic articles of significance left behind in any of the hundreds of *ksars*. People were not driven out suddenly, by war or disaster: the desert gave them plenty of time to decide there was nothing for it but to leave, to carefully pack up all their belongings, load up their beasts of burden, and set off for a new life elsewhere.

Now that we're nearing the next village, a bunch of children has raced out to accompany us. Children here have their hair shaved right down short – nits must terrible in a place like this – with just a single odd little tuft left, plaited into a tiny pigtail. It is never right in the centre – is that because only God is perfect? Moussa informs us that all children must have a topknot like this, because, if perchance they should die, they would need it to be pulled into paradise. I can't get any more out of him on this interesting topic; looking a little shame-faced, he claims that's all he knows. Not proper Islam, then, we deduce.

The children mill around us. Overheating badly, I head off alone towards the next *ksar*, along the side of a sandy hill, seeking easier walking and a bit of shade. Walking so far on soft sand does some-thing very strange to all sorts of foot-muscles you never knew you had. The sun is terrible. I am a black spot on a yellow surface, vibrat-ing with light.

The shade of the fortress, granary, whatever it may have been, is a welcome relief. Down below me now is a deep well – once a corn-store, a home, a prayer room? Higher up, the doorways are just two feet wide, crumbling away: on some of them the iron hinges still hang. One more human achievement being slowly digested by the desert. How old can it be? Could it be from the times of the Talmud?

Across the valley a sand dune has thrown itself at the base of a red cliff like some wild animal exhausted from the hunt. Down below, at the bottom of the hill, a racket has broken out: Gérard, Guy and Moussa are playing with the kids, who have brought sheets of corrugated cardboard, bits of plastic grain-sack. Gérard and a tiny child are climbing to the top of a dune together. Gérard seems to be taking orders from the boy, or maybe girl: he sits on the sheet of cardboard. The child sits on him. A quick scull with their hands, and off they both shoot, wild laughter, tobogganing down the slope.

I head for the exit and, blinded by the light, bang my head hard on what was once somebody's doorway. Race down the hill regardless. Up onto the dunes to grab myself a small child and a slab of cardboard. Wheeeee!

A lovely game. These desert children know a thing or two. That precipitate rush downhill creates a fantastic cooling headwind. On my third go, beginning to feel that the running back up rather cancels out the cooling effects of the skid down, I pause at the top before prostrating myself beneath my favourite child, a very squeaky little girl with the best chance of any of them of getting into paradise: she has not one but three little topknots on her head. From here you can see a broad dune behind us, higher than the others, wearing a strange frill of dead palm-leaves along its crest. Beautiful from up here, this luminous snaking curve outlined in shadow, the fringe of palm-leaves marking the sharp divide between sun and shade. Down below, nestled in its curve at valley level, the children's village, which must be the replacement to the *ksar* I was just in. Its palm trees are planted, one by one, down in deep, deep troughs in the sand, only their heads showing. That way, they can reach the water themselves, no need for hard bucket-work. The same decorative fringes of dried palm-leaves sprout from the crested tops of their craters as along the top of the snaking dune. And for good reason, as Moussa now explains. The palm-leaves have not been stuck in along the crests. It is the other way round: the leaves have created the crest. They are sand-stops, *afreg*. The villagers choose where they want the sand to halt, and place their row of palm fronds along the line. The sand dune will grow: every few months you must go up and add another layer of fronds. But – *inshallah* – the *afreg* will usually hold the dune where it is for many decades. You have to treat the desert sand delicately, with respect. To try building an impassable barrier is to tempt the dunes – and the djinns – to show you what they can do. Sand will build up behind the barrier, then begin to overflow it. Soon you have created exactly the menace you wished to avoid. Your village, your gardens, will vanish beneath the giant dune of your own making. As the *Pouvoir* found to their cost when they tried to build what they called a socialist village, says Moussa, up at the head of the Gourara. They would create palm groves for the propertyless, they said, and new homes for the landless poor. It was part of the plan to rescue the Haratine from their bondage. The water was easily accessible – just a few feet below ground level. Wells were built, sand cleared to find the clay level, palm trees planted. They had some frenchified archi-tect who had designed a village in the form of a spiral. He said the sand would be carried through it and away. People came from miles around to look. But nobody moved in. The landless came to help with the building, all right, and plant the groves: the *palmeraies* would be good for a few years, they could see that, and they got paid to do it, anyway. Moussa's father was one of them. But as soon as they'd set eyes on the place, they knew it could never be a permanent home. Why bother moving themselves and their families here? They would just use the gardens – at least they'd been provided free – until they vanished under the sand. Because somehow – nobody knows if it was part of the architect's original plan – the builders had begun by putting up a twenty-foot protective wall to the sandward side of the village. Before they'd even finished building the first half-dozen homes, the sand was already half way up it. The intended occupiers laughed bitterly into their *chèche*-tails and went off home. No point in it at all, they said. That was twenty years ago. Today the place has all but disappeared.

A torrid wind is rising now, abrasive and dry. It is midday and, in spite of the wind, absurdly hot. The children all scamper off home towards their village: we start heading back to Timimoun, crossing the path of a man riding a little donkey, heading for a gap between the dunes, his gandoura and *chèche* of indigo cloth so faded it's almost white. His feet dangle in time to the creature's steps, the tips of his babouche slippers grazing the ground. Slipping between the dunes, he and the donkey vanish into the sand.

Moussa tells us, as we trudge on homewards, that the Gourara is situated in a world wind tunnel, a place where the winds from both sides of the earth meet and crash into one another. Is this possible? And that if the winds start to come strong from the south-east in the next week or two, the whole date harvest may be ruined, shrivelled on the bough. The pollination will not take. Women must tie their headscarves tightly, never loosen them outdoors, once that wind starts up. It is well known that the loosening of headscarves can conjure up a wind, even on the calmest of days.

I'm not sure how to take this. Perhaps it is a reference to the fact that I've got my *chèche* wrapped man-style, and we're almost back in town, where this will embarrass our escort? I unravel it and put it on like a proper ladies' *khimar*, just in case. The wind dies down as suddenly as it arose. Moussa turns and gives me a big grin.

We seem to be going a very roundabout way back into town, heading for the farthest end of the *ksar*. Moussa has something he wants to show us, he says, giving us a mysteriously gleeful look as he leads us on through the alleys on the edge of town, the head-high walls behind which the domestic palm groves lie.

We stop at a big iron gate. With a squeal of hinges, Moussa swings it open for us. We step out of the glaring eyeball-shrivelling sun and into another world.

21

A green and shady paradise: green foliage rustles above us, and all around us is the sound of trickling water, constant and miraculous. The air is cool and fresh. Rays of light penetrate the palm-fronds far above, picking out bright peppers, tomatoes, pumpkins. Beside us are pomegranate trees in flower, palest green leaves still barely in bud, their blossoms red stars against bare dark wood. Way above us, strings of date-flowers cascade from the heads of the palms; their fringed crowns are darkest green against the glimpses of blazing sky. After so many miles of harsh sand and arid stones, it is hard to believe this is not a hallucination: the classic desert mirage, in impossible close-up.

The water trickles on. A lemon tree stands just inside the gate, a little grove of oranges over against the far wall. In the centre are more fruit trees, peaches or apricots; below them rows of onions, carrots, maize, chilli-peppers. A big clump of cactus-leafed barbary figs stands spiky against the wall in the corner. There are other plants I don't recognize – some kind of dark-green shiny bush, long thorns hidden among the leaves, its heavy clusters of pale pink flowers giving off a strong, warm perfume, of tobacco, roses, chocolate, a perfume that pervades the whole garden.

Henna, of course, says Moussa. Have we never seen henna before?

And those tall plants that look like huge parsley running to seed? They are cumin, a plant I've only ever met as a dry powder in a cellophane packet. Green and lively here, though. The bright sun-dappled grass in the centre of the grove is not a lawn, but a tiny field of barley. Some small children away on the far side of it are picking off barley-heads, and beyond them two women are heading their way.

Moussa seems to be waiting for the women to draw close. Are they friends of his? Family? They arrive, and we are all introduced. Oddly, though, Moussa seems to be introducing himself to them first. Do they not know one another already?

The older woman is called Rashida and is wearing, wrapped around her head, the exact pink-and-gold fringed shawl that looked so terrible on me. Taiwan must have flooded the entire Algerian market with the things. She looks gorgeous in it. The younger woman is Aisha, her daughter.

We three foreigners shake hands politely, waiting to be given more information. There is an odd air of expectancy. All of a sudden, Rashida, who has seemed all along to be trying hard not to laugh, claps her hands together as if she can no longer contain herself and with a peal of laughter throws her arms in the air – and then around me. Her daughter, laughing too, seems to be remonstrating with her in her own language, but suddenly gives up and joins in the hug.

Rashida has gone and spoilt the surprise, now! says Aisha. Have I guessed who they are?

I think I have. Moussa has set us up. Are they perhaps the same Rashida and Aisha who once prepared a very luxurious picnic for a certain train journey to Paris? Aunt Rashida and Cousin Aisha?

Yes, they are indeed, says Rashida. So young Moussa really did tell us nothing? What a good boy he is, she says, giving him a pat on the cheek. And there is a better surprise still to come, says Aisha: Kebir is here too, and Mohammed. Look, there they are, heading this way!

Where? With so much vegetation in here, shaded green broken by blinding fingers of light from above, it's hard to see anything at all. But yes, two figures in white have detached themselves from the background of foliage, way down the other end of the grove, and are hurrying this way, threading through the crops. It really is Kebir! And Mohammed behind him!

But did Rashida even know who I was at all, I ask her, when this surprise was arranged with Moussa?

Of course she did, she says. She had heard all about me! It was a funny thing to see those boys so worried about someone else going off on a train into the unknown, just the exact way she'd been so worried about them!

Moments later, I am getting a public hug from a Muslim man. And then from another. Who would believe it? Uncle Kebir and Mohammed at last! I really have made it all this way – and found them!

I have gone all sniffly. So have Rashida and Aisha.

An hour later, we are still catching up with a couple of decades of news. Only Mohammed, out of all the brothers, is actually here in Timimoun for now, but we will soon be seeing Rashid again, who has succeeded in getting the flock of sheep he dreamed of, and the camel too. And if we're lucky, we'll get to see Karim and Sayid as well.

Karim is due back from his building job in In Salah, though no one's sure exactly when he'll arrive, now, says Aisha, with all this political trouble, and the roads inundated with soldiers. Mohammed has ended up joining his uncle Kebir as he was planning, but not at his old trade, because hardly anyone uses mud-bricks any more. New homes – if they get built at all – are just thrown up with cinder-blocks these days. So he and Kebir have gone back to farming the dates. Not just in this *palmeraie*, no; this one is mostly for the family's own food. They have a couple of much bigger groves they rent over the far side of town, to grow their yearly cash-crop. Between times they work with Brother Rashid and the sheep – Mohammed bought a lorry with his French savings, which has turned out to be the saving of the project, as luck would have it. It was Karim, in the end, and not Mohammed, who became a builder, Mohammed tells us. Karim even went and studied architecture for a bit, though he never finished his degree. Sayid, meanwhile, still a very serious boy, did his engineering training as planned and is working now – but hundreds of kilometres away, at Hassi Messaoud, in the oil complex, away on the other Grand Erg, the eastern sand sea that borders with Libya. The only sad story is Hassan, who has vanished completely somewhere in France. He was last heard of threatening to marry a French woman and stay there – then complete silence. Did that bad man Le Pen and his racist friends get him? Or did he maybe marry the girl and decide to forget his religion and his roots? Rashida fears the worst. Nothing at all has been heard from Hassan for five whole years.

On a more cheerful note, we have been introduced to Aisha's and Karim's three children, who have presented us with pretty bunches of barley-heads, which they were collecting for our *leben*, they tell us, the buttermilk we'll be drinking with our lunch. Because of course, yes, we will all be eating here together – they have prepared a surprise picnic lunch in our honour.

I have grasped now, not before time, that Rashida is Kebir's wife, and Aisha his daughter. (Of course he was married, says Kebir. Who did I think the famous Aunt Rashida was?) And I have at last had the chance to thank both women for saving my life with their delicious food, after that terrible time on bread and fishbones. I still remember every mouthful as if it was yesterday!

Rashida remembers cooking it too, she says: preparing the chicken, shaping the patties, her heart full of fear for the boys going so far away, so young, and maybe never to return. And doing her best to pretend not to be afraid for Aisha's sake, Aisha making the date pastries beside her, all excited – only a little girl, and so fond of Karim already! Though look at her now, married to him, a mother, and a good job in the town hall too! (Naturally I have to tell Aisha that it was obvious, even then, aged sixteen, that Karim was dead keen on her too – he couldn't stop himself pulling out that little packet of family photos at any excuse, and there was no doubt which cousin his eye lingered over the longest!)

We have, of course, been shown around every corner of this beautifully groomed *palmeraie*. It is Kebir's reward to himself and his family, he says, for all those years spent far from home, on the building sites of France. We have also learned that the local Berber word for these palm-grove gardens is the same word they use for 'paradise'. It's not hard to see why.

We have seen the raised stone pool into which the *fouggara* water flows, ready to be used for the irrigation later, when the midday heat dies down; and the row of basketwork beehives against the back wall, where the bees make the best honey, having such a multitude of flowers to choose from – especially the henna flowers with their built-in *baraka*. We have inspected the vegetables and the fruits, and been shown the the barley crop and the wheat crop. Kebir says this grain-growing is a recent development. Once upon a time people here hardly bothered with more than a patch or two of wheat or barley in Timimoun. You were better to concentrate on your date harvest. The nomad tribes would always bring corn down aplenty, come autumn, grain they received from the lands to the north, in exchange for the wool and cheese from their sheep. Once they arrived at the oases, they would swap half of it for dates: concentrated nuggets of calories, easy to transport. But things are all upside down these days. You can't depend on that any more, not even when you have family among the nomad tribes, like Kebir.

Kebir has introduced us to his rows of tobacco plants – don't tell the *intégristes*! – and to the family's bewildering array of varieties of date-palm. Some have fruit that is sweet and juicy and to be eaten fresh; others grow dates that will dry out all by themselves up on the tree and last all winter – to be pressed into blocks for sale to the nomads. Now for the broader-trunk palms that produce feed-crops for animals – to sell, and to feed the two sheep they keep back in the yard at the house. Livestock don't just eat the date-fruits, but even their pits, which the women crush in their mortars so the sheep can get at the nutritious kernels. Dotted here and there are some younger, lower trees of yet another variety of date: a palm that hates the smell of humans and has to be cajoled into growing by trickery. Each tree is hung with bunches of a pungent herb which in French is called *armoise* – until it has raised its head high enough above its owners and is no longer disturbed by their offensive presence.

Mohammed and Aisha have shown us how you pull out the fibre from the palm-trunks and twist it into rope – thick and sturdy, to be coiled into baskets and beehives; or thin like string, to be woven into mats or sacks, The leaves too are woven into containers of every kind: once a major export industry here, they say, before the invention of the plastic bag! We have seen the stone combs set into the water-channels to measure out the garden's allotted quota of water. The rate of flow is set up by the *kiel el maa*, the town elder in charge of the water, and tampered with at your peril. Kebir has told us how the government's new scientific wheat seeds, supposedly developed for desert oasis conditions like these, do not have the *baraka* of the ancient local varieties. The bread made from the government corn, Kebir says, tastes all wrong, and, moreover, its stalks are too short, so you don't get enough straw for the compost. Compost is vital to keep these groves fertile – especially now that the camel caravans have been replaced by lorries, while beasts of burden, and their manure, have become so scarce . . . because, after all, how much manure does a Toyota make?

We have been introduced by Rashida to the crop with the most *baraka* of all – her own rows of waist-high henna bushes, their leaves gleaming and shiny, their flowers pyramids of starry florets, their warm scent even better from close up, and as sensuous as the Song of Solomon would have you believe. She has shown us the new growth of young leaves, their veins flushed red with the colour of rejoicing – a quality this generous plant is happy, she says, to share with us humans. This afternoon she will be harvesting the flowers, with the help of the children, to be taken to her neighbour Fatima, in whose distilling copper their perfume will be preserved for the rest of the year, transformed into a precious attar of henna, to be used at weddings and feasts – firstly by Rashida's nearest and dearest, and secondly by whoever can afford it! The process takes twenty whole days on the fire, or twenty-five for the really high-class attar. Henna, in its every possible form, is essential at weddings, where – unless you want to look like people of no consequence! – display and ostentation are a necessary part of the festivities. Henna being a holy plant of immense and soothing powers, it will defuse the Evil-Eye-provoking envy that such celebrations might conjure up in the hearts and eyes of the guests – and maybe of the *djnun* too! – and turn that harmful and negative emotion into its opposite: a joyful pleasure in the good fortune of others.

The smell of the flowers certainly is heavenly, I say.

Rashida agrees. Of course it is. Attar of Henna was, naturally enough, the favourite perfume of the prophet Mohammed.

What exactly is *armoise*? I ask Gérard and Guy as we brush past another grey-green bundle of the stuff hanging beneath a palm, on our way to the domesticated corner at the far end of the grove, where rugs and mats lie spread in the shade.

It is, Guy explains, the herb that is used to make absinthe.

A herb which is very good for the digestion, says Kebir, and will be going into the pot of tea we're about to drink. Come on!

Over in the far corner of the garden, beside another henna hedge, are two small bonfires of palm-prunings. One, right over by the wall, already has a pot simmering over it on a trivet, a *couscoussier* on top. Rashida has filled the tea-kettle from the *fouggara* and hung it from the tripod that stands poised over the other.

We take our seats on the palm-fibre mats under the orange trees. I am a bit nervous about the absinthe aspect of this tea, but I am assured by Kebir, who is now doing a very flash type of tea-pouring that involves filling every single glass, then re-emptying it into the teapot to be repoured from an even greater height, that *armoise* in its unfermented state does nothing but help the digestion. I sip gingerly at my glass. It tastes good and astringent, anyhow, and I don't seem to be going blind, or starting to hallucinate – even after two whole glasses.

Just wait till I see what he has brought to surprise me, says Kebir.

Do I remember how he tried to make a *bekbouka* in Paris? The thing with the sheep's stomach, that he was missing so badly after a year in that Portakabin, but it came out all wrong?

Yes, I do indeed – he went to a great deal of trouble to find a butcher who would find him a sheep's stomach, then stuffed it with meat and spices into something like a very delicious haggis, minus the oatmeal. The rest of us enjoyed it a lot, but it was a great disappointment to the chef.

Well, this time he has the real thing, he says, made for him by the nomad boys who work up in the hills with Rashid, real specialists of the dish. And that's what's boiling in the pot over there. At last I will get to taste it as it was meant to be!

There's a chance we may see Sayid, we now hear, as we work our way through the last of the regulation three glasses of tea. He is supposed to be coming soon, bringing his wife and children back home to the safety of Timimoun. He has decided they must be got away from the madness that has broken out since last year, when the Americans came in to reorganize the Algerian oil industry, and then the Islamists went out of control. Sayid himself has been threatened twice over working for the Americans, Mohammed tells us, even though he is doing no such thing: his contract is with the Algerian Sonatrach. And his wife is scared to leave the house at all. Any woman outdoors is either menaced by angry religious *barbus*, who take her for a prostitute, or propositioned by sex-starved oil men, for the same reason. The town, these days, is a nightmare.

Gérard and Guy are startled to hear the name of one of the American multinationals in question, famous for its close links to the CIA. (This corporation will, by a strange coincidence, soon be bidding for the contract to build a new secure barrier across the thousands of miles of frontier between Mexico and the USA. Who can say whether Tobias, if he has struck lucky with his Marla, may not be working upon it at this very moment?)

The boys are right to be horrified, says Kebir. Hassi Messaoud has become a place riddled with violence and poverty, and surrounded by

shanty towns of penniless ex-villagers and ex-nomads, who do deals
with corrupt binmen to get priority access to the rubbish of the
rich. Prostitution has grown into a major industry there, with all
the oil men. *The filles de joie* are brought in as cleaners and caterers
by contractors who double as pimps. There are plenty of young
women available for the role: mass unemployment has seen to that.
Now there is the new religious violence into the bargain.

It sounds like hell on earth, I say.

Exactly, says Mohammed. Forget the good salary; all the family
thinks Sayid should come right back home to stay.

Kebir and Mohammed will be taking off in the lorry in a few days'
time, as soon as they've finished work on the palm-pollination, to take
some extra fodder up to Rashid's sheep – and of course, they say, we
must pile into the lorry with them, come up and stay a few days in
the tents. This is the best time of year up on the high plains, and
if we treat Rashid right, we might even get a ride on his camel.
Mohammed can't wait to see his face when I turn up in the wilderness with them! He won't believe his eyes!

And it's a good thing for us, says Kebir, that they do have to go
up into the hills, because we've made a fine mess, when we finally
get ourselves all the way to Timimoun, in going to stay with Hadj
Mouloud. We can't possibly leave his place now, and come to stay at
Kebir's as we ought to do. It would be unimaginably rude and disrespectful – it would look as if we were publicly criticizing Hadj
Mouloud's hospitality. Kebir and his family would make an enemy
of Hadj Mouloud for life, and he is much too powerful a man to
have as an enemy! The Hadj is a man who is very protective of his
good name. To leave at all – unless it was to leave town – would be
a terrible insult. But to leave to stay at the house of much poorer
people – it doesn't bear thinking about!

Aisha, who is pounding up the barley in a big wooden mortar for
the buttermilk drink, thinks I could maybe leave Gérard and Guy at
Hadj Mouloud's and come on over by myself.

But everyone decides this would look even stranger. And, says Rashida, even if the Hadj didn't take offence, the rumour would soon be all round town that Kebir was putting her out to grass and taking a second wife! No, no, we'll just have to wait a few days and all go up into the hills.

Time to eat, and after a salad of produce from the *palmeraie* – grated carrots with fresh coriander, honey, lemon, and some kind of kale-like leaf – we are going to have couscous with *klila*, a kind of sheep's cheese. This is the children's favourite, and they are clinging to Aisha's skirts as she mixes it, to make sure they don't miss a second of eating-time. She stirs a sort of compote of dried apricots and dates into the hot couscous with a big knob of butter from a deep earthenware jar, and then crumbles the sheep's cheese into it. Another stir, and it's ready. The cheese is deliciously sharp, a lovely contrast with the sweetness of the fruit and the buttery couscous – I'm not surprised the kids love it. The *klila* itself reminds me of nothing so much as the matured, dry ricotta that southern Italians use in place of Parmesan on their pasta. I check with the chefs, and yes, *klila* is made from the whey of the sheep-milk, just like ricotta. I'll be able to watch them making it when we go up into the hills, too, if I'm lucky.

Does this mean, I ask, that they make a full-fat cheese with the whole milk first, like the Italians? No, it doesn't – they make sheep butter instead, something I've never heard of till today. But I've already gathered from our diet at Hadj Mouloud's that people here are as much butter addicts as we northerners, though they eat so little meat I don't suppose they could develop a cholesterol problem if they tried.

Now comes the Saharan haggis. As delicious as the one I remember from Paris – with major improvements in its flavour as far as Kebir is concerned, now that it has the correct down-home spices in it. But – woe is me – one of the spices in question is ferociously hot chilli-pepper. I am reduced to watching Gérard and Guy stuffing greedily – again – and gloating along with Kebir about how delicious the *bekbouka* is, meanwhile making sure that my own mouthfuls are composed mainly of the pancake-style bread that Aisha has served us as accompaniment. With copious swigs of the lovely green-barley buttermilk to damp down the fire, I can just about tell that it really is delicious.

Moussa and Aisha are chatting away in the Berber tongue, and I notice the name of Hadj Mouloud cropping up; Mohammed is looking very gripped by their conversation. I wait hopefully for a translation. Aisha, it turns out, working at the town hall, has her fingers on the pulse of the struggle we heard about among the *moksirin* – the Haratine man's bid to buy that *palmeraie*. Hadj Mouloud and friends, she says, are trying to reactivate an ancient Berber law, designed to stop family land getting broken up; a law which allows any relative, however distant, of the owner to step in and buy a piece of land – at half the price offered by any non-family member. Which basically means, if the Hadj can find such a relative, that our Haratine man will be out of the bidding. Normally, Aisha says, nobody would even have thought of trying to reactivate such a law. But since the privatization of everything, and the kowtowing to Islamists, the government has brought back the local *djema'a*, the council of elders, a body abandoned years ago as not properly democratic, not least because only landowners could sit on it. Hadj Mouloud evidently thinks that, in the present climate, other feudal institutions that suit his purposes may successfully be slipped back into the pot.

What makes her despair, Aisha says, turning to me, is that thirty years after the French left and Algerians achieved democracy at last, men down here still can't see one another as equals. Haratine are born inferior and naturally they should have less rights: that's how they see it. If they can't even learn to see one another equals, what hope is there for women?

Well, when she puts it like that, I tell her, I realize there is plenty of hope. Look at my own country – we were a third of the way through the twentieth century before the British state finally admitted that women were as fully rational as men. First the vote was only for male property-owners – just like the *djema'a*. Then it was only for men. Then women finally got a vote, but only if they were over thirty. There are women still alive in my country who grew up in those times, taught that they were too stupid to have a say in the world, and men's natural inferiors. But look at the difference nowadays: anyone who seriously tried to assert such a thing would be taken for a madman.

Mohammed and the boys are all busy admiring the lorry, and getting it ready for the trip. It is another Gak, just like Youssouf's haystack transport back in Morocco. Strange that I've never heard of such a brand, when they seem to be all the rage here in the Maghreb. Mohammed tells us that they are – or were – made by Berliet. I have heard of the company, at least. My interest in lorries being just about exhausted by this information, I wander off into Timimoun's weekly souk, on today in the main market place: a walled square, dirt-floored, surrounded by broad mud-brick arches.

Starved as I am for female company at Hadj Mouloud's, I soon fall in with a bunch of Haratine women, lively and cheerful and loud and dressed in bright primary colours, all with their hair done up into those long tresses of beaded braids that fly and tinkle as they move and laugh. They have bright, open faces and smile a lot, lovely white teeth in gleaming ebony faces. A bunch of paler-skinned women go past as I examine the wares on the Haratine stall, covered head-to-toe in pale *haiks*. You can't meet their eyes, which are the only part they have showing, and they don't even smile, never mind look as if they're having any kind of a nice time. Repression? Social status to be maintained? Born grumpy? No idea, but it is certainly not attractive. But then, what about all the lively women at the wedding the other night? Do the non-black women have split personalities, one private, one public?

I am certainly beginning to see Youssouf's point about white brides being stuck up, and black ones more fun. It occurs to me now that the home town Youssouf was heading for isn't so far from here

– the long curve we've taken south-westwards from Algiers has brought us right back round towards the southern oases of Morocco and the Tafilalet. Maybe his black beloved is actually a Haratine? The national borders, in these nomad lands, are an artificial, colonial invention, after all. Would they have Haratine over in the Moroccan oases too, in the same lowly social position? That might explain what was so shameful about the liaison in his family's eyes.

The Haratine women are soon plaiting my hair into beaded braids just like their own. How could I resist? I have only stopped at their stall to check out the wares – I am now addicted to kohl-containers and have to buy another to add to my collection at every market. Next I inspect some strange necklaces, pyramid-shaped beads of some dark-brown shiny stuff. They mime at me to sniff one. Cloves! They have mixed some sort of resin with ground-up cloves and moulded these tiny, perfumed shapes between their fingertips. They act it out for me, and I realize you can even see their finger-prints on some of them. They give me a lot of necklace information I can't understand – we don't have more than a few words of French in common – but in amongst the laughter and linguistic confusion I gather that the necklace either protects you from headaches or cures them. I don't exactly want one, not being a dangly-necklace type of person, but somehow I end up festooned with three of them and not allowed to pay. The word *baraka* crops up a lot – do I not have to pay because I am bringing them *baraka*? Will the necklaces bring me *baraka*? Whatever. It is all good. Now I compliment them on their amazing hair – one of the older women, with so many glass beads on her braids that you can hardly see the hair, lets me feel the weight of them. One thing leading to another, as it so often does; suddenly there I am, squeezed in round the back of the stall, having my hair plaited up, three of them at it at once, sides and back, building lots of silky threads into the plaits to bulk them up, giving me a stylish corn-rowed fringe at the front, and adding a good pound weight of green and blue beads to the ends. A lovely feeling, as you move your head, those long swaying tinkling tresses. I feel like the business. My best hairdressing experience ever. I have never before had anything as interesting to look at, while having my hair done, as hobbled camels and date-flower-laden donkeys, nor been serenaded by beturbaned old men with hand-drums. Or had such entertaining stylists, in such numbers – even though they do, at one point, prod my bosom in such a lively manner that, still not too stable in the hunkered-down position, I fall flat on my bottom in the dust.

Moussa will tell me later that they certainly do have Haratine in Moroccan oases. *Shurfa* and *m'rabtin* too. And that over in Morocco the *djema'a* is still as it was in the old days, going strong, and for property-owners only: under that king of theirs, who would even dare try to change it? But just like here, he says, thanks to emigration, some of the Haratine actually own property these days. Which has, I gather from the cheering tale of Haratine resistance he now tells me, set the cat among the pigeons in a big way.

It seems that in some small oasis town, once part of the Sijilmassa complex – an olive-growing town, thanks to its plentiful water supply – the Haratine decided to stand their own property-owning candidate for the *djema'a*. And this Haratine having won his seat, the owner of the only olive-oil-mill in town, a *sharif*, was so outraged that he banned all Haratine from using it. That would teach them. Their whole harvest would go to waste.

But lo and behold, in the nick of time, another Haratine, recently returned from a long sojourn in Germany, stepped into the breach – and spent all his savings on a brand new mill. Ultra-modern, much cleaner and faster than the old *shurfa* one, extracting more oil per kilo of olives into the bargain! And now, indeed, members of the aristo-cratic classes, out of pure self-interest, are slowly succeeding in overcoming their prejudices and giving him their custom.

Things have been going swimmingly with Hadj Mouloud since we were forgiven for that first looking-at-his-women mistake. Now I bounce in all excited about my braids, waiting for his reaction, only to receive no comment at all. Hadj Mouloud just pretends he hasn't noticed. And so does everyone else in his household. Not that I was expecting much joy from his womenfolk. I asked if I could eat with them the other night and was sent to join them in the kitchen. Six women of varying ages sat on cushions on a sandy floor around the couscous bowl and the fruit and blanked me completely. Hardly a smile, hardly a word addressed to me, not that we had any language in common, but still, that doesn't stop people communicating if they want to, as I very well know. And they hardly spoke to one another, either.

It dawns on me now, as the tea-tackle is brought in as usual by the silent women, that since Hadj Mouloud and family can have no idea how this type of hairstyle is viewed in Northern lands, they must imagine that I've intentionally disguised myself as a Haratine. Which would be pretty odd behaviour if you happened to think, as people of their class seem to, that nobody in their right mind would wish to identify with a Haratine. Still, it'll be a good lesson to them all.

Hadj Mouloud seems to get over it pretty quickly, anyhow, and as we sip, I decide to ask him about second, and indeed third, wives. I know I'm not supposed to ask him about his own ones, of course – though I am very curious to know the status of the various women of this household – so I just ask him if he agrees with the taking of more than one wife?

Hadj Mouloud, good-mannered as ever, answers – if rather curtly – that he is in perfect agreement with the Koran: that a man should only have as many wives as he can afford to keep at exactly the same standard of living, each one in her own separate establishment.

And what about the Haratine, I ask, still thinking of Youssouf. Do you really never intermarry with them, then, not even as second or third wives?

You would only marry a woman of the Haratine, he says, even more curtly, if you already had a full complement of three white wives. Then you might take on a Haratine, who would work as a servant to the others.

Really? So there actually is intermarriage, then. And yet, in spite of that, the communities have stayed so separate for all these centuries? I can't make head or tail of it, till Gérard comes up with the solution.

Does that mean then, he asks, that any children of such a marriage would also count as Haratine – as members of the servant class?

Of course they would. Like the illegitimate offspring of slave-owners in the USA, once upon a time. We realize, at last, from the extremely stiff responses we're getting, that this is not a decent topic to be pursuing and politely change the subject.

Later, we will hear from Abdallah that Hadj Mouloud has a fourth, black wife himself, whom he keeps right over the other side of town. Which means, come to think of it, that if only poor Yous-souf was rich enough to marry three pale-skinned women first, nobody would disapprove at all of his marrying the dark-skinned girl of his dreams.

22

Abdallah's and his wife Amina's home is in one of the newer, French-colonial houses: nothing at all like Abdallah's father's. It has tiled floors instead of sand, and we sit on divan-sofas arranged round a coffee-height table, in a living room – yes, it has a definite function! – open to the walled interior courtyard and the palm trees that protect it from the burning sun.

Amina too has been to university – and even spent a year in Algiers, chaperoned by an aunt who kept house for her. She receives us in a tightly tied *khimar* and reminds me of Mariam – in her strict-teacher persona, that is, not her relaxed Casablanca mode. Amina seems to have been seriously influenced by the puritan version of Islam up in the North: she wears no kohl on her eyes nor jewellery of any kind and chaffs her husband for having taken us to the *Ahellil*, a primitive country entertainment, she says, and of very dubious religious significance. She is a teacher too but holds no brief for the Berber tongue, even though it is the language of her own parents. It keeps the children back, she thinks. It is better for them to be taught in Arabic. Arabic helps detach them from superstition and backwardness.

The couple had some trouble, they tell us, when they first married, in getting Hadj Mouloud to agree to their setting up a separate establishment, but really, since they have nothing to do with the farming life and the *palmeraies*, and they both work full time, there was no point in it.

Naturally, as soon as they reveal that theirs was an arranged marriage, the three of us are agog to learn more. First preconception to bite the dust: they are obviously mad about one another. Whichever one is speaking, the other gazes proudly and fondly on. Amina tells us that their engagement was arranged in the traditional way: by agreement between their families, but with both of them free to refuse if they didn't like the idea. No decent family here would ever force their children to marry someone they were dead set against, a person they knew they would be unhappy with!

But how, I ask, could they tell any of that, if they didn't even know one another? Did they get to meet up and talk about it?

No, certainly not! But of course they knew all about one another. And when they were children they knew each other well – before puberty children meet often, at family celebrations, weddings and Eids, or with their mothers at the *hammam*. And then, Amina was always great friends with Abdallah's sisters at school, she tells us. They all said she would get on brilliantly with him, like a house on fire, they had so much in common, even their sense of humour. And the same went for Abdallah, he knew all her brothers. Everyone said they were made for one another. Then, the two families got on well, and had a lot in common – of course your own family would have the best idea of who you'd be happy with! Here you would never even start being interested in a boy until you knew that you liked his family. Because what else will he turn out like, but his family? Here, when your parents start looking for the right man for you, they will say they are 'looking for good uncles for their grandchildren'.

Amina did manage to sneak a few secret looks at Abdallah, really, she admits. Girls are let out of school an hour early to make sure they will be back home and out of the way before the opposite sex hits the streets; but there are always ways and means! She and his sisters hid on the way home one day, waited till the boys came down the road so she could check him out. (Amina looks at him under her lashes, giggling with delight at the memory!) And the second time, she says, she even managed to say hello to him!

Amina and Abdallah turn the tables on us now. Europeans are insane, they say, the way we base our futures, and our children's futures, on some casual encounter in a public place with loud music and drink to befuddle us. What kind of basis is that for a happy life together? Then we go off and set up home with a person of whose family, background and proclivities we know little or nothing, just because we find them physically attractive. Surely there is more to marriage than just physical attraction? It is a social duty, a moral duty, to make it work. The couple should be well matched in background and in temperament. And in social standing. Otherwise there will be too many sources of potential discord. No wonder our European marriages fail so often.

But what, Gérard asks, about love and passion?

It seems a silly question in the present circumstances, when Amina and Abdallah have clearly fallen head-over-heels for one another, but still, it can't work out like that for everyone, can it? It is also a very personal question, and I am torn between wanting to kick Gérard for asking it and a keen desire to hear the answer. Boldly, Amina takes over answering. If you have remained pure until your wedding night, she says, with a little gleam at Abdallah, it would be hard, with the pleasure you are giving one another, not to fall in love! Would we not agree?

And what about second wives? Abdallah takes over here. He doesn't fundamentally disagree with the idea, he says. In the old days, when there were no labour-saving devices, it was a way of letting a wife retire – she didn't want to get pregnant any more, and the work of the household gets harder as you get older, doesn't it? So a fresh young woman could take over, and give her some relief, take over the heavier jobs. And more children were always needed, too, once upon a time . . .

But what about this business of having separate homes for each wife, like his father? Does that make life easier for any of them? Once a respectable man will have a separate establishment for each wife, that hardly makes sense, does it? I say.

But of course, that is just an ideal people aspire to. Most people are nowhere near Hadj Mouloud's exalted status and never have been:

their wives have to share a home, like it or not. It has never bothered Abdallah, he says, having lots of brothers and sisters from the other mothers. There are fifteen of them altogether, so you just get lots of company when you're a child – and a fine network of connections, when you're grown, in every possible area of life!

That may all be true, says Amina. But she has no intention of any such thing happening in this household!

And the *hijab*? The *khimar*? The seclusion of wives in the home? Abdallah says that we Westerners have simply forgotten our own religion. We are Peoples of the Book too – and we have the same traditions, underneath the differences. Why does a Christian bride wear the veil? Why is the epitome of good Christian womanhood the nun, who like any devout Muslim woman wears no make-up, covers her hair and dresses in such a way that her body is modestly concealed?

Amina isn't too interested in the modesty angle on the veil. It is a brilliant option, she says, and has become a great weapon against being kept shut up the home. In her grandmother's day, everything needed in the home was produced by women's labour in their own courtyard, while the husbands' job was to bring in the raw materials from the outside world. There was no reason why women should be out and about. But these days, young women who want to get out of the house can argue that the family honour, and their own virtue, is being protected by the use of a few scraps of cloth, and get away from the stifling internal courtyard! That is how she herself got permission to go away and study: by promising to wear the full *hijab* whenever she left the house. Look how many girls – even from poor backgrounds, the daughters of migrants – are getting themselves university educations these days. Soon the face of Algeria will be changed for good. Did we know that almost half of all judges in the courts here are women? That women are taking over medicine and the law as well? Young men don't bother with education – they put all their energy into trying to get abroad. You don't need a degree to mix concrete in Europe, do you? But young women don't have those choices. It's study, or stay indoors. And they're voting with their feet.

Sixty per cent of university students now are women, Amina says, and the *khimar*, the *hijab*, even the face-covering *niqab* are no sign of oppression, but the woman's undercover victory flag!

We all wish we could go and stay at Kebir's and Rashida's. The atmosphere there is so much more relaxed and cheerful than at Hadj Mouloud's, and nobody cares if Gérard and Guy come and sit in the courtyard with the women, never mind not even being allowed to look at them. We are spending a lot of time round there. We have even rolled and eaten our own couscous, with the help of Rashida and her mother, an extremely ancient lady with an infectious cackle of a laugh and startlingly bright orange hair under her many loops of scarf: the effect of henna on white, I deduce. Aisha and the children – and Karim, when he's home – all live here too, each family with its own rooms off the courtyard, traditional style.

Still, only a day or two left until we all go off into the hills together. We have decided to say goodbye to the Hadj then, as if we were leaving for good. By the time we get back, it really will be time for Gérard and Guy to set off southwards, if they want to get across the Sahara before the heat comes. In the meantime, we can stay at Timimoun's red-mud-brick extravaganza of a hotel and let Hadj Mouloud know that something went wrong with our travel plans – we'll say we didn't want to inconvenience him with a surprise visit.

I still haven't worked out what I'm doing next, or how I'm getting home. I am beginning to wonder if it wouldn't be easier just to go on across the desert with Gérard and Guy to Mali, where at least nobody wants to kill me. As yet.

The plane is not flying to Algiers until further notice. The state of emergency continues, and all air transport down here has been requisitioned. Even if it did reappear, the flights cost a fortune, Aisha tells me. More than the boys are planning to spend on whole of the the rest of their trip. The bus-and-*niqab* option does not appeal, either. I did a test run with Rashida, Aisha and her granny, and dressed up in one of those tent-shaped *haiks* – certainly a lot easier to keep on than the twenty-yards-of-material Tlemcen version – and added the veil too, by which time I felt seriously claustrophobic, and the granny had my bosom checked out most thoroughly. Verdict? My public laughed their heads off. When the only part of me you can see is my eyes, they are very noticeably the wrong colour. Mohammed went off indoors and came back with a pair of sunglasses to complete the disguise. I'm sorry to say that, like most homes here, they don't have a full-length mirror at Kebir's. Otherwise I might have got as much entertainment as everyone else out of my new pious-Muslim-lady look. Apparently I looked like a Saudi Arabian tourist. All very well, but I'd have to wear the sunglasses at night, too, wouldn't I? And not speak to anyone for the whole two days – not even to get food or if the bus broke down. And if the person sitting next to me turned out to be very chatty, what then? The last straw was Kebir's pointing out that a woman who looked as devout as I now did would obviously be saying her prayers five times a day, whenever the bus stopped for that purpose. I'd better get into training now, he said, if I wanted to be word perfect for next week. I think he was only joking.

He and Mohammed have offered to drive me in the Gak to Algiers, or maybe over the border into Morocco, if things don't improve soon. The place where Rashid and the sheep are camped is not too far from the Moroccan border – we could go along the old nomad trail into the Tafilalet, or the northern road that leads to Figuig, which must, I think, be the one Mohammed the father was recommending back at the Rif *funduq*. That seems ridiculous, though. Eight hundred miles in a big, slow sheep lorry to Algiers, or seven hundred to Oujda. And they won't hear of just dropping me off at the Moroccan frontier.

Forgetting these worries, we go off to enjoy the next event in the week-long wedding festivities: a music-and-drumming night with a dancer. Aisha and Rashida are not coming. I will probably be the only woman there, they say. Still, I am an honorary man, after all. Hadj Mouloud said so. Though Mohammed did suggest, I admit, that it might be best if he got Kebir to find me a nice green towel and a pair of hobnailed boots for the occasion.

The dance is the only part of the public festivity not held out-doors: that's how louche it is. It must be the Algerian oasis equivalent of a stag night, and is held in a sort of school hall with rows of seats, a place that doubles as Timimoun's cinema when the film-lorry comes to town. I should have known from the tale of the women of the Ouled Naïl that dancers are certainly women of dubious reputa-tion, if not actually prostitutes. That is why the respectable population needs to be protected from them by walls. Still, a famous dancer coming to town, big excitement, party night – how could I resist? Eating kebabs and making merry, I hardly notice there isn't a single woman here, I am getting so used to it – and to my own strange hermaphrodite position, not exactly a man, but certainly not a woman either, to whom all those strange and irksome rules apply.

The music is strings and massed drums, a slow rhythm building up with the dancer's first tiny, shimmying movements, louder and faster until it fills the room and nothing is left but the beating of the blood, while now, with shiny red lipstick and lashings of blue eye-shadow, hair out and flying, jewellery jangling, the dancer shakes and stirs for all she's worth, stamping and twirling, framed by the vibrating hands of her musicians, working up a film of sweat. Soon men from the audience are starting to rise as if hypnotized from their seats, brandishing banknotes on high, then walking entranced, in time to the beat, up the central aisle to the dancer's side. They pause as close as they dare to the gyrating, hip-twitching dancer, join her in the dance for a moment, then plaster the money onto her as she dances, taking their time about it, sticking it to her forehead on her own sweat, or on her cleavage, or tucking it into the broad belt of jin-gling coins she wears slung low on her hips.

Moussa, standing next to me at the back of the hall, remarks envi-ously that not one of them has a chance with her, anyway, whatever they may think.

What does he mean? Are they expecting to get some private time with her if they stick enough money onto her?

Well, he says, he thinks she must take the highest bidder to her bed. Or maybe, he adds, receiving a sceptical look from Kebir, she already has some rich man lined up anyway?

Kebir pooh-poohs the whole idea. The men are poor saps, showing off. Not impressing the dancer, but one another – and all imagining exactly the same thing as Moussa!

Moussa, when challenged, doesn't seem too sure of how it works – but he is certain that only a rich man would get the chance . . .

Early in the morning, before we leave, Mohammed and Kebir take us off to see a *marabout* – a living *marabout* at last, a real Sufi sheikh, not just the tomb of his dead ancestor. Though we'll be going to the tomb as well, because Kebir has promised to take a few pinches of sand, impregnated with the ancestor's *baraka*, back up to one of the nomad shepherds who look after the sheep. And a charm, too, if Sidi Haddou will make us one.

And what, we enquire, are these items needed for?

Two different matters, he says with a grin. One is for, er, men's problems. And the other for – rain!

We set off along a narrow track around the bottom of a hill crowned by the ruins of another abandoned *ksar*, crumbling away like the fingers of a mud skeleton. We're into serious dunes here, soft sand that gives way under you: the muscles of my feet and ankles are soon crying out in agony. A good mile from the nearest dwelling now, we are tormented all of a sudden by swarms of flies. How on earth do they appear from nowhere in the middle of a desert?

Mohammed starts grumbling about being dragged off miles through the dunes to collect cures and spells he doesn't really believe in – and to pay homage to a man who has never lifted a finger in his life and expects his whole village to keep him – just because his great-great-great-great-grandfather was a holy man! Mohammed is ashamed that we have to witness this superstitious nonsense.

Not so different from priests back in France, says Gérard comfortingly. Every French worker has to pay towards their upkeep, too, taxed straight out of their wage-packet . . .

But Mohammed says it's worse here. Double the number of parasites to support. Not just the *imams* and the mosques, but the sheikhs and their *zawiyas* too, sitting on your back. Though the sheikhs are men of peace, at least, who seek harmony and reconciliation, and may well be worth their salt, while *imams* and mullahs do nothing but cause trouble!

Perfume of wood smoke, trails and wisps of it up ahead, signal a village at last. And here on its outskirts is a threshing floor, just like the ones you find in the Spanish Alpujarras. I recognize it right away. A round, cobbled area, with a wooden post in the centre where the threshing party attaches the livestock that are driven round and round over the crops, the tramp of their hooves separating the grain from the chaff. By the side of the threshing floor stands a little shelter of woven palm-leaves – the sentry box, Mohammed says. Each village piles its compost on the threshing floor over the winter – manure, straw, palm prunings, vegetable peelings, everything and anything that will rot down into good dark earth. So precious is this stuff, and so vital to the survival of the *palmeraies*, that the villagers mount guard over it by night, all through the winter months.

Although there is no manure here now, oddly enough there is a guard in the sentry box – or at any rate, an inhabitant. A somewhat wild-eyed and ragged-looking individual is hunkered down inside the shelter. He glares angrily out as we pass, but says nothing. No greeting is passed with him.

This man, Mohammed tells us, lowering his voice, lost his reason years ago, when his father cursed him from the house for disobeying the patriarchal authority. A father's curse is called *sakht*; it is the exact opposite of *baraka*, and means that everything you do will go wrong, for the whole rest of your life. Nobody wants anything to do with you any more: nobody will join you in any enterprise, or let you join them. Because from now on, your presence will be like a black hole, sucking out all the grace and good fortune that might have been theirs. Your only way out is to leave town, go somewhere you are unknown. But not everyone has the strength of character to do that. Far less if they truly believe that they are doomed, now, to fail at everything they undertake. Probably he is living off the charity of the *marabout* Sidi Haddou these days . . .

Sakht! It sounds as horrible as its meaning. Poor man!

A vile tradition, Mohammed agrees. He gets angry, he says, with the people who turn up here – from French universities, from America even, all the -ologists fascinated by local culture, studying Timimoun's ancient traditions, wanting to save them. It may be fascinating to them, but they don't have to live with it. Personally, Mohammed can't wait for the whole lot to die out. What is good about *sakht*? About the seclusion of women? About the exclusion of the Haratine? In France, he discovered what it was to be ostracized, excluded, presumed inferior on sight. I was there with him in Paris, wasn't I, at his first experience of it! And he wants no truck with such horrors, traditional or not.

We turn off the path at a tiny whitewashed dwelling, the home of the *marabout*, Sheikh Haddou. Inside, the place is floored with sand like Hadj Mouloud's. But the *marabout* has an even better way of keeping cool. What we've taken for the main house is just the entrance hall. His rooms are down below, a whole storey beneath the desert. And there sits a little old man, cross-legged on a palm mat in the cool sand, who rises to greet us, displaying a piously modest short-and-narrow white robe and a set of very bad teeth. The teeth, I now find, get seriously in the way of my believing that he is truly wise or holy. A terribly unworthy reaction. Where do I think he would find a dentist?

There are deep, decorated alcoves built into the ancient walls down here – was the whole building once above the sand? – which are filled to overflowing with books and rolled parchments in grandiose disorder. I wander over to inspect them, complimenting him on his library, and Sheikh Haddou tells me in no uncertain terms not to touch anything. His library is doubly precious, he says through Mohammed, the translator, since so many documents were lost over the last century. When the Tuareg attacked Timimoun, in the year 1908 of your Christian calendar, he says, they took almost every book and parchment in the place – all that were not hidden – and burnt them. Only the writings held in the outlying villages, and in the *zawiyas*, survived. The rule nowadays is that nobody but a *marabout* must touch them. In the case of Christians like ourselves, he is not permitted even to display them to our eyes, which may suck out their *baraka*.

Mohammed gives us his gloss on this. When the French first appeared in these parts, he says, they came up with many ruses to get at the documents held by the *zawiyas*. The French historians and archaeologists, begging the sheikhs as one learned man to another, were allowed to borrow many items, which very often were never returned. They didn't stop at books, either. There is an ancient well, now dried up, at the entrance to this village, at whose mouth, once upon a time stood an ancient stone with an inscription carved into it in Hebrew. It was sacred to the memory of a certain Sarah, who had died in childbirth, and whose husband deeply mourned her passing. It had stood there since time immemorial – until 1926, when a party of French archaeologists came visiting. They denied any knowledge of its disappearance, but it was clear that if no local person had disrespected that woman's memory in a thousand years, they were unlikely to have suddenly started now. Various outrages of this kind occurred, until the educated classes of the Gourara concluded that the only solution was to refuse to show their sacred possessions to any visiting Christians at all. That way, they were safe from envy, greed and covetousness.

Sheikh Haddou gets down to business with Kebir: business that involves much muttering at close quarters, the perusal of various books from the shelves and the making of sets of strange marks – which may be Arabic letters, though they don't look much like any I've seen so far – on a small piece of squared paper, which is then folded up even smaller, wrapped in a fragment of soft red leather and stowed away in the pockets of Kebir's gandoura.

Now, says Sidi Haddou. Time for the Nazarenes! What would the Christians like his help with?

We can't think.

Mohammed can, though. A question about me. What should I do next? Make tracks for the north as soon as possible, before things get any worse? Stay in Timimoun until the trouble dies down? Or head on south with my companions towards Mali, where peace still reigns?

The *marabout* has a think. Finally, he says something long to Mohammed, in his own language. And I wait with bated breath to hear my doom.

He is saying, translates Mohammed eventually, that I must decide whether I want a handful of honey, or a basket of bees. He says that life is a choice between the one and the other. I must ponder on that, and the answer will become plain.

A positively gnomic utterance, the meaning of which does become somewhat plainer when, as we walk back across the sand, Mohammed explains that a basket of bees means a beehive. Still, that certainly leaves plenty to ponder upon.

As we wait at the whitewashed tomb for Kebir to scoop up some Sand of Good Fortune, Gérard starts battling with his *chèche*, which – unlike Guy's, of course – unravels when he tries to tuck in its trailing side-tail to cover his nose and mouth against sun and sand, the way the locals do so casually. Mohammed pulls his own *chèche* off and shakes out the cloth, ready to deliver a full-blown *chèche*-winding lesson, from A to Z. His one is even longer than Gérard's. How many yards of cloth can there be in it? How vain you Algerian men are, I say. Surely there is some rule in the Koran about not having too much cloth in your *chèche*?

Precisely the opposite, says Kebir, ducking back out of the shrine. A *chèche* must be long enough to double as your shroud: enough cloth to bury you in. It is meant as a constant reminder that life is short, and that you should always behave justly, never do anything you would be ashamed of, were you to meet your Maker tonight.

But then, says Mohammed frivolously, he himself finds that wrapping your own shroud around your head each morning can often have the opposite effect, and remind you that you'd better enjoy life as much as you can, before it's too late.

Once we and Hadj Mouloud have made our lengthy and formal *adieux*, Abdallah says he will accompany us to the square where we are to meet Kebir, Mohammed and the Gak. On the way, he finally reveals to us what a bad time his father has been having since we came to stay. He would never dream of mentioning it himself: he is too good a Muslim. But Abdallah wants to warn us that Hadj Mouloud has actually written a letter to Jean-Pierre asking him not to send him any more guests, claiming that it's because he's too old to cope. But what Hadj Mouloud has really found impossible to cope with is having me about the place, confounding all his mental – and social – categories.

Mohammed, who has joined us en route, is cracking up laughing as Abdallah reels off the list of my offences, showing how badly I have brought Hadj Mouloud's honourable name, and that of his household, into disrepute. Starting from the beginning, the list goes like this. Firstly, turning out not to be married, or even related, either to Gérard or to Guy: an unmarried woman roaming the town with no officially designated protector is an abomination. Then, hanging around with the *moksirin*, amongst whom alcohol is known to be drunk. And asking to eat with Hadj Mouloud's women, when I should have realized that, as an honorary man, I couldn't suddenly decide to inflict my dubious company on decent, God-fearing ladies. Still, I had to be humoured: Islamic rules of hospitality dictate that you must never refuse a guest anything. Then, publicly attending the dancing soirée, in front of the whole town, when I was known to be staying with Hadj Mouloud, thus associating his name with women of ill repute. And lastly, as if all that wasn't enough, cavorting with female Haratine – in front of the whole town, again – and actually presenting myself for a meal at his home dressed up as one.

His father was convinced I was intentionally trying to make him look a fool over that one, says Abdallah, giggling. And apparently, whilst disguised as a Haratine, I not only asked him about second and third wives – by implication asking him about his own – but also disagreed with him about something. You are not meant to disagree openly with your host, especially not if he is a generation older than you, and you are female.

All in all, Hadj Mouloud's nerves are wrecked. And he feels that his standing in the community may have been irreparably damaged.

And I, on the other hand, feel that small-town morality is the same the world over.

23

Into the big grey Gak lorry with Kebir and Mohammed. We're off to the plains, the sheep and Rashid. Gérard and Guy are riding shotgun behind us, in the truckbed of the vehicle, amongst bales of hay and bags of sheep-nuts, hidden beneath a wigwam of palm and eucalyptus branches which, if the sheep turn out to need moving, will be roped on across the lorry's open back to shade them.

We stopped at a chaotic roadside animal market some way back, amid swarms of other antique lorries and of milling sheep raising immense clouds of dust, to buy the fodder. Ruinously expensive, was the verdict on the hay. I was torn between sympathy for my present companions and hope that this would have brought Youssouf the good luck he hoped for – and a family of his own.

Now, back in the lorry, Uncle Kebir is enjoying Mohammed's recitation of my sins against Hadj Mouloud for the third time. It does not seem to be palling yet. He is quaking with laughter all over again. Though he does agree with him about the hair, he says. It doesn't look right on a white woman.

Mohammed disputes this hotly. He thinks it looks great. I sit quietly and say nothing. I would certainly feel a complete idiot, back in Europe, with my hair in braids and beads – so maybe Kebir is right. Fortunately, I can't bring myself to care. It feels good. And the incidence of mirrors larger than three inches across is so rare in this part of the world that I have not been able to form any opinion myself, and am not expecting to. I am pleased to report, though, that suntan is now nicely filling in the spaces between my freckles. Hardly anyone has commented on them all week.

We are heading north-east now, through dunes that are growing more and more massive, skirting the eastern edge of the Grand Erg. Eighty-thousand square kilometres of baking nothingness. It's hard to believe, with barren mountains of sand as far as the eye can see, that we can possibly be heading for grassland. Plenty of desert to get through first, says Kebir. In this landscape of heat and bulging yellow sand, an alien apparition heads towards us through the heat haze, silver and red and gleaming, a giant's toy in an overheated sandpit. We are about to meet one of the massive Saharan oil-industry lorries that Mohammed himself described to me all those years ago on a Spanish train. As it draws close, its true proportions become apparent. It looms over our lorry, dwarfing us, its wheels so huge that the tops of the tyres are level with our heads. We can't even see the driver, he is perched so high. With a whoosh of wind it passes us and vanishes into endless yellow as suddenly as it appeared, leaving nothing but a trail of flying sand.

An inhabited place at last: a palm grove and a set of shacks by the side of the road, built from palm-fronds interlaced, and shaded by a dozen eucalyptus trees. Two other lorries are parked outside it, as ancient in style as our own. A transport café, desert style.

We pile out and head for one of the shacks. The place looks oddly reminiscent of an African village from south of the Sahara – and with good reason, it turns out. The people who serve us our coffee, at wooden benches set beside a palm-log table, are Malians, migrants who set out long ago on the long trek towards Europe and riches, but ended up staying here instead. A collection of strange objects hangs suspended from the branches of one of the eucalyptus trees: a head of corn, a fragment of shattered mirror, a piece of cloth and what looks like the arm and hand from a plastic doll, hung fingers-upwards in the style of the Hand of Fatima.

Some kind of gri-gri, says Kebir. An amulet to protect the proprietors. People from across the Sahara often believe not in the One God, but in many. Each element of nature has its own spirit, to be praised and placated. You call it *animisme*. But you can combine animism, if your tastes run that way, with a single Master God who rules over the others, and rub along just fine with us People of the Book – so long as nobody starts going into the fine print!

Mohammed and Kebir have ordered *café-poivré* – peppered coffee – and, glutton for punishment that I am, I have followed suit. Not chilli-pepper, as I half suspected, but ground black pepper and a dash of cinnamon, go into the brew. Surprisingly good. Also on offer is coffee with *armoise*. Funny, I've always imagined it was the North Americans who invented flavoured coffees. Wrong again.

Mohammed has returned from the bar with one of the other lorry-drivers, an acquaintance from the trans-Saharan transport trade. Ali is a Cha'amba nomad, keeping up the old trading traditions of his tribe, using the internal combustion engine in place of the camels. Though in the old days, he says, the Cha'amba did not usually go as far south as Mali. He has stolen the route from the tribesmen of the Tuareg. Once upon a time all hell would have broken loose over such *lèse-majesté*, but nowadays, everything's a free-for-all. Dates and salt go south to Mali, we hear, while sheep and camels – to our surprise – come north. Nothing surprising about it, says the driver. There are endless grasslands to the south of the desert, around Gao.

But of course there are – I recall now the English cannons, used at Gao to scatter that defensive shield of Malian livestock.

The Malian café-owners, Kebir tells us, built the first of these palm shelters as a temporary home while they worked on the local palm groves to top up their travel money – they'd found some seasonal work, rebuilding the local *afregs*. But there were plenty more jobs in the *palmeraies*. The Malians stayed on and started up this café for the trans-Saharan lorries – and an unofficial employment agency, finding other migrants, in their turn, jobs on the palm groves. The émigrés from Mali, Niger, even Senegal and the Ivory Coast, have ended up doing the jobs that the Haratine, now free men and with some resources of their own, will no longer do – or not at the wages on offer. More shacks soon sprang up around the first one, and there is a whole set of service industries here now, catering to the passing trade of dates, sheep and migrants. One enterprising man – an Algerian from the north, come to get away from the unemployment and all the religious trouble – has even managed to set up a phone booth here in the middle of nowhere, and does a roaring trade charging for phone calls back home to sub-Saharan Africa.

Remembering Yazid, I enquire about the cassette method of home communication. But no. It's no use down here. These days, a developing country will have the telephone long before it gets round to a reliable postal service.

Mohammed's friend Ali occasionally brings humans back across the desert among his truckloads of livestock, he confesses. It's against the law, in theory, because they're supposed to have visas to come here to Algeria, too. But what is he going to do? Leave them there by the roadside to walk?

Arrangements for receiving the not-quite-legal migrants are well organized here, he tells us. You drop them at the edge of the palm groves outside the town, where children will be waiting among the trees to take them onwards to work and shelter. Here they will get over the first part of their journey. Some of them, in really bad shape or completely penniless, are fed and nursed by the Sufi brotherhoods in the local *zawiyas* until they are able to work. Then they can begin to prepare themselves for the onslaught on the Melilla barriers – and Fortress Europe.

And when, Gérard asks, will he be going back over to Gao? Would he take a couple of passengers the opposite way, for once? It's fine by Ali. Just be here, in this café, seven days from today, he says. He will look out for them. And any help with the petrol money is welcome!

Seven days from today in the morning? asks Guy. Or the afternoon?

Ali shrugs his shoulders. Travelling here is not like driving around Paris! He has been to Guy's country, where everything is so precise.

But here, anything can happen. Ali has travelled a lot, he tells us. And he doesn't just mean France – or Mali, for that matter. He was in Vietnam, with the French army, when it was defeated at Dien Bien Phu. Airlifted out of there. Then the Americans took over the job. A lovely country, green and fertile, he says. The Vietnamese could grow anything they wanted, given the chance. The only thing their country really lacked was palm trees.

Gérard pulls out the *Petit futé*, seeking information on this strange spot, and on the highlands we're heading for. Alas, *The Little Cunning One* has nothing at all to say to us on the topic. We are, it seems, nowhere. And heading into nothingness.

Disconsolately, he shuts it again. Guy has the good grace not to crow this time. He takes the book gently from Gérard's hands and stows it away from him. We'll be flying blind from now on, then, he says.

Kebir is sorry for the Malians, he says as we climb back into the lorry. They are rootless like truffles, with no kin to help them over the hard times.

We are surprised by the simile. Do truffles grow here in Algeria, then?

They certainly do. We'll see, if it rains while we're up there – *inshallah!* – that the high plains will be stuffed full of them a few days later. The nomads use them for couscous sauces, slice them and dry them for winter, sell them to the cities of the north.

The eyes of the Frenchmen light up. Yet another reason to hope for rain.

At last we are up on the high plains – an open, craggy landscape, a huge, wide, pale sky, a green veil over the stones – but when you get up close there is hardly anything there in the way of edible plants, not much beyond stunted and heavily chewed thyme and *armoise* bushes. But that doesn't bother Kebir and his nephews, or the nomad relations. They have always bred and grazed their animals up here;

now they are breeding without the grazing. It is lambing time, and till that is over, at least, they are staying put. And standing up to the big business sheep-men who are trying to put the small ones out of business.

The plains are still *'arsh* land, which means they are collectively owned – land that was left to the Algerians, since the French settlers weren't interested in it. So it still belongs to everyone, and anyone can use it. This was fine under the old tribes, who once upon a time had huge areas to wander, and in any case were bound to use the pasture with care – for the survival of their own people. But now with their shrunken acreage and everyone out for themselves, collectively owned land makes no sense. Everyone wants to exploit it to the maximum, nobody wants to take care of it. That, we hear, is why the *djema'a*, the council of elders, was reintroduced – or re-legalized, rather, because it had never really died out 100 per cent. The government hoped that by putting the old clans back in charge, acknowledging the power of their leaders, the degradation of the land would be stopped. But it hasn't worked. What authority do the old nomad tribal leaders have? It was destroyed generations ago. Who would listen to them now? The market talks louder. And now the big fish have realized they can put the small ones out of business altogether by cutting their water supply. They have blocked up several wells on purpose – to drive small nomad farmers off the grazing. You only need to throw a load of cement down a couple of water-holes, and the remaining ones are farther apart than a herd can walk in a day. Big money has big water-tankers and can take water to the livestock between-times. But the small people can't move any more, and, stuck in the one place, the sheep soon have nothing left to graze on. The owners have no choice but to sell up. But Rashid and his partners are fighting on, staying put, in this arid, almost grassless desert. There may be hardly any pasture left – unless, by the Will of God, it rains – but at least they are within a day's travel of the water-hole. That is why we are bringing in extra feed by lorry.

*

It is evening by the time we arrive at the encampment – to find nothing at all like the couple of horny-handed shepherds I've imagined, all alone with a couple of dozen sheep. There must be several hundred sheep and a good fifteen adults all living up here, and as many children again, in half a dozen of those broad, wide tents made of woollen strips – not red and black striped, this time, but a warm browny-beige. The Ait Atta use a mixture of camel-hair and the brown wool of Jacob's sheep, Kebir tells us, as we pull in onto the stony land and park, annoying two hobbled brown camels, who gurgle crossly at us before hopping lopsidedly off towards the tents.

We head for the centre of the camp, the circle of palm mats around a fireplace. There must be other cooking places beneath the wide awnings of the tents, too, judging by the wisps of smoke rising about them. The ground smells of thyme with every step we take, but there is no sign at all of the plants here, until you bend right down to discover sad little woody stumps, chewed to the quick. The poor sheep must be desperate. Beyond the tents, two horses are tethered. And beyond the horses, the women of the camp are finishing milking the sheep.

How do you make a sheep stand still to be milked, in a wide empty, stony landscape? You tie it, by the horns, head to head with another sheep. Flummoxed, unable to move either backwards or forwards, both sheep go into a trance and wait quietly and patiently while the job is done. Each woman has a row of twenty or thirty sheep immobilized like this and is working her way down the row with a bucket; when it fills, she walks over and empties it into the massive ceramic pot over by the tents.

Kebir is off wandering round the tents, seeking Rashid. Mohammed introduces us to everyone – too many names to remember, though I do grasp that Rashid's business partner is called Nazir, and his son is another Sayid, and his wife is Dahlia, just like the English name, except that here you pronounce the 'h'. And also that, here among the nomads, women count as full human beings: they are included in the introductions, even while busily milking.

A wild and frenzied bleating has been coming from inside one of the tents: the lambs have been taken from their mothers while they are milked. Now, milking over, they are let out, and their mothers released from their confusing bondage. A loud and joyous *baa*-ing reunion takes place amid a blinding cloud of dust.

Two men are coming towards us through the dust-cloud, one leading a camel – the noble white kind with the extra *baraka*. Kebir and Rashid – amazed, as predicted, to see me up here. He hands the camel to Kebir, who gets on with hobbling its front leg, while Rashid and I both squeak and jump up and down and have a few hugs, and I introduce him to Gérard and Guy.

Soon we are all sitting round the fire trying to catch up, while the sheep, too, seem to have decided they need to keep warm. They are all slowly crowding up around us, more and more of them, a woolly *maa*-ing sea pressing in closer and closer, bringing their dust-cloud with them, until Nazir, fed up, jumps to his feet, stomps off into the middle of the flock, grabs a ram by the back leg and drags it off, bellowing with rage, a hundred yards away. The others all follow. Peace at last – and time for tea.

We discover from Nazir, with the help of Rashid as translator, that nomads like himself call us sedentary people 'wet chickens', and take great pride in the fact that they, unlike wet chickens, do not engage in manual labour. (Obviously they don't count their women, who never seem to stop labouring, and are now carrying the heavy jars of milk off into the tents, two by two.) This is a new type of alliance, they tell us, oasis-dweller and nomad, Rashid and Nazir, even though they are second cousins by blood. The nomads, Rashid and Mohammed say, have always regarded the oasis-dwellers as their inferiors, as dirt-digging clodhoppers, whose lowly destiny was to provide the fruits of the earth that a noble nomad needs to continue his travels.

Nazir nods his agreement, grinning happily. Rashid liked to think of himself as a herdsman, though he knew nothing about sheep, says Nazir – until his nomad cousins took him under their wing. Those creatures they keep in Timimoun are not real sheep, but overgrown rabbits. Do we know that a Saharan lamb at four months weighs as much as a two-year-old ram of their sickly oasis breed?

And Nazir, meanwhile, says Rashid, getting his own back, knew nothing of scientific sheep-rearing methods. Do we know how he would cure a sick sheep, until Rashid forced him to use the services of modern veterinary medicine? He would walk it seven times around the nearest *marabout*! And a fine sight it was, when the whole flock got foot disease one time, to see Nazir trying to get a hundred wayward sheep seven times round a whitewashed tomb!

Night-time round the camp-fire. Mohammed has pulled out the precious *marabout* sand and given it to one of the older men here, another of Nazir's cousins, I think, who is going to wait till moon-rise, then sprinkle it in a circle around the fire. Kebir and Nazir are sure they can smell rain in the air, anyway. But the cousin is determined to use his sand while it is fresh and extra-full of luck and holy grace. Gérard hopes it works. He wants to try those truffles. Guy says, po-faced, that he personally wants sheep-pasture more than truffles. Has Gérard no fellow-feeling for our hosts?

But Gérard hasn't, at the moment. He did not enjoy witnessing the death of the animal we are about to eat – or, to be more precise, its very efficient skinning, which is done here by cutting a small hole in the animal's back leg, applying the lips to the hole, and blowing very hard, until its body puffs up like a big woolly balloon, signifying that the skin is now fully detached. The only way to proceed, though, Mohammed said, if you want the skin in one piece for your water-skins.

Our fire is of camel dung, dried in the sun: the only free fuel in this wood-free zone. The men add bundles of aromatic *armoise* to perfume the roasting meat. Over by one of the tents, two of the young boys are duelling in rhyming couplets, while their friends alternate between applause and howls of laughter. Can they have heard rappers, then? We are amazed.

Rashid thinks this is very funny. Of course they have. They don't live their whole lives up here! They have villages they go home to for a good half of the year. But this verbal jousting is a tradition of their own, anyhow – something kids have done for centuries, in this part of the world, to entertain themselves. In Timimoun, if they're really good at it, they'll get trained up to the *Ahellil*.

The moon has appeared; Nazir's cousin gets up and begins sprinkling his sand in the finest of streams, making it last till he's circled the fire seven times for extra power – much to the annoyance of the two teenage girls who are trying to baste the meat, and of many other members of the group around the fire, whose commitment to the efficacy of the charm is seriously undermined by the fact that they have got nice and warm and comfortable and don't wish to move. I am with them, though I'm too polite to mention it, since everyone else is doing my grumbling for me.

Round the shared meal, conversation turns to the *marabout*'s charm for Men's Problems – which turns out, somewhat to our disappointment, to be for a horse, a stallion whose love-life, it seems, leaves a lot to be desired. The charm in the red leather needs to be stitched up carefully and put around his neck as an amulet. But not until the other piece of paper has been put into a mixture of water and vinegar and stirred up with pinches of powdered cloves and of henna. Once the powerful words have dissolved off the paper and into the liquid, it will be massaged into the affected area. It is best, though, the company agrees, to wait for the full moon – the day after tomorrow – when both treatments will be more efficacious. Fingers crossed.

From horses and astrological conjunctions we move on to the trouble in the north – the link is a little obscure to us, but we can't expect people to translate every word, after all. Nazir says that it is the oil that has ruined Algeria – it has given his country two left hands. This is hotly disputed by many of those present. Everyone fears for Mohammed Boudiaf's safety – the army may have called him in, but they are not going to put up with him for long. He is too brave for his own good, challenging the powers-that-be at every turn. He has threatened the *Pouvoir* by actually suspending five officials for corruption. And then turned around and sacked a general of the armed forces! There was a shocked silence for a few days, but now, we hear, the army has picked the general up, brushed him down, and put him into the Ministry of Defence.

Kebir laughs bitterly at this. The general, he says, was out of favour with the *Pouvoir*, anyway, from what he's heard. He was thrown to Boudiaf as a sacrificial lamb, along with the evidence of his corruption: French bank accounts and investments in some Paris clinic. It was only when Boudiaf called for a public trial that they suddenly changed their minds. Because how had the general annoyed those above him? He'd refused to rubber-stamp a defence contract with France, which stood to make the powers-that-be a fortune, and keep Algeria in debt for decades! That, Kebir thinks, is why France so happily provided the evidence against him. But the *Pouvoir* certainly didn't want their own dirty laundry washed in public, which was bound to happen if the general took the stand. And look – now he has landed himself a nice new job!

Deep waters indeed, says Nazir, to growls of assent from all around the bonfire. Everyone here thinks it won't be long before Boudiaf gets assassinated by a mystery assailant.

And they are right. By the end of June, just a couple of months from now, Boudiaf will be dead: shot by a member of his own bodyguard who, according to the powers-that-be, claims to have killed him 'for personal reasons, and for religion'. A perfect formula. Was it the army? The *Pouvoir*? The Islamists? All sides can now blame one another, and virtual civil war break out, while the economy is quietly re-formed into a shape more pleasing to Algeria's advisors.

The debate gets more and more heated. Soon, nobody can be bothered translating to us any more. Their conversation is too exciting. Or, for some, too boring. Rashid, who has evidently not lost his love of music since we last met, is over among the rappers now, join-

ing in the dance and percussion section with a will. I have long lost
the thread and am drifting off to sleep on my lovely pile of sheepskins, warmed by the fire, belly full of lovely roast lamb, when I am
suddenly awoken by an outbreak of major excitement all around me.
And, yes, by drops of rain on my face! Big, fat drops of rain! Everyone is standing now, congratulating one another, shaking hands,
holding hands . . . Was it the Lucky Sand? Would it have happened
anyway? Have we Europeans brought them extra *baraka*?

Who cares? says Nazir. If only it will keep on all night, *inshallah,*
everything is going to work out fine!

We settle down snug under Rashid's tent and fall asleep listening
to the happy sound of the thundering rain on our oiled-wool roof.

In the morning I am awoken by a much less welcome sound: the
tramp of marching feet. In big chunky boots. Nobody here wears
such a thing. Soldiers, of course. The fighting has come to get us, all
the way up here. I close my eyes tight and dig my head deeper under
my blanket, a cosy burnous on loan from Rashid. I don't want to
know. The tramping goes on and on; my heart goes on pounding; and
still nothing seems to come of the marching boots.

At last, I give up trying to ignore it, and open my eyes – to a sight
worse than anything I have imagined. There is a deep hole in the
ground, right next to my face, and inside it a horrendous snake-like
creature with a monstrous hairy tassel of a head is flailing about, in
time to the marching feet. A moment of utter panic, and the snake-
thing comes flying out of its hole, to reveal that it is attached to the
back end of a pair of furry ears and two bright, intelligent eyes. I have
inadvertently made my bed, right at the edge of the tent, on top of a
desert gerbil's nest. The thumping was the poor creature desperately
digging its way out from under my pillow.

The next sound to awake me is a rhythmic flapping one, accompanied by a strange guttural gurgling. Too weird altogether. I can't
come up with any explanation of it at all, never mind one I could

panic about. I crawl across the rugs and sheepskins, and poke my head out of the tent.

Of course! Naturally! It is the sound created by four goatskins full of sheep-milk being shaken vigorously back and forth on tall bentwood tripods by a pair of nomad housewives, already up and busy, preparing breakfast for thirty. They are churning the milk, as predicted by Mohammed, till it separates into breakfast butter and *leben*. And I am happy to say that as far as the eye can see, the ground is looking distinctly damp.

People soon begin straggling towards the fireplace. Breakfast is lovely hot *galette*, the flat pancake-bread, with lashings of newly made butter melted onto it, and a novel kind of jam: date jelly from the fruits of the Timimoun groves. The buttermilk to drink, with or without added dates to sweeten it. Perfect in this fresh mountain-after-rain air. And some *klila* cheese next, with sweet, strong absinthe tea. If you want something more protein-packed, there is a wind-dried version of *bekbouka*, to be sliced wafer-thin, salami-style.

Guy accidentally spills the date-buttermilk all down the front of his brand new white gandoura – purchased only yesterday in Timimoun, at Kebir's instigation – and to his surprise gets a hearty round of applause. Guy, mystified, sits and stares. The man next to him claps him heartily on the shoulder. Now Nazir calls for a speech. Another round of applause.

Dates and buttermilk, it is eventually explained, are purposely thrown down the robes of a successful candidate to the *djema'a* before he addresses its members for the very first time – to humble him and remind him that, though he may now have great powers, he is still as fallible as everyone else.

Naturally, it is not long before we tourists are demanding a go on a camel. We can come later to the water-hole, Nazir says, when a whole convoy needs to go down. And for now, we can just have a quiet seat on Rashid's one, like the wet chickens we are.

I get first go – and very disconcerting a camel turns out to be. It stands up back legs first, so you think you're about to be thrown over its head, then at the last moment jerks up onto its front legs and saves you. A much more endearing feature of camels is the way they chew the cud. It's hilarious to watch. I didn't know the camel was a ruminant like the cow, but it is. You can actually see the bolus of food creeping up its long curvy neck, taking for ever, till it finally arrives in its mouth: whereupon the creature – taken, it seems, completely by surprise – suddenly widens its great soppy eyes with the absurdly long thick eyelashes, utterly amazed. Making me laugh out loud every time.

One of the nomad cousins has a grumpy brown camel that does horrible, throat-gurgling growling and is constantly threatening to spit – they really can spit their stomach acids at you, our host tells us. Everyone steers well clear of the cousin and his ill-humoured steed. The cousin's wife, impressed by my courage in the teeth of the ferocious beast – a courage born, did she but know it, from utter ignorance – takes a liking to me and brings me in to visit the women's side of the tent, separated off by a thick curtain, where she shows me, as if it was a great secret between us, the contents of an amazing bag of medicines: herbs and spices and coloured powders, and odd things like a dried chameleon, each one wrapped up in its own little square of pristine white cloth. Women's mysteries, it seems, into which I need to be initiated. Or is she just showing me the contents of the medicine cabinet, in case of emergencies? Alas, I can make very little of its contents, all unrecognizable – apart from, of course, the chameleon. The medicine bag itself is clearly the whole body of a small sheep, skinned by the blowing method. The sheep-bum has been sealed with a leather spiral, its legs have been extended by leather thongs into handle-straps, and its neckline has been carefully folded into a concertina, the thongs passed through a set of holes punched around the top. Pull the strings and the neck of the bag closes neatly. Don't know if I've described it well enough, but when you see it, you are in no doubt that you are looking at the antecedent and inspiration for: the duffel bag!

We have no shared language, alas, as so often happens when

I meet women here, so I can glean no information about the contents of the fascinating bag, though naturally enough we have a giggle about my breasts, and this time I squeeze hers in return, causing even more hilarity.

Mohammed and Rashid tell me later that the nomads supply many of the herbs and spices sold in those perfume-and-chemist type shops in the cities. And that one of the uses for a chameleon was, once upon a time – they hope no longer – to attract would-be fiancés to your daughters. If nobody had made an offer for a young girl's hand, the chameleon would be set on a little brazier, and the girl in question would stand over it, keeping the fumes inside her skirts, for as long as she could bear it.

Thank goodness Rashid is here, these days, with his scientific spirit. Hopefully there is a brighter future for chameleons. And for young women, too.

Afternoon prayers now, and the few men who are going to bother praying start to wash themselves – hands, face, behind the ears and all – using a smooth pebble instead of water. Apparently there is a special dispensation for this type of symbolic washing in the Koran, for times of water shortage. What water there is left must be saved for the sheep. The two horses get buttermilk to drink: easier come by, here, than water. Time for the water-caravan to depart. I get to ride one of the brown camels to the water-hole – only, I suspect, because it doesn't really need a rider anyway, being just part of the string. It's an hour's walk there and back and it really is like being on a boat. Not a ship of the desert, though, as the camel always seems to be described. Much more like a small rowing boat lurching through a billowing oily sea. I soon feel horribly sick, although I do my best to cover it up. Bad enough being a wet chicken, without acting like one.

There is sheep chaos at the water-hole. Everyone who is anyone has brought their flock here. No wonder Rashid and Nazir have decided to take the water to the sheep, and not vice versa. Thousands of *maa*-ing woolly backs stretch for miles, their cloven toes churning the rain-soaked earth into mud so deep that you sink in up to the ankles as you step down from your camel. I back off as far away from the mud-sea as I can while the big water skins and plastic cans are filled and loaded onto the camels, finally to find myself pressed up against a very stylish black leather tent, dome-shaped, held up on bentwood supports. I am, I gather, among a family of blacksmiths. Tuareg nomads, I guess, since the men's faces are veiled right up to their eyes. Dad and Granddad Tuareg are both working away at their anvils, round the far side of the tent. While one sits grinding antimony into kohl with the flat of his hammer, the other has a powerful fire going, and a little girl of seven or eight pumping the bellows while he heats a strip of red-hot metal held in a pair of tongs.

He is hammering a knife blade out of the leaf-suspension steels from a defunct lorry, says Kebir, who has come over to see what I'm at. Fine steel: the knife will be a good one. Blacksmiths here, unlike most people in this part of the world, don't travel with a tribe or clan, but in family units. And people are afraid to associate with them. They are something like scary magicians, their work too inexplicable, maybe – and too necessary. Didn't the Jewish metal-smiths of Chefchaouen have the same problem? The Tuareg wives and daughters are busy making those little hide bottles to keep the kohl in, like the first one I bought, up in Kabylia. And, as I suspected, beneath the sleek fur covering of the kohl-pot lurks some unappealing body part, a bit of stiffened dried gut. Still, waste not, want not. This is the exact opposite of the thriftless European abattoir. Even thriftier is the mended earthenware pot they show me to illustrate their husbands' prowess. Where its base has worn right through from years of resting on stones over their camp fire, it has been beautifully patched with two fine metal plates, welded within and without.

The women tell Kebir to tell me that they have just come all the way from Gao.

Really? From right across the desert? I gaze upon them with a wild surmise.

Yes, they say, as if it was the most ordinary thing in the world. They always come up here in the spring; there are plenty of repairs to be done once the herding of the flocks starts, harnesses, horse-shoes, pots and pans . . .

The women's dresses are spectacular. Voluminous indigo robes, the same colour as their husbands' *chèches*, with huge, wide, flowing sleeves and a kind of built-in veil that winds round from the back, two decorative button-like items on either side of a kind of sweetheart neckline. Their faces are uncovered, unlike their husbands'. Among the Tuareg only the men bother veiling themselves.

It takes me a rather rude amount of staring to work out that, complicated though the Tuareg dress may look, it is amazingly simple – just one long piece of fabric that must be exactly three times the length of their outspread arms.

Luckily, the lady in question is not offended but entertained by my interest in her outfit, and shows me that the two button-things that hold the whole outfit together are nothing but small, round pebbles. This, I am sure, must be the original ancestor of the button-and-hole. Evidently, I am at the fountainhead of human civil-ization here. First the duffel bag, and now the button! You simply put the pebble beneath the two bits of cloth you wish to unite, hold onto it through the cloth, and tie a bit of coloured thread around it, anchoring both pebble and fabric into place. Genius. The huge wide sleeves, meanwhile, are not really sleeves, but a cowl-like drape, where the fabric is pulled over the shoulders from behind and ur-buttoned at the front. The last third of the cloth, wound back round behind them, forms a hair-covering veil in a Virgin Mary style, and is held between the teeth for modesty as they come to the well to draw buckets of water. As they lean forwards to the well, they throw the sleeve-part of the robe back over their shoulders, out of the way, and bare their naked breasts to the view of all and sundry. Nothing pri-vate about breasts round here, not compared to chins, it seems. And why should there be, indeed?

What an eccentric race we are, we humans, the way we randomly select some body part to make a big fuss about. Bare your head, cover your head. Bare your legs – no, cover them up! In my own culture, the nipple is certainly one of the few taboos left. No problem at all here, though. Another member of the family is sitting happily on a nearby rock, one sleeve thrown back, suckling her small baby, no worries.

Stupidly, I go over and admire the child. Whoops. The mother does a weird gesture at me to ward off my Evil Eye. She makes a fist, leaving only her thumb and little finger outstretched, which she now pokes several times towards her own eyes, obviously trying to interrupt the dangerous rays of potential envy glancing from mine.

I surprise her by bursting out laughing. Hardly believable, but this is another Calabrian gesture. Except that I think I've now understood its true meaning better than my friend Ciccio, back in Italy, who uses it all the time, whenever he's praising something ironically, and means the exact opposite. Lovely curtains, you might say to him. Yes, aren't they just, he will reply, stabbing away towards his eyes. And I am so used to this southern Italian gesture that, just, for a second, I think the mother is trying to tell me that her baby is not lovely at all. Which, of course, in a certain sense, she is. Evidently the precise meaning of the gesture has wandered somewhat over the centuries, but the connection is undeniable. I can't wait to tell Ciccio what he's really doing!

Night time, another camp-fire. It is two days later, and the moon is full. The *Marabout*'s charm for the horse's love life is now soaking in its liquid of Power. Clever that the *marabout* suggests adding henna and cloves: at least it is bound to have an antiseptic effect, whether the charm itself has any curative property or not. Somebody has brought out a drum, a big ceramic bowl with a goatskin stretched over it: he is tapping out rhythms on it, playing with the children inside one of the tents, who are weaving their own rhythms on sticks and tea-glasses to answer him. Amid much ribaldry, Nazir's cousin, the man in charge of magic – or do I mean religion? – around here, sets off to anoint the horse with his potion of melted words.

Conversation turns to the miraculous powers of Sidi Haddou, and thence to his remarks, made for my own edification, about handfuls of honey and basketfuls of bees. What did the *marabout* mean? Many interpretations are proffered. Honey is more pleasant than bees, and less risky, but it is only a momentary pleasure. Bees, if you're daring enough to choose them, will give you honey for years. Is the handful of honey the world of the rich West? And the bees everyone else? Is the honey my life in Europe, or this trip to the Maghreb? Are the bees what I will make of it? But no, that would be honey again . . . You can't hold on to honey, it slips out of your hand . . . I should be brave and go the whole hog; that is the general verdict. Unless (from one of the older men) it is better to be content with the honey, and not go after the dangerous bees?

Whatever. Like so many of the words of Holy Men, the interpretations are infinite. Use them to feed your own decisions. I'm beginning to prefer the one where I carry on across the desert. I could follow the road of those Elizabethan cannons to a land of many gods, spirits of nature beyond the reach of the Book. The collective efforts of its People may, as Pedro told me so long ago, have led Europe to America. But then, were the locals pleased to see us come – a race of gold-grubbing plague-bearers?

Since I am free, give or take a few *intégristes*, to wander this earth as the fancy takes me – unlike so many of its inhabitants – it seems churlish not to seize the chance. From this close, the desert has lost its terror; it hardly seems an obstacle at all. Wind the *chèche* back on; remember that life is short, and that most people in the world are hard put to it to get so much as a drop of honey, though they may battle whole swarms of bees. Look at that blacksmith family, all the way up from Mali. They came right across the Sahara, tents, babies and all, without so much as a vehicle, trusting to the kindness of passing lorry-drivers. The desert is a lot less scary than the forces that stand in my way if I take the road north: the *drogués de la religion* and their Macchiavellian opponents. And why should I be in such a rush to get home to Europe? Those olive trees have survived thirty years of neglect. What difference could another month or two make?

The stars are bright in a black-velvet sky, the fire is warm . . . and I am half asleep beside it now, on my own pile of snug sheepskins, wrapped in Rashid's old brown camel-hair burnous. Its hem got a bit chewed by a hungry sheep, but it will do me fine, he says, if I just trim the bottom off. I can keep it for the journey, if I want. And I think I will.

Another two days have gone by: it is early morning, dew still on the ground, and all around us the land is greening. The mountain thyme, coming back to life, perfumes everything. Tomorrow, Kebir says, there will be truffles. The women are taking down the tents: the men are packing them onto the camels, the bentwood supports hanging snugly across their humps, as if designed with just such transport in mind. The lorry won't be needed to move the flocks now. They can walk on, grazing as they go, getting nice and plump on the way. If I want, Mohammed and Rashid will drive me north to the border. I can be on my way back across the Mediterranean, to home and safety, in forty-eight hours.

No. I can't do it. Not yet.

I have learned, now, what a small, snug place Europe is. A life in London town, or an olive grove in Italy? What sort of a dilemma is that? There's hardly anything to choose between them.

Onwards across the desert it is. I'm going for the basket of bees.

Visit **www.panmacmillan.com** to read more about all our books and to buy them. You will also find features, author interviews and news of any author events, and you can sign up for e-newsletters so that you're always first to hear about our new releases.

www.panmacmillan.com

GIFT SELECTOR
YOUR ACCOUNT
WISH LIST
WAITING LIST

HOME ABOUT US IMPRINTS TRADE/MEDIA CONTACT US ADVANCED SEARCH SEARCH GO

BOOK CATEGORIES WHAT'S NEW AUTHORS/ILLUSTRATORS BESTSELLERS READING GROUPS

Coming Soon...

Reading Groups

Competitions
Feeling Lucky?

Extracts
Sneak Previews

Interviews

Events
Meet Our Stars

Reviews
What The Critics Say

News & Awards

Editor's Choice
What We're Reading